HOW CLOUDS HOLD IT TOGETHER

INTEGRATING ARCHITECTURE WITH CLOUD DEPLOYMENT

Marvin Waschke

technologies

Apress®

How Clouds Hold IT Together: Integrating Architecture with Cloud Deployment

ISBN-13 (pbk): 978-1-4302-6166-7

ISBN-13 (electronic): 978-1-4302-6167-4

Managing Director: Welmoed Spahr
Acquisitions Editor: Robert Hutchinson
Technical Reviewer: Efraim Moscovich
Editorial Board: Steve Anglin, Mark Beckner, Louise Corrigan, James DeWolf,
    Jonathan Gennick, Robert Hutchinson, Celestin Suresh John, Michelle Lowman,
    James Markham, Susan McDermott, Matthew Moodie, Jeffrey Pepper,
    Douglas Pundick, Ben Renow-Clarke, Gwenan Spearing
Coordinating Editor: Rita Fernando
Copy Editors: Jana Weinstein, Kim Wimpsett
Compositor: SPi Global
Indexer: SPi Global
Cover Designer: Anna Ishchenko

Distributed to the book trade worldwide by Springer Science+Business Media, LLC., 233 Spring Street, 6th Floor, New York, NY 10013. Phone 1-800-SPRINGER, fax (201) 348-4505, e-mail orders-ny@springer-sbm.com, or visit www.springer.com.

For information on translations, please e-mail rights@apress.com, or visit www.apress.com.

Apress and friends of ED books may be purchased in bulk for academic, corporate, or promotional use. eBook versions and licenses are also available for most titles. For more information, reference our Special Bulk Sales–eBook Licensing web page at www.apress.com/bulk-sales.

Dedicated to my friends and colleagues
at CA Technologies

Contents

About the Author. vii

About the Technical Reviewer ix

Acknowledgments. xi

Introduction. xiii

Part I: **Services, Virtualization, Handhelds, and Clouds. . .1**

Chapter 1:   The Imperative 3

Chapter 2:   The Merger. 37

Chapter 3:   The Bridge 59

Chapter 4:   The Buzz. 83

Chapter 5:   The Hard Part 105

Part II: **Service Management. 135**

Chapter 6:   The Foundation 137

Chapter 7:   The Edifice 165

Part III: **Enterprise Integration. 191**

Chapter 8:   The Harder They Fall. 193

Chapter 9:   The Contenders. 223

Part IV: **Virtualization 247**

Chapter 10:   Not in Kansas. 249

Chapter 11:   Splendid Isolation. 269

Part V: **Clouds. 289**

Chapter 12:   Slipping the Surly Bonds. 291

Chapter 13:   Tricky Business. 311

Chapter 14:   Fish nor Fowl 331

Chapter 15:   Conclusion 353

Index 365

About the Author

Marvin Waschke was a senior principal software architect at CA Technologies. His career has spanned the mainframe to the cloud. He has coded, designed, and managed the development of many systems, including accounting, cell tower management, enterprise service desks, configuration management, and network management.

He represented CA Technologies on the DMTF Cloud Management Working Group, DMTF Open Virtualization Format Working Group, DMTF Common Information Model REST Interface Working Group, OASIS Topology and Orchestration Specification for Cloud Applications (TOSCA) Technical Committee, DMTF Cloud Auditing Data Federation Working Group (observer), DMTF Configuration Database Federation Working Group, W3C Service Modeling Language Working Group, and OASIS OData Technical Committee (observer).

He was the editor-in-chief of the CA Technology Exchange (an online technical journal) and the author of *Cloud Standards: Agreements That Hold Together Clouds*.

About the Technical Reviewer

Efraim Moscovich is a software architect and software engineering leader.

He has more than 25 years of experience in IT and software engineering in various capacities.

His areas of expertise and interest include cloud computing, automation, large-scale software architecture, complex event processing, usability, and ideation and innovation skills.

He served as the senior principal architect in the Architecture group at the Office of the CTO and the senior director of engineering for the Server Automation product suite at CA Technologies.

Efraim was a member of the CA Council for Technical Excellence and of industry standards groups such as the OASIS TOSCA technical committee, and he served as the lead and mentor on the CA Patent Review Board.

Acknowledgments

I have learned a great deal about cloud architecture and deployment from my many colleagues on the various standards working groups in which I have participated. Notable among these are Larry Lamers of VMware, Shishir Pardikar of Citrix, Alan Sill of the Open Grid Forum, Jacques Durand of Fujitsu, Eric Wells of Hitachi, and Ali Ghazanfar of ZTE Corporation.

I would like to give recognition to Paul Lipton, my friend and CA Technologies representative on the DMTF board of directors. Paul is also co-chairman of the OASIS TOSCA Technical Committee. Paul is a longtime participant in many computing standards groups and has been a friend and colleague for several years.

Jacob Lamm of CA is the executive sponsor for this book. Jacob and I have worked together for many years on enterprise management solutions, including service desk and configuration management systems. I have learned a great deal from Jacob about the business side of IT.

Efraim Moskovitz served as technical reviewer for this book. Without his help, there would have been many more gaps and gaffes. Efraim and I worked together on the CA Council for Technical Excellence for several years, and Efraim contributed several articles to the CA Technology Exchange, which I edited. He is a good friend and valued advisor.

Karen Sleeth is the director of the CA Press who encouraged me many times when I was feeling down about this project. The book would not exist without her.

I also am grateful to the folks at Apress: Robert Hutchinson whose wit and insight shaped many aspects of the book; Rita Fernando, the project manager who gently and tolerantly nudged me forward; and Kim Wimpsett, whose patient copyediting pruned away the excess shrubbery and clarified my obscure and twisted prose.

Finally, I must gratefully acknowledge my wife, Rebecca; my daughter, Athena; and my grandsons, Matthew and Christopher. They tolerated my erratic and reclusive ways while I was working on this book. I cannot thank them enough for this.

Introduction

Cloud computing is changing the computing industry and our daily lives. Without clouds, the search engines like Google that have become an ever-present source of information on every subject would not be possible. There would be no social networking sites like Facebook. Online shopping sites like Amazon would be cramped in scope and unpredictable in performance. Scientific projects like the Human Genome Project would be much more difficult. Businesses are moving more of their IT to cloud implementations every day.

Centralizing data into a cloud that is accessible to mobile devices such as laptops, tablets, and smartphones, as well as desktops on the enterprise premises, has proven successful and has aided in expanding the boundaries of the workplace far beyond the walls of the enterprise office. The nature of the workplace and work styles have changed and forced enterprise governance to change also.

The basics of enterprise software design apply to all enterprise software, but cloud implementations bring new requirements and challenges.

Greater participation in planning by business management is one requirement. Clouds supplied by a cloud service provider rather than owned by the enterprise have distinct advantages, but the presence of a third party complicates the relationship between the enterprise and its IT systems. The involvement of a cloud provider can raise questions about governance, security, and auditability that require the participation of business management. Business factors such as costing methods and accounting for ownership are also likely to change.

Technical solutions may help, but they cannot resolve these business issues. Consequently, cloud projects require intense cooperation between business managers and technologists that similar projects confined to the enterprise premises do not require.

Cloud implementations also require new technical skills that stem from the greater role of network communications and the use of a virtual environment. These issues can be especially challenging when implementing enterprise integration. On the other hand, clouds also present important opportunities for rationalizing and increasing enterprise integration, and the central nature of cloud implementations simplifies and increases the opportunities for integration. On the other hand, the rise of mobile devices and wider geographic distribution of enterprises bring on new technical challenges.

Cloud implementations can be central to reducing the investment in enterprise computing while increasing its functionality and reach. It can also be the key to enterprise integration, but to fully realize the potential, enterprises must undertake cloud computing projects as both business and technical efforts. These projects require a planning, development, and operations methodology that brings these aspects together systematically. The IT Infrastructure Library (ITIL) is a proven set of practices for bringing together business management and technical expertise for the development and management of successful IT services. This book brings cloud computing and service management together with detailed recommendations for successful services built on cloud technology.

Services, Virtualization, Handhelds, and Clouds

The Imperative

The Challenge of the Information Age and IT

SUMMARY

There is debate among economists and skeptics from other disciplines on the significance of the Information Age. For the last fifty years, Moore's law has accurately predicted the exponential growth of computing capacity. If exponential growth continues, exceedingly rapid growth will occur at some point, but when the curve will become steep is hard to predict. IT has seen rapid growth in the first decade of the twenty-first century. The rate of change seems to be increasing and IT is penetrating into lives in ways that were impossible a few years ago. IT may have reached escape velocity. Service-orientation, cloud, and IT integration are critical in harnessing the blast of new capacity.

For many people today, *information technology* (IT) is troubling.[1] The benefits from computing have always been apparent. But from the beginning prophets have warned that humans might someday become dominated by their machines. Yesteryear's dystopic speculation has given way to today's icy realism. The stagnant unemployment rate and the soaring stock market following the 2008 financial crisis raise questions. Have we reached a point where businesses can increase output and profit without employing more people? Have the machines really begun to replace humans? Where does IT fit in?

---

[1]The term *IT* is used differently in different contexts. Among engineers, it usually refers to the combination of hardware and software that makes up networked computer systems. In service management, the term usually also includes the department or group that is charged with developing and maintaining these systems and includes people, processes, and governance. IT is often also used as a general term for computing disciplines. In the present work, *IT* is almost always used in the service management sense.

Rumination over the potential elimination of jobs by computers has been a popular topic for many intellectuals, from science fiction writers to economists and statesmen. The standard retort to the fear of job elimination has been that computer-driven increases in productivity go hand in hand with increases in demand that generate more, not fewer, jobs. This answer has been borne out through decades of prosperity. Has the balance changed? Did the triumph in 1997 of the IBM supercomputer Deep Blue over the reigning World Chess Champion, Garry Kasparov render grand masters obsolete? Did the defeat in 2011 of *Jeopardy!* champion Ken Jennings by Watson mark a turning point in the economy?

Information technology has evolved rapidly since its inception, and enterprise computing has changed with it. Cloud service management is an approach to designing and managing enterprise IT that represents much of the progress that has been made in computing, particularly the progress of the last decade and a half.

This book examines three related strands of recent IT development: enterprise integration, service management, and cloud. These three strands all have roots deep in the history of computing, but they are combining and blossoming, beginning to dominate both enterprise and consumer computing, and changing national economies. I will explain these aspects of IT architecture, how they influence business and society, and how to plan and design projects based upon them.

I am a software architect, development manager, and a developer; not a stock market analyst, a business executive, or a product manager, but this book is meant for all these roles. Stock market analysts want to know where the next big thing will drive the market; executives look for a map to guide their company to success; and product managers are on the prowl for attractive new products and features to offer to their customers.

Inevitably, the software architect in me will often show in this book. This is not to slight the other important participants. Architects are often in the background supporting visionary leaders who introduce new products and concepts to consumers. Architects also have vision, but it is of a different type. They envision the software and its interaction with physical or virtual hardware, its strengths and limitations, how it can be made reliable and efficient in production. They must also anticipate that successful software continually changes and adapts to evolving business and technical environments. The architect's view encompasses the entire IT system, the integration of all its components, both those deployed on a cloud and traditional components on the enterprise premises. The architect's down to earth concentration on the workable and feasible often offers insights critical to entire cloud projects.

Until outsourcing became popular, IT management assumed that every aspect of the datacenter was under direct control of the IT department. Cloud further reduces IT control. When a cloud is public, personnel outside the enterprise reporting structure have control of equipment, data and production processes that were traditionally entrusted to enterprise IT.

These changes affect everyone. Executives must institute new ways of assuring that systems deliver services that align with corporate goals and are accountable to enterprise governance. Product managers have a range of challenges and opportunities to transform into products for their customers. Developers have new technologies to master and new ways of working on projects that have unfamiliar requirements and new goals.

An architectural view of cloud straddles the visionaries who anticipate the final product, the executives and managers who guide IT, and the developers who design components and write the code. The architectural view provides both perspective and practical patterns and guidelines for planning and creating a successful cloud implementation in an environment that combines cloud and on-premises components. Visionaries can gain insight into what is feasible and what is not and increase the depth of their vision. Executives and managers will see aspects of clouds that will change the way they conduct business. Developers will get some well-deserved help in understanding the both new and perhaps strange requirements and technologies that cloud puts before them.

Advances in Computing

Computers have become more accessible and even indispensable to a wide swathe of the population in both developed and less-developed nations. Some of the new ways in which we interact with computers are obvious. Social networking applications such as Facebook have worked one kind of transformation. Social networking takes the near-universal access to networked computers now prevalent and adds content with universal personal appeal. This means that computers are used by segments of the population that would not have touched a computer a short time ago. For example, my octogenarian mother-in-law got her first computer only a few years ago. She now sends and receives email and posts photographs and comments for friends and family daily, but she would not have considered owning a computer in 2000.

When I took a chemistry class with a computing project at university, students were not allowed to touch a computer. We passed in punch cards and received printouts through what looked like a bullet-proof security window for a check-cashing service in a bad neighborhood. The irony is that the old IBM 7094 behind the security wall did not have a hundredth of the computing or storage capacity of my mother-in-law's laptop. The computing power, network capacity, and storage required for a single Facebook page were not available to a major research lab in 1967, when I took that class.

The success of phenomena such as Facebook depends on the technology that makes social networking possible, but it also depends on a society that has evolved to the point that both the technology is accessible and the content that people want is available. This requires computing and storage capacity that far exceeds the requirements of IT of the past.

The smartphone has worked a related transformation by changing where we compute. When we roll up our sleeves to do some computing today, we don't go to a datacenter. There are desktops in our offices; we tote laptops to and from work; and a fourteen-year-old packs more computing power to the beach in a smartphone than NASA could muster for the Apollo moon mission.

Networking technology, especially the Internet, has transformed the independent, isolated computers of the past developed by the great innovators such as Gates, Jobs, and Wozniak. Computers are now embedded in an enormous network that links millions of end-user and server computers together. If it were not for security walls, checkpoints, and other intentional barriers, naughty computer users today would have direct access to nearly every other computer on the planet for fiddling with their data and flashing annoying pictures on their screens.

The amount of storage available today is difficult to describe with the terms used when computers first became consumer products. When the PC was introduced, storage was commonly on floppy disks and measured in thousands of bytes. Internal hard drives were quickly added to standard PCs. Early PC hard drive capacities were measured in millions of bytes (megabytes), and then billions of bytes (gigabytes). Today, trillion-byte (terabyte) PC hard drives are common and data centers have much more storage. Amazon Web Services (AWS) S3 storage service describes their storage in "objects." These objects can contain up to five trillion bytes (five terabytes) of storage. In early 2012, AWS reported storing 762 billion objects.[2] Facebook is said to deploy seven quadrillion bytes (seven petabytes) of new storage a month.[3] To put these quantities of data in perspective, the books in the Library of Congress are estimated to contain less than ten petabytes of data.[4]

---

[2]Rich Miller, Data Center Knowledge, "Amazon: 762 Billion Objects Stored on S3 Cloud," http://www.datacenterknowledge.com/archives/2012/01/31/amazon-762-billion-objects-stored-on-s3-cloud/, January 31, 2012.

[3]Rich Miller, Data Center Knowledge, "Facebook Builds Exabyte Data Centers for Cold Storage," http://www.datacenterknowledge.com/archives/2013/01/18/facebook-builds-new-data-centers-for-cold-storage/, January 18, 2012.

[4]The estimate is imprecise. See Leslie Johnston, Library of Congress, The Signal: Digital Preservation, "A 'Library of Congress' Worth of Data: It's All in How You Define It," http://blogs.loc.gov/digitalpreservation/2012/04/a-library-of-congress-worth-of-data-its-all-in-how-you-define-it/, April, 2012.

The implications of *big data* have captured the public eye.[5] Big data is a response to the burgeoning scale of computing. We now have the capacity to store previously unimaginably vast quantities of data, the computing power to process it, and ways to collect data that were unheard of ten years ago. Big data is technology to cope with this explosion of resources and to marshal them to generate useful knowledge. Without storage capacity, computing power, or abundant data collections, big data would simply not exist. But with the confluence of these resources, we are able to extract buying patterns, predict trends, detect terrorist plots, and make other discoveries that were not possible before. This ability presents challenges to governance and privacy, but with the challenges, there are opportunities.

Businesses generate whole new lines of business and make others obsolete with computing innovations such as the MP3 file format, network bandwidth, and small players with large audio storage capacity that turned the recording industry upside down, or digital processing that has largely eliminated paper from the US payment system.[6] The military, prime mover of the early stages of computing, now must counter the threat of cyberwarfare no less assiduously than it does the threat of nuclear weapons.

Enterprise architects, designers, and planners face a call to action for the benefit of enterprises, individuals, and society. They must harness and extend the changes, expansion, and innovation in computing that stand before us.

Historical Background

The history of the development of the industrial, technical, and information society in which we live is a history of economic and social change driven by technical advances. Engineers may ask why this is important. Most software engineers I know are not out to reshape society. Instead, most of them want to participate in the construction of projects and products that serve a useful

---

[5]*Big data* has no crisp definition. It was coined in response to the increased size and changed nature of data that has begun to be collected and processed in the last few years. Generally, big data has three characteristics: it is large, measured in terabytes, petabytes, and larger units; to be useful, it must be processed rapidly; and it may not be in traditionally structured form.

[6]Use of paper checks by consumers has declined sharply, but the Federal Reserve estimates that they will survive for another decade. Behind the scenes, paper has almost completely disappeared. Prior to September 11, 2001, paper checks were hauled by truck and airplane from bank to bank for clearing. Aircraft grounding following 9/11 brought a near crisis in the financial system by delaying check clearing. Regulations were changed to allow electronic transfers of images. A decade later, almost all physical movement of paper checks has been eliminated. See David B. Humphrey and Robert Hunt, "Getting Rid of Paper: Savings from Check 21," working paper 12-12, Philadelphia: Federal Reserve Bank of Philadelphia, http://www.philadelphiafed.org/research-and-data/publications/working-papers/2012/wp12-12.pdf, May 2012.

purpose and find a ready market. Like everyone else, they want to earn a good living and to create something they are proud of. In seeking those goals, they make decisions daily, even hourly. With a better understanding of how the work fits into the overall pattern of society and how products have changed lives and perspectives, those decisions will, in small and large ways, be better and the overall results more satisfying for everyone.

The Ages

Economists and cultural commentators often call the age of computers and electronic data processing the *Information Age*. This age began in the second half of the twentieth century and continues today. IT integration, service management, and cloud computing are important developments in the progress of the Information Age.

Two preceding ages helped shape the world we live in today: the Industrial Age and the Technological Age. To place the Information Age in perspective—especially in economic perspective—you must know something about the preceding ages. It is especially important to identify the forces that have been deemed powerful enough by historians and economists to distinguish one age from another. These forces give us a clue as to what is most important in IT today.

The Industrial Age

The Industrial Age marks the beginning of the modern world that we all recognize: the world in which machines began to contribute substantially to human well-being. The age began in the late seventeenth century and extended into nineteenth century. It started with the invention of the steam engine. Early steam engines drove fans to ventilate coal mines in Britain. Dangerous gases and lack of ventilation limited mine depths and coal production. These steam engines, much less sophisticated than the engines of a few decades later, dispelled the gases and made deeper mines practical. The increased coal supply replaced wood as the dominant fuel source. The supply of wood was dwindling as Britain's forest had nearly disappeared at the end of the seventeenth century. The Industrial Age began.

The introduction of the steam engine delivered a one-two punch: first, a new way to transform raw energy to useful work; second, an abundant source of energy to fuel the transformation. Coal was the source and the steam engine was the transformer. Enormous changes began. With the power to transform raw materials rapidly into saleable goods, opportunities flourished. Tenant farmers migrated to factory towns where new industrial jobs, dismal by present standards, were far better than starvation on inefficient remote farms.

New means of transportation, such as steam trains, opened larger markets and furthered accelerated development. Agriculture increased in efficiency and a smaller rural population could provide food for a growing urban population.

The steam engine did not have a role in all these changes, but it was a catalyst that started the transformation. Macroeconomists point out that these changes represented major changes in the exchange of goods and services. Formerly, agriculture had produced scarcely enough food for the farmers themselves. Stimulated by new markets, farmers began to adopt new cultivation methods, and food supplies multiplied. This enabled the growth of cities and entire populations became consumers of rural agriculture.

Previously, the expense of transportation limited commerce to the exchange of rare and expensive commodities. Steam trains and ships decreased the cost of transportation and made the distribution of ordinary consumer goods practical. Before the appearance of industrial manufacturing, artisans exchanged their wares within small communities. In the Industrial Age, manufacturers produced the same wares centrally and used advanced transportation to distribute them cheaply to large markets.

These changes redistributed wealth. Before the Industrial Age, wealth was in the hands of aristocrats whose riches derived from hereditary privileges such as the power to tax and royal bequests. During the Industrial Age, industrial production and commerce became growing sources of wealth, and the relative wealth of the aristocracy diminished as the new wealth accumulated among the upstart classes.

The Technological Age

The next age, the Technological Age, also transformed markets, population distribution, and sources of wealth. The twentieth century was the age of technology. Some of the achievements of technology include advances in chemistry that brought explosives, herbicides, pesticides, synthetic fertilizers, plastics, pharmaceuticals, synthetic fibers, and a host of other substances. Technology also created the electrical power distribution grid, electric lights and appliances. Just as steam power characterizes the Industrial Age, electricity and petroleum-fueled internal combustion engines characterize the Technological Age. The current transportation system based on airplanes, diesel-powered trains, highways, automobiles, and trucks are all innovations of the Technological Age.

Technology reduced the number of agricultural workers needed to produce food for the rest of the population, causing further migrations to urban areas as small family farms consolidated into the equivalent of agricultural factories, furthering the restructure of the landscape.

Increasingly, automated electric machinery made factories more efficient and reduced the relative cost of ever-more-complex products. Electric appliances replaced much of the drudgery involved in simple housekeeping. This decreased the need for domestic servants, which were a large segment of urban populations in the industrial nineteenth century.

Efficient transportation transformed markets. Fresh fruit and vegetables shipped in refrigerated railroad cars and transport trucks changed diets as fresh produce became available in all seasons. Telephone, radio, and television transformed communications and homogenized culture.

Technology enabled the rise of an educated and skilled middle class prepared to perform increasingly sophisticated tasks in growing industries. Populations that had been concentrated in urban areas used their growing wages to move to suburban areas surrounding the cities.

The Information Age

From the macroeconomist's point of view, both the Technological Age and the Industrial Age generated new sources of wealth and new markets. Because the next age, the Information Age, is still in progress, we don't know how the age will end—but some economists and historians are not even sure that the Information Age qualifies as an economic age on the same order as the Industrial and Technological Ages.

Why do some economists and historians deprecate the significance of the Information Age? They maintain that, although much of the progress in computing has brought about improvements, these improvements have not dramatically changed the structure of society and the economy.

In their view, although computing has made agriculture more efficient, we have observed only an incremental continuation of the trend toward more efficient cultivation and distribution, which has reduced the number of farmers and increased overall output, but not engendered new directions in farming. Just-in-time inventory depends on computing and has made manufacturing more responsive and more efficient, but manufacturers still create the same types of products without major changes to the distribution system. These contrarians argue that the Information Age has brought important improvements but not dramatic change. In their view, the Information Age has had little impact on sources of wealth and distribution of markets and therefore does not qualify as an economic age at all. This is an assertion that bears examination.

What we call the Information Age began when computers emerged from wartime laboratories and began to influence the conduct of business in the mid-twentieth century. At first, the main focus of computing was military and scientific. Computers cracked codes, calculated complex weapon trajectories, and solved complex equations for weapons development. Military and scientific computing will always be important,[7] but the application of computing that soon gained the most attention was business.

From midcentury on, computers became more and more prevalent in business. At first, computers primarily automated back-office functions—the activities that customers only indirectly participate in, such as maintaining accounts, billing and accounts receivable, and tracking inventory. In contrast, customers interact directly with front-office functions, such as online stores.

Mainframe

Mainframes are direct descendants of the computers designed for military and scientific purposes. Early computers were designed to solve a single problem. If confronted with a different problem, the computer had to be rebuilt. Since rebuilding was expensive and troublesome, the earliest electronic computers were only applied to the most critical problems.

Of the many innovations that drove the beginning of the Information Age, arguably the seminal innovation was the one proposed by John von Neumann. In early single-purpose computers, the instructions for solving a problem were in the wiring of the computer. The instructions were changed by rewiring the logic controls. The von Neumann design converted the control instructions into input that was treated like the data for a specific problem.[8] This meant that a single computer could solve different problems by consuming a different set of control instructions instead of rewiring. Von Neumann's EDVAC was the first design for a programmable general-purpose electronic computer.[9] All modern computers, from mainframes to handhelds, even embedded control chips, have roots in von Neumann's design.

---

[7]Military computing has taken a new twist recently as cyberwarfare has transformed computing from a tool for developing weapons into both a formidable weapon in itself and a valuable and ubiquitous asset that must be protected. This transformation is important in assessing the growing significance of the information age and IT integration.

[8]Von Neumann's original description of a programmable computer appeared as "First Draft of a Report on the EDVAC" was published in 1945. The document was published prematurely and the concept inadvertently became unpatentable. A reproduction of the document can be found at http://virtualtravelog.net.s115267.gridserver.com/wp/wp-content/media/2003-08-TheFirstDraft.pdf

[9]The priority claims of EDVAC (electronic discrete variable automatic computer) and the slightly earlier ENIAC (electrical numerical integrator and computer) are controversial. The ENIAC was programmable in the sense that its modular design permitted reprograming by physical rearranging jumpers and cables. The EDVAC could be reprogrammed without physically changing the hardware. The EDVAC was designed by the same team that designed the ENIAC and construction of the EDVAC began before the ENIAC was complete. At the core of the controversy, von Neumann was a latecomer to the team. Although only von Neumann's name appears on the EDVAC design paper, other members of the team assert that the EDVAC concepts were developed prior to von Neumann's participation in the team.

Automating the back office was, and still is, the main thrust of mainframe computing. In the early days of business computing, the day's transactions would be collected—often via messengers collecting decks of punched cards—and then run through a batch program to update the accounts at the end of the day. The result was a new deck of punch cards representing the state of the accounting system at the end of the day. This system was not far from that of the nineteenth century by which clerks were condemned to balance the books to the last penny before leaving the counting house. Before direct-access persistent storage (typically disk drives) became widely available, the updated books were stored on punch cards or magnetic tape and a printed master listing of all the data in a long report. When someone needed data on an account, he looked it up in the printed report, which was not that different from a merchant in 1850 opening a handwritten journal or a ledger to check on the status of an account. At this stage, the computer had made accounting faster and more accurate, but business was still conducted in the same manner—a good example of computing improving and accelerating an existing process, leading to incremental growth, but not a transformation.

I have been describing a serial computing environment in which jobs run one at a time in sequence. In this environment, integration meant designing output that the next program could read as input. If an accountant wanted to compare data from two departments, she had to go to the paper reports for the two departments and look up the data, or someone had to write a program that would take the output for two departments and combine them to produce an answer. This corresponds to our nineteenth-century merchant going to two sets of journals and ledgers for two divisions of his business. Integration had not progressed much beyond the level in manual systems, although updating accounts had become much faster and more accurate. Again, incremental growth.

Batch programs are less often written now. Programs that segment activities into many independent transactions that are executed when the transactions occur are much more common. In a *transactional system*, as soon as the customer makes a purchase, the system processes the transaction and balances the books as the transaction occurs rather than waiting until the end of the day for a batch update. Thus, in a transactional accounting system, account balances are always available and up-to-date.

Instant availability of account information presents opportunities. Not only do the traditional back-office functions run much faster but the state of the system is always, at least in theory, available. Using a transactional accounting system, executives can check the balance of any account at any time and expect up-to-the-minute information instead of waiting until a batch job completes. Transactional processing meant that businesses, especially large businesses, could make informed decisions anytime without waiting for batch jobs to complete.

It took time for transactional processing to expand and become more sophisticated. In the early days of mainframes, software and its source code were bundled with hardware. Mainframe owners were free to modify the programs to fit their needs. Often the modified code was donated back to the hardware vendor for sharing with other customers, somewhat similar to open-source code today. The foundations of many of the early transactional processing systems were developed in this way. This included the IBM *Information Management Transaction Manager* (IMS TM) and the IBM *Customer Information Control System* (CICS).

Instant availability of the accounting information and other information such as inventory levels had wide implications and potentials that far exceeded the capabilities of the computing infrastructure of the time.

Transactional systems with their up-to-the-minute information had much more potential than early systems could support. Continuous maintenance and accessibility of the system state adds another level of sophistication and complexity to information processing, because systems can share state. This is powerful. In 1966, Douglas Parkhill anticipated that integrated systems would combine information from every aspect of a business into a single model.[10] This model provides current information in near real time and is also capable of simulating and projecting future states for planning, enabling businesses to adjust their investments to optimize for the future.

Businesspeople have always done this kind of planning, but they had to rely on estimates based on experience and intelligent guesswork without the aid of current, comprehensive, and accurate information. In addition to affording predictive value, comprehensive and accurate data spurs innovation and inspires businesses to modify processes and offer new services that could not be supported by earlier technology.

Timesharing

Until the advent of distributed systems and desktops, computers were expensive—often too expensive for a smaller business to purchase and providing more capacity than the business could use. Nevertheless these businesses had processes ripe for automation. Timesharing was a solution to this need.

Operating systems were designed to support more than one user at a time. This was done by doling out short intervals of processing time to each user and switching fast enough and separating data well enough to give the users the illusion that each was in complete control and the only one on the system.

---

[10]Douglas F. Parkhill, *The Challenge of the Computer Utility* (Reading, MA: Addison-Wesley, 1966).

Users were usually connected to the timeshared central system by leased lines: private connections from their key board and display to the computer. If the line were fast enough and the central computer were sufficiently powerful for the number of users, it would appear as if a timeshare computer miles away were in the same room.

Timeshare computing made computing available to many businesses that could not afford their own computer, and it also began the spread of knowledge of computing outside the largest companies and institutions, but it was still expensive and not widely available to individual consumers.

Distributed Computing

When distributed computing began to take the place of mainframes in the public eye, mainframe back-office computing continued to be important, but distributed computing began to move computing capacity from sacrosanct glass-house datacenters and into the hands of ordinary office workers.

Distributed computing adds both value and complexity to computing. A distributed computing system is made up of relatively small networked computers instead of a single central computer. In distributed systems, large numbers of small and powerful computers perform computing tasks. The small computers rely upon networking technology to transfer data and control between them. There are advantages to both distributed and centralized mainframe approaches. Although the distributed approach is now prevalent, there are many productive mainframe systems active and not likely to be replaced soon.

Both mainframes and distributed systems are dependent on networks, but in different ways. Mainframe networks connect the mainframe in a sort of hub-and-spoke pattern (Figure 1-1). The primary network data path is between the central computer and an end-user terminal or other peripheral such as a storage unit or printer. Today, the scenario is more complicated because mainframes usually intermingle with distributed systems and mainframes are linked together. A mainframe user terminal is often a workstation in a distributed system and the mainframe itself may also be a node in a distributed system, but the primary data path remains between peripherals and the central processor.

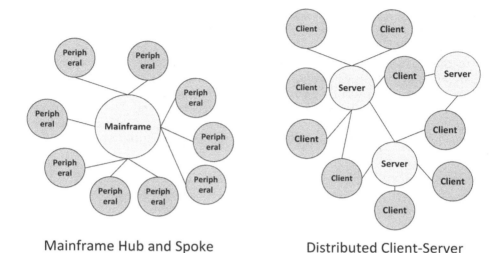

Mainframe Hub and Spoke   Distributed Client-Server

Figure 1-1. Mainframe and distributed systems have different characteristic network patterns

The components of a distributed system are often simpler and less sophisticated than the components of a mainframe system, but distributed systems as a whole can be more complex than mainframes. The network in a distributed system does not have a central computer. Instead, a distributed system is usually described as a client–server system. A client requests operations and data from a server. A server executes client requests and returns data and status to the client. A computer in a distributed system may switch around and act as a server in one transaction and as a client in the next. Often, to fulfill a client request, a server reaches out as a client to another server and acts as a client and a server at the same time.

Distributed computers are independent of the others in the system. If one fails, the others continue to operate, although the total system may be impaired because the software running on one computer may be dependent on the performance of software running on other computers.

Part of the challenge in building distributed systems is to prevent isolated failures from affecting the entire system. Failures in distributed systems can be complex. A hardware deficiency in one computer—a fragmented disk drive that delivers data more slowly than expected for example—may cause the entire system to perform more slowly, but the source of the slowdown may not be apparent and may require extensive troubleshooting.

Distributed systems also have dependencies on the network that mainframe systems do not have. Mainframe systems are usually dependent on a network for connecting the users to a central computer, but all computing occurs on the central computer with relatively little dependence on a network. In a distributed system, the same connection from the user to the system exists, but because servers interact with other servers and clients and servers can interchange roles, there is an added dependency on a connection between the computers that are performing the distributed computing work. A request from a client often will be parceled out to a number of servers and it may not be easy to determine where a problem has occurred. These issues can become even more complex when systems are virtualized, in which case computing may appear to be centralized but in fact be distributed over many networked physical machines.

Another important characteristic of distributed systems is scalability. A scalable system can be expanded to handle greater loads, often characterized by greater numbers of clients; it can also be shrunken when the load decreases. Often scalability is equated with supporting vast numbers of clients and huge loads. This is not exactly correct: a system designed to handle a specific load, no matter how large, is not scalable if it is not designed to be "scaled up" to even larger loads. "Scaling down" usually does not get the attention that scaling up receives, but under some circumstances, decreasing the capacity of the system can also be important.

Although mainframes handle very large loads—often larger than comparable distributed systems—distributed systems typically scale more easily; when the load is too large, additional servers are added to the system. If the system is designed well, there are few limits on the number of servers that can be added. Scaling up a single central computer can be more difficult because there is only the central computer to expand and there is a limit to the size and number of processors that can be added.

Computer theorists of the 1960s, such as Douglas Parkhill, did not anticipate the appearance of distributed systems. As discussed, distributed systems rely on compact powerful computers that are strung together into a system. Without the powerful desktops that began to appear in the 1980s, the current common architecture of distributed systems connected by the Internet would look far different. In hindsight, small and powerful computers were inevitable. As long as the processing power packed into a single electronic chip follows Moore's law and increases exponentially, as it has since the invention of the transistor, computers will become smaller and more powerful with each year.

This means, on the one hand, smaller and more powerful handhelds that can interpret speech more accurately and play movies flawlessly and, on the other hand, giant datacenters stuffed with hundreds of thousands of the same powerful processors closely linked together to perform monumental tasks such as searching the Internet or managing a large and growing social network.

Distributed systems have affected business computing in many ways. Desktop computers are cheap—very cheap, compared to mainframes. Purchasing or expanding a mainframe usually requires corporate budgeting, because mainframes are expensive. Desktop computers can be purchased under departmental or even individual budgets and often crept into enterprises with little strategic input from upper management. They proved to be so useful that they became a runaway success, often to the consternation of the professionals in the datacenter.

Soon every office desk had a desktop PC, and homes were not far behind. This presented an opportunity for software programmers and vendors who unleashed a flood of useful (and occasionally not so useful) applications for individual and departmental groups. Cheap desktops and equally cheap and innovative software rapidly spread through enterprises and began to affect productivity and business methods.

The proliferation of desktop distributed systems had several important implications. Activities were automated that had never been automated before. Word processing together with electronic filing is one example. Automated staff scheduling is another. With increased automation, productivity increased, and the amount of data that could be analyzed electronically also increased. The flaw in all this growth was lack of coordination and strategic direction. Artificial barriers to communication, such as departments with incompatible systems to manage the same task, proliferated. Although the data available for analysis grew rapidly, much of this data remained inaccessible. Data that could be used by the entire enterprise might be stored on a hard drive on an administrator's desk and protected and backed up at the whim of an untrained user.

Although independent personal applications, such as office productivity tools, are still important, management of distributed systems has evolved. Many applications that were once individual or departmental have been taken over by the enterprise and managed and maintained by the corporate IT department. Even personal applications such as word processors and spreadsheet tools are usually managed by corporate IT so they can be supported efficiently for security and reliability.

Distributed System Integration

Bringing diverse processes and data together is called *integration*. As IT systems become more integrated, the enterprise becomes more efficient and agile. Increased integration is at the heart of many of the advances in IT that we are so familiar with.

Although distributed systems have come to dominate IT, they present an integration challenge. The benefits from integration of distributed systems are the same as in mainframe systems. However, distributed data can be more difficult to bring together and analyze. Communication between distributed processes is often difficult. Integration of distributed systems is dependent on innovative use of the network. Many of the advances in system architecture of the past fifteen years are related to communication between distributed processes.

Impact of the Information Age

As mentioned, some economists maintain that the Information Age does not qualify as an age because it has not had social and economic consequences comparable to preceding ages. Looking at some of the characteristics of IT today is more revealing than arguing one side or the other. It may be that the changes the economists are looking for are not here quite yet but loom on the horizon.

Many advances in the last decade are obvious. Many people go for days without touching paper money, coins, or a checkbook. Credit and debit cards and online payment systems take care of it all. You can buy almost everything you need to live over the Internet today. You could probably go for months without entering a store, except perhaps a grocery store for fresh produce, although even fresh grocery shopping services are available in some cities.

It is possible that you have stopped reading paper newspapers and magazines, choosing to view them instead on laptops and tablets. You probably buy books online, and a substantial number of those are probably electronic, not paper. If you are a budding author, you may eschew traditional publishers to publish and sell your book online for only a few dollars. Many musicians record and self-publish their music electronically, circumventing the once all-powerful record companies.

Banking and insurance are two examples of industries that have been transformed and made more efficient by IT, but the industries themselves have not disappeared. Banks are able to transfer funds and track accounts much more efficiently now than they did fifty years ago, but they still provide services that are similar to those they offered in 1960. I am old enough to remember when banks closed their doors at 3 PM to balance their accounts, a check took weeks to clear if you did not take it to the bank that issued it, and everyone took hours each month to reconcile paper cancelled checks with the bank's accounting. Debit cards and online bill payment are much more convenient and the accounting is almost instantaneous, yet the services—relieving me of the risk of carrying large amounts cash and of the necessity of visiting payees in person in order to make payments—are the same services provided by bankers since the Middle Ages.

These kinds of instrumental and incremental changes are less radical in nature than the changes brought about by the Industrial Revolution, which transformed what people ate and where they lived, or those of the Technological Revolution, which gave rise to an entire educated middle class.

Nevertheless, the potential for IT to drive societal and economic changes is staggering. Parkhill predicted in 1966 a significant list of the features of the Information Age today: computerized shopping, the declining use of physical money, universal computerized access to most of the planet's information, and automated paperless publishing. But he also predicted high rates of unemployment and social change as the human role in the economy declines and is replaced by computing. If this prediction is realized, the Information Age will achieve full recognition as an economic age.

Parkhill saw the decline in employment as a benefit, not a detriment. Although he expected a period of transition that might be difficult, he predicted that eventually society would adjust and employment would be directed toward humanistic goals. Whether this prediction will prove as prescient as his others remains to be seen.

Moore's Law

The Information Age is essentially different from the other ages owing to *Moore's law*. Moore's law is not a law in the formal sense; rather, it is an inductive prediction that has proven correct for over fifty years, since the invention of the transistor in 1958. Moore predicted that the density of transistors on integrated circuits would double every two years. The impending failure of Moore's law has been predicted many times, but so far it has held up with remarkable consistency and the end is not in sight. Entirely new approaches to computing, such as quantum computers, portend a whole new realm of expansion beyond the limitations of silicon technology.

Moore's law projects exponential growth. Most people know what exponential growth means, or have at least heard the term, but the implications are often surprising. Let's examine exponential growth more carefully.

Exponential Growth

There are many stories of clever mathematicians using their knowledge of exponential series to trick the unknowing. One goes like this: a poor mathematician does a service to the king and the king offers to pay. The mathematician offers the king two payment plans: an arithmetic plan and an exponential plan (Figure 1-2). The first plan is to pay the mathematician one dollar today, two dollars tomorrow, three dollars the day after, increasing the payment by a dollar each day for thirty days. The second plan is to pay the mathematician half a cent today, one cent tomorrow, two cents the day after, and four cents the day after, doubling the amount each day for only thirty days.

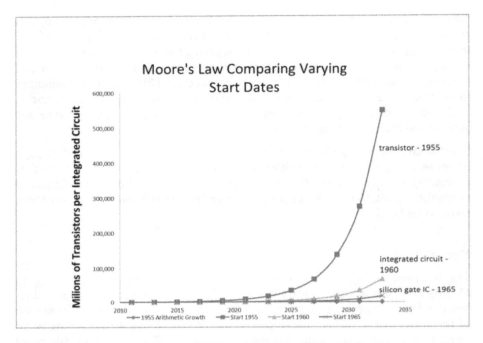

Figure 1-2. Changing the start date of Moore's law from 1955 to 1965 postpones a radical increase in computing power

The king chooses the second plan. We all know the outcome. If the king had chosen the first plan, he would have paid a total of $465. But by choosing the second plan, he will end up paying a total of **$5,368,709.**

We also know the real outcome. By the end of the third week when the payout to the mathematician exceeds $10,000, the king has the mathematician's head removed to prevent further disruption.

But there is a very important point in this story. Halfway through the month, on the fourteenth day, the first plan's total payout would have been $105, whereas the second plan's payout was $82. In other words, for the first two weeks, the exponential plan favored the king.

If the mathematician had made the exponential plan more attractive and reduced the first payment to five thousandths of a cent (0.005¢), the total payout would still be over half a million dollars, but the first plan would favor the king until the eighteenth day, and the payout would not exceed $10,000 until the twenty-fourth day. The mathematician would have lived an extra week.

By adjusting the starting point of the exponential payment plan, we can adjust the mathematician's life span. If we reduce the initial payment to 0.000005¢, he might live to old age because the total payout over thirty days is less than $6,000.

The Industrial and Technological ages were analogous to the first payment plan. The first steam engine was built, then the second, then the third, and so on. Each engine became more powerful; building the second steam engine doubled steam power, but building the third only added a third more power. Each additional engine added something to the previous, but there was not continuous doubling of power. The inventions of the Technological Age were similar: innovations were continuously added but there was not exponential growth. Society was certainly transformed by the innovations of each of these ages, but the transformations of these ages proceeded through incremental processes rather than exponential series.

The differences between incremental and exponential series are important. The rate of change in an incremental series stays constant. In the real world, increments differ in size, so the rate of change varies, but over the long haul, progress follows a straight line. At least in retrospect, incremental progress is easy to understand and projections are relatively simple and reliable.

Exponential series are less intuitively stable. To interpret an exponential series, you have to know where you are in the series. This tells us something important about the growth of the Information Age. If we accept Moore's law and peg the growth of the Information Age to the exponential growth of computing power that the law implies, we don't know if the starting point in 1958 was a dollar or a hundred-thousandth of a cent. The year 2014 might be analogous to the third week of a sequence that started at half a cent, in which case the Information Age is about to become exciting. But the sequence might have started at 0.005¢, in which case we have another couple decades to wait before the real excitement starts. We know the series is exponential, but we don't know where we are on the curve (see Figure 1-2). Moore's law does not tell us whether we have already entered the steep part of the curve, in which case the Information Age is a wash-out, or whether the curve is about to take off and we will soon find out what the Information Age is about, or we have decades to wait before the acceleration takes off. Figure 1-2 shows that if the Moore's law progression started in 1955 (the start date usually ascribed to the law), chip density will begin to take off in 2010 to 2020. If we have decades to wait, maybe Moore's law will finally fail and the Information Age will wash out in another way.

Have we reached the fast-growing end of the computing curve? Or are we still in the flat initial segment, slowly doubling in microscopic increments, decades away from escape velocity? Or are we on the threshold of fun greater than we ever imagined? And are we always in danger that technology will hit a physical wall that stops the progress of Moore's pilgrim?[11]

Searching for the Acceleration Point

Surprising developments in recent years suggest we may be entering the steep part of the curve. The sudden ubiquity of social computing with Facebook, LinkedIn, and a number of other social networking sites indicates that computing influences everyday lives in new and profound ways. Facebook's datacenters are as large as or larger than the "serious" datacenters that power computation-intensive industries like banking or insurance.[12] Who would have thought that sites devoted to pictures of cute puppies and birthday greetings would consume more computing power than the insurance industry in 1990?

This change is not incremental. Social networks did not exist in the twentieth century. Without the increase in available computing power, storage, and high-speed network capacity, social networking on the current scale could not exist. So far, the impact of the social network use of computing capacity has been more social than economic. The assets of a social network such as Facebook are for now better measured in number of users than dollars of revenue—but with a market capitalization of over ninety billion dollars invested by shareholders into Facebook, someone must anticipate profitability.[13]

---

[11]Speculating on potential walls to Moore's law is interesting. Resource depletion is a possibility. Silicon (sand) is not likely to be a limiting factor, but perhaps other elements that are used in trace quantities in computer chips may limit growth. Ray Kurzweil, suggests a different kind of limit, at which computer intelligence completely exceeds human intelligence (*The Singularity Is Near: When Humans Transcend Biology*, New York: Penguin, 2005).

[12]Numbers are scarce, but Internet companies such as Facebook clearly have the largest datacenters. See Rich Miller, "Who Has the Most Web Servers?," http://www.datacenterknowledge.com/archives/2009/05/14/whos-got-the-most-web-servers/, May 14, 2009.

[13]Many dispute the significance and benefits of social networking and the Internet in general. Evgeny Morozov is an articulate exponent of the anti-triumphalist view of the Internet. (See Noam Cohen, the New York Times, "The Internet's Verbal Contrarian," http://www.nytimes.com/2013/08/15/business/media/the-internets-verbal-contrarian.html?pagewanted=all&_r=0, August 14, 2013.) Morozov focuses his critique on the political influence of technology rather than the technology itself—in other words, what is done with the Internet rather than what it is.

The storage and processor time lavished on Facebook kittens and puppies are available courtesy of the huge increases in computing power predicted by Moore's law.[14] It is easy to assign too much significance to an observation like this, but worth considering that we have entered a period when massive amounts of computing power are available for purposes that the pioneers of computing would have dismissed as a waste of valuable resources.

There are other indications that something big is happening. Giant datacenters are one aspect of burgeoning computing power. The other end of the spectrum is the number of small computing devices that have entered our lives. The growth in mobile devices depends upon computing devices that are incredibly more compact than the computing machinery of the last century. A smartphone today has several orders of magnitude more computing power than a room-filling computer of fifty years ago. Cellular connectivity is also dependent on the computing power required to track roving smart phones and maintain connections to other phones and web sites. The entire BYOD ("bring your own device") phenomenon results from the rise of ever-more-powerful personal devices. Handheld devices have extended the reach of computing to the third world where computing did not exist until recently.

And the number of handheld computers may soon be exceeded by the number of computers that are being embedded all around us. Computers are being built into many things and these embedded computers are frequently being connected to the Internet. Some have speculated that the real driving force behind IPv6 network addressing is not to accommodate increased numbers of human computer users. A human being with a keyboard only needs a single network address, whereas the computers embedded in the cluster of devices around that human being may soon require tens or hundreds of addresses.

The control components in automobiles are one example of the use of tiny computing units to control and assist mechanical devices in their operation. Computers in automobiles now usually operate independently, controlling your automobile without connecting to other cars on the road or a central data collector and processor. However, we are not far from navigation systems that connect with highway traffic control systems to steer you around traffic congestion and even take over driving itself and consign highway deaths to system defects.

---

[14]This is not to dismiss the many more practical uses of social networking today, but the prodigious consumption of computing resources on pure sentiment is an indication of the wealth of resources available.

In the future, your toaster and coffee pot may carry on their own conversations with applications running on a cloud hosted in another country. Conceivably, an energy utility might anticipate current loads from the information from coffee pots and toasters (and many other electrical devices) and use this information to make load switching decisions. Coffee plantations might regulate their crops based on consumption data contributed from your coffee pot.

For better or for worse, we are becoming embedded in a maze of computing devices, all made possible by the availability of smaller and cheaper computational power. And these little processors are all connected. The interconnection of all these devices is what is called the *Internet of Things* (IoT). The IoT is closely related to clouds because to truly take advantage of this profusion of data, there has to be a datacenter that consolidates the data and converts it to usable information. These hubs of the Internet of Things can be well accommodated in clouds.

For some people, this may sound like a horror story, but there is no certainty that an apocalypse of centralized control is on the horizon. Previous economic ages each have generated fears, but it is at least possible that society will muddle its way through the Information Age as it did the previous ages. We do know that as long as Moore's law continues to operate, information technology will continue to acquire new capabilities.

An important question on the historical scale is whether the Information Age has finally reached the point that it is as influential as the Industrial Age and Technological Age that preceded it. The developments of the last decade—cloud, mobile computing, and ubiquitous network connections—have certainly changed our lives. Whether they have changed them sufficiently to usher in a new "age" remains to be revealed.

Cloud Computing

Advances in technology have moderated the difficulty of building enterprise applications, but the recent explosion of data and computing capacity has also increased the challenge. For decades, delivering applications as a service running on a provider's premises has been an important business and architectural model for managed IT service providers. Relatively recently, however, the model has risen in prominence in the form of what are now called *cloud implementations*.

CLOUD DEFINED

The National Institute of Standards and Technology (NIST) defines *cloud* as a model for rapidly deployed, on-demand computing resources such as processors, storage, applications, and services. NIST describes four deployment models—private, public, community, and hybrid—and three service models—infrastructure, platform, and application as services.[15] In practice, a cloud is usually implemented as a pool of physical resources that supports configurable virtual resources and services. The virtual resources are deployed for and owned by consumers. The consumers have access to their virtual resources and services until their relationship with the cloud service provider ends and virtual resources are released.

A cloud implementation shares characteristics with timesharing, but there are also fundamental differences, which stem from technical changes. See Figure 1-3 for a glimpse of the differences. Both cloud consumers and timeshare consumers use a computing service without owning the computers. The differences between cloud and timeshare are largely due to differences in the technology. Timeshare customers typically had terminals on their premises, devices that were little more than remote displays and keyboards without any computing capacity. These terminals were connected directly to a central computer whose computing time was shared among other connected terminals.

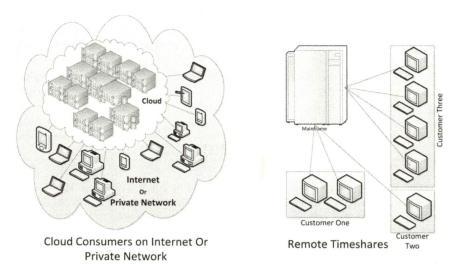

Cloud Consumers on Internet Or Private Network

Remote Timeshares

Figure 1-3. Cloud and timesharing differ

[15]Peter Mell and Timothy Grance, "The NIST Definition of Cloud Computing: Recommendations of the National Institute of Standards and Technology," http://csrc.nist.gov/publications/nistpubs/800-145/SP800-145.pdf, September 2012.

Clouds use more advanced equipment and technology that are based on distributed systems. Instead of a single central computer, the physical implementation of a cloud consists of many connected computers. Instead of a single timeshared computer, cloud consumers see the cloud as a collection of virtual resources, which include virtual computers that are reserved for them. Their connection to the cloud is through a network, often the Internet, to a portal that provides access to their reserved virtual facilities. The devices on the consumer's premises are usually computers with computing capacity of their own. They may be desktops, laptops, handhelds, or other devices. The cloud services may be accessed directly by the consumer, or processes running on the consumer's devices may access cloud services without the consumer's active intervention.

Cloud implementations present more options and flexibility for both the consumer and provider. Cloud implementation has become important in almost every recent IT project.

Later chapters have much more to say about cloud architecture.

Service Orientation

In the beginning, von Neumann computers ran programs. When a program was useful to an end user of the system it was often called an *application*. Today, computers still run programs and applications, but, for most in IT, computers are beginning to be more often thought of as providing services. This has been an important change. Later chapters will have much more to say about *service orientation*. Programs are single entities that start, perform a task or tasks for a period of time, and then stop. Batch programs usually proceed from beginning to end with little or no interaction with other programs or users. Interactive programs respond to user requests and events from other running processes, but in general they are thought of as independent entities.

SERVICE ORIENTATION DEFINED

Service orientation starts with the concept of a consumer and a provider. Consumers may range from a person, a company, or an agent to a software process or a thread within a process. The provider offers a real or implicit contract such that, when presented with certain inputs, certain results may be expected. On the business level, one of the inputs is usually a fee for the service. Both the consumer and the provider are expected to stick to the contract. In business, a provider or consumer that does not stick to the contract can expect penalties. On the technical level, consumers and providers must also follow the rules of a contract, often embodied in an interface specification. If the rules are not followed, the expected outcomes will not occur. Business discussions of services often focus on the transfer of costs and risks between the consumer and provider. Technical discussions usually concentrate on the modularity and granularity of services.

Services are designed to respond to requests for service. Service is both a business and technical concept. In business, following the *Information Technology Infrastructure Library* (ITIL) definition,[16] a *service* is a vehicle for delivering value to a consumer while transferring specified costs and risks to the provider.[17] A dry-cleaning service delivers cleaned clothes (value) to the consumer, and the dry-cleaning provider takes on the risks of damaging the clothing and the cost of cleaning equipment. The consumer compensates the provider by paying for the service.

In business and economics, services are contrasted with goods. *Goods* are tangible or intangible assets that have lasting value, unlike services in which value production ceases when the service is complete. The distinction is similar to the distinction between hardware and software in computing.

In IT technology, the concept of service is related to its business concept, but the two are not identical. Both the business and technical definitions of service involve the separation of the concerns of the consumer and provider. The technical definition is not directly concerned with value and risk. Instead, the technical definition concentrates on separating the consumer and provider to achieve greater modularity and a decoupling.

Unlike applications, which usually are a bundle of functionality directed toward performing one or more related tasks, a well-designed service executes a single fine-grained task that can be used in many higher-level services or is composed of many such services. Fine-grained services are much more easily reused and repurposed than monolithic applications, and the separation of services from consumers tends to create a more resilient architecture that recovers more easily from failures (Figure 1-4).

---

[16]ITIL will come up often in this book. ITIL began as collection of documents on IT published to guide IT practice in the UK government. It has evolved into a collection of best practices that are recognized globally as a compendium of practices for service management of IT.

[17]David Cannon, David Wheeldon, Shirley Lacy, and Ashley Hanna, *ITIL Service Strategy* (London: TSO, 2011), p. 451.

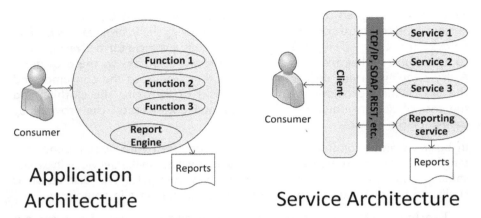

Figure 1-4. A service-oriented architecture decomposes applications into individual services

Service orientation on both the business and technical level is one of the architectural principles that have propelled the growth of the complex IT systems that we have today.

Integration

System integration is a long-established practice in enterprise IT. *Integration* often refers to the practice of stitching and wiring new applications into an IT system, or adding a new application to an existing system. The term is to be taken here, however, to mean something broader: the entire process of building applications and architecting system and function as a single coordinated whole. One way of looking at the progress of IT is to see it as an ever-increasing integration of the IT environment. The level of IT system integration profoundly affects the role of IT in contemporary business.

Like most business and engineering endeavors, IT projects seldom start by inventing an entire infrastructure. Instead, they build upon a set of established architectural patterns, best practices, and off-the-shelf technologies. Innovation is at its best when it avoids duplicating previous achievements by redesigning and rebuilding facilities that already serve their purposes. Using best practices and established technology that builds on proven resources makes it possible to focus on the innovation that will move the project ahead of its peers, instead of wasting energy on rebuilding foundations that already work well.

Applications always have target functionality. A service desk application creates and manages incidents and problems. A performance management application measures system performance. When these applications are developed, the goal is usually what developers and product managers call "best-of-breed": the best service desk among service desks; the best performance manager among performance managers. Best-of-breed is software built to the highest standards that does its job better than all its competition, whatever the criteria for excellence in the product area.

The best-of-breed goal inspires outstanding software products. In this, software is like most industries. Best-of-breed products have been the foundation for many great industries, not just software. Ford became a great car company by aspiring to build the best economically priced cars and Boeing became a great airplane manufacturer by striving to manufacture the best airplanes.

But best-of-breed products do not always ensure the success of the user of the product. Sometimes success for users depends upon the fit of a product to their environment rather than the superiority of the product itself. Fleet operators with a large stock of GM parts and trained GM mechanics may discover a Ford vehicle that fits their needs better than a corresponding GM product, but they still pass on the Ford because their support infrastructure would have to be revamped to maintain it.

This is often so in IT management. A service desk may be counted the best-of-breed because it has an intuitive and attractive user interface and the finest service-level management system, but in an enterprise with heavily instrumented infrastructure, this best-of-breed service desk may fail if it cannot work with the instrumentation to automatically create an incident when the system detects an anomaly. A service desk with fewer features but able to create incidents automatically may be more effective than the best-of-breed competitor under those circumstances. Success in automatically creating incidents depends on more than the surface features in the service desk. It also depends on the ability of the entire system to communicate with the service desk at the right moment in a form that the service desk can use.

Most of the time, the overall value of an application depends on the functioning of the application in the total environment. This requires integration. In a totally integrated system, every application is aware of every other application in the infrastructure and is able to communicate freely.

Free communication within an integrated environment is a challenge as well as a goal, because most situations require governance and administrative control. Unauthorized persons and applications must be barred access to certain data and services for legal or management reasons. Management policies may control when and how operations can be executed to accord with enterprise goals. Administrative policies limit activities to maintain order. In an ideally integrated system, all services and data are accessible from anywhere, but policy controls and other mechanisms can prevent access from anywhere or anything when management or administration demands.

INTEGRATION DEFINED

Generally, *integration* means combining diverse complex parts into a whole. The composed parts remain distinguishable, but they work together harmoniously, with some level of control that reaches through the entire composition. Each integrated application exposes data and operations that all the other applications in the infrastructure are able to access and use subject to security, management, and administrative policies.

IT Integration

Integrated applications work together. When applications are not integrated, they cannot, or do not, communicate. We usually talk about data and application integration. Data integration means that data is shared between applications. An example of data integration is a service desk application and a *customer relationship management* (CRM) application that share the same list of employees. This saves effort and reduces errors that arise from discrepancies between the two systems. It also makes reports that span the two systems, such as a report by a customer of all the employees who have been involved in resolving the customer's incidents.

Enterprise-wide reporting and dashboards are other common examples of data integration. Data from many applications are combined into views to present the overall state of the enterprise. These reports and dashboards become much easier to develop and are more accurate if data is shared between applications rather than independently maintained.

Application integration is more complex and a step beyond data integration. Integrated applications use each other's processes. If a service desk and a CRM application integrate as applications, the service desk might automatically annotate a customer's history when it logs an incident related to the customer. Application integration can take many different forms. Applications may interact without user involvement; a user can use one integrated application from another integrated application or work from an interface that blends integrated applications together. Users do their jobs with less effort and greater accuracy when they don't have to jump from one application to another to complete a single task.

Another aspect of integration addresses the management of the IT system itself. In a distributed system, failures or impairments can sometimes be easily traced to a single source, but failures often cannot be traced to a single malfunction. The failure or impairment may be the result of an unfortunate series of situations, none of which is consequential in isolation but which are disastrous in concert. To manage this kind of complexity, integration of the entire management system is necessary.

Data versus Application Integration

The distinction between data and application integration helps us understand how integration works. Most applications that share functionality also share data. On the other hand, applications often share and combine data without sharing functionality.

Data Integration

Many integration requirements deal only with data. The need for consolidated and combined reports is an important reason for data integration. The need may span organizational barriers, such as a report that combines human resources data from several distinct business units.

In other situations, a report may be required to cross application boundaries when it requires data that is contained in more than one application. For example, a CRM application tracks the products a customer has purchased. A service desk program often is used to record issues opened by customers on products. A design department that wants to know if certain types of defects affect a few users intensely or touches all users may request a report that lists the issues opened by a customer on each product purchased. Such a report requires data from both the service desk and the CRM applications.

Data integration challenges such as these may have a simple and quick solution. For example, many applications can generate reports in the form of spreadsheets. It may be a simple job for someone skilled in spreadsheets to obtain spreadsheets from different sources and merge them into a single sheet. In the human resources data example, the data from different divisions is likely to be contained in spreadsheets, and obtaining the desired report may involve no more than summing a few columns.

If both the CRM application and the service desk applications generate spreadsheet output, merging the data into the desired report may be more difficult because data must be combined in more intricate ways. However, this is still a relatively simple task. A combined report that shows issues per product per customer can be created using the spreadsheet tool's ability to create joins between tables.

Data integration is often much more complex.

Data Redundancy

Failover and disaster recovery are heroes poised to save the enterprise. When something goes wrong, *failover* transfers activity from the failing system to a backup system so business can carry on. If a disaster utterly destroys some portion of the system making failover impossible, *disaster recovery* kicks in to rebuild the system as rapidly as possible. Redundancy increases the stability and resiliency of a system for failover and disaster recovery. When a component fails or becomes inaccessible or data disappears, a redundant component or data storage may be able to take over. However, *data redundancy* is not always beneficial.

When a discrepancy appears between two versions of anything—a gauge reading, a transcription of an oracle bone inscription, or a computer file—questions arise: Is one or the other correct? Or are both correct? Is the discrepancy a mistake? Or are both versions legitimate?

In IT, the problem is with data sources, not oracle bone transcriptions. Management applications are often data sources.

If a server is performing below expectations, how do technicians diagnose the problem? Their first step is to go to the applications that manage the ailing server. If one management application—say, a network management— reports that ailing server has 2 gigabytes (GB) of random access memory (RAM) and another application—say, an asset management system—has recorded that the server has 8 GB of RAM, which is right? If the network management system is correct, the problem could easily be a memory module that has worked its way out of its socket. If the asset management system is correct, RAM is probably not the problem and the technicians have to look elsewhere. Perhaps a disk should be defragmented or a RAID level changed.[18] But who knows which application is right?

Faced with this uncertainty, technicians must spend time diagnosing the problem. They may have to go out on the floor, find the physical server, open the case, and visually inspect the memory modules. If they are lucky, they will find a loose module. Or else they will find that they must look elsewhere.

In a large and tightly run IT department, a trip to the physical server is not trivial. It wastes technician time and lengthens the time during which the server underperforms. If the server is supporting critical business, the extended server slowdown could be disastrously costly. If the server is supporting external customer-facing services, customers could become disgruntled and the business end up losing both customers and its reputation for reliability.

This example may not cause any substantial problem, but as the delays build up over time, productivity decreases and inevitably a big blowup will occur, for which the enterprise will incur substantial expense.

---

[18]*Redundant arrays of independent disks* (RAIDs) are arrays of hard drives that work in coordination to provide greater reliability and performance than a single drive. The data distribution pattern of the array can be configured for varying tradeoffs between performance, error resilience, and capacity. These data distribution patterns are called levels.

A single data mismatch is not likely to cause all the consequences described here. Enterprises have run for many years with disconnected asset and network management systems. But the errors that result from the disconnection are not limited to the obvious kind of problem described above. For example, missing RAM is not the problem it once was, because it costs orders of magnitude less now than it did—but inventory shrinkage is always a problem. Shrinkage is most likely to be detected in asset management, not network management, although network management is more likely to have accurate information because it has automated means of detecting configuration. It is hard to determine what the cost of this lack of synchronization has been.

Application Integration

Communication between applications is often an afterthought—something for services personnel to tear their hair over on-site, but a side issue for product managers and application designers dialed in on producing best-of-breed applications. While striving for that critical best-of-breed status, it is easy to forget that an application seldom stands alone. The task of designing applications that can work with other applications requires knowledge of more than the technology and business area under development. It requires broad knowledge of the workings of many different applications and a comprehensive view of the entire business ecosystem. This is intimidating and often unappreciated work that few want to tackle. When deciding between adding a best-of-breed feature and communicating with applications that are difficult to understand and even potential competitors, the arguments for neglecting communication are strong.

This has mixed impact on customers. Product managers promote best-of-breed features because customers want to buy them. Presumably, if they vote with their dollars for the features, they are happy to get them. It is easy to blow off these features as "bells and whistles," but usually a new feature is neither a bell nor a whistle but a capability that substantially increases the value of the application for the customer.

Consequently, support for an application is often an afterthought left to the IT staff or hired services consultants after best-of-breed applications are installed. Since the applications have been designed with scant attention to integration requirements, stitching the applications together results in a system that is easily broken, squanders resources, and may provide integrated data and services that are far below expectations.

A much better approach is an IT system architecture that places application-and-data integration in the foundation of the system rather than built into each application in the system. Recent developments in IT system architecture—service orientation and cloud in particular—have made IT system integration more important, easier, and in some cases harder.[19]

Most important, the rate of acceleration in IT has increased. Methodologies such Agile and DevOps are symptomatic of the appetite for better systems that deliver more quickly.[20] This new appetite is related to the growing role of IT in our lives. As IT becomes more common, consumers have become less tolerant of failures. Online companies such as Amazon support staggering numbers of users with uptime that would have been considered stellar a decade ago, but a few minutes down in several months raises the ire of an uncompromising user base. If an application has a few users, they tend to accept a few flaws as long as the application delivers value, but when an application becomes a constant element in people's lives, they want their services all the time with no exceptions, and they want their features, many of which depend upon integration, now, not eighteen months in the future.

Conclusion

Today, software architects face an imperative that has grown from explosion of available computing power in the last decade and the related expansion of the role of information technology in our culture and economy.

Moore's law has proven to be an accurate prediction of a critical aspect of the increase in computing power: the exponential increase in the density of transistors on computer chips. This increase in chip density has reduced warehouse-sized mainframes of the mid-twentieth century to today's handheld tablets and smartphones. If Moore's prediction of exponential growth continues to hold, computing power will increase even more rapidly in the future.

---

[19]In general, web services, standards, and more uniform architectures, all of which are characteristic of clouds, make integration easier. On the other hand, platform and software as cloud services can make integration more difficult because they sometimes hide the some of the interior workings of the service from the integrator.

[20]Agile and DevOps are two methodologies that are strong influences today. Agile is a development methodology that emphasizes iterative incremental development over methodologies that advocate complete detailed designs before writing code. DevOps is a methodology that combines well with Agile. DevOps emphasizes close cooperation between development and operations groups. Operations participates in the design, construction, and testing of a project. When Agile and DevOps combine, code is delivered to operations teams in small increments. The experience of the operations team is then incorporated into the next drop of code.

The increase in computing power has had implications for society and the economy. We have entered the Information Age in which computer storage, transmission, and storage of information touches many aspects of life, from e-books and debit cards to massive search engines and social networking applications.

Applications are designed differently today. On average, they are more complex, require less knowledge to operate, and access much more information than the applications running on standalones of the past; and more and more often, they are services rather than intangible goods that their users own. They make use of concepts such as virtualization and cloud computing. They rely on far-reaching networks and they are closely tied to management concepts such as service management.

The challenge for software architects springs from the dynamic intersection of computing power and the influence of computing on society and economy. There is an enormous gap between the programs that ran on the standalone desktops of thirty years ago and the apps that run on the tiny tablets and smartphones of today. The critical imperative of the software architect is to design software architecture that harnesses and extends the direction and power of computing that is currently available and likely to expand rapidly in the future.

EXERCISES

1. Name and describe three of the most important advances in computing in the twenty-first century.

2. Compare and contrast the Information Age with the Industrial and Technological ages.

3. Using a spreadsheet or other tool, experiment with arithmetic versus exponential growth. Try different timelines, starting points, and rates of change.

4. How is cloud computing similar to timesharing? Different? How do these similarities and differences affect IT architecture?

5. How are services different from applications? Can a traditional application be used as a service? How?

6. Compare and contrast data integration and application integration. Is one more difficult to implement than the other?

The Merger

Enterprise Business and IT Management

SUMMARY

Business and IT are two distinct disciplines. In most enterprises, they are also interdependent but not necessarily cooperative. Cloud service management decisions need both business and technical input to be made wisely. Cloud utility computing is a significant change to the way IT works. A thorough understanding of what utilities are and how they work is required by both business and IT because they influence many decisions. The development of electrical and other utilities is frequently compared to the development of utility computing. Their similarities and differences help explain the value and difficulty of cloud computing.

From the outside, enterprise and IT management appear to be in harmony. On the inside, this is probably the exception rather than the rule. Often, the IT department and the business units appear to be armed camps, not harmonious partners.

It is easy to argue that such antagonism is wrong, but the roots of the antagonism are also easily discernible. Most IT professionals have degrees like a bachelor of science or higher in computer science (BSCS) or electrical engineering (BSEE). The signal degree on the business side is an MBA (Master of Business Administration). These disciplines have different subject matter and disciplines. They speak different languages; their scales of value are different. Software engineers seldom admire well-constructed business cases, and business managers rarely appreciate elegant and tightly written code.

Technologists and business managers have a hard time communicating. Both use words and phrases that the other does not understand. REST (representational state transfer) to a software engineer and rest to a business manager are not even slightly similar.

In addition, their goals are different. Technologists aim to get the most out of technology. They plot the most efficient way to accomplish a task and exercise new features of the technology with the same acumen with which a business manager coaxes an improved bottom line. Both technologists and businesspeople must make an effort to understand each other for IT to be an effective contributor to the enterprise. Lack of mutual understanding leads to business regarding IT as sunken overhead and losing opportunities offered by new technologies; and to technologists whose efforts repeatedly miss the requirements of business.

Business and IT Architecture

ARCHITECTURE DEFINED

Architecture is the underlying organization of a system and the principles that guide its design and construction. An architecture identifies the components of the system, the relationships between the system's components, and the relationship between the system and its environment. IT architecture not only describes the physical computing infrastructure and software running on the infrastructure but also details the relationship between IT and other business units and departments and the structure and content of the data stored and processed by the system.

The architecture of an enterprise is a nested hierarchy. At the top of the hierarchy is the overall enterprise architecture. Within the enterprise architecture are the architectures of its components. They may be business units, organizations, or other entities. For example, within an enterprise architecture, the human relations department, the engineering department, and the manufacturing business unit may all be components with their own architecture.

The hierarchy depends on the organization of the enterprise. In Figure 2-1, a single IT architecture serves several departments and business units. This arrangement is common but by no means the only way to organize an enterprise architecture. For example, each business unit may have its own IT architecture while the functional departments such as human resources share an IT architecture.

The reasons for differing enterprise architectural patterns vary. A business unit may have been acquired with its own IT department, and enterprise management may decide to leave the business unit structure undisturbed. In other cases, a business unit or department may be geographically remote from the enterprise premises, making centralized IT awkward. When regulations dictate that two departments must be strictly separated, distinct IT architectures may be required. A division or unit with special technology, such as *computer-aided design* (CAD) or *computer-aided manufacturing* (CAM), might work better with a separate IT architecture. Other reasons may relate to either business or engineering requirements.

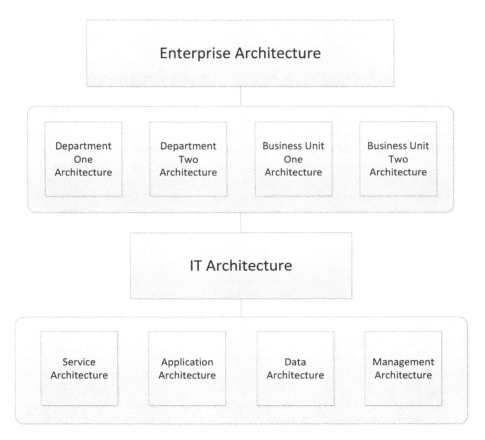

Figure 2-1. An enterprise architecture contains the architectures of subunits. IT is both a subunit and a link among other subunits.

The boxes on an enterprise architecture diagram do not exist in isolation. Just as application architecture and data architecture must coordinate to be effective within the IT architecture, the IT architecture must coordinate with the entire enterprise architecture as well as each subunit. IT architecture has to be planned and implemented in accordance with these considerations and it must also evolve along with the other components in the enterprise architecture.

When IT architecture is designed and evolves in isolation, the enterprise as a whole suffers. The damage is both technical and managerial. IT cannot support the business units and departments in achieving their goals and the enterprise does not get the full benefit of innovation in IT. This becomes a classic "impedance mismatch" in which the business asks for things IT can't supply and IT provides things that business can't use. The consequences can be ugly. Unsatisfactory outsourcing is one result. Inefficient departmental IT projects that duplicate and work around the IT organization are another.

Cloud and Enterprise Architecture Fragmentation

Cloud facilitates IT projects both inside and outside the IT department, because any employee with a credit card can have entire datacenters, advanced application development platforms, and sophisticated enterprise applications at their fingertips. The situation is reminiscent of the days when anyone could buy a PC, put it on her desk, and automate her department. IT can anticipate something similar to the course of distributed computing, in which desktop IT projects slipped out of IT's view and basics such as disaster recovery and security suffered until management was forced to reassert IT control.

The relationships between enterprise architecture components are always *full-duplex* (such that communication between the two connected components flows in both directions simultaneously). Departmental architectures that ignore the architectures of other components are as counterproductive as IT that ignores enterprise and departmental architecture. Both cause problems. Departmental systems that run contrary to the enterprise architecture may not communicate or integrate with similar systems in other departments. When a department has an activity that relies on IT processes, IT may not be able to help if they do not understand the role of IT processes in the departmental activity. IT departments have sophisticated performance monitoring, fault detection, and incident systems that manage the reliability of the IT system, but these may be of no help to a department that has its own private system running in isolation.

Fragmentation is a problem for both technical and business management. Technically, systems must be designed for integration and sharing. Too often, applications are designed to meet a specific set of requirements that disregard the possibility that the application will eventually have to communicate with and serve many departments. Even when integration is addressed in the requirements, they can be deferred or ignored in the rush to put the system in operation. When this happens without a clear plan for remediation, fragmentation can become permanent. Cooperation between business and IT management in the form of strategic planning is a solution to fragmentation.

Closing the Architectural Divide

The relationship between IT and business determines many outcomes. Technologists who are deep into the hardware and software heart of IT sometimes forget that IT exists to support business and may even be the business itself for businesses that rely heavily on software, such as insurance companies and online businesses. These technologists are often frustrated by businesspeople who do not understand the mechanisms that make their business work. Businesspeople sometimes forget that IT is vital to their present and future business and listen more to outside business advisors than to their own dedicated technologists.

The edges of these architectures are critical. IT technologists do not have to understand the details of the core of enterprise and departmental business architectures. For instance, IT does not need to understand the mesh of relationships between sales and production, but they do need to thoroughly understand where IT touches the enterprise and each of its business units and departments. IT can legitimately expect that the business units and departments understand in business terms the resources available to IT in meeting their requests. In addition, IT can expect that the business understands the implications of ignoring IT requirements.

Fortunately, the divide between IT and business has become less severe. In the heady days of the first Internet boom, business sometimes gave IT a blank check to pursue the next big thing. That may have appeared to be good for IT, but it left a hangover. Freewheeling attitudes lead to ill-planned projects that delivered less than was promised. The pendulum swung to the opposite extreme and business became excessively skeptical of IT claims. In the sober light after the boom, the mutual dependence of business and IT became evident, and conscious efforts were made to set up frameworks that would avoid antagonism and promote constructive cooperation.

A fundamental step toward closing this divide is a comprehensive architecture that integrates the enterprise, enterprise subunits, and IT department. There are a large number of enterprise architecture frameworks available from the academy, industry analysts, enterprise integrators, standards organizations, and other sources. Each of these has its own strengths and weaknesses, and each enterprise must select the best fit. A comprehensive architectural framework has value because it clarifies the relationships and dependencies between entities in the enterprise.

This need for an IT architecture that coordinates with the overall enterprise architecture is only accentuated by cloud offerings that make it easy for non-IT groups to float their own IT projects. An enterprise IT architecture is a tool for avoiding that form of chaos, because it makes it easier for business units and departments to see the services that the IT department provides and so disinclines them to strike out on their own.

The key is to pay attention to enterprise goals and plans in developing an IT architecture that aligns with the enterprise. IT itself seldom represents a revenue stream. Its role must be to enhance other revenue streams and provide other units with the capacity to expand and transform their business. This puts an extra burden on IT to know their customers: the business units that depend on them.

The challenges discussed here are not limited to IT. Any subunit of an enterprise faces a similar problem in working with the other parts of the enterprise, and all can benefit from taking a similar approach. Nevertheless, given the general challenge, there is much that is specific to IT.

Computing as Utility

Computing as a utility is an important concept that has been discussed for a long time. Both technology and business are being affected by the transformation of some aspects of IT into utilities.

UTILITY DEFINED

In its most general sense, *utility* is what a service does, and it is the basis for deciding if a service will meet the needs of the consumer. When discussing computing as a utility, the meaning is more specific and derives from the concept of a *public utility*, a service that maintains an infrastructure for delivering a specific service to a wide range of consumers. The service provided by a utility is a commodity. Some utilities are implemented by government agencies; others are private or a combination of public and private. Utilities may be regulated or they may follow industry or de facto standards, but in any case the services they provide are interchangeable.

Utility is a business and economic concept that applies to a wide range of services. A utility is a broadly consumed service that is offered to the public. Utilities are standardized, at least in following a de facto standard. Therefore, consumers can switch relatively easily among utility providers.[1]

Utilities often do not yield value directly to their consumers; the utility has to be transformed before the consumer gets value. For example, electricity from the service panel only has value to a homeowner when it is connected to a light bulb or some other appliance.

---

[1]Changing your cell-phone provider is difficult, because the providers have an interest in keeping their existing customers. However, the difficulties are far less than the obstacles to switching your brand of printer and continuing to use the supply of print cartridges for your old printer.

Utilities are often government-regulated to enforce uniform interfaces and safety standards. For example, building codes enforce standard 240-volt receptacles that will not accept a standard 120-volt plug. This prevents damage to 120-volt appliances and injury to users.

When utilities are monopolies, their pricing structure is often government-controlled. They may be publicly or privately owned. Some electric companies are public, often operated by municipalities. Others are private, but regulations limit the prices that can be charged—which benefits consumers where there is no alternative to a single electricity supplier.

COMMODITY DEFINED

A *commodity* is a good (as opposed to a service) that is assumed to be of uniform quality so that one can be exchanged for another without effect. Commodities are more or less fungible. Fungible assets are those which can be exchanged freely and have the same value. Money is frequently held up as the exemplar of fungible assets. A dollar debt can be paid with any dollar; it does not have to be the exact bit of currency that changed hands when the debt was incurred.

Utilities are closely related to the idea of commodity. *Commodity* can refer to any good, as opposed to service, but it has the more specialized meaning of a good that is sold with the assumption that it meets an agreed-upon standard that is applied to all goods of that kind, no matter what the source may be. Commodities are fungible; a commodity may always be exchanged for an equal quantity of a commodity of the same type. For example, a bushel of commodity wheat purchased today could be resold six months later at a higher price, because today's commodity wheat is interchangeable with expensive future wheat.

Utilities deal in commodity services. A *utility provider* is separate from a *utility consumer*: the utility is supplied uniformly over a wide consumer base, and the economic incentive for using a utility stems from an economy of scale and the transfer of risk to the provider. Consumers are usually charged based on the service consumed, and are not charged directly for the investment in the infrastructure needed to generate the service. These concepts, inherent in the nature of utilities, translate into questions that can be asked about the potential of a service as a utility:

- Can the service be effectively supplied by a provider? Or would consumers be better off supplying the service themselves?

- Do economies of scale exist? Is it substantially cheaper to supply the service to many consumers?

- Will consumers benefit substantially from being charged only for the service used? Can the service be metered? Does the benefit offset the cost and effort of metering the service?

- Are there meaningful risks that the utility could mitigate, such as physical dangers in generating the service or financial risks in equipment investments?

- Is the service a fungible commodity that is used identically by all consumers without regard to the source? Is the service uniform? Or must it be customized for most consumers?

An example of a service that would probably not be a good candidate for becoming a utility is a dry-cleaning service. All the questions above but the last can be answered affirmatively. Dry cleaning is a specialized task that uses dangerous chemicals and requires expensive equipment. Large dry-cleaning plants with automated equipment can do the job cheaply. Then why isn't dry cleaning a utility? The reason is that customers who accept one dry-cleaning service may not accept another. People are fussy about their dry cleaning. They search for a dry cleaner that cleans their clothing just the way they like it. They have special requests. Occasional rush jobs are important. Consequently, few consumers would be satisfied with a utility dry-cleaning service that allowed few options or custom service.

These concepts are independent of the technical implementation of the utility. Technology typically makes a utility possible, but technology alone will not qualify a service as a candidate for becoming a utility.

When a service is transformed into a utility, the technology may change. Small generators might be replaced by huge dynamos driven by huge hydroelectric projects, mountains of coal, or nuclear reactors. The business and financial basis of the service will change also. Consumers will sign contracts for service. The utility will guarantee minimum quality of service. Regulators may become involved. Small entrepreneurial ventures may be consolidated into larger utility suppliers.

The notion of computing as a utility arose naturally when timesharing began to become common (Chapter 1). It was a short step from customers sharing time with a large datacenter to the idea that timeshare terminals might become widely available and treated as a utility. This vision did not materialize. Timesharing thrived for a time, but terminals did not appear everywhere. Instead, new devices called *personal computers* (PCs) began to pop up everywhere. The first PCs were little more than expensive toys not connected to any other computer, let alone the massive hub the timeshare utility envisioned. But with the aid of ever more powerful integrated circuits and miniature processors, they rapidly rose in importance.

The Birth of a Utility: The Electrical Grid

It is a commonplace that IT is undergoing transformation to a utility, in a process analogous to the emergence of electric power as a public utility around the turn of the nineteenth century.[2]

Early Adoption of Electricity

The transformation of power generation to a utility has parallels with the progress of IT. Before electric power utilities, large electricity consumers like manufacturers had their own private generating plants. These dedicated private industrial facilities were among the largest generation plants, much like the private mainframes owned by large institutions and corporations. Smaller concerns and residences relied on small generation companies that supplied electric power to clusters of consumers in limited areas. A small generation plant might supply a few small businesses and a handful of residences within a mile radius.

As electrical engineering advanced, the small generation companies expanded to supply larger and larger areas at lower and lower prices. Gradually, concerns began to shut down their private generators and rely on cheap and reliable power from the generation companies specializing in generating and distributing comparatively cheap electrical power over wide areas. Eventually even the largest electricity consumers such as aluminum smelters shut down their private generators and plugged into the growing grid.

Productivity and Electricity

Surprisingly, the adoption of electricity did not result in immediate gains in productivity. Prior to electricity, power distribution in a single plant was done through a system of rotating overhead shafts, pulleys, and belts. This arrangement dictated the layout of factories. It had been much easier to transmit power upward than to spread it out horizontally. Multi-floor factories with limited square footage on each floor used less power than factories with the corresponding square footage on a single floor. Placing machines close together also made more efficient use of power. Layouts like this were inflexible and hard to use. Moving or replacing a machine required moving precisely

---

[2]A prominent proponent of this theory is Nicholas Carr, whose article "IT Doesn't Matter" (*Harvard Business Review*, May 2003, http://www.nicholascarr.com/?page_id=99) has provoked a great deal of discussion, both for and against his proposition, since it was published in 2003. Carr included all aspects of computing in his prediction that most enterprises would outsource their current IT activities to computing utility providers, which is more than simply outsourcing computing.

aligned shafts and pulleys. Changes required highly skilled millwrights and could stop production in the entire plant for days. Narrow aisles made moving materials difficult. Equipment positions could not be adjusted as needed to speed up work.

These limitations caused inefficiency. Modern plants tend to be single-floor structures that cover large areas. Most machines have their own electric motors and power is transmitted to the machine via electric cables and wiring. This arrangement permits ample space for moving materials using equipment such as forklifts and conveyers. There is room for maintenance. The plant configurations can be changed to accommodate new processes, equipment, and products. Running a cable and plugging it into an electric panel usually has little effect on the rest of the plant, so the rest of the plant is not affected by maintenance and changes. These flexible layouts depend on the ease of running electrical cables and moving electric motors to where they are needed.

When electric motors replaced steam engines, electric motors were seen as replacements for central steam engines connected to manufacturing equipment with shafts and pulleys. Instead of immediately installing an electric motor for each machine, the shaft-and-pulley system was preserved and only a few central electric motors were installed. This meant that individual machines would not have to be modified or replaced to accommodate an electric motor.[3]

Adoption in this manner resulted in some immediate reduction in production costs, but large increases in efficiency did not appear until the old plant designs were replaced or changed to take advantage of the innovation. Replacing and redesigning plants and equipment was a slow process that involved rethinking plant design. It was not complete a decade or even two decades after electric power had become prevalent. Consequently, the real economic impact of electrification did not appear until electrical power had been available for some time.

This is important to keep in mind when examining the adoption of computing in the Information Age. If the pattern of the electrical industry holds true, the first appearance of innovation—such as the von Neumann computer or the application of computers to business—is not likely to result in the immediate transformation of an economy. The first stage is to insert the innovation into existing structures and processes with as few changes as possible. But a significant innovation, such as electricity, will eventually drive a complete transformation, and this transformation is what determines the ultimate significance of the initial spark. Unfortunately, the ultimate significance is hard to identify except in retrospect.

---

[3]Nicholas Crafts, "The Solow Productivity Paradox in Historical Perspective" (CEPR Discussion Paper 3142, London: Centre for Economic Policy Research, January 2002), http://wrap.warwick.ac.uk/1673/. This paper presents a rigorous discussion of the consequences of adopting electricity and compares it to computer adoption.

Pre-Utility Electricity and Computing

The pre-utility stage of electricity generation has similarities to IT departments and datacenters today. Although there is some outsourcing of IT services, similar to the early stages of the electrical transformation when an occasional manufacturer used electricity from a local public generation plant, most computing consumers own their own computing equipment. Large enterprises have datacenters; small consumers may only have a smartphone—but almost all own their computing resources. However, with the advent of cloud computing and the ancillary technologies such as high-bandwidth networks that make the cloud possible, consumers are beginning to use computing equipment as a sort of portal to computing utilities accessed remotely, similar to the wall receptacles and power cords that electricity consumers use to tap into the electrical power grid.

The concept of *utility computing* is exciting to business because it promises lower costs, spending proportional to the utilization of resources, and reduction of capital investment in computing hardware. Utility computing is also exciting to the engineer, just as designing and building the colossal electrical infrastructure and power grid were exciting to electrical engineers of the twentieth century.

Analogies Are Dangerous

Thinking by analogy is often helpful, but it is also risky. The high school physics analogy between water in a pipe and electricity is helpful in understanding Ohm's Law, but the water-electricity analogy can be deceptive.[4] If the aptness of the water analogy when applied to Ohm's Law tempts you to stretch it to include gravity and conclude that electricity runs downhill, you will be wrong. IT is similar to electrical systems and may be in the midst of a transformation similar to that of electricity at the beginning of the twentieth century, but a computing grid is not the same as an electrical grid. IT is also similar in some ways to railroad systems and various other systems pundits have compared with IT, but, as the stock fund prospectus says, "Past performance does not guarantee future results."

---

[4]Ohm's Law is a basic electrical principle that states that voltage is directly proportional to amperage and resistance. Most people learn Ohm's law through an analogy with water in a pipe. The resistance corresponds to the diameter of the pipe, the voltage corresponds to the pressure, and the amperage corresponds to the volume of water that flows. If the pressure is increased, the water flowing will increase. If diameter of the pipe is decreased, the pressure must be increased to get the same volume. This analogy is excellent because it leads to an intuitive understanding of one aspect of electricity and is used frequently for teaching Ohm's Law.

The history of analogous utilities may lead us to questions about computing utilities, but analogies will not answer the questions. The pattern of the adoption of electricity certainly has similarity to mainframes taking over back-office functions such as billing without changing the essential nature of business. The analogy suggests that we ought to look for something similar to the redesign of manufacturing to take advantage of the properties of an electric motor. Internet commerce is one candidate; online advertising is another. But there is no assurance that the Information Age will follow the pattern of previous ages. For example, we cannot argue that social networking will bring about economic change because electricity changed manufacturing. We are forced to wait and observe the changes that occur.

In the meantime, it is the job of the IT architect to work with business and IT management to respond to the changes that are occurring now.

IT Utilities

Utility computing gets a lot of attention, but there are also many commodities and utilities within IT. For example, anyone can pull a Serial Advanced Technology Attachment (SATA) standard commodity hard drive off the shelf and expect it to perform as advertised in any computer that has a SATA interface. These drives come from several different manufacturers that compete on read-write speeds, data capacity, and mean time between failures. Periodically the standard is revised to support innovations in the industry, but the drives on the same version of the standard remain interchangeable. When possible, standards are designed to be *backward compatible*, so that drives built to different standards remain compatible.[5]

There are many other commodities in IT. Network equipment and protocols connect together computers and computer systems with as little regard as possible for the kinds of systems that connect to the network. Although there are large differences in capacity and speed, networking equipment is also interchangeable. *Domain Name Service* (DNS) is a utility. It is a service that is offered by many different providers and is freely used by everyone who connects to the Internet.

The largest IT utility is the Internet. Consumers establish wired connections to the Internet by entering into a business relationship with an Internet service provider (ISP), which acts as a gateway to the Internet. Consumers are free to switch from provider to provider, although they may be limited by

---

[5]If the standard is backward compatible, a drive built to an older standard can plug into a system built to a newer standard. If the standard is *forward compatible,* a drive built to a new standard can be plugged into a system built to an older standard.

the providers available in their geographical location. In most cases, there is a clear demarcation point that distinguishes the provider's equipment from the consumer's equipment and premises.

IT Utility Providers and Consumers

IT differs from other utilities in important ways. Fundamentally, computers are designed to be used for many different purposes with great flexibility. The electrical grid, on the other hand, exposes electrical power in fixed forms with little flexibility. On the electrical supply side, innovation and progress come from producing more electricity at less cost delivered more efficiently. People don't buy more electricity from suppliers with more exciting flavors or colors of electricity. If consumers have alternate providers, which they seldom do, they only shop for a lower price, greater reliability, or better customer service. The product is always the same.

Utility Computing Providers

In the early days of electricity, the product of generators was always electricity. The voltage varied, some was alternating, some was not, but the generators all produced electricity. By setting standards for voltage and phase, generation plants became interchangeable. Electric current is a physical force that can be measured and controlled, not an abstract concept. A utility does not deal in abstract concepts; the utility charges for something that can be metered and used.

Computing is an abstract concept. In the days of timesharing as a utility, measuring the computing abstraction was relatively easy because it could be equated to a few measurements such as connection duration, *central processing unit* (CPU) time, and data stored. These were measurable by user account, and consumers could be billed based upon them. Because there was only one central computer with a limited number of CPUs in a timesharing system, the measurements were straightforward. When distributed computing became prevalent, measuring computing became much more complex.

User accounts are not as meaningful in a distributed system, where a server may not be aware of the user account associated with a service request from a client. Measuring computing in this environment is possible, but it is more challenging than on a timesharing system based on a limited number of central computers. Cloud computing also approaches metrics somewhat differently than timesharing did. Clouds abstract the notion of computing consumption from the underlying hardware. Instead of directly measuring the consumption of hardware resources, clouds measure consumption of the computing abstraction. The abstraction hides the complexity of the underlying hardware. Metrics based on the abstraction at least appear to be understandable, even though the underlying measurements and calculations may be quite complex.

Measurement was one more obstacle to utility computing in an environment where the cost of computers had plummeted. Small businesses and individuals found it more economical and convenient to cut costs by using new, cheaper computers instead of subscribing to timesharing utilities. This undercut the economic basis for timesharing.

Unlike electricity, where establishment of a utility power grid was a slow but linear progression, utility computing has developed in fits and starts, encountering technical difficulties and economic diversions along the way.

Utility Computing Consumers

On the consumer side of the electrical service panel demarcation point, there is an enormous range of competitive products that can be plugged or wired in (Figure 2-2). The innovation and diversity in electrical products are on the consumer premises. Ordinary electricity consumers have only one control over the electricity they receive: they can cancel electrical service. They cannot signal the utility to reduce the voltage, increase the frequency, or change the phase by a few degrees. The types of output from the utility are very limited.

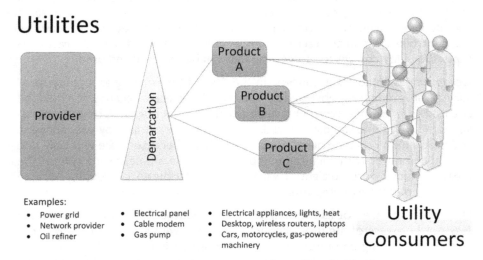

Figure 2-2. Utilities are separated from consumers by a distinct demarcation point. The commodity is uniform at the demarcation point, but it is used in different ways by consumers.

Other utilities such as railroads are similar. A railroad moves cargo in a limited set of types of railcars, but the contents of those railcars may vary greatly. The contents of a hopper car may be coal or limestone, but the car is the same. When you go to a gasoline station, you are offered three types of gas that can be burned in any gasoline-powered car.

IT Progress toward Utility Computing

In the days of timesharing, there was a vision of utility computing. In the vision of those days, there would be one enormous computer that would share resources such as data, and all users would log on, forming a great pool of simultaneous users of a single computer. That vision crumbled with distributed computing. Instead of one enormous central computer, each user got a private computer on his desk. Computing would have to evolve further to get back to the utility computing vision.

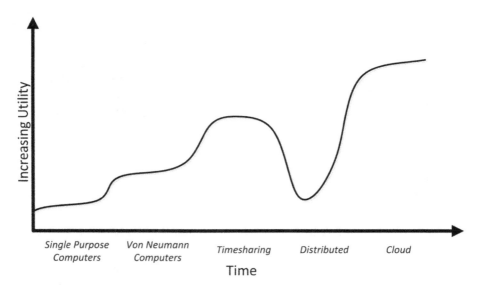

Figure 2-3. Progress toward utility computing was not linear

When distributed computing became prevalent, computing was anything but a utility. It was as if the consumer electronics industry preceded the electrical grid. The computing consumer had a range of platforms, each with its own set of software products, but there was nothing that they all plugged into to make them work. The Internet appeared, but the Internet was primarily a connecting medium that computers used to exchange information. Most computing occurred on single computers. Instruction sets varied widely between vendors. Higher-level languages such as FORTRAN, COBOL, and C improved portability, but differences in the input and output system and other peripherals almost guaranteed that moving programs from one platform to another would have problems.

UNIX was one step toward utility computing, because it was ported to different platforms. This is still evident today. The Big Three in server hardware—IBM, HP, and Sun (now Oracle)—all run UNIX. Unfortunately, although the companies all wrote UNIX operating systems—IBM wrote AIX, HP wrote HP-UX, and Sun wrote Solaris—each did so in a slightly different way. The result is almost a utility, in the same way that a horse is almost a camel inasmuch as both have four legs. To produce utility-like portability, developers had to write different code for each UNIX platform to account for tiny but critical differences in low-level functions such sockets and thread handling. It was an improvement over the days before UNIX because almost all the code stayed the same, but a handful of critical differences made porting difficult.

Java was another step forward. Java isolates the platform idiosyncrasies in a *virtual machine* (VM). The virtual machine is ported to different platforms, but the code for an application stays the same. This yields greater portability than C or C++ on UNIX, but a separate computer for each user is still required.

At the same time, Microsoft and Windows made steps toward utility computing by sheer dominance in the computing arena. Microsoft Windows was an early winner in the desktop operating system wars, and Microsoft made progress toward establishing Windows as the de facto standard for distributed servers.

Microsoft had competition. Linux is an open-source version of UNIX that has won great favor as a platform-independent alternative to the IBM, HP, and Sun versions of UNIX. A few years ago, it looked like a David and Goliath battle was being waged between tiny Linux and mighty Microsoft.

A new twist, *virtualization*, has dimmed the operating systems' spotlight. Virtualization separates the operating system from the underlying hardware. A virtualization layer, often called a *hypervisor*, also called a virtualization platform, simulates the hardware of a computer, and operating systems run on the simulated hardware. Each operating system running on the hypervisor acts as an individual virtual computer, and a single hypervisor can run many virtual computers simultaneously.[6] Adding to the flexibility, a hypervisor can run on several physical computers at once, moving VMs from physical computer to physical computer and optimizing the use of the physical system.

Large systems can be deployed as VMs. Virtual deployments have many advantages, but one of the most important is that hypervisors can run most operating systems virtually. Consumers don't have to make all-or-nothing choices when choosing operating systems and hardware. The mix of virtual hardware and operating systems available on hypervisors makes a new kind of computing utility possible. The uniform commodity is made available in the form of VMs and other virtual hardware. This uniform commodity is the foundation of clouds.

---

[6]These virtual computers are usually called *virtual machines* (VMs) or *virtual systems* (VSs). The Java VM referred to above is a VM that runs on operating systems rather than a hypervisor.

Utilities and Cloud Service Models

Cloud and utility computing are not the same thing. Some uses of cloud fit the utility definition well. Other uses do not fit so well.

Of the cloud service models (described the next section), *infrastructure as a service* (IaaS) is the most likely to become a utility. In some countries, IaaS could be a candidate to become a regulated utility like the power grid or telephone. An IaaS cloud could become government monopoly like the old postal service. It is tempting to imagine a future landscape where every IaaS provider offers a standard interface that consumers can use interchangeably. More likely, market forces may force IaaS providers to agree on a reasonably uniform de facto interface, not unlike the network of gasoline stations that blanket the country having settled on three choices of gasoline. There is no regulatory body dictating what gas may be pumped, but when every petroleum refiner and gasoline station owner wants to sell to every vehicle on the road and all automobile manufactures want to produce cars that can be gassed up anywhere, the industry has arrived at great uniformity.

Platform as a service (PaaS) and *software as a service* (SaaS) differ from traditional utilities. Since they compete on the uniqueness of their service, they are less likely to become utilities in the traditional sense.

Utilities providers follow many of the same practices as all service providers do, but there are also differences. Supply and demand in the market tends to force utility prices to converge on a market price. Utilities can be very profitable because they have an assured market and great demand, but their profitability is more dependent on supply, demand, and the regulatory climate. They benefit from innovation in the way their product is produced, and not so much from innovation in the product itself. Non-utility services compete more often on offering innovative services that are attractive to consumers and garner a premium price.

Cloud Computing Models

The three National Institute of Standards (NIST) models of cloud service—IaaS, PaaS, and SaaS—illustrate some of aspects of clouds as utilities.

Infrastructure as a Service

The most basic NIST service model is IaaS. It provides the consumer with a virtual infrastructure made up of a few basic virtual entities such as virtual computers, network, and storage. Consumers are free to deploy and use this infrastructure as they see fit. This is closest to the electricity model. IaaS competition has begun to look like competition between electric utilities. The supplied infrastructure is quite uniform. There are a few variations but the range is limited.

Platform as a Service

PaaS provides platform utilities for developing and supporting applications such as *integrated development environments* (IDEs), databases, and messaging queues. This is in addition to the infrastructure an IaaS provides. Competition still focuses on the basic variables of IaaS: price and performance. However, the offered platforms vary greatly and PaaS services also compete on the effectiveness and ease of use of their development-and-support platform.

Software as a Service

SaaS competition is similar to that of PaaS. The consumer of SaaS is not exposed to the infrastructure at all, and there is little direct competition on that level. Consumers see only running software. The software is unique to the SaaS provider. If a budding SaaS *customer relationship management* (CRM) startup were to copy the Salesforce.com CRM service, the startup would probably be quickly bound up in a lawsuit. To compete, the startup has to develop better CRM software.

Do IT Utilities Matter?

Whether or not computing becomes a utility has great significance to both business and IT. Carr's article "IT Doesn't Matter" urged the possibility that computing will become a utility.[7] In such a discussion, it is important to make clear the demarcation point between provider and consumer. For the electrical grid, the demarcation point is the service panel. A commodity—a standardized electric current—passes through the service panel and is used by a lot of different appliances and devices. In the century since electricity became a commodity in the United States, the electrical product industry has boomed. The millions of devices that are powered from the electrical grid are unique and often innovative products, not utilities. Vacuum cleaners, for example, are not interchangeable. Some are good for carpets; some better for hardwood floors. Some are lightweight and easy to use; others are heavy-duty and require strength and skill.

Virtualized computing is similar to electric current and can be standardized into an interchangeable commodity.[8] Software is not as easily characterized as a utility. The most important characteristic of software goes back to the

---

[7]Carr, supra.
[8]The *Distributed Management Task Force* (DMTF) standard—*Cloud Infrastructure Management Interface* (CIMI)—is an example of such standardization (http://dmtf.org/standards/cmwg). See my book *Cloud Standards* for discussions of many standards that contribute to IT and clouds in particular.

day when von Neumann thought of inputting processing instructions instead of wiring them in. Software was invented to make computers easily changed. From that day, computers were general-purpose machines.

When discussing computing utility, the distinction between hardware and software is important. Software is malleable: it originated in the desire to transform single-purpose computers into multipurpose machines that could easily and quickly be restructured to address new problems. Software invites change and innovation. It resembles the electrical appliances on the consumer side of the electrical service panel.

Computing hardware is certainly continually innovative and flexible, but software is expected to change more rapidly than hardware. In addition, hardware designers have tended more toward compatibility than software designers have. For example, the Intel x86 instruction set, dating from the late 1970s, is still is present in processors built today, though it has been expanded and adapted to more complex and powerful chips. The same computer hardware is used to run many different software applications. Enterprises have many different software applications and many are bespoke applications that are built for a single organization; whereas enterprise hardware infrastructures vary in size and capacity but are all similar compared to the software that runs on them.

The analogy between the development of electrical utilities and computing breaks down a bit when we compare software to electrical appliances and hardware to utility electricity. A lot of software will run on any hardware built with an x86. It is as if the electric service panel were designed and widely deployed before electrical utilities were designed. A consequence is that utility computing may not follow the same sequence as electrical utilities. The great gains for electrification of manufacturing occurred when factory builders began to take advantage of using many small motors instead of shafts and pulleys. Many large gains have already occurred without utility computing and these gains have some similarity to the flexibility offered by electric motors.

This difference can be seen in what has happened since Carr asked his provocative question. Carr made a number of recommendations to CIOs based on his prediction that IT would soon become a utility. His recommendation was to be conservative with IT: Don't overinvest, don't rush into new technology, and fix existing problems before acquiring new ones. This is cautious advice and businesses that followed it certainly avoided some losses, but they may also have missed out on opportunities.

At the same time, IT departments were dismayed by this attitude. Carr's recommendations boiled down to tight IT budgets based on advice that was both business and technical analysis—a business recommendation based on a prediction of an impending technical change. In the best of all worlds, such a decision should come from collaboration between the business and technical sides of the house.

IT departments that followed Carr's advice, anticipated cloud utility computing, and were cautious about investing in and expanding their physical infrastructure have probably already begun to use IaaS utility computing. Such departments consequently reduced their capital investment in IT without compromising their capacity to expand the services that they offer to their enterprise. This is a clear benefit from Carr's advice.

But following Carr's advice may not have been all good. Departments that were also reluctant to expand or modify their software base may have fared less well. There have been important software innovations in the past ten years that these organizations may have missed while waiting for software to become a utility. They may be behind the curve of big data analysis (Chapter 1) of the their customer base, use of social networking tools for fostering customer relationships, or even the more mundane improvements in integrating different segments of the business. Again, software is closer to the electrical appliances on the consumer side of the electrical panel. It changes more rapidly and is more closely tailored to the needs of individual customers.

IT clearly does still matter, but it has changed since Carr wrote his article in 2003. Carr predicted the change toward utility computing, but there are some aspects that have gone in different directions. No one is likely to say that the IT services provided by most IT departments have all become interchangeable commodities. Email, for example, is often treated as a commodity because email providers are largely interchangeable, but even the SaaS service desk services are not particularly interchangeable among SaaS providers. SaaS has moved the maintenance and administration of the service desk out of the local IT department, but it has not converted the service desk into a uniform commodity. On the other hand, the infrastructure that supports the back end of SaaS service desks has become a commodity. SaaS consumers are purchasing that infrastructure indirectly though their SaaS fees. Many other enterprise services are similar.

The move from an on-premises application to a SaaS service or deploying on-premises applications on a PaaS or IaaS service is likely to be a business decision, but it is also a technical decision. For business, reducing the capital investment in hardware by replacing it with cloud services has significant financial implications. Not only does it affect the cost of IT services, it also affects the distribution of capital expenditures and operating expenses.

At the same time, these decisions have a highly technical component. For example, the performance of a cloud application is unlikely to be the same as that of the same application deployed on-premises. It may improve or it may get worse—or, most likely, it will be better in some places and worse in others. Predicting and responding to the behavior of a migrated system requires technical knowledge. Even a self-contained SaaS application may have effects on network traffic distribution that will require tuning of the enterprise network.

Although some technologists may regret it, moving the infrastructure and administration of a service to an IaaS provider is often a good use of utility computing provided it does not compromise security or governance. Switching from an in-house application to a SaaS application may be a good decision, but perhaps not if a SaaS application is not available that fits the needs of the enterprise, the same way a home vacuum cleaner may not work for a cleaning contractor. These decisions can only be made wisely when there is both business and technical input.

Conclusion

IT decisions—especially strategic decisions that affect the long-term direction of IT and the enterprise—always have both a technical and a business component. Decisions made entirely by one side or the other are likely to have compromised outcomes. Even highly technical decisions about areas deep in the infrastructure or code eventually affect business outcomes. This problem—the coordination of business and technology—is a fundamental aspect of the service management approach to IT, which is the subject of the next chapter.

EXERCISES

1. Define architecture in your own terms. What is the relationship between architecture and enterprise planning? What makes IT architectures different from other enterprise architectures?

2. What makes a utility different from an ordinary service?

3. Compare and contrast the development of the electrical power grid to utility computing.

4. Explain why the decision to move to a cloud computing utility model is a joint technical and business decision.

5. Does IT matter?

The Bridge

Service Management

SUMMARY

Service management as a discipline grew out of efforts to improve manufacturing quality and efficiency in the mid-twentieth century. These efforts lead to recognition of IT as a collection of services that could be planned, implemented, studied, and adjusted in the manner of a production line in a factory. ITIL is a set of practices for following this pattern. Service strategy is the first phase in the ITIL service management plan, in which enterprise goals and requirements shape a high-level plan for IT services.

The shadow cast by the service-management umbrella is broad, extending into the organization of the enterprise as well as IT. Service management practices can also guide the design and operation of enterprise clouds. This chapter introduces service management and the Information Technology Infrastructure Library (ITIL). A basic understanding of the goals of service management and ITIL is useful in building cloud-application architectures because many businesses have adopted ITIL practices and expect IT to support these practices. Most ITIL discussions and publications are about strategies for adopting ITIL practices in an enterprise and the effect of the practices on the organization. Service management adoption requires management buy-in training programs, and the enterprise organization may often be restructured. This is a big and difficult job, and the discussion in this chapter is about designing cloud architectures that support a service management approach to IT. The executives, managers and architects who implement the technology behind IT that is managed as a service have to understand service management practices, but they have a different set of questions and needs than the typical ITIL practitioner who guides an organization through the process of adopting service management practices. This chapter also discusses the service management strategic planning phase in detail. Chapters 6 and 7 will discuss service design, implementation, and operation.

Importance of IT Service Management

Other than a few paper reports, which are rapidly disappearing, IT has few direct physical outputs and the final products of IT services are seldom tangible. Unlike a factory, IT does not provide its consumers with goods. Instead, IT, for the most part, performs services for its consumers. Unfortunately, the fact that IT exists to provide services is sometimes forgotten. Traditionally, IT has required considerable physical assets. Management and IT practitioners are both occasionally overwhelmed with the wealth of expensive computers and other devices in the care of the IT department. When this is the case, the enterprise may start to think of IT as a sort of steward for the IT infrastructure instead of the service provider that it genuinely is. This illusion can be detrimental to the IT department.

In the days when a single computer required a specially designed floor, an expensive cooling system, and cost millions of dollars, it was easy to think that the investment was an end in itself; that keeping up with the latest innovations in computing was paramount. The enterprise assumed that valuable services would inevitably follow.

Experience shows that this was and still is a shaky assumption. Without concerted effort, value-generating services do not just pop up. In a few cases, a service may be developed without heed to its value and turn out to have great value, but many more failures can be ascribed to lack of consideration of the value of services that are developed.

IT departments that continue to be hardware stewards instead of service providers eventually suffer. The speed of IT advancement causes computing equipment to become obsolete quickly. Desktop computers, for example, are often replaced in a year or two, not because they are no longer functional but because their replacements have so much more functionality. In contrast, factory equipment may retain value for decades. To compensate for the rapid decrease in computing equipment value, the return on an investment in IT infrastructure must be rapid and large if it is to compare favorably to other enterprise investments. Consequently, when management takes a hard financial look at IT, it has often been disappointed and resolves to put IT under tighter fiscal control.

For the most part, the IT fairy tale days are over. Executive management measures IT departments on their contribution to favorable business outcomes. Unless they can be shown to contribute in proportion to their size, the large investment in IT infrastructure is a burden, not an asset.

Business alignment has risen in importance, but the complexity and breadth of the IT infrastructure has also increased steadily. IT services have also become more mission critical. For example, increased Internet merchandizing and dependence on online financial transactions have increased the dependence of business on the smooth functioning of IT.

As the infrastructure has grown in size, complexity, and importance, business alignment has become more critical and significantly more difficult. Instead of supporting a few back-end accounting and inventory services that are hidden from customers, IT now provides hundreds of services that still depend on the traditional back-end services, but also include a wide range of customer-facing services. Businesses provide customer support through social media, field mobile apps, and stream video—to name a few of the diverse services that appear on the IT agenda. The list goes on and on with new services appearing all the time.

Each of these services must be properly provisioned to operate appropriately and align with business. This is both a technical and business challenge. All these services must be coordinated into a coherent business plan that will meet enterprise goals such as growth and profitability. The services must be technically reliable and attain required service levels while keeping within financial constraints on infrastructure investment. In order to do this, the services have to fit within an IT technical architecture that provides an agile and extensible platform and makes the best use of the IT investment.

This is a challenge. IT service management is an important approach to meeting the challenge.

What Is Service Management?

IT must pay attention to the services it provides, but the processes required to enable IT to drive solid business services are not simple. Without an adequate process, IT often gets a list of business requirements that it does not understand and bears little relation to what the IT department needs to know in order to build or modify a service. Worse, the requirements may not take into account existing IT resources or advances in technology that would provide an excellent return on the investment.

SERVICE MANAGEMENT DEFINED

The goal of service management is to optimize the efficiency and value of services within an enterprise and those used by the customers of the enterprise. The first step in service management is to analyze the nature of services to be managed. Service management often requires improved communication within the enterprise and with enterprise customers. At the core of service management is a process for continuous improvement of services, generally based on a continuous cycle of design, implementation, observation, and feeding observations back into new or improved designs. Service management can be applied to many different areas such as manufacturing, hospitality, or retailing. There are many frameworks that address aspects of service management. ITIL and Microsoft Operations Framework (MOF) are two that apply specifically to IT.

IT service management (ITSM) is a special form of service management that aims to increase cooperation between IT and all the elements of an enterprise to further enterprise goals. Often those goals are increased revenues and decreased costs, although some enterprises, such as government agencies or nonprofit organizations, will have other goals. The service management process assures that the goals are directly or indirectly represented in every action taken in the IT department and that every investment is optimized for accomplishment of these goals. Business alignment is a state where actions and investments are all tuned to provide maximum support for enterprise goals.

Value of a Service

ITIL provides some conceptual tools for understanding the value of a service. Two of these are *warranty* and *utility*. These concepts are useful for analyzing what makes a service successful.

Utility of a service

The *utility* of a service refers to what it does. If you recall, the ITIL definition of a service suggests that it is a means for delivering desired business outcomes to a consumer that transfer some of the cost and risk of delivery from the consumer to the provider of the service. The utility of the service is the business outcomes that the consumer gets from the service. Put more succinctly, the utility of a service is what the service does.

UTILITY OF A SERVICE DEFINED

The utility of a service is the functionality of a service, what the service does. A service with adequate utility is described as "fit for purpose." (Note that *utility of a service* defined here is not the same idea as a *public utility*, defined in Chapter 2.)

A service that does what the consumer expects is described as "fit for purpose." This is another way of saying that the utility of the service provides the functionality the consumer wants.

Warranty of a Service

Utility is only one aspect of the value of a service. The other aspect is *warranty*, which is related to risk. Warranty is the fitness of the service for use by the consumer. A service that does the right thing but is not available when the consumer needs it is fit for purpose (its utility is adequate) but not fit for use (its warranty is inadequate).

WARRANTY OF A SERVICE DEFINED

The warranty of a service describes how the service is delivered. If the service meets its warranty, it is fit for use, which means it is adequately secured, reliable, performant, and any other requirements related to delivery of the service.

For a service to be suitable for a consumer, it must be both fit for purpose and use. On the technical side, it is easy to obsess over utility and slight warranty. This is a dangerous mistake. Services that are not fit for use are not acceptable to the consumer. When a service unfit for use is delivered to a consumer, the results can be very bad. The developers usually feel blindsided—they did their work. The service does what it is supposed to, but the consumers feel betrayed—they are tantalized by the service functionality they want, but it is unusable. Learning to pay as much attention to warranty as utility is perhaps the most important lesson a developer can learn from service management.

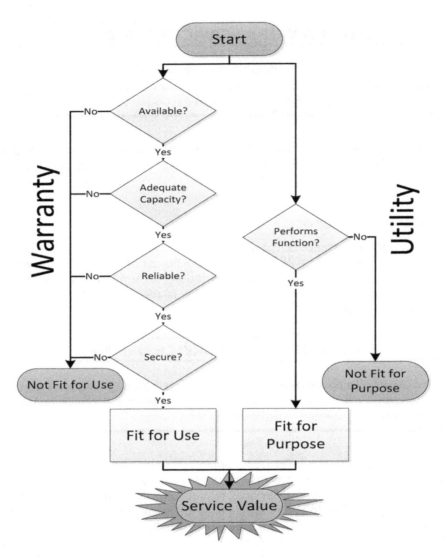

Figure 3-1. Warranty and utility are both required to realize service value

Much of the entire process of service management is devoted to making clear both the utility and warranty of a service. There are many practices devoted to making the warranty of a service clear and ensuring that the warranty is met.

Perhaps the most prominent of these are service-level agreements (SLAs). SLAs are contracts between the consumer and provider. They contain specific, measureable levels of service that must be met by the provider, and obligations the consumer has to the provider. In addition, they may contain incentives and penalties. Well-written SLAs are characterized by the mnemonic acronym SMART—specific, *m*easureable, *a*chievable, *r*elevant, and *t*ime bound.

Service Standards

Service management is a way of approaching IT management that has changed the way IT is developed and delivered. Service management in IT is hard to separate from ITIL because ITIL was an early advocate of service management of IT and has received wide acceptance in IT circles. ITIL is also notable for its extensive certifications and training programs. ITIL calls itself a collection of best practices rather than a standard. For an army of service management experts and consultants, however, the ITIL collection of books is the authority for the practices under the *service management* umbrella.

ITIL is not the only source of service management practice. The ISO/IEC 20000 standard covers most of the same practices as ITIL. The Microsoft Operations Framework (MOF) is closely related to ITIL. The TM Forum, formerly the TeleManagement Forum (TMF) publishes Frameworx, which is management guidance for communications service providers. Frameworx is directed toward communications networks rather than IT, but it touches on many of the same topics as ITIL. There are also other frameworks for quality improvement that apply to IT service management such as Six Sigma, Total Quality Management (TQM), Capability Maturity Model (CMM), and others. However, ITIL dominates the IT service management world; and most of these frameworks have a mapping to ITIL.

Service Management Pitfalls

Few will argue that service management as a concept is faulty, but, in practice, ITIL and service management can be frustrating.

Implementation of ITIL practices is as much about business organization and management as it is about technology. It affects the way IT service requirements are gathered and how services are deployed and supported, but it affects even more the way the people and processes in an enterprise work together. Unfortunately, this strength can easily turn into a weakness. Service management promotes wholehearted cooperation between the business and the technical aspects of an enterprise. But in order for this to happen, both business and IT must endorse the service management discipline and be fully engaged in the service management process. If either side holds back, the effort becomes an exercise in seeking sound from a single hand clapping—it won't work.

Consequently, implementation of service management practices seldom succeeds as a grassroots movement. Success requires spontaneous cooperation and commitment from departments that often have trouble speaking the same language. Service management practices are likely to do the most good where the IT department and business units are downright antagonistic, which is also the situation where implementing service management practices is most difficult. The quickest and surest way to implement service management practices is for upper management to fully commit to service management principles and be willing to take long-term decisive action.

It is important that the participants commit for more than a single quarter or year. Implementing these practices changes basic patterns of thought and organization. This takes time and can generate opposition. Breaking down resistance is not easy. There is always a chorus waiting to declare the new processes a failure and fall back into the old ways. Without long-term commitment, service management practices are likely to be dismissed as another faddish initiative that will disappear as quickly as the morning dew.

Executive commitment has its own perils. The entire set of service management practices exemplified by ITIL is intricate and all-encompassing. Establishing even a modest practice can be a big and difficult job. A service management implementation requires strong executive backing to overcome organizational inertia toward change. But strong executive backing can also mean that service management becomes a high-stakes initiative with heavy incentives for quick adoption. This can encourage early superficial practice adoption that offers few real benefits to the enterprise.

ITIL training is almost an industry itself, with a hierarchy of degrees culminating in the ITIL Master certificate. Swarms of consultants with PowerPoint slides and training materials are ready and able to help an enterprise manage services in the ITIL way. These classes and consultant services are all valuable, but there is a hidden risk: ITIL and all its trappings sometimes threaten to become ends in themselves. When an organization begins to score itself on the quality of its ITIL implementation rather than the quality of its business outcomes, it runs great risks.

An implementation of any quality framework, especially a complex framework like ITIL, can earn high scores for conformance to recommended practices without ever addressing business or technical goals. Awards get passed out, but, without addressing the issues, favorable business results do not appear and the bottom line does not change. When the bottom line does not change, other, almost always less palatable, changes are sure to come. This is especially ominous when the framework has been oversold to executive management.

ITIL History

In 1957, a British government agency, the Central Computer and Tele-communications Agency (CCTA), was established to advise the British government on the adoption of computing. In the 1980s, the CCTA began to develop a series of books on IT practices as guidance for various offices and agencies in order to promote consistency in implementing IT. These books became the original ITIL library of ten core books, covering service support and delivery. Other books were added on subjects like cabling and business continuity management. These books were issued in the late 1980s and early 1990s. The official government publisher for the UK, the Stationary Office (TSO), published the original ITIL library and all the later editions of ITIL.

Since the original collection of books, there have been three major releases of ITIL. In 2000, the second version, ITIL, volume 2, was released. ITIL, volume 2, consolidated the sprawling ITIL books into two core areas: service support and service delivery. In 2007, a third version, ITIL, volume 3, was released. ITIL, volume 3, is in five books, four devoted to stages in the ITIL service cycle and a fifth on continual service improvement. In 2011, a revision to ITIL, volume 3, was released, which made some additions and corrections to the 2007 release, but left the five-book structure intact.

Statistical Quality Control

Even though ITIL is the predominant set of practices for IT service management, service management was and is a wider movement than ITIL. Service management practices were developed in service industries such as banking, airlines, and insurance, where customer-centered services are critical. Service management is also related to the statistical quality control movement, formulated by thinkers such as W. Edward Deming and Walter Shewhart.

During World War II, statistical quality control was used in the war effort with good results. Walter Shewhart was a physicist and mathematician who is often called the inventor of statistical quality control. When he was an engineer at Bell Labs, Shewhart was assigned to improving the quality of telecommunications equipment—especially buried equipment that was hard to repair or replace.

Common- and Special-Cause Variation

Shewhart noticed that variations in part quality could be statistically divided into common-cause variation and special-cause variation.

Common-cause variation is variation attributed to randomness and the limits of the manufacturing process. For example, a milling tool may be designed to machine parts to within two-tenths of an inch of a target length. Any length that varies less than two-tenths of an inch from the target is due to the design of the machine. The variations from the target length that stem from the milling tool design are common-cause variations.

Special-cause variation is not caused by the limitations of the process and has an assignable cause. Suppose milling waste was allowed to build up and began to cause variations in addition to the common-cause variations inherent in the process. These variations could be eliminated by clearing away the accumulated waste. These are special-cause variations.

Common-cause variation cannot be reduced without fundamentally changing the process; special-cause variation can be reduced by identifying the cause and eliminating it. A frequent error is to mistake common-cause variation for special-cause variation. Because common-cause variation comes from randomness in the process itself, common-cause variations can only be reduced by reducing randomness, which can only be done by changing the process. Trying to eliminate common-cause variation by assigning it to a special cause is likely to disrupt the process and decrease quality rather than improve it. For example, adjusting a machine that is functioning within statistical limits is likely to put the machine out of adjustment rather than improve its performance.

Using statistical analysis, quality engineers can identify special-cause variations that can be eliminated. Suppose in our milling example, a goal of one-tenth-inch accuracy had been set, and at a point in the production process the length piece was checked and those that are out of standard were rejected. Assuming a normal distribution, even though the cutting machine is only designed for two-tenths-inch accuracy, most of the pieces will fall within the one-tenth-of-an-inch standard, but there will be some outside the standard. When milling waste builds up, more pieces will be off-standard, and when the waste is swept away, fewer pieces will be off-standard. By statistically examining the occurrence of off-standard pieces, the quality engineers can find the special-cause variations like the buildup of waste and work to eliminate the special causes. In this example, sweeping away the waste more often would eliminate the special cause and improve quality. At the same time, the engineers would discover the level of common-cause variation and be able to look to changing the process by switching to equipment with more precise tolerances. This is the basic principle of statistical quality control.

Although it may not be immediately apparent, statistical quality control has been influential in the development of service management. Statistical quality control places the process above the product. Instead of relying on inspection of the end product to identify quality issues, statistical quality control examines the production process. Following traditional quality control methods, when quality must increase, inspections increase in rigor and more parts are rejected or sent back for reworking. Statistical quality control starts by determining the statistical limits of the process and then identifying and eliminating the special causes of variation. Then, there may be a move to improve the process itself to further eliminate undesired variations. This is a continuing activity that may continue through the life of the process as special causes and new quality goals are set. This is also the continual cycle that service management imposes on IT services.

The Deming Cycle

Shewhart, and his later student and colleague W. Edwards Deming characterized the process of continual improvement by statistical quality control in what has come to be called the Shewhart Cycle or the Deming Cycle. Deming gave credit to Shewhart for the cycle, but it is more frequently called the Deming Cycle because Deming popularized it.

The cycle consists of four stages that repeat in a continual cycle. The steps are "plan—do—check–act" (Figure 3-2). In the *plan* stage, the production process is strategically defined and the expected results are decided upon, constraints identified, and goals set. During the next stage, the *do* stage, the process is implemented and goods, services, or whatever its output may be begin to be delivered.

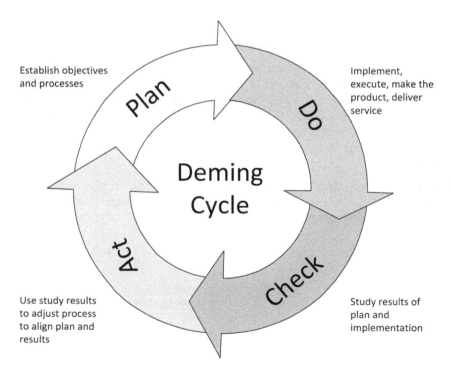

Establish objectives and processes

Plan

Do

Implement, execute, make the product, deliver service

Deming Cycle

Act

Check

Use study results to adjust process to align plan and results

Study results of plan and implementation

Figure 3-2. The Deming Cycle is a feedback loop for process improvement

The third stage, *check*, Deming preferred to call "study" because the word check implies that the results are checked against standards set in the planning phase. Some checking against standards is often done in the checking stage, but the point is to examine the working process carefully and consider all aspects of its operation and output. Statistical methods of distinguishing common and special causes of variation are often important in this stage.

Studying the working process carefully and systematically is at the heart of Deming's approach to quality. In the checking stage, the impact of the process on the entire production line and enterprise is under scrutiny. This may involve questioning the effects of the scrutinized process on steps that occur later in the overall process and the effects on customer satisfaction.

The fourth stage is *act*. This stage takes the conclusions of the previous stage and adjusts the process to align with the original plan and other conclusions of the check stage. Special-cause variations may be eliminated and the limitations of common-cause variations are studied and understood.

The act stage is followed by another cycle of planning, implementation, study, and adjustment. The cycle does not end, but it may quiesce when a process reaches mature stability.

Continual Improvement and the Birth of ITIL

This methodology of continual improvement[1] is carried through in service management. Most business and IT services do not lend themselves easily to the control charts[2] and the quantitative methods of statistical quality control. Nonetheless, the emphasis on improving process rather than imposing ever-more-rigorous inspections on the end product, and the practice of identifying special causes and eliminating them apply to service management as well as manufacturing.

The software version of emphasizing process over product puts less emphasis on more rigorous quality assurance and more emphasis on identifying special causes in the development that generate defects. It also advocates improving

---

[1]Some practitioners carefully distinguish between *continuous* and *continual* improvement; others use the terms interchangeably. Strictly speaking, continuous improvement is a continuum—that is, continuous improvement implies a smooth upward curve with no gaps or steps. Continual improvement can be continuous, but it may also be a series of step-wise incremental changes, which is often the case with change in IT.

[2]A *control chart* is a basic tool of statistical quality control that plots a significant metric against time. The mean and standard error of the points in the chart are calculated and indicated on the chart. Various methods are used to spot variations that are outside statistical control on the chart.

the development process itself to reduce random-variation defects. A developer in need of additional training is an example of a special cause. Adoption of methodologies such as Agile and DevOps are intended to reduce defects that stem from the process itself. They do not add new tests to identity more product for recoding. Instead, they fix process that generated the defects.

Deming led the way in promoting quality as the key to making enterprises more cost-effective and efficient. Deming's reputation was made in his work with Japanese industries as they recovered from their defeat in World War II. Deming applied Shewhart's approach to statistical quality control to Japanese industries. He also emphasized that effective application of statistical quality control requires changes in management of production as well as changes in production itself.

Deming convinced Japanese industrialists to apply statistical quality-control principles to Japanese industry with striking results. The Japanese made strides in quality that would lead the world. The ascendance of Japanese automobile manufacturers in the 1980s and '90s can be traced directly to Deming's work with the Japanese auto industry. Other countries had to struggle to match Japanese quality and innovations, and statistical quality control became well established.

Toyota was among the Japanese enterprises that were influenced by Deming. Toyota developed its own system known as either lean manufacturing or the Toyota Production System (TPS). TPS emphasizes avoidance of waste, which it characterizes as anything that does not benefit the customer. It also assigns importance to avoiding disruptions in the production process.

The ITIL authors were working in the 1980s in a milieu saturated with Deming, statistical quality control, and systems such as TPS. The practices described in ITIL, volume 1, were profoundly influenced by this ferment, and the influence continues through the current release of the library.

Interest in and analyses of the production process in addition to its output was an important consequence of statistical quality control. In the old style of quality control, defective products got attention, but the causes of the defect were only loosely analyzed. The basic remedy for low quality was more rejection and reworking. If a reason could be found for the rejection, the reason was corrected, but there was no mechanism for examining the process.

Service management brings the same emphasis on process to the management of IT services. Instead of focusing on elimination of bad outcomes after they occur, ITIL strives for a system that avoids bad outcomes from the beginning and has a systematic method for correcting conditions that lead to bad outcomes.

ITIL divides the IT service management process into the following four phases, which correspond to the four stages of the Deming Cycle:

- *Service strategy*: corresponds to the plan stage
- *Service design*: corresponds to the do stage
- *Service transition*: corresponds to the check stage
- *Service operation*: corresponds to the act stage

The four phases do not necessarily occur in chronological order, although each phase provides input to the next phase. Unless a service is created tabula rasa, all of the phases are likely to occur at the same time. Management may strategize new roles for a service in operation while enhancements are designed and other fixes are in transition. Nevertheless, each phase has its own inputs and outputs and all contribute to the overall improvement and success of the service.

In this chapter, we concentrate on service strategy and service design.

Service Strategy

Service strategy is the first phase in the development of a new service. The documents and guidance produced in the service strategy phase continue to play a role though the entire life of the service. Business strategy is the driver for service strategy. The service strategy team must be aware of the long- and short-term goals of the enterprise and recognize the role of IT services in meeting these goals. The service strategy determines requirements for new services and scrutinizes existing services for modifications needed to meet changing enterprise directions. In this stage, business requirements are the primary concern. Technology helps define the limits of possible implementations and suggests directions opened by new or unfamiliar technologies.

Methodology

Senior enterprise management is usually represented on the service strategy team. The team identifies and prioritizes the importance of existing and future services. The team is responsible for gathering business requirements and identifying the enterprise resources that might be used in implementing requirements.

An example of a strategic business requirement is a directive that a financial organization must reduce dependence on a particular outside customer credit rating service. Exactly how the dependency must be reduced would probably not be part of the directive. One solution might be development of a complete independent in-house credit rating service. A more moderate solution might reduce dependence on the undesirable external service by combining the results of several services. A yet-more-moderate solution might be to continue using the outside service but supplement the outside information with the enterprise's own account, sales, and demographic records on the customer.

The strategy team would explore these solutions, comparing them to the original directive and other business requirements. There may be conflicting business requirements. For instance, a long-term contract with an outside service may increase costs if usage drops. The strategy team would have to sort out possible conflicts with the overall directive, resolve them, and properly prioritize the requirements.

The team also examines existing resources that may be available. For example, the team might determine if the enterprise has easily accessible records and data to supplement external credit assessments. Financial resources might be among the resources examined and IT financial management could be brought into the discussion.

The team also investigates the enterprise-level constraints on the service. For example, a Sarbanes-Oxley regulation may require audit controls on some aspect of a new service. The service strategy team is expected to identify this constraint and point it out to the service designers.

The strategy team also examines the impact of services or customers. Although the team may leave to the design team the exact metrics and service levels for customer and user satisfaction, they look at and document the critical factors that affect customers and users.[3]

The determinations of the strategy team take the form of a set of documents that are associated with the service. These documents are the foundation for the next phase in the service management cycle, design. They also are the basis for the checking phase of the cycle. The key activity at the check phase compares the operational service to the requirements and constraints laid out in the strategy phase.

IT technologists can make important contributions to the strategy phase. Although technology does not have a leading role, technologists can often add much-needed information on the resources already available in the IT infrastructure that may not be apparent to business strategists. They may also be able to suggest strategies enabled by new technologies or extensions of

---

[3]Customers and users are not exactly the same thing. A customer is the purchaser of a service. The purchaser may also be the user of a service, but not necessarily. For example, management may purchase an e-mail service for corporate employees. Management (the customer) may be satisfied with the service due to low cost and robust data-retention support, but the employees (the users) may be dissatisfied with delivery latency and limits on e-mail attachment sizes.

existing technologies that are unfamiliar to the business side. They also often have a better understanding of the costs of implementation than those more distant from the IT operations.

Engineering, on the other hand, also has much to learn from strategy discussions. By being aware of the service strategy, engineering is better prepared to make decisions that have implications for the ease and expense of expanding or contracting the infrastructure in strategic directions. Tactics should always align with strategy. With an understanding of strategic motivations and direction, technologists can make informed tactical decisions that support both short- and long-term strategy. Sometimes this might involve a decision such as implementing on a public cloud instead of a private cloud. Other times, it might be a decision to expand an existing network switch or purchase a new switch with capacity for the future. These may be tactical decisions to address an immediate and limited need, but they have strategic implications and should align with strategy.

Service Portfolio

The most important tool for service strategy is the service portfolio. The portfolio can be paper, but it usually is an electronic document or document management system. The portfolio is used to manage services from inception to retirement.

A service portfolio is not the same as a service catalog. As ITIL uses the term *service catalog*, it is a document for current or potential service consumers. The catalog lists all the services currently available and serves as a sort of menu that consumers can use to choose services for subscription. It contains a description of what the service does and how it is used, how it is billed, and the service-level agreements that are in place.[4]

Unlike the service catalog that contains information that is useful for operations, the service portfolio contains all the information needed to manage the full-service life cycle. The portfolio contains services that are operational, but it also contains services in various stages of planning and design that may never become operational. In addition, it contains services that were once operational but are now retired. Thus, the service catalog only contains a subset of the services in the service portfolio.

---

[4]There are service catalog applications that go beyond the ITIL service catalog. Consumers can subscribe to services from the service catalog application and the application may automatically set up billing and provision the consumer with access to the service. Often these service catalog applications are linked to the enterprise service desk. Although service catalog applications are natural extensions to ITIL practice, the ITIL service catalog is a listing of services, not a service subscription portal.

The service portfolio also contains information that a service catalog does not have. One of the critical functions of service strategy is to charter services. The charter bears some similarity to the description of services in the service catalog, but it has a different emphasis and often is not suitable to present to service consumers. The portfolio contains all the information the strategy team has collected on each service.

Service charters are an important part of the service portfolio. The charter is the main input to the service design team. It contains the scope, requirements, and directions from which the service design is developed, but it is not the design itself. For example, the charter for a customer purchase tracking system used for sales lead generation might designate the types of sources for the tracking system, the governance for access and privacy, and how frequently the system must be updated. However, designating the format or contents of specific data elements would be inappropriate unless the elements were strategically significant.

More detailed implementation characteristics are specified in the next phase of the cycle: service design. Some products of this phase also go into the service portfolio. After the design phase is completed and service begins transition to operation, a description of the service is usually compiled for the service catalog. The catalog description will go into the service portfolio because it is important information about the service and useful for managing the service life cycle. However, as a consumer document, the catalog will probably contain a selective condensation of the design documents contained in the portfolio.

Service retirement plans will probably not be included in the service catalog although retirement is important in the service portfolio. Strategic service retirement planning is concerned with issues like the criteria for a decision to retire a service and the business implications for retirement. Although retirement plans may not be made at the inception of the service, eventually they will be needed and should be included in the service portfolio when they are created.

The strategy team uses the service portfolio as a compendium of information for managing the service. In addition to the information previously mentioned, the service portfolio usually contains an analysis of the alignment of the service's capacity and the enterprise's demand for the service along with the documents used to assess and manage the risks involved with the service. All this is input to make strategic decisions for the implementation and operation of the service.

The key functions of the service strategy team are to approve the final charter and authorize entry into the design phase. However, the responsibilities of the strategy team do not end there. The service management Deming Cycle is not a waterfall methodology. It is closer to agile development. Agile development progresses by completing a part of the project and delivering the part to users. The results of the first delivery influences the requirements and design of the next delivery. This process is repeated until the project requirements are met. A little strategy, some design, and maybe a step forward to transition—but just as likely, to design—may reveal a need for more strategy and transition may show up strategic or design flaws. The Deming wheel can spin very fast. The phases work together, each contributing, and always keeping, to the basic principle that results are checked and fed back into the cycle.

Financial Management of IT

The ITIL service strategy also includes the financial management of IT. Financial management, including IT financial management, is a complex and specialized subject that requires experts. However, enterprise IT architects and IT professionals need to understand some of the problems in financially managing IT. Only a few high points are touched on here.

Financial data goes into the service portfolio and is included in many IT service decisions. The goal of financial management of IT is to assess and manage the cost of IT service delivery in a way that makes costs, values, and investments clear and unambiguous. IT financial management is the basis for guiding prudent enterprise investment in IT. This job is not as easy as it may appear.

IT is highly abstract and not as readily financially analyzed as other aspects of the enterprise. The products of a production line can be counted and measured relatively easily, but services are not so easily measured. The value of a service is often dependent on the satisfaction of the consumer. Consumer satisfaction measured through an IT business-reporting service depends on easily measured variables like the number of data elements in the report and the timeliness and reliability of report delivery, but its value also depends on intangibles such as the aptness of the data in the report and the ease of drawing significant conclusions from the report presentation. The intangibles are not so easily measured and consumers may not agree on the value of the service.

IT COST DEFINITIONS

Capital cost or expenditure (CAPEX): A capital cost continues over time and appears on the balance sheet. A capital cost may depreciate or appreciate over time.

Operational cost or expenditure (OPEX): Operational costs are paid out over time and do not accumulate. Rent and payroll are operational costs.

Direct costs: Direct costs can be assigned accurately and unambiguously to a service.

Indirect costs: Indirect costs contribute to the cost of a service, but cannot be directly assigned to it. Overhead is usually an indirect cost.

Variable costs: Variable costs change in proportion to the usage of the service.

Fixed costs: Fixed costs do not change as the usage of the service increases or decreases. Payroll is a fixed cost if workers cannot be reassigned as service usage decreases and increases.

The investment in IT services may also be confusing. IT involves several different types of costs. Some are capital costs, like investment in a facility whose value continues over time and appears on the balance sheet as an asset. Capital costs are distinguished from operational costs, which do not accumulate value over time or appear as assets. Payroll, for example, is an operational expense. Some costs are traceable directly to users of IT services, such as payroll for subject matter experts whose time can be billed to the service transactions they handle. Other costs are indirect—that is, not directly attributable to a given consumer transaction—but nonetheless are a necessary cost of a service. Payroll for network engineers whose work contributes to many services is an indirect cost because it cannot be allocated directly to consumer transactions. Yet other costs are fixed, such as most capital costs, and do not change in proportion to usage of services.

Most of the time, charges that vary in proportion to usage are desirable. IT service consumers want to pay only for what they use and expect to pay less when they use less. But a mixture of capital costs and direct, indirect, and fixed costs can make usage-based charges difficult to ascertain. The cost of a service is often only partially related to the usage of the service. For example, if a service requires four servers of a given capacity in order to be available, the hardware cost remains the same when the service has one user and when it has a thousand. Some costs like electricity and cooling may increase slightly for a thousand users, but for the most part, this increase is negligible and the costs remain constant. If the IT department charges per user, the department may show a serious deficit during a business downturn when fewer users access the service. With fewer users, revenue from the service decreases, but the fixed costs do not. This can squeeze the IT budget into a deficit.

Charges can become particularly confusing when the provider and consumer of the service are in the same organization. When business is down, the consumers all want to pay less for services, but the IT department's costs are fixed and do not change with the business cycle. When usage goes down but fixed costs do not change, charge-back formulas can generate anomalous results. If the fixed costs are allocated between departments in proportion to usage, departments may find their charge back increasing even as their usage goes down because other departments have cut back more on their usage and the fixed costs come to dominate the charge-back formula (Figure 3-3). Part of the challenge of IT financial management is to avoid confusing anomalies like this.

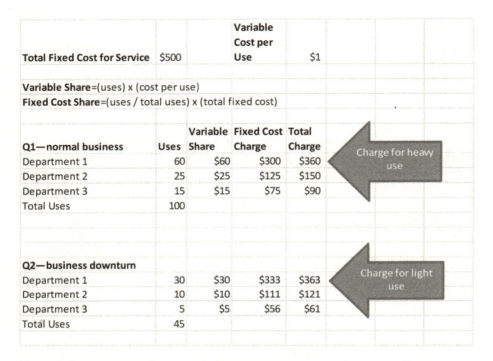

		Variable Cost per Use		
Total Fixed Cost for Service	$500		$1	

Variable Share=(uses) x (cost per use)
Fixed Cost Share=(uses / total uses) x (total fixed cost)

Q1—normal business	Uses	Variable Share	Fixed Cost Charge	Total Charge
Department 1	60	$60	$300	$360
Department 2	25	$25	$125	$150
Department 3	15	$15	$75	$90
Total Uses	100			
Q2—business downturn				
Department 1	30	$30	$333	$363
Department 2	10	$10	$111	$121
Department 3	5	$5	$56	$61
Total Uses	45			

Figure 3-3. An example of a service becoming more expensive when it is used less

IT finances directly affect technical architectures. The anomalies previously described are one of the most important reasons for businesses moving to cloud implementations.

Much has been made of the benefits of shifting CAPEX to OPEX, but the shift is probably less important than the need to align service costs with service usage. By and large, IT infrastructure costs are fixed and do not vary by service usage. When IT infrastructure is moved to a cloud implementation, usage of cloud resources aligns much more closely to service usage. Even if the cloud is a private cloud owned by the enterprise, the cost of the service is clarified and the total enterprise infrastructure resource requirement may be reduced.[5] When the cloud is public, the cost of the service will follow usage more closely, and the total cost to the enterprise will be rationalized and perhaps reduced.

---

[5]Actual costs may not be reduced, but the infrastructure capacity available to the enterprise may be increased, which means services can be expanded with less new resources required. There are many factors that influence the available capacity. For example, if peak usage times for a number of heavy-hitting services coincide, available capacity increases are likely to be eaten by the need for peak usage capacities. However, the financial clarity provided by the cloud implementation is always helpful.

ITIL for Developers

Architects and developers should pay close attention to the service management concepts in this section. They may seem distant from software and hardware engineering, but the principles here are some of the most basic drivers of enterprise software design. Creating a system that delivers a service is a significant achievement, but creating a system that the business side can use profitably advances the enterprise.

ITIL can be frustrating for developers. ITIL training is usually oriented toward enterprise adoption of ITIL and how an organization that follows ITIL practices should function. There is often little in this training that developers can take away as a useful advice in their jobs.

Much of the ITIL message is that IT is more business than technology. That can be disheartening to engineers and technologists whose chosen vocation is to understand and use technology to its fullest; to create software that does new things; to utilize the infrastructure at peak capacity; to design and manufacture new devices; and to extend the infrastructure to support new tasks. For them, technology is the most important part of IT.

However, the fact that the ITIL literature does not dwell on IT technology does not mean that technology is not critical to service management. Without technology, there would be no IT services and without hardware and software innovation, IT services would not improve and provide services to meet future needs.

For engineers, it is unfortunate that ITIL training and literature appears to slight the technical side of the interplay between business and technology. This neglect is perhaps explained by the number of expensive projects in the past that failed to deliver value to their owners because inadequate attention was paid to business requirements and goals. Engineers have to remember that ITIL bridges the gap between business and technology. When ITIL practices are working the way they are intended, services make better use of technology, but technology's role is enhanced, not diminished. The best job security is a job well done. Technologists should see ITIL as a way of increasing the value of their work and their esteem within the enterprise.

The challenge to engineers and technologists is to understand what ITIL practices are trying to accomplish and how to use input from ITIL practices to build better IT services.

The ITIL provides some technical advice on the overall support management infrastructure, such as what a service desk ought to track and the data to be kept in a configuration management database. ITIL also provides insight into the requirements-gathering process and the service-deployment process. Developers and business managers often use their own language and see issues differently when looking at requirements and deployment plans. Opening up these processes to all parties is often one of the most important implications of ITIL practices for developers.

Enterprise software and hardware engineers should not look at ITIL superficially and shrug off ITIL training as irrelevant to their concerns. They may not realize that they need to understand service management concepts because the classes and presentations seldom directly address the problems facing development. However, without the kind of systematic attention to collecting requirements from all the stakeholders and continual examination and feedback of results, IT risks building services that fail to advance business goals.

ITIL practices help answer questions like these for development:

- Who are the stakeholders who must be satisfied at a given stage in service development and maintenance?

- How do I prioritize and resolve competing and contradictory technical and business requirements?

- How do I design applications that align with enterprise goals and do not require reworking as soon as they are released?

- How are development processes affected by ITIL practices?

This chapter and the ones that follow address these challenges.

Conclusion

Service management as a discipline grew out of efforts to improve manufacturing quality and efficiency in the mid-twentieth century. These efforts identified the importance of processes in quality and efficiency, and lead to recognition of IT as a collection of services that could be subjected to the same regimen of planning, implementation, study, and adjustment as a production line in a factory. ITIL is a set of practices that can be implemented to follow this regimen. Service strategy is the first phase in the ITIL service management plan. At this stage, enterprise goals and requirements shape a high-level plan for IT services. The service portfolio is the most important tool for service strategy. IT financial management is one aspect of service strategy.

EXERCISES

1. Explain what it means that IT is primarily a service provider.

2. What is the Deming Cycle and why is it important?

3. How do utility of a service and warranty of a service contribute to service value?

4. How does warranty of a service affect developers?

5. Describe the differences between a service catalog and a service portfolio.

6. What is the goal of service strategy?

7. How are cloud implementations and service costs related?

The Buzz

Mobile Devices in the Workplace

SUMMARY

Handheld mobile devices present new challenges to the enterprise architect. Many of the popular apps installed on mobile apps are based on cloud implementations. Much of the buzz surrounding mobile devices comes from the synergy between cloud and mobile. Cloud has contributed greatly to the popularity of mobile devices. Conversely, mobile devices drive cloud innovation and support for mobile apps can be the motivation behind cloud implementations.

Mobile apps for handhelds are wildly popular, but they have both advantages and disadvantages compared with traditional web apps and hybrids. Enterprise architects must weigh the alternatives. The choice is often driven by where logic will be implemented: in the cloud or on the device. "Bring your own device" (BYOD) is a popular trend that has gained wide acceptance. BYOD goes hand in hand with cloud implementations. The combination threatens enterprise security and governance, pushing enterprise architects to reevaluate security and governance concepts in the architecture and development of cloud projects.

Despite the growing pains, mobile devices increase the reach of computing far beyond the traditional home and office. They are already transforming the way work and leisure combine in our lives. By keeping people in continual connection with the resources of the Internet and each other, they promise to extend individual capabilities in ways that were previously unknown.

The Apple iPhone and iPad immediately come to mind when mobile devices are mentioned. These beautifully designed consumer products have captured the market and sent Apple stock soaring. More important, these devices have been described as the death knell of the desktop and laptop computer. There are some dissenting voices, but it is clear that the combination of mobile devices and cloud services is irrevocably changing the way computers are used.

The mobile devices are not just the latest gadget to catch the consumer's eye. They are a force in transforming the IT environment and they are changing more than consumer buying habits. The devices are small and portable, but these characteristics alone do not explain their effect on enterprise IT.

Cloud services and mobile devices intertwine. Many of the most important mobile applications rely upon cloud implementations. This is especially true of enterprise mobile apps, which interact with enterprise data and processes. Music services such as iTunes rely on a catalog of music stored in a cloud. Social networking applications such as Facebook rely on an enormous cloud implementation. Search engines such as Google also rely on cloud. These and many more cloud applications turn tiny mobile devices into expansive portals.

What Is a Mobile Device?

A *mobile device* is a computer designed to be portable and small enough to be held in the hand instead of sitting on a desk or a lap. Mobile devices are certainly mobile, but they have other distinguishing characteristics, as noted in the following sidebar.

MOBILE DEVICE TERMINOLOGY

- *Mobile device*, a *handheld computer*, or a *handheld device*: A computing device that is intended to be held in the hand and carried by the user. The terms indicate a form factor and not an operating system or computing architecture. Most mobile devices rely on wireless or cellular network connections and touch screen input. Sometimes laptops are considered mobile devices, but not always.

- *Tablet*: A larger mobile device that is usually seven inches or more measured diagonally. Touch screen input is the norm, and detachable keyboards are usually available. The term *tablet*, like *mobile device*, is a form factor. Most tablets have wireless network connections; some have cellular network connections. High-resolution electronic pens, general-positioning circuitry, digital cameras, gyroscopes, and accelerometers are common. Some smartphones are intermediate between a smartphone and a tablet.

- *Smartphone*: A device that combines a miniature computer with a cellular phone. Simple cellular phones may have applications such as a personal calendar, but these are usually proprietary and users have few or no application choices. Smartphones are supported by app marketplaces where new applications can be bought or downloaded. Smartphones are now expected to have a camera, global positioning circuitry, and a growing range of other resources, as well as wireless and cellular connectivity.

Mobile devices are designed to be used with a network connection, and they can be crippled if they do not have access to external resources—network connectivity and storage being the most important. Mobile applications compensate for connectivity lapses by storing data locally and syncing up later, but everyone who travels in areas where cellular access is sporadic or nonexistent knows how frustrating a smartphone or tablet can be when it is separated from the network.

CELLULAR VS. WI-FI

Cellular and Wi-Fi are two distinct technologies that can be used to connect mobile devices wirelessly to a local area network (LAN) or the Internet. Cellular connections are designed to support continuous connections while traveling between the service areas of cell towers maintained by cellular telephone providers. Seamless switching from tower to tower is a distinctive characteristic of cellular technology. Wi-Fi is a trademark of the Wi-Fi Alliance, a trade association that certifies compliance with the IEEE 805.11 standard and its extensions. Wi-Fi is designed to support LANs that are connected by radio instead of wires. Unlike cellular connections, Wi-Fi does not support movement between Wi-Fi service areas. When a Wi-Fi client moves out of a service area, the connection is dropped and the client must sign on to another Wi-Fi LAN to continue communication. Smartphones and tablets usually support both Wi-Fi and cellular network connections. Wi-Fi is typically faster and cheaper than cellular, but is only available if there happens to be a Wi-Fi transmitter close by that the user can access.

Several types of cellular service that support data transmission are available, including 3G (third generation), 4G (fourth generation), and LTE (long-term evolution). The terms are used somewhat loosely. They are based on standards sanctioned by the International Telecommunications Union (ITU). The 3G service is gradually being replaced by 4G. The actual speed of 3G and 4G networks depends on the implementation, but the 3G standard supports 200-kilobit-per-second transmission, while 4G supports 1 gigabit for stationary or slow-moving phones and 100 megabits for phones traveling at ground transportation speeds. The 3G service supports analog voice and digital packet transmission. The 4G does not support analog transmission, so all 4G voice is transmitted in packets rather than over switched circuits. LTE is faster than 3G, but it is not full 4G, although LTE Advanced is.

Mobile devices that move about freely and yet connect with voice and data networks are the product of evolution that influences the way many people think about mobile computing. When DOS and Windows were designed, network connections were not common; operating systems for personal computers were built without assuming that the computer would be plugged into a network. Until recently, most Windows applications were designed to perform their work without calling on resources other than those on the computer. Conversely, these desktop devices were built with the assumption that external access to the machine would be limited—an environment where desktop security was easier to maintain. This thinking still lurks in the background and can be the source of dangerously poor decisions in mobile and cloud architecture.

As computing progressed, network connections became more common and personal computers became more connected, but until wireless networks became widely available, connection to the network was an exceptional condition, not the norm, especially for laptops. In conference rooms all over the world, laptop users scrambled to plug into network ports that were never plentiful enough to go around. The quest for network ports also applies to desktop personal computers. Although setting up fixed physical desks with network drops is less of a problem than it is for laptops, decisions on locating wired desktops are often determined by proximity to drops.

Consequently, until recently, desktops and laptops had to be designed to function offline nearly as well as they did online. A typical word processor was designed to work offline. It read a document stored on the computer, edited it, and stored it back to the computer. This offline operation required program code that was physically present on the local computer.

To support that mode of operation, the word processing program had to be installed locally and the PC had to have substantial local storage. The code had to be installed and updated from physical media such as floppy disks, CD-ROMs and DVDs, or downloaded when the computer was online. In addition, the local processor and memory had to be adequate to perform all the computing necessary to process the text.

Today, traditional word processors such as Microsoft Word and LibreOffice depend on the network to provide help text, but all normal operation, except installation and update, takes place locally. In 1995, reading a document from a remote server into a word processor, editing it, and storing it back to the remote server was an extravagant and impractical idea. This has changed. Today, with document servers such as SharePoint, the practice is commonplace.

Online office suites, such as Google Docs and Microsoft Office 365, go some-what further. Rather than a downloading a copy of the document to be edited to the local machine, the document stays on the server in its store. The local client gets a representation of the document and generates operations, such as "Insert a string of characters at this point" in the document, which it transmits to the server. The server performs the operation and returns a representation of the result to the local machine. This system makes it possible for many users to edit the same document at the same time. Most processing occurs on the server. The client displays the server's representation and generates commands from the user's input; the server processes the commands and publishes a modified representation. When more than one client is modifying the document, the server coordinates the activity by accepting and executing commands serially.

Online office suites have greatly increased the appeal of mobile computing, especially tablets, by offering an office environment that greatly exceeds the capacity of the mobile device. A user has access to many more documents than the device holds. Consequently, working from mobile tablets and even mobile phones has become practical. Online office suites also enable laptops to be lighter, cheaper, and more easily portable.

Despite innovation in online computing, the concept of the stand-alone per-sonal computer remains strong. Personal computers are designed to store every document, photo, and chart the user is likely to want access to at one time. Processors are designed to handle the computing loads generated for any task a user might reasonably undertake. With the progress that has been made in CPUs, memory, and hard disk storage in the past decade, independent per-sonal computers are more powerful than ever before. To users who have been accustomed to stand-alone computing for decades, the current computing and storage capacity available on the desktop is what they have been looking for. They finally have the power and capacity to do what they want.

But today's desktop capacity is not enough. Now that computers connect to the network almost anywhere, at least in urban and suburban areas, the stand-alone assumption is seldom valid and users are seldom willing to accept it. They have become accustomed to the instant information and communication offered in the online world. In addition to information and communication, services are now online. An example of a service is the weather web service offered by the National Oceanic and Atmospheric Administration (NOAA). This service provides current weather information from a national database and NOAA weather stations. This service is the source for current tem-perature and weather conditions found in many web sites, applications, and operating systems.

The transition from the stand-alone desktop to a portal into a world of remote resources is profoundly significant—certainly as significant as the rise of distributed computing and perhaps as significant as the invention of the programmable electronic computer itself.

But the concept of the personal device as a portal has critics. Those who insist upon having a self-contained personal computer have legitimate arguments. A private machine is private, easily secured, and its reliability is under the control of the owner. The stand-alone model affords better privacy, security, and reliability than a system that is implemented largely using remote resources. This disparity presents a challenge to mobile and cloud-based services to become as private, secure, and reliable as their local counterparts.

With the advantages to stand-alone computing, why are users rushing headlong into a massively connected environment? The answer is that the perceived advantages outweigh the perceived disadvantages. As computing has expanded, the demands we place on computing have also expanded.

Keeping all your resources on your own machine may be safer, but it is bothersome. The connected paradigm places resources in a central location that all the players can access. Under this paradigm, resources are "in the cloud"—not any place in particular. If you want to work somewhere besides your own desk, the cloud and your documents are as accessible from a hotel room a thousand miles away as they are from your office. If you want to listen to your music on the beach as well as in your living room, if you have several devices, your music in the cloud is accessible everywhere. If you want to collaborate with others, you can share resources by placing them in the cloud. If you want to take on a computing-intensive task like analyzing big data, a stand-alone computer lacks the capacity, but through the cloud you can tap into capacity that is limited only by your willingness to pay for it. And when you are finished using the capacity, you can release it and quit paying for it. Under the connected cloud paradigm, the capacity of the device on the desk or in the hand is not the limiting factor on what can be accomplished.

Our notions of security, privacy, and reliability are changing as the transition to using remote resources progresses. Traditionally, security, privacy, and reliability were tied to the idea that you can only trust is what is locked behind your own physical door. This has been a valid assumption for a long time, but there are other ways to establish trust. You can establish your physical security and privacy by triple locking your doors and putting bars on all your windows, but that strategy fails when driving an automobile. It seldom matters if the doors are locked during an accident on the highway because drivers are exposed to other drivers whom they cannot lock out of their personal driving environment, but instead of refusing to venture onto the streets, drivers manage the risk by purchasing insurance and supporting good roads, effective traffic laws, and law enforcement.

Computing security, privacy, and reliability in a connected, cloud service-supported environment is like driving on a highway, not a castle reinforced for a siege. The growing pains of entering the service-supported environment appear every day: security breaches, disregard of privacy, and resource failures. These are serious problems that will not go away without effort. Some of the problems have already been partially addressed. Others have not yet been discovered, let alone addressed, but the challenge is not insurmountable. On entering a new paradigm, old issues are transformed, and often their solutions are unexpected in the new environment. Most important, there are powerful incentives for resolving these issues because the benefits, both to the problem solver and the problem sufferer, promise to be enormous.

A mobile device is much more than a small form factor. It is a device designed to be so portable that it can easily be taken anywhere and architected to be a gateway to vast resources that are not physically on the device.

A mobile device places the whole world of computing into the user's hand. Work, play, explore, experiment. Contact, collaborate, just hang out with anyone anywhere from anywhere. Audio, photo, and video data were all once considered too bulky to transmit easily, but mobile devices exchange audio files, photos, and videos without difficulty. All of this becomes possible when resources are universally accessible through the network. Unfortunately, some of these resources are dangerous.

Mobile devices and the connected, cloud service-supported environment are all related, and, like most things that change in computing, can be related to Moore's law. Mobile devices are an example of an innovation made possible by packing more computing power into less space, but they would also be impossible without the increasing reach and capacity of the network. It is somewhat paradoxical that shrinking handheld computing hardware has caused even more computing power to become centralized in clouds and available over the network.

Programming Mobile Devices

At this time, there are three kinds of applications being built for mobile devices: mobile apps, web apps, and hybrids. They are comparable to the fat and thin clients of the last decade. A mobile app is an application that is coded to interact with the operating system of the handheld. A web app is an application that is coded to run on a server and interact with the user through a browser. The server is most likely in a cloud. A hybrid combines some characteristics of both a mobile and a web app. The advantages and disadvantages of mobile apps and web apps parallel the differences between on-premises local processing-based clients and browser-based clients.

Web Apps

Mobile device web apps have the same architecture as familiar browser-based applications, sometimes called thin client architectures. In thin client architectures, a browser displays and manages interaction between the end user and the application. The data and logic for the application all reside on the server, not the client (Figure 4-1).

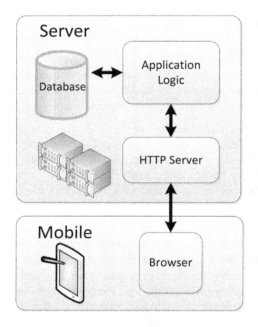

Figure 4-1. Web apps resemble a thin client architecture

This architecture has proven to be very effective for many kinds of enterprise and consumer applications. Readily available standard browsers, such as Internet Explorer, Chrome, Safari, and Firefox, hide the architecture of the underlying client. A web application designed to run on Firefox can be used by any desktop, laptop, or mobile device that supports Firefox and provides nearly the same user experience on any client platform. Performance is largely dependent on the server, the network, and the efficiency of the browser code, so neither the user hardware nor the user operating system greatly affects the experience. Further, developers can expect to deliver similar experiences on most browsers.[1] Consequently, the developers can write one set of server code that will reach all clients, including handhelds, with the same functionality.

Also, since the application code is on the server, maintaining the application is simplified. Application code, particularly JavaScript, is often cached and executed on the client, but the canonical code for the application is on the server. Unlike older fat client architectures, updates and patches are made to the code on the server, which then triggers refreshes of cached code on the client. In the fat client model, updates must be installed on the client, a more arduous process than web app cache refreshes. It is not necessary to keep track of which machines have the web app installed and request, or force, downloads and installations of upgrades or patches on each installed client.

FAT CLIENTS

Before the HTTP (hypertext transfer protocol) servers and browsers began to flourish in the 1990s, client–server applications were almost all based on a client that contained the logic for the application and interacted directly with the client operating system. These clients often used a substantial portion of the client hard drive and other resources. Therefore, they were called *fat clients*. Since the clients were usually written in compiled languages, they were also called *compiled clients*. Because enterprise desktops were predominately Windows PCs, Windows was the almost-universal fat client operating system.

Fat clients interacted directly with the operating system for access to resources like displays, keyboards, and mice. For performance, fat clients often cached data locally, but most data was stored on the server to be shared among all clients. Because both servers and networks had less capacity than today, fat clients often minimized communication with the server to avoid network latency and to avoid overloading the server.

A fat client server is often little more than a transactional database shared among many clients. Many of these servers have Windows operating systems, although UNIX variants, such as IBM AIX, HP-UX, or Linux, are common in large installations.

Until browsers and HTTP servers were perfected and developers got the hang of working through browsers, fat clients provided a richer and more elegant user experience than thin, browser-based clients. Eventually, fat clients lost favor because the thin client experience improved and the maintenance and support issues became overwhelming.

---

[1]This statement has to be qualified. Although the browsers all support the standards, their support varies. Interpretations of the standard can differ. No browser supports every feature defined in every applicable standard. To keep the user experience acceptable on all browsers, developers have to restrict themselves to the features shared by their target browsers and use conditional code that executes differently to suit each browser. This annoyance is unfortunate but a fact. Developers have become adept at working around it.

For application developers and IT departments, these advantages are significant. Instead of developing several different versions of a fat client that had to be ported to each platform require, developers can write server code that will be accessible everywhere. Although they still may have to port to different server platforms, that is more manageable than the nightmare of combinations and permutations of mixed server-and-client platforms that boils up when an application becomes widely distributed. The effort required to write patches and upgrades is also reduced when all the clients act identically.

Web applications reduce the effort required from IT departments. They no longer have to stage major campaigns to manage distribution and installation of fat client code for each user of the application. When a defect is found, a single patch applied to a server solves the problem. There is no need to push down or manually install patches to each client.

Clients based on local code are much different. Patches must be sent to and installed on each client. Clients on different local platforms require different patches. You cannot patch a Linux client with a Windows patch. In the worst case, the IT department has to segment their user base by platform and send out the proper patch to each user. Not only does the IT department have to keep track of who their application users are and how to contact them, they also have to keep track of which platform they are on and hope they have not changed platforms. These activities not only absorb the time of IT professionals, but their users often see patch installation as efficiency sapping and close to harassment. Under this level of duress, IT departments often prefer to defer improved new releases and even run known defective code to avoid upgrading or patching a fat client architecture.

It is no surprise that web applications have become very popular among application providers and IT departments. Web application architecture is the foundation for *software as a service* (SaaS). In a non-SaaS deployment of a web application, the consumers run their servers on their own equipment in their own datacenters. In a SaaS deployment, a service provider replaces the consumer's on-premises server with a server running on the provider's premises. This is possible because the server holds the entire application and the provider can offer the application service to the users as a pure service over the network. This relieves the consumer, who may be an individual or an enterprise, of the chores of keeping the physical server running and administering the application.[2]

---

[2]SaaS has its own challenges. Applications were traditionally designed for a single installation supporting a single enterprise. SaaS can be architected that way, but that architecture is hard to scale and maintain. From the consumer's viewpoint, on-premises architectures are under the governance of the consumer. They can be secured and customized easily. The consumer decides when and how to patch, not the provider. The challenges can and are being addressed.

Native Apps

With all the advantages to web apps in enterprise applications, why is there so much interest in *native apps*? There are several characteristics of mobile devices that make native apps attractive.

Like fat clients, the application logic of native apps is usually implemented directly on the handheld and executed locally, not on a server, interacting directly with the mobile device operating system. Rather than passing HTML screens, they send and receive brief messages to and from web services on the server (Figure 4-2).

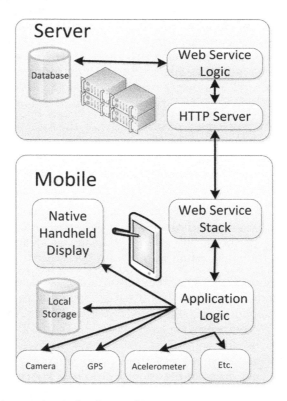

Figure 4-2. Native apps have a fat client architecture

Mobile (native) apps have attractions similar to those of fat clients. The user experience with native apps is generally superior because app developers have direct access to the mobile device operating system. Browsers have trouble with accessing the native features of mobile devices that users love: the cellular interface to telephony and messaging, GPSs, accelerometers, cameras, and so on. Native apps easily access local data storage, which makes caching and local databases easier to implement. This is important on devices where connectivity may be sporadic. Mobile device processors have steadily become more powerful. Devices based on these processors can perform well without depending as much on network speed. This is important because mobile device network connectivity has become ubiquitous in urban areas but is often not as fast as that of typical desktops, and laptops. Rural areas sometimes have issues with basic connectivity.

Even native apps that do not interact with mobile device native features have a distinct advantage over web apps. A web app server is aware of some of the characteristics of the device and browser it interacts with and can tailor the interface accordingly, but a native app has more information. This affects appearance and behavior. Web apps frequently force users to pan over the display and fiddle with the magnification to use the app. A well-constructed native app does not require panning and avoids the peephole appearance of many web apps on a mobile device. Even though gesturing on a mobile touch screen is more natural and quicker than manipulating a desktop or laptop screen with mouse and keyboard, native apps require less user effort.

Native apps also can implement business logic on the local device rather than relying on a server in the cloud for all logic. This can be an advantage for apps that perform intensive interactive processing of data. By processing locally, the app avoids the network latency in passing data back and forth with the cloud server and can make better use of local device features.

At present, native apps are usually preferred to web apps. Perhaps the main reason for this is that browsers running on mobile devices cannot yet provide a user experience of the quality and functionality of a client that interacts directly with the device operating system.

The mobile device operating system vendors, Google Android, Apple iOS, and Microsoft Windows Phone/Windows 8, have stepped up to helping with the maintenance and support problems by following Apple's lead in setting up markets—"app stores" from which applications are purchased and downloaded—making the whole installation process uniform and relatively pain-free. These markets also manage upgrades and patches, automatically upgrading client when necessary, taking some of the sting out of those chores. However, users still experience pauses when the updates are downloading.

One of the drawbacks to fat clients was the necessity of providing different client code for different platforms. In many cases, a single client for Windows was enough because Windows dominated the desktop user market. However, large enterprises and institutions sometimes did not use Windows in some departments. For example, engineering departments often have tools that require UNIX or Linux desktops. Application providers were forced in that situation to provide one client a version for Windows and others for the variant platforms like the flavors of UNIX.

This fat client problem may also be an issue for mobile native apps. There are two contending mobile device operating systems, Android and iOS, that split the market. Although Microsoft has lagged in the mobile device market and Windows 8 and 10 hold only a small slice of the mobile device market today, Microsoft has engineering and product design resources that are hard to discount and they may be making headway in the tablet market. A three-way split among mobile device operating systems is conceivable in the next few years. Developers who want their applications to reach all mobile devices will have to plan for at least two and possibly three versions of each mobile application. Like the fat clients of old, extra rounds of quality assurance testing will be required. Different versions of patches will have to be developed and managed.

Changes to a native app go through the app store. This is both an advantage and disadvantage to the developer. The app store takes care of distribution and installation of the new versions an app, which removes a major drawback to fat clients. However, there is still the need to go through more than one app store to support more than one mobile platform and each store has its own requirements which may be difficult to work with for an app with unique features.

Hybrid Apps

There are also *hybrid apps*, which are designed to run on more than one mobile device platform with little modification. A hybrid app uses components of the browser engine, but not the browser itself like a web app. A hybrid app is installed on the mobile device like a native app and has access to local resources, but it uses components of the browser engine to run JavaScript code and render HTML and Cascading Style Sheets (CSS) screens. Although the user has to install the hybrid app, by using the browser as the platform, the hybrid has some of the portability of a web app.

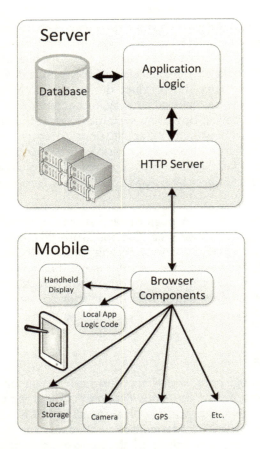

Figure 4-3. Hybrid apps combine both local and remote processing

Mobile or Web App?

Developers have a difficult decision. Native apps provide pleasing interfaces that can use all the features of the mobile device hardware. There are features that handheld device users expect and they may react negatively to their absence. In addition, in some circumstances, a native app can lessen the effects of network latency and interruptions by performing more processing on the local device instead of a cloud server.

Unfortunately, in the current mobile device market, supporting a single platform is seldom viable. At a minimum, both Apple iOS and open-source Android[3] are usually required. Future conditions may introduce more platform variety. Some enterprises may be committed to less common platforms, adding more complications. Multiple platforms multiply the development effort.

Web apps, on the other hand, provide a usable interface that has greater reach and is easier to maintain. Existing browser-based applications will often run on mobile device devices without changes, but they usually need to be modified for usability, sometimes greatly modified. Web apps designed for both traditional desktops and laptops and mobile devices usually detect which device the browser is running on and modify the appearance and controls to match the display. However, these seldom match the elegance and functionality of a native app that takes full advantage of the mobile device environment. Native app development environments and plentiful prebuilt widgets make native app development easier, but web apps use techniques that have been used longer and experienced web app builders are plentiful. Development staffs may already have the training and resources to build web apps or modify existing browser-based applications to run on mobile devices.

Hybrid apps can be seen as having the advantages of both web apps and native apps, but they also share some of the disadvantages of each. Hybrid apps have access to local resources, and the core code is the same for all platforms. However, there still must be a distinct version for each platform the app is installed on. Patches may be similar, but developers have to create separate patches and updates for each platform. Integrated development environments (IDEs) help, but they are not the entire answer.[4] In addition, since hybrid apps use the same browser components as web apps, hybrids are subject to the vagaries of the browser implementation and still have some of the limitations of a browser display.

There is no easy answer, although, like the thin vs. fat client wars of a decade ago, time will sort things out. For the time being, developers have to balance the benefits of the reach of web apps, the compromise provided by hybrid apps, and the rich user experience provided by native apps.

Enterprise applications are probably more suited to web app implementation than consumer applications. To minimize user training, enterprises often try to duplicate the experience of desktop web apps on the handheld. They may be able to make a few modifications to their existing thin client application to become both a desktop application and a mobile device web app that

---

[3] Android code is released under the Apache license.
[4] IBM's Worklight is an example of a hybrid IDE that plugs into Eclipse. See an overview here: www.sitepoint.com/build-a-mobile-hybrid-app-using-ibm-worklight-part-1/.

meets all their requirements. Also, enterprise applications tend not to use features like cameras that are dependent on handheld resources. Therefore, enterprise developers may gain more from the reach of web apps to more platforms with minimal increase in support and maintenance.

Consumer application builders are usually eager to use mobile device resources and they probably do not have to duplicate the functionality of an existing thin client application. As they see it, they are probably competing against other native apps and they have to top the experience provided by their competitors. If providing an interface to the desktop and laptop world is not important to them, consumer application builders are probably better off with a native app and contending with the multiple code bases for the platforms they want to address. If only one platform serves their needs, all the better.

The field may be shifting. HTML5 includes support for many of the native mobile-device features and enhances web app developers' control over appearance. HTML5 was released in October 2014 by the World Wide Web Consortium (W3C). The major browsers all have added support for HTML5 elements and application programming interfaces (APIs) as they have appeared. The Windows 10 Edge browser, which replaces Internet Explorer, includes HTML5 support.[5] However, HTML5 coverage is not complete or consistent. Nevertheless, as HTML5 evolves and browsers extend support, building web apps that satisfy mobile device users will become easier.

If HTML5 is successful, mobile and web apps may follow the pattern of fat and thin clients. As the functionality of web apps improves, the maintenance and support issues of native apps may become an overwhelming disadvantage just as they did for fat clients.

Mobile Devices and the Cloud

The cloud and mobile devices are a good match. Their appearance at roughly the same time shows the effect of two sides of the increasing density of logic on computer chips. Mobile devices are made possible by highly compact yet powerful processors and dense memory chips. Clouds are made possible by using the same power and density to build datacenters of tremendous capacity. The same low-level advances have made possible faster, higher-capacity, and further-reaching networks that support clouds and mobility.

---

[5]For a comparison of browser HTML5 support, see https://html5test.com/results/tablet.html. Accessed August 2015.

The combination of mobile devices and the cloud makes it possible for computing power to penetrate much more deeply into everyday life. This penetration ranges from family groups that communicate over social media like Facebook on their smartphones, exchanging photographs of new babies and cute animals in near real time. Authors can collect whole libraries of research in cloud repositories and check a fact on their smartphone during a casual conversation; they can conduct research from a public computer in a library with the same resources they have at the desktop in their office. A scientist in a research institute can check on data for a critical experiment in real time from a tablet. If we are careful about the way we store data, losing a device through a crash or a mishap is no longer a crisis—we just access our pictures, music, and documents from another device.

All these advantages are wonderful—but not without their headaches for the enterprise cloud architect. The connections between mobile devices and the cloud open a whole new realm of performance, integration, security, privacy, and regulatory issues that all have to be resolved.

Bring Your Own Device

Bring your own device (BYOD) is a practice that exhibits the benefits and challenges of the wide popularity of the combination of clouds and mobile devices. Many employees now prefer to work from handhelds or laptops they own and carry with them rather than enterprise-supplied devices. This gives them the freedom to work from anywhere in an environment of their choice, using devices they have chosen for themselves (Figure 4-4).

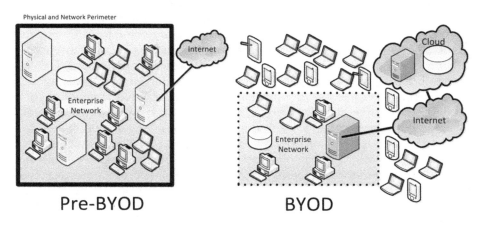

Figure 4-4. BYOD has changed the overall structure of enterprise computing

Employers welcome this because they may believe workers who are available round the clock are more productive than workers who are only available during regular working hours on the office premises. Many also believe that allowing employees to work in an environment of their choice enhances productivity and job satisfaction. Employee-owned equipment is equipment the enterprise does not have to purchase, carry on their books, or maintain. The *total cost of ownership* (TCO) of an employee's device like an iPad is the employee's problem, not the employer's.

Pre-BYOD-and-Cloud IT Management

Before BYOD and clouds, enterprise IT security built a physical and network wall around the enterprise to keep out intruders and control data moving both in and out of the enterprise. The wall existed both as locked doors and restricted access and private networks protected with firewalls and proxies.

Locked doors and tight control of network access blocked intrusions from outside the enterprise. Within a secure perimeter, the IT department could focus on preventing unauthorized employees from accessing and changing information and stopping unauthorized interference with critical processes. When the enterprise owned all equipment within the perimeter and employees were only allowed to work within the perimeter, the enterprise exercised total control of access to its network and everything connected to it.

Tight perimeters are still maintained in high-security settings. However, the typical perimeter is becoming more penetrable and security has been forced to change. The portable laptop that can be connected to public and home networks has been common for some time. Access to outside networks, particularly the Internet, has become embedded in many business practices. All but the most security-conscious enterprises grant some form of Internet access. Although protected by firewalls and proxies, this access can become a portal for malware. Social engineering exploits can trick employees into granting access and privileges to unauthorized outsiders. Operating systems, applications, and services built under the outmoded assumption of a friendly environment have inadvertent or naïve security flaws, which are readily exploited by malefactors. With this in mind, development practices have been tightened up with security awareness training and security checklists, and security reviews and patching processes have become more reliable and prompt. However, as individuals, business, and government use interconnected computers more, the stakes and opportunities for abuse and crime have also grown. Laws and regulations like Sarbanes-Oxley, Gramm-Leach-Bliley, and the Health Insurance Portability and Accountability Act (HIPAA) have raised the standards for computing security.

These are challenges that have pushed enterprise computer security far beyond the state of a few years ago. BYOD heightens these challenges and adds to them.

BYOD and Cloud Security

Both clouds and BYOD weaken the enterprise perimeter. Aside from the issues of third party governance involved with cloud, cloud implementations make data and processes accessible outside the perimeter. When combined with mobile devices, enterprise data is exposed on a moving target that may be using insecure connections like the public wireless in a coffee shop or on the beach. Even when an employee works from home, the enterprise may have no assurance that the employee's network is secure.

The combination of cloud, mobile devices, and BYOD is potent; both utility and vulnerability are enhanced by the combination. A cloud makes processes and data much more available than when they are locked up within the enterprise perimeter. Mobile devices add another dimension to availability by freeing users from desktop machines. BYOD completes the troika by giving employees control of their detached devices.

When the employee owns the equipment, the perimeter becomes more porous and in some areas effectively disappears. Many issues arise. IT department control of an employee-owned device is often unclear. An employee may object when the IT department requests to scan an employee's smartphone for apps that are dangerous to the enterprise. An employee may protest when the IT department requests removal an unsafe app used for sharing baby pictures when the app could also be used to share critical enterprise data.

If the IT department detects an imminent threat, such as a missing critical patch, the department may need to remove the threat immediately without permission from the employee. If, in the course of removing a threat, the IT department damages or exposes personal data, the employee may look for legal recourse.

Many departments have policies and tools to erase and obliterate all the contents of a company laptop or mobile device that IT identifies as lost or stolen. A personal laptop is somewhat different. Instead of stolen, the laptop might have been innocently borrowed. The employees may react harshly when their personal data is deleted.

In addition, BYOD brings consumer services, such as cloud data-storage services into the enterprise. An employee might install a cloud file synchronization service on his personal laptop. These services often do not meet rigorous security standards that businesses rely on for safe storage of data. The consumer services are meant to be convenient, but convenience is often antithetical to security. Therefore, some consumer services are far from secure by business standards. The consumer cloud service has all the vulnerabilities of any cloud implementation, but the enterprise does not have a service agreement with the consumer service provider nor is the consumer service likely to have audit certification.

Although BYOD is a reality in many enterprises, in some cases enterprise management and governance has lagged behind the reality. Explicit, written BYOD policies are relatively rare, which is unfortunate because without clear guidelines that employees explicitly acknowledge and agree to, BYOD security is problematic. Employees have to give up some rights to their devices if enterprise security and governance are to be upheld. Explicit agreements between employer and employee on BYOD are desirable to lay down the limits and expectations on both sides.

There are technological solutions, such as encryption, that can help BYOD security. For example, a public key-encrypted document can be set up to be inaccessible without a private key on a limited set of devices. In theory, such a document would remain secure no matter where it is stored. This arrangement depends on the security of the public key encryption, which has been something of a cat and mouse game between the encryption developers and the encryption breakers. Mobile device operating systems can be designed to separate company activities from private activities, perhaps similar to a multiuser operating system. Other possibilities include running virtual machines on the mobile device to separate company from private activities, also similar to some multiuser implementations. There will no doubt be considerable improvements as BYOD becomes more prevalent and the enterprise perimeter continues to fade away.

Mobile Devices and the Enterprise Architect

Enterprise architects designing cloud applications should never forget that mobile devices from outside the enterprise may access the cloud system. Even applications written for an enterprise that bans BYOD should probably anticipate that BYOD will be allowed at some time.

An app on a mobile device served by a cloud implementation is not much different from a fat or thin client interacting with a server in an on-premises system. Web services work in the same way with mobile devices on the Internet as they work with on-premises clients connected to the enterprise network. Within the enterprise perimeter, where every user is part of the organization, applications can reduce security a bit if it buys greater convenience. This is not the case for an application interacting with a mobile device over the Internet.

Within the enterprise perimeter, a simple username-password challenge, corresponding to HTTP basic authentication, is often adequate to authenticate a user already known to the organization. In the Internet world, basic authentication is usually inadequate. HTTP basic authentication transmits passwords in clear text, open and available to the person sitting next to you at the coffee shop with the packet sniffing software. The same packet sniffer can also read all the data sent to and received from the server because the packets are unencrypted. There are other problems. Web sites can be hi-jacked and spoofed, so clients need proof that the site they have connected with is the site they intended to connect with before they start sending out valuable data.

These issues are largely resolved with Secure Sockets Layer (SSL) or more accurately, Transport Layer Security (TLS.)[6] When HTTP uses TLS, the protocol is called Secure HTTP (HTTPS). HTTPS encrypts data both going to and coming from the server and requires third-party certified authentication of the identity of the server. The encryption scheme is negotiated between the client and the server. The security of the connection can be reduced by negotiating a less secure scheme. HTTPS is well established and supported, and it is used by many sites on the web. An enterprise mobile app that handles critical information should always use HTTPS and require the latest encryption scheme.

Nevertheless, HTTPS is often not enough. A protocol that relies solely on a password is not as secure as it could be. Passwords are easily spied upon; users tend to use passwords that are predictable, and social engineering exploits can sometimes obtain passwords. Users frequently forget their passwords, necessitating password resets, which are themselves vulnerable. Alternatives that use personal artifacts like fingerprint and retinal scans can be compromised by clever reproductions of the artifact. When this happens, the artifact cannot be replaced like changing a password. A solution that has seen some success is two-phase authentication where the user enters a conventional password, and then receives a short-lived password that is sent to a pre-arranged place, like a cellphone or email address. A malefactor must know both the conventional password and obtain access to the temporary password.

Moving data and processes from inside a corporate perimeter to a cloud that can be accessed externally and offering that access from mobile devices offers new freedom to enterprise systems, but security has become more challenging for enterprise architects who must meet equally pressing demands for security and convenient access.

Conclusion

Computing has been tied to the display-keyboard-mouse form factor for three decades. It is now breaking free of this paradigm with small, light, powerful, and, above all, portable devices that work with data and processes that run on a public or private cloud. One result is further decay of the enterprise security perimeter, which is springing leaks as more and more highly portable devices are used from outside the perimeter. The cloud makes these problems worse because the core of enterprise computing and data storage is also slipping outside the perimeter. Enterprise architects must meet these challenges.

---

[6]TLS replaced SSL fifteen years ago. SSL is no longer considered secure. There have been several revisions of TLS, each closing security holes in the previous version. SSL is still the more common term, but it nearly always refers to TLS.

EXERCISES

1. What is a mobile device? What are its architectural characteristics? How does it interact with clouds? How is a mobile device different from desktops and laptops?

2. Distinguish between web apps, native apps, and hybrid apps.

3. Which is closer to a fat client architecture: web apps or native apps?

4. What is the enterprise perimeter?

5. How does BYOD and the cloud challenge the enterprise perimeter?

The Hard Part

Clouds

SUMMARY

For a business or other organization, deciding to use a cloud implementation and then choosing a cloud service model and how the cloud will be deployed are difficult problems. The decision depends on the role of the cloud service within the organization and the relationship between the cloud consumer and provider and the service provided. The decision is financial, managerial, and technical. It requires an understanding of what a cloud is, the benefits from cloud deployments, and the risks and obstacles to a successful deployment. And it requires an understanding of the unique requirements of managing a service deployed on a cloud.

Individual consumers are in a different position. Cloud services are usually offered to consumers as complete services that they either accept or reject. They may seem to be less concerned about the details of the implementation. However, the choice to use a service is often an architectural choice and means placing some aspect of their affairs into the hands of a third party, whether the consumer realizes it or not. To be an informed consumer, some knowledge of the underlying architecture and management is required.

This chapter addresses the concerns of both businesses and individual consumers.

What Is a Cloud?

Like any service, two groups participate in cloud services: consumers and providers. ITIL defines service providers as suppliers of outcomes that consumers want while avoiding the risk or direct costs of producing the outcome themselves. Providers generate outcomes that consumers are willing to pay for.[1] For consumers, the alternative to using a service provider is to do the job themselves. In the case of clouds, providers supply computing services. These services can take several forms. Cloud service models are a high-level classification of cloud services based on the type of resources the cloud provider offers.

NIST CLOUD DEFINITION

The National Institute of Standards and Technology (NIST) published a definition of cloud computing[2] in 2011. The industry has widely accepted this definition although any definition in the lively and developing cloud arena dates quickly.

According to NIST, *cloud computing* is a model for easy and wide network access to computing resources that can be rapidly configured, provisioned, and released.

The NIST definition lists a number of characteristics of cloud computing, including the following:

- *Self-service*: A cloud consumer can provision cloud services without the intervention of the cloud provider.

- *Broad access*: Connecting with a cloud does not require a private network connection or special, dedicated devices.

- *Resource pools*: The provider presents resources to the consumer as an undifferentiated pool that can be configured and provisioned by the consumer's request.

- *Elasticity*: The resources used by the consumer can be expanded and contracted automatically to respond to varying consumer loads. The resources appear unlimited to the consumer.

- *Metered service*: Service use is metered, and consumers are charged for the services used.

NIST delineates three service models.

- Software as a Service (SAAS)

- Platform as a Service (PaaS)

- Infrastructure as a Service (IaaS)

---

[1] Note that consumers do not always pay with money. Often, using a service yields valuable information about the consumer to the provider of the service. The provider then uses that information for a profit. For example, a search engine may use information it obtains about consumer interests for a directed advertising service and charge the users of the advertising service.

[2] Mell, Peter; Grance, Timothy. "The NIST Definition of Cloud Computing." Recommendations of the National Institute of Standards and Technology. September 2011. Accessed November 2013. http://csrc.nist.gov/publications/nistpubs/800-145/SP800-145.pdf

NIST also lists four deployment models.

- Private cloud

- Community cloud

- Public cloud

- Hybrid cloud

Cloud Service and Deployment Models

The NIST cloud definition addresses several service and deployment models for clouds. (See the "NIST Cloud Definition" sidebar.) Service models describe the service that is provided by the cloud. Deployment models describe the relationships between the consumers and providers of the cloud.

Service Models

NIST defines three service models that are based on three basic types of services: infrastructure, platform, and software. The standard NIST definition of cloud computing is well known, and most cloud practitioners know the definitions and classifications well. In the intervening years since NIST published the definition, the field has evolved. Many cloud services and implementations have appeared, and the number of "aaS" acronyms has burgeoned. These new services are specializations or extensions of the basic NIST models. See Figure 5-1.

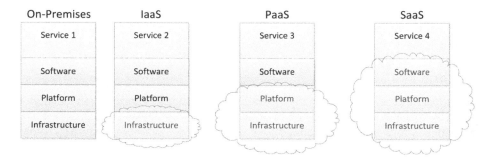

Figure 5-1. IaaS, PaaS, and SaaS each address a different level of IT management

Infrastructure as a Service

The most basic cloud service is Infrastructure as a Service (IaaS), which offers virtual computers, storage facilities, and networks to consumers.[3] An IaaS architecture is at the bottom of most PaaS cloud architectures. SaaS architectures are sometimes based on an IaaS architecture and sometimes not. See Figure 5-2. Consumers use these virtual cloud resources as if they were physical hardware on their own premises. The consumer acquires software and installs it on the cloud virtual devices and then administers running the software. This software includes utilities such as database management software and HTTP servers as well as applications. Some IaaS providers offer preconfigured machine images that already have some software installed, eliminating some of the effort involved in standing up a system on an IaaS platform. Some software vendors offer their software in packages ready to install as complete or partial systems on designated IaaS provider clouds.

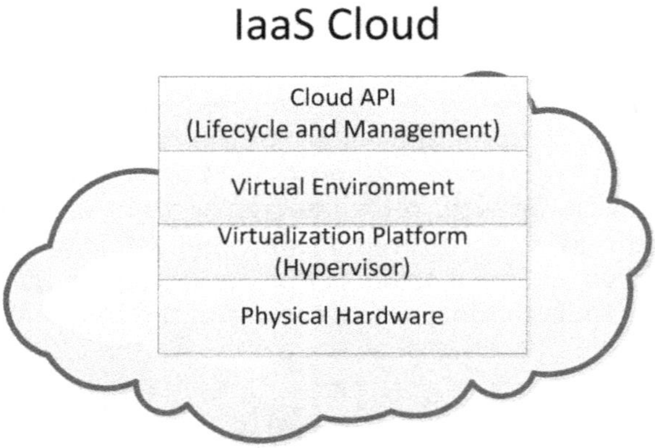

IaaS Cloud

Figure 5-2. A typical IaaS architecture

Platform as a Service

A Platform as a Service (PaaS) cloud provider supplies more than bare virtual hardware to the consumer. In addition to virtual infrastructure, the PaaS provider offers software utilities and services. For example, they may offer development environments that supply design tools, specialized code editors, compilers, testing tools, and a framework for moving the resulting production application into production on the PaaS cloud. Utilities such as databases and load balancers are another frequent offering. The range of platform facilities

---

[3]Clouds do not always supply only virtual resources; they can offer physical resources as well. However, many of the advantages of cloud implementations are dependent upon the speed and flexibility of virtual deployment. Therefore, clouds only rarely are used to supply physical resources.

offered by PaaS providers is varied and extensive. However, the core of an application running on a PaaS cloud is usually still owned and maintained by the consumer. For example, the Microsoft Azure PaaS platform supplies several utilities, including SQL Server. Azure consumers can code applications on Azure and use the included SQL Server instance, but the code is theirs, and they must maintain it themselves.

Software as a Service

Software as a Service (SaaS) moves the ownership and administration of software applications to the cloud provider. The provider supplies the software, manages the underlying hardware (or delegates the hardware to an IaaS or PaaS provider), and administers system backups, patches, and updates. Aside from a limited consumer-specific configuration that the consumer must perform, the consumer is not involved in provisioning, configuring, or maintaining the service. Some SaaS applications support customization, but SaaS customization is typically much more limited than traditional enterprise application customization, which sometimes is so extensive that the customer writes some application code. To use a SaaS service, the consumer uses the application and usually pays based on usage. Some SaaS are offered without direct charge. These are often stripped-down versions meant to attract customers to full-featured pay versions or other paying products. Some SaaS applications, like Facebook, are offered without charge because the provider wants to collect information on the clients or use the application as a platform for advertising or similar activity.

Other Service Models

Software developers and providers have not hesitated to expand and specialize the three NIST service models. A specialized cloud service that home consumers are likely to use is Storage as a Service. A typical storage service will provide storage resources, reminiscent of an IaaS service and an SaaS interface. The result is an easy-to-use service that backs up data to a remote site and makes the data available anywhere with an Internet connection. This is convenient for users who use several different devices but want to access the same data on each device. A music service like Apple iTunes is a form of Storage as a Service in which a consumer stores specialized data, audio files containing recorded music, and can access their stored files from many different devices through an Internet connection.

For businesses, Storage as a Service often takes the form of a remote backup service that performs backups and stores the data or a cloud storage facility. Other forms of business Storage as a Service is storage of data that is not frequently needed but must be retained. Unlike home consumers, business consumers are usually more interested in secure storage of large quantities of data rather than convenient access from multiple devices and locations. Of course, bring your own device (BYOD) and off-premises workers have added multidevice access requirements in many business situations.

Other service models that have appeared are Network as a Service, Backup as a Service, IT as a Service, and many others. Each is a specialization, extension, or combination of the basic NIST models. The rapid proliferation of service models is a sign of the growth and entrenchment of the cloud concept.

Deployment Models

Clouds are also classified by deployment model. Ownership and consumer groups characterize the public, private, and community deployment models. The fourth model is different and is discussed next. The public cloud provider that offers cloud services to the public is at one extreme in the deployment spectrum. Private clouds are at the other end of the spectrum in which an organization owns and offers a cloud service limited to its own organization. There are advantages and disadvantages to each deployment model. See Figure 5-3.

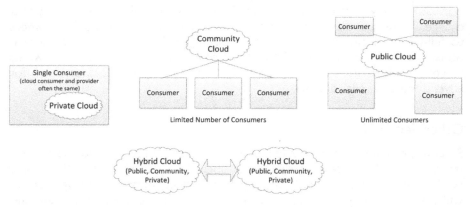

Figure 5-3. Private, community, public, and hybrid clouds are NIST deployment models

Public Cloud

Public clouds are often thought of as the archetype for clouds. They probably are closest to the notion of utility computing that has been discussed almost since computers began. Utility computing was discussed in detail in Chapter 2. A public cloud resembles a public utility like an electricity supplier. Both deal directly with the public and are open to all comers. Public clouds differ from classical utilities in that they are not regulated like many public utilities, and although the services of each public cloud are similar to other public clouds, the services are not as interchangeable as you usually expect from commodities. When you fuel your car from different gas stations, you do not expect to adjust your car's engine to accommodate the new gasoline or connect a hose adapter to fill your car's tank. Public clouds are open to all consumers willing to accept the terms of use, but consumers cannot now expect switching from one public cloud to another to be transparent. Some adjustment, perhaps substantial changes, may be required.

Market forces may compel public clouds to evolve to be closer to utilities in the future. Standardization efforts, such as the Distributed Management Task Force (DMTF) Cloud Infrastructure Management Interface (CIMI),[4] promise to speed this process. OpenStack[5] is an open source project with wide support in the industry. It appears poised to become the default cloud implementation stack, just as Linux has become the default non-Windows operating system.

For most public cloud users, metered usage is an important characteristic of a public cloud shared with the classic utility model. If cloud resources sit idle, public cloud users do not expect to pay for the resources, just as homeowners do not expect to pay for electricity they do not use.

Private Cloud

For all their advantages, the jump to deploying on a public cloud is not easy for many enterprises. Security and governance issues can prevent delegating responsibilities to third-party public cloud providers. Many enterprises are cautious and want to test the cloud waters before they commit to relying upon a cloud provider. A private cloud is often a good alternative. In its simplest form, a private cloud is built on the organization premises, often by the IT department, perhaps from equipment already owned by the organization. If the goal is IaaS, the equipment is configured as a cloud by isolating it from the rest of the environment and then providing a virtualization layer and a set of utilities that provide an interface for creating, configuring, controlling, and metering virtual infrastructure on the designated cloud hardware. The interface to the cloud is offered to the rest of the organization. There may be a chargeback system, only usage reports, or no metering at all.

Metering in a private cloud owned and operated by a single organization is not a necessity, but it can be useful. When business units or departments are aware of their computing resource usage, they are better able to gauge the efficiency their usage and become more cost effective.

---

[4]See http://dmtf.org/standards/cloud for a discussion of CIMI and other DMTF cloud initiatives.
[5]See www.openstack.org/ (accessed August 24, 2015) for more information.

IaaS is not the only service model that private clouds can support. A SaaS application implemented on a private cloud can provide easy access and maintenance for applications used across an organization. PaaS deployed on a private cloud can be particularly well suited to providing flexibility for software development and quality assurance testing.

Private clouds do not have to be built by the private consumer or hosted on the owner's resources. Third parties can operate private clouds on an organization's premises or operate them on premises not owned by the cloud owner. The necessary and sufficient characteristic that differentiates a private cloud from other deployment models is that it is not shared with other organizations or unrelated consumers.

Community Cloud

A community cloud is an intermediate deployment model between public and private clouds. Similar to a private cloud, the consumers of a community cloud are limited, but instead of limiting consumption to consumers from one organization, a community cloud is offered to members of an associated group of organizations. Often, community clouds are owned by consortiums, such as groups of educational or scientific institutions. Like private clouds, they can be built and hosted by third parties.

Hybrid Cloud

A hybrid deployment model is not an ownership model like public, private, and community clouds. A hybrid cloud is defined by a relationship with other clouds. A typical example of a hybrid cloud is *cloud bursting*, in which one cloud reaches capacity for some activity and "bursts" by transferring some of the load to a different cloud. The load may stem from any activity.

A common hybrid cloud bursting scenario supports a large web site that is heavily used for short periods, such as a site that appears in a Super Bowl halftime ad. During or immediately after the ad, the site could get millions of hits, far more than normal load.[6] The number of hits depends upon many factors and is hard to predict with any accuracy. One solution is to provision a server farm with enough capacity to handle the highest estimates, but a hybrid cloud presents a more elegant solution. The site starts out during the low-usage pregame period deployed on a single cloud implementation. As the hits increase, the first cloud bursts to a second cloud. If the number of hits soars beyond all but the most optimistic estimates, the system could burst to a third cloud. At that point, three clouds would be supporting the site. The second

---

[6]Advertisers' site hits during the 2014 Super Bowl were reported to average nearly a two-thirds increase over normal traffic levels. See www.cmo.com/articles/2014/2/6/mobile_the_real_winn.html. Accessed March 25, 2014.

and third clouds are decommissioned when the demand diminishes. Flexibility and scalability are crucial to services that are offered to national or global consumers, and hybrid clouds are a way of providing flexibility and scalability with excess capital investment in infrastructure.

The ability to transfer between clouds characterizes hybrid clouds. Bursting is a popular example, but other hybrid clouds may not involve bursting. An application that has processes running on several separate clouds runs on a hybrid cloud. An application that runs on one cloud and stores data on another cloud is also running on a hybrid. An important requirement for hybrid clouds is for interfaces that support rapid and efficient transfer of loads, events, and data from cloud to cloud.

Cloud Benefits

The many benefits from cloud implementations justify the effort required for cloud service management. Individual consumers, small organizations, and large organizations benefit, although the benefits are not the same.

Separation of Consumer and Provider

One key to understanding the benefits of clouds is to understand the value of separating cloud consumers from providers into distinct roles. This separation is the essence of the concept of a service. Cloud services separate the consumers of a computing service, such as the users of an application, from the providers of a computing service, such as the system administrators who install and maintain the application. When an organization both uses and maintains an application, one group has to be organized and trained to support the application, and another, usually much larger, group has to be organized and trained to use the application; and infrastructure must be available to support the application. In some organizations, this may not be a problem because they have the resources to support the application efficiently.

Until the advent of clouds, organizations—especially startups and other small-to-medium businesses—had little choice: either administer complex and demanding applications or find less demanding alternatives, which were likely to be weak compromises. Today, cloud implementations are a viable and powerful alternative. Organizations can use SaaS management tools like sophisticated sales force and service desk management applications that they do not have the personnel or infrastructure to support. These applications used to be reserved for larger organizations. Using SaaS, these smaller organizations can skip ahead to large organization efficiencies while still small. In addition, these smaller organizations may be able to gain large organization efficiencies while forestalling the bureaucratization that restricts the agility of large organizations.

Larger organizations benefit also, but they have the option of implementing the service on their own premises in addition to a cloud implementation. In this, larger organizations have a range of choices. They can implement on IaaS and avoid ownership and administration of infrastructure but retain control of all the software. Organizations with in-house written applications or highly customized off-the-shelf applications often opt for IaaS. PaaS offers similar software flexibility, but some software utilities are handed off to the cloud provider. SaaS moves the most responsibility to the cloud provider and works best where there is little or no customization of the application. Often, when an organization is spread over a wide geographic area, a centralized cloud provider offers additional benefits because the implementation can be concentrated in a small area offering additional efficiencies.

The individual consumer also benefits from the separation of consumer and provider. It may seem odd to think this way, but until networking and network applications appeared, users were their own providers. Any resource they wanted to use had to be present on their personal computer. As networking became more prevalent, more resources came from the network. For example, network file servers and client-server applications were a way of providing resources to the consumer without the consumer owning the hardware or the complete software. Employees connected to a corporate network were the main beneficiaries of these remote resources.

For individual consumers, current cloud implementations are mainly an extension of the benefits of those that used to be limited to corporate networks. Instead of keeping terabytes of photographs and videos on personal hard drives, consumers today delegate storage to a cloud storage service, just as corporate users stored files on corporate file servers. Instead of having dozens of processors on their laptops, they play games using the banks of processors on a cloud implementation. The consumer now can consume cloud services in place of services they provide themselves. Typically, the SaaS nature of these services is transparent to consumers. It does not matter to them if an application runs on their tablet or phone or on a remote cloud. They only know that they are enjoying a service that they did not have before.

Consumers also benefit from IaaS and PaaS. The benefits are indirect and hidden but still important. The SaaS products used by consumers are often implemented on IaaS or PaaS clouds. For example, the popular entertainment streaming application Netflix is implemented on an IaaS public cloud, not on on-premises company servers. Because Netflix relies on a cloud provider with huge computing resources, Netflix subscribers can reasonably expect that they will have a pleasant and pause-free experience watching a movie at a peak time on a Saturday night.

Specialization

Economic progress is often associated with specialization. When a person or an organization narrows its focus and becomes proficient at supplying a specific good or service that a supplier of many services supplied at lower quality or efficiency, the result is often improved quality and decreased cost. The specialist acquires tools and skills to perform the work quicker and better and can therefore offer a superior value for lower cost. When a vital good or service is supplied at dramatically improved quality or decreased cost, major changes may occur in the economy and society. For example, during the Industrial Revolution, many costs were lowered by the application of steam power to specialized manufacturing, replacing unspecialized village workshops. Consequently, economies changed, populations moved, and society was transformed.

Computing clouds are also specialization. The operator of a large public or community cloud can afford to develop skills and acquire equipment that one person or a single organization cannot. Large cloud installations are deployed in specialized data centers that are built for energy and computing efficiency. A large cloud operator can design and have manufactured special computers, storage units, switches, racks, and other gear to optimize their systems. They can design and implement high-speed interconnects between their computing units that may number in the hundreds of thousands. They can locate their data centers where energy and cooling costs are low. These efficiencies are not possible without the large scale that clouds achieve by supporting large numbers of consumers. At the same time, by specializing, the cloud suppliers develop the skills and assets necessary to scale to the levels that offer these efficiencies. By becoming specialized suppliers of computing capacity, cloud providers have, and continue to develop, expertise that would not otherwise exist.

Enterprise cloud consumers benefit from their own specialization. Each organization has its core capacities, skills, and assets that they alone possess and enable them to compete in their own business area. Management experts often urge businesses to focus on their core capacities and avoid investing in auxiliary efforts that do not offer competitive advantages. Using a cloud is one way that business can do this. Instead of developing IT expertise and investing in a large data center to track parts and inventory, an equipment manufacturer might decide to invest more in new product design and leave the data center infrastructure management to a cloud supplier.

Scale

In addition to specialization, the scale of clouds has benefits. A common problem in smaller datacenters is spare hardware capacity. Service desk systems provide a good example. They have hours of peak usage, perhaps one early in the week, a lesser peak near the beginning of the weekend, and monthly and yearly peaks when books are closed or other periods of elevated activity.

These peaks are exactly the time when the service desk is most critical and has to be most reliable and perform best. In the past, organizations would buy a server or servers big enough to handle the largest expected load with an additional percentage of "headroom," usually an additional 20 to 50 percent capacity. Most of the time, the server would run at below 20 percent of its total capacity. In other words, 80 percent of the investment would yield benefits only a few days a year.[7]

A private cloud helps avoid some of these sunk investments. If different applications have different peak periods, a private cloud that shares capacity among the applications allocates the spare capacity of one application to other applications that need it. If the organization happens to span time zones, they may be able to garner further efficiency.

A large public cloud is in an even better position. This supports the applications of a large number of consumers with all different consumption patterns and locations, which offers greater opportunities for load leveling and efficient utilization. In addition, large clouds, through economies of scale, have lower energy and equipment costs, and therefore large clouds, can operate more efficiently and reduce the cost of spare capacity.

Financial

Usage-based charges are financially beneficial to business in many ways. The benefits of being charged by the service used rather than the fixed cost of implementing and operating the service are clear. However, Chapter 4 discussed some of the difficulties in internal chargebacks for IT services in which chargebacks may increase rather than decrease when use of a service decreases because of inelastic IT costs. Public or community cloud implementations with metered usage-based billing can increase the elasticity of IT costs, which makes IT service chargebacks more practical.

But metering is not the only benefit. Much has been made of the benefits of transferring *capital expenditures* (CAPEX) in IT infrastructure to *operational expenses* (OPEX), and there are undoubted benefits. However, most organizations agree that reducing expenses is more beneficial than transferring expenses from capital to operations.

---

[7]Organizations have tried in some ways to use some of this spare capacity. Hardware virtualization has been the most successful of these ways but works well only when there is a substantial pool of hardware and loads with different peak usages. Virtualization is one of the first steps toward a private cloud implementation.

There are some areas where clouds are especially effective in reducing expenses. Software development is one of these. Software development often requires hardware and software that are not needed after a project is complete. Traditionally, this equipment is leased. In addition to the cost of the lease, there are transportation, cabling, setup, and takedown costs. These fixed costs may exceed the cost of a short lease. The fixed cost of leasing 10 servers for a week is not much different from the fixed cost of leasing 50 servers for a year. In contrast, a virtual machine from a public cloud provider can be used for a few minutes at a time at a low cost.

Software *quality assurance* (QA) testing is also a beneficiary. Marshalling 1,000 client machines to test an application is a formidable job if the machines are physical computers in a test lab, but the same test is much easier and less expensive if the test machines are virtual machines deployed on a cloud. Tests can be performed using cloud implementations at a lower cost and less effort compared to the expensive and laborious physical hardware tests of the past.

In these areas where usage is highly fluid, cloud computing comes into its own. The capital required for a technical startup drops considerably when equipment does not have to be purchased or leased, and software development projects within large enterprises become cheaper and more agile with this kind of flexibility. This is especially significant for startups. They are always strapped for cash, and they struggled to scrape up the capital to provision even a modest development lab. By using cheap computing power from public cloud providers, they are now able to undertake development that would have been possible only with massive venture capital or in a well-funded established development house. This has changed the dynamics of software development in general.

Connectivity

Clouds also provide benefits from their connection through the Internet. In some cases, this is good; in other cases, it's not so good. The Internet is all about global connectivity. Data stored in a cloud and applications running in a cloud become accessible outside the enterprise perimeter. The accessibility raises the possibility that illegitimate access may be obtained from outside the enterprise perimeter. On the other hand, external connectivity can be useful. For example, data on roving employee laptops can easily be backed up remotely using a cloud-based application. SaaS applications that are available outside the corporate network can make remote employees more productive. However, despite these advantages, security issues increase.

ON-PREMISES

On-premises[8] is a term used frequently in cloud discussions. The term derives from telecommunications terminology. The term was used to distinguish between wiring and other infrastructure owned by the customer and wiring and equipment owned by the communications provider. The term was later used for software running on equipment on the consumer's premises and software running remotely on a cloud. The term is anomalous when used in combination with *private cloud* because the software is still running on the customer's premises even though running on a cloud.

Large organizations spread over wide areas may find that cloud architectures help them provide uniform services to remote offices by replacing local *on-premises* implementations with cloud implementations that serve all locations. Both private and public clouds can be used for these implementations. A private cloud owned and implemented on the organization premises can consolidate services without inserting a third-party cloud provider. If the organization is comfortable with a community or public cloud, the organization can offload more of the administration.

Most mobile apps have at least portions implemented as SaaS. Many basic products, like office suites, have cloud implementations such as Google Docs or Microsoft Office 360. Other products, such as Dropbox and Carbonite, use cloud storage to provide file synchronization and remote backup. Other services such as Apple iTunes and Amazon Kindle sell music and e-books that can be accessed from all the consumer devices. These patterns permit consumers to perform activities that require more computing power or storage than they have on their own machines and avoid intricate installations and maintenance that some of these products require when they are implemented locally.

Often individual consumers have more issues with connectivity than businesses because individuals are usually more dependent on public networks than businesses. Networks are no faster than their slowest link, which is often the "last mile." The last mile is the final connection between the user and the network. For consumers, the last mile is usually a telecommunications copper wire or a coaxial cable, originally for television. Residential users do not often have much choice in their last mile, and that often means restricted bandwidth and high latency.

This is changing somewhat with mobile devices that can use the cellular network for connecting to the network. Connection speeds are getting faster, although a cellular connection is usually more expensive than a land home Internet connection.

---

[8]*On-premise* is also used frequently. Sticklers point out that this is contrary to standard English in which *premise* refers to a proposition that is agreed upon as the basis for a succeeding argument. *Premises* refers to the facilities that house a business.

When one looks at a map of broadband availability in the United States,[9] metropolitan areas are covered, but much of the country is not supplied or under-supplied. This limits the market for consumer cloud applications and affects some cloud product development decisions.

Cloud Risks and Obstacles

Cloud services provide a user with a kind of connectivity that was previously unavailable or difficult to achieve, and cloud services give users access to computing power that governments and the largest corporations would have been hard-pressed to amass only a few years ago. They all rely on a pool of shared resources that contains private data and supports private processes. These private data and processes are entrusted to the cloud provider.

Privacy and Security

There are many privacy and security risks in IT. Privacy can be compromised, resulting in identity theft, loss of intellectual property, and a whole range of other losses. Security breaches can interrupt and subvert processes; outcomes may be far from desirable. Before clouds, users relied on the isolation of their devices to establish ownership of their data and control of processes. Cloud complicates the challenge.

Prior to the cloud, data security and privacy were easier to understand but not as convenient as the data services provided through a cloud. When ownership of data was tied to ownership of devices, consumers could depend on their own diligence to keep their data out of the wrong hands. When their data is in the cloud, consumers are dependent on the integrity of their cloud provider.

Processes are equally vulnerable. They can be halted, overwhelmed with input, given incorrect input…the list is long. On-premises applications rely on operators who are answerable to enterprise management. The competency of these operators can be verified, and other measures can be taken to assure the enterprise that its interests will be maintained. When an application is deployed on a third party, the enterprise loses this level of assurance and control.

The cloud can be safer than private implementations. Cloud providers can and do build datacenters that are orders of magnitude more difficult to break into than the best secured private residence and many private datacenters. The providers know more about protecting data from remote intrusion and can take better protective measures than a private person or an enterprise

---

[9]See www.fcc.gov/maps/broadband-availability. Notice how quickly service drops off away from metropolitan areas. A Federal Communications Commission report (www.fcc.gov/reports/eighth-broadband-progress-report) reports that 19 million Americans do not have minimal broadband connectivity.

without a large IT staff. Providers can require background checks on every person on their sites. Only a rare homeowner requires a background check on their furnace repairman. Cloud providers are in the business of providing security and privacy, and they have, or should have, substantial incentives to do their job well. None of this guarantees safety, but it does undermine the assertion that cloud implementations are inherently unsafe.

Nevertheless, the fact that a provider *can* protect data and processes does not mean that a provider *will* protect the data and processes entrusted to them. It is up to the consumer to require an appropriate level of security. The level of security of any given provider changes often, generally for the better, and is reported with alacrity in the trade press. Consumers would do well to pay attention.

The most important task of the enterprise architect in security and privacy is to understand the vulnerable points in the system. This requires an understanding of both the technical construction of the application and its business role. Technical knowledge is required to identify what is vulnerable. For instance, a process that uses TCP/IP sockets rather than HTTP for some incoming data has different technical vulnerabilities than a process that uses only HTTP.[10] However, this fact is not enough. The criticality of the data passing through the socket also is important for evaluating security and privacy, and the criticality is a usually a business decision rather than a technical decision.

Auditability

Audits play an important role for verifying the governance of any enterprise. An audit is a systematic and planned review of the records and processes of an enterprise. An audit has defined goals and methods that are often sanctioned by an independent certification organization. Audits may be performed internally or by an independent external team. For many enterprises, audits of various aspects of their finances and operations, including IT operations, are required. Processes that cannot be audited may not be permitted in sensitive areas by statute, regulation, boards, or management.

Cloud implementations can present challenges to auditing. Cloud implementations have varying degrees of transparency and accessibility to audits. Private clouds are not more difficult to audit than other forms of on-premises computing. Public clouds, on the other hand, bring a third party into the situation and delegate some control to the third party. Consequently, the third party

---

[10]Transmission Control Protocol/Internet Protocol (TCP/IP) is the protocol used for most computer-to-computer network communications. Hypertext Transfer Protocol (HTTP) is used for most Internet communication. HTTP uses TCP/IP as its lower-level transmission protocol. Read more about TCP/IP and HTTP in Chapter 10 of *Cloud Standards* (Apress, 2012).

may have to participate in the audit. Unless provisions for auditing access are included in the contract between the consumer and provider, the cloud provider may be unwilling or unable to provide the desired access. Audit agreements have become more common, and auditors have become more cloud aware; so, auditing has become less of a problem than it was a few years ago, but it is still frequently cited by businesses as a reason not to proceed with public cloud projects.

Enterprise architects should keep in mind that auditing issues will stop a project summarily. When designing for cloud implementations, especially systems that either are targeted at a public cloud implementation or are likely to be ported to a public cloud, the systems must meet audit requirements when deployed on a cloud. Audit requirements vary from organization to organization and may even change over time as business practices and the regulatory environment changes. Architects should make it a practice to be aware of audit requirements in their business and act accordingly. In some businesses, audit requirements may be limited to a few important financial reports. In other businesses, such as pharmaceuticals, audit requirements may be much more stringent and touch many aspects of IT.

Lack of Independence

Reliance on remote resources that are not under the direct control of the consumer reduces the independence of the consumer of computing resources. In the days when mainframes and timesharing were the primary source of computing resources, users were accustomed to working in an environment they did not own. That all changed with the personal computer. Users became accustomed to owning their hardware and the software on the hardware.

One of the goals of the open source movement was to increase the autonomy of computer users by giving them access to the source code of the processes running on their hardware so they could determine exactly what their software did and change it if they wanted. Of course, few personal computer users took time to read the code of the open source software, and even fewer changed the code. For most, the attraction of open source software is the low price. Nevertheless, the transparency is there.

SaaS, as Richard Stallman has pointed out,[11] reduces the software user's control of the software that processes their data in return for ease of maintenance and setup. Users should realize that they have delegated a share of

---

[11]Richard M. Stallman. "What Does That Server Really Serve?" *Boston Review*, March 18, 2010. Accessed January 13, 2014. www.bostonreview.net/richard-stallman-free-software-DRM. Stallman is the founder of the open source movement and holds strong opinions about access to software. Many disagree with his views.

control, and they must trust the integrity of their provider. Sometimes trust can be problematic. Providers may be constrained by law, for example, to reveal information to legal authorities that the consumer might rather keep private. Less threatening, but still problematic, a provider may reveal usage information, which is then put to target marketing use or other purposes.

Performance and Outages

Many consumers, especially businesses, are concerned about performance and outages of public cloud providers. A lapse in performance or a complete outage can become a finger-pointing match. The consumer blames the provider, the provider blames the network, and so on. Usually, outages and performance are handled in a service level agreement (SLA) that spells out penalties and incentives for meeting performance and availability[12] requirements. In many cases, SLAs are written by public cloud providers and offered on a take-it-or-leave-it basis, which leaves the consumer in an undesirable position.

Good enterprise architecture can alleviate performance and availability issues. One way is to configure cloud implementations to take advantage of options for distributing virtual machines for performance and availability. For example, some providers allow the consumer to designate that two virtual machines must run in different data centers for availability. For performance, the consumer may be able to designate that two processes must run on blades in the same rack. There are other ways to tailor architectures to the requirements of cloud implementation. More of these will be discussed in Chapter 12.

Consumer Clouds

When the cloud consumer is an individual, the benefits gained from clouds differ from those obtained by business. Although there are exceptions, individual consumers now get cloud services that have no previous equivalent. Businesses, on the other hand, more often use clouds to more efficiently implement services they have had in the past.

Individual consumers receive connectivity and mobility from clouds, which were previously available only in limited forms on corporate networks. Consumers are able to share data and access it from different devices and

---

[12]*Availability* refers to the percentage of the total time a system is expected to be available that is actually available. A system that is supposed to be available for 100 hours but is unavailable for 1 hour of the 100 hours has 99 percent availability. 99.999 percent (4 seconds down in 100 hours) availability is often held up as a high level of availability. This level is commonly called *five nines*. One hour down out of 100 hours is called *two nines*, and so on.

locations. For example, most social networking depends on storing data in a central space that is accessible to a designated group of fellow consumers.

Consumer cloud services depend more on the availability of broadband and high-speed network services than business cloud services. Enterprises are more often prepared to invest in leased or owned network infrastructure to ensure adequate support for their cloud applications. Individual consumers usually depend on public service providers such as cable and telecommunications companies. If there is not adequate network capacity available in an area from a service provider, individual consumers will not fully appreciate cloud services such as streaming video. This limits the reach of cloud service providers.

Social networking applications are significant consumer applications that could not exist without cloud implementations. One reason is the bulk of information that these applications store. Without enormous cloud storage facilities, the constant flow of text, audio, photographs, and video could not be sustained. In addition, social networks assume that data will be available on any desktop, laptop, tablet, or phone the user cares to use. This too would not be possible without clouds.

Storage

End consumer–oriented services frequently involve some form of cloud storage and often blend into other kinds of services. For example, users of Amazon's Kindle books use a cloud service for storing their books and notes, although they may not think about the storage aspect.

It's worthwhile considering the Kindle service for a moment. It is more complex than may be immediately apparent. A user purchases a Kindle book from Amazon. A copy of the file that represents the book is downloaded to a device. The device may be one of several models of Amazon Kindles, reader software on a desktop or laptop, or reader software on a non-Kindle tablet or other mobile device. The download is from the Amazon cloud. After the book is downloaded, the user reads the books, makes notes on it, and sets bookmarks at important spots. If the user gets a new device, such as a new smartphone, the user need only register the new device, select books from those they have already purchased, and begin reading. If the sun on the beach is too bright for their smartphones, they can read their book on screens that use technology better suited to sunlight.

The downloaded file on the reader remains joined to the Amazon cloud. For example, if the book is revised, Amazon may offer to revise the books on the user devices. Usually, this is with the user's permission, but permission is not technically necessary. In one startling licensing case, Amazon deleted books from Kindles without permission from the owners.[13] Perhaps the most surprising part of this service is the simplest: no matter where or on which device a book is opened from, it is always on the last page read. In addition, the user's notes and bookmarks travel with their books to every device the user chooses to read from. This is accomplished through a cloud implementation.

Paper books exist in the user's hand; an electronic book, as implemented by most electronic book services, does not. A file of data does exist on the device, but that is only a temporarily cached representation. If the network were faster and connections more reliable, that copy would not need to exist. When the user goes to another device, a similar representation with notes and bookmarks either already is present and updated or is created from the prototype in the cloud. The book with its notes is detached from the device held in the user's hands and exists in an abstract sense in the cloud.

The book in the cloud like this is also a virtual entity; it usually does not exist as a single physical record that embodies the book. In theory, only one copy of the file containing the book need exist on the book service cloud, with auxiliary copies propagated on the cloud for backup and caching for more rapid download. Each book owned[14] by a consumer references that single master copy. On the cloud, each book owned by a user is a reference to the master copy and to data specific to the user's copy of the book, such as their notes, bookmarks (including an implicit bookmark at the point where the reader was last reading), a list of all the devices from which the reader reads, and so on. The real situation is no doubt more complex than this. An electronic book service would certainly maintain more than one copy of the master copy both for insurance against disaster and perhaps for performance. The data on a person's books would be also copied as a backup and cached for performance.

Music services that store music libraries for users to access from different devices and permit them to have much larger libraries than any device they own could store are similar to electronic book services, storing music files rather than book files. Similar to an electronic book service, these services can use master copies of music files.

---

[13]The deleted books were, ironically, written by George Orwell. See www.nytimes.com/2009/07/18/technology/companies/18amazon.html. Accessed August 24, 2015. In another case, Amazon deleted the entire contents of the Kindle of a consumer suspected of objectionable activity. See www.theguardian.com/money/2012/oct/22/amazon-wipes-customers-kindle-deletes-account. Accessed August 24, 2015. In both cases, the company later admitted to making a mistake.

[14]*Owned* when applied to e-books is not traditional possession. In fact, the relationship between the reader of an electronic book and its supplier is more accurately characterized as licensed or leased than owned, but having a book on your reader at least feels like you own it.

Backup and storage services are different but still similar. These services offer storage for any kind of data, and they do not have master copies that are shared among consumers. Each file or block of data is the unique to the user who stored it with the service. These services take various forms. One variety designates a directory or group of directories as linked to a master directory tree in a cloud. Files placed in these directories are automatically uploaded to the cloud master. From the cloud master, the files are downloaded to other corresponding directories on other designated devices. Whenever any device modifies or creates a new file in one of these directories, the change is automatically propagated to the other devices. Using this kind of service, an author can have an upstairs and a downstairs desktop and a laptop for excursion, all with synchronized manuscripts and notes so he can work upstairs, downstairs, or at the library and always have the latest copies in front of him.

Other consumer cloud services operate at a somewhat higher level. For example, backup services install an agent that automatically sends backup copies to a cloud server. The user does not have to do anything until the day they need a restore and the backup is automatically restored on request. Other services are built into applications, such as a note-taking service that can be configured to store data on a cloud and make notes available to copies of the application installed on other devices. Unlike the storage service described earlier, the user may not be aware that files are involved. They only see that their virtual notebook is accessible to more than one device.

File synchronization and sharing services, such as Dropbox or Microsoft's OneDrive, use cloud storage to store master copies of files. When a synchronized file changes, the master is updated, and the changes are sent to the owner's designated devices. The file owner can also offer a link to other users with whom the owner wants to share. The master copies stored in the cloud can also act as backups or archival storage.

Streaming video services are also examples of using shared cloud storage to share videos. Streaming video is particularly susceptible to variations in network speed and capacity.

Cloud Applications

Yet another type of consumer cloud service is SaaS. Many SaaS applications make some use of cloud storage, but they also process data remotely on computers in cloud data centers. These applications range from massive efforts to turn over the status quo of a major product, such as Google Docs and Microsoft Office 360, moving office software from the personal computer to the cloud. Cloud gaming services, such as Nvidia Grid, offer games that run on a central server and stream video to the user browser. Almost all mobile apps use some form of cloud storage for user profile information, which allows consumers to switch from device to device. These patterns permit users to perform activities that require more computing power than the user has available on their own machine.

There are two main benefits to consumers. Like cloud storage, these applications promote collaboration. A group of users can work on the same application at the same time when the application is hosted on a cloud. Users of cloud office suites can collaborate on documents. Gamers interact with each other in cloud-hosted games.

Enterprise Clouds

Enterprises can be both cloud consumers and cloud providers. As cloud providers, they may provide private clouds to their own organization, or they may be a cloud giant like Google or Yahoo that offers public services to vast numbers of users.

Enterprise Cloud Consumers

Enterprises use many of the same cloud services that individual consumers use, although the services are often tailored to business purposes. Many business use backup services similar to consumer backup services for backing up the data on their employee's computers and other devices; the business edition of these tools often have features such as centralized administration of many individual accounts and support for departmental structures. Microsoft Office 360 is an example of a service that is used by individual consumers but is also tailored toward business use with business-oriented features and licensing.

However, enterprises and other organizations also approach clouds in ways that are conceptually different from most individual consumers' usage. Enterprises may have requirements that render one-size-fits-all SaaS applications unacceptable.[15] Typical enterprises have many legacy applications that either were written in-house or are heavily customized versions of commercial packages. These enterprises have trained and skilled IT departments that develop, implement, and support computing for the enterprise. Although they may be interested in converting to cloud-based versions of these applications, conversion is a slow and expensive process. These enterprises may prefer to deploy their applications on IaaS and PaaS clouds to gain some of the benefits of cloud computing without giving up the advantages of their bespoke and in-house software.

---

[15]This is changing. Heavily customized and carefully tailored applications used to be the hallmark of a large application installation, but many enterprises have acknowledged that the maintenance and support of bespoke software is a burden. This has led to a reevaluation of requirements and often a decision to use off-the-shelf or SaaS solutions.

Cloud Providers

Another view of enterprise cloud is from providers of cloud services. These are represented by the giant search engines such as Google and Yahoo, the social network providers such as Facebook, the public cloud providers and others who view clouds as opportunities to provide services rather than a better and more cost-effective way to consume services. Unlike individuals and other businesses, their goal is not to offload some of the computing infrastructure to another entity. Instead, their goal is to convince others to make use of their services by designing and deploying efficient cloud services with sufficient capacity to offer high-quality services to all comers at competitive prices.

Cloud Management

Managing services supplied by a cloud has challenges, even for individual consumers. Some challengers are similar to the management of locally installed applications and services supplied on the premises; others are quite different. The challenges faced by individuals and business are also different because individual consumers and businesses use clouds in different ways. Individuals seldom interact with a cloud directly. Instead, they engage with applications that have cloud implementations. Businesses, on the other hand, frequently deal with clouds directly. Although they use SaaS applications in the same way as individual consumers, they also run applications on IaaS or PaaS clouds and use cloud storage directly.

Cloud Service Management for Individual Consumers

Individual cloud consumers are faced with relatively simple decisions. Almost all cloud services offered to individual consumers are forms of SaaS because the consumers ordinarily don't concern themselves with platforms or infrastructure.[16] They must decide whether to use Dropbox or OneDrive or whether to use Google Docs or Microsoft 360.

Consumers should realize that the price and features of the service provided are only one part of their decision. For example, Word 360 may provide features that a consumer wants that are not available on Google Docs. An informed consumer may base their decision on those features, but they should also realize that they delegate responsibility and management of their documents to the provider when they choose the service. Just like businesses, they should ascertain the reliability and integrity of the provider. In this example,

---

[16]This situation may be changing. Network as a Service (NaaS) is being offered to businesses, and wireless networks as a service for home networks may not be far behind.

both third parties are well-known, reputable, and financially sound enough to meet their obligations. However, consumers should realize that they could be damaged if the service provider fails to perform as they expect.

Consumers should also realize that the click-through agreement[17] on a cloud service is not the same as the click-through license for software. A software license usually spells out the limits on the consumer's use of the vendor's software and spells out the responsibilities of the vendor if the software fails. For most consumer software, the consequences of a failure, say the crash of a word processor, are annoying but not catastrophic.[18]

A click-through on a cloud service describes, among other things, the limits on the provider's responsibility for delegating the consumer's property to the vendor. This trust relationship goes beyond ordinary use of a vendor's software product. With software licenses, vendors protect themselves from users. Users might get less out of the software than they were expecting, but they ordinarily don't bear a great risk of losing substantial assets. Cloud service users do risk losing substantial assets. For instance, if a backup service were to lose backups and the consumer lost their primary copy, valuable documents or data could be lost. If the provider does not maintain adequate security, damaging breaches of privacy or data tampering may occur.

For both software and services, the vendor writes the click-through agreement, and the customer can only accept or reject it. In the backup service example, backup service agreements typically limit the provider's liability for consumer losses; some even accept no liability. Therefore, blithely clicking through a cloud service agreement, more so than a software license, could result in a serious misunderstanding and loss of significant assets or treasures.

As important as these questions are to individual consumers, they are not as far-reaching as the management decisions that business cloud users typically make.

Business Cloud Service Management

Business cloud users must decide on service and deployment models. These decisions have greater reach than choices between services. A decision to port existing applications to run on an IaaS cloud can involve significant ongoing investment and may be difficult to reverse.

An alternative is to switch to a SaaS service. That too has implications. Switching from an existing highly customized application to a generic SaaS application will force groups of users to reconsider the requirements that

---

[17]A click-through agreement is a license or other legal document that a user accepts by clicking a screen, typically when a system is installed.
[18]Operating systems may be the exception here.

drove the customizations, modify their processes, and retrain personnel to use the new application. This is expensive, time-consuming, and likely to generate resistance. On the other hand, organizations often find that reduced maintenance and availability of third-party training programs make up for the lack of customization and conversion costs.

Further complicating the decision, SaaS applications are typically easy to set up and use, and the cost per user is often low. If individuals or departments are dissatisfied with an application supplied by the corporation, they may simply start to use the SaaS application and pay for it from the department budget. This may work for the department, but divergent processes can be difficult to manage and inefficient on the corporate level. For example, using an on-premises corporate customer relations management (CRM) system and a SaaS CRM system at the same time could cause embarrassment if a customer appears in only one system and the person who responds to a customer's call has the wrong system.

In addition, cloud services often present integration challenges. For example, a SaaS service desk that does not integrate with on-premises network management will not automatically generate tickets on network failures. This can result in slow incident recognition and resolution.

Cloud management is a more complex topic than it may appear. It can mean both managing services deployed on clouds as well as managing the operation of clouds themselves. To make matters more confusing, clouds provide services that are platforms for providing other services.

Cloud as a Form of Outsourcing

The practice of contracting with a third party to replace an in-house service is called *outsourcing*. It has become common practice in both IT departments and other business functions. Outsourcing can involve supplementing or replacing employees with contractors, such as outsourcing the job of answering customer service calls to an outside contractor. Sometimes, the contractor may hire a former employee to perform the work they previously performed supporting the outsourced service.

ITIL addresses cloud implementations as a form of outsourcing. Each of the cloud service models outsource some aspect of IT management. An IT department usually manages on different levels. At the most technical level, they are responsible for the acquisition, maintenance, and operation of hardware and software. On a higher level, they are responsible, with the cooperation and guidance of the business and upper management, for modifying existing services and designing and implementing new services. Finally, they are responsible for the day-to-day operation of services. The three basic cloud service models—IaaS, PaaS, and SaaS—roughly correspond to these three levels of IT management. See Figure 5-1.

The decision to deploy on a cloud must take into consideration the position of the IT department as a service provider within an organization. IT service providers are often described as Type I, II, or III. See Figure 5-4.

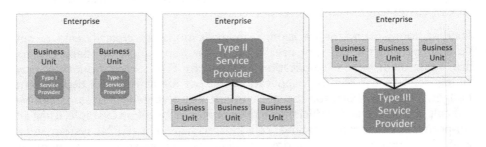

Figure 5-4. Service providers are divided into three types

A Type I provider is an internal provider. An IT department that is part of a business unit and is a provider of services only to its own business unit is a Type I provider of services to a single business unit. A Type I IT department may offer a private cloud services to their business unit, or they may use external cloud providers to provide services to their business unit. See Figure 5-4.

An IT department that provides services to more than one business unit is a Type II shared service provider. A private cloud implemented by this type of IT department could be used to implement services shared among several business units. A Type II provider may also use external clouds to implement shared services.

A Type III service provider is an external provider. A Type III IT department might provide a public cloud open to all comers, a community cloud offered to a limited set of organizations, or remotely hosted private clouds limited to the organization that request a private cloud services. A Type III IT department could be a business unit of an enterprise or an entire business devoted to providing external services.

IT departments are often mixtures of the types. For example, a Type I department might supply some services to other business units while its primary role is to supply services to its own business unit. A Type III department might also be a Type II or even Type I provider to business units within its own enterprise.

Depending on the IT department's type of service provider, the decision for outsourcing to a cloud occurs on different levels in the enterprise. A cloud deployment for a Type I department may well be only a business unit decision. For a Type II provider, the decision often requires approval on the corporate or even board level. Type III service providers are a different case, depending on their relationship with their own enterprise.

All outsourcing delegates some responsibility for a service to a third party. When the outsourced service contributes to a mission-critical service, delegation of responsibility can be extremely important. Although outsourcing decisions are often based on cost, the decision to outsource should always be preceded by the analysis of the implications for privacy and security, auditability, and accountability as well performance, reliability, and suitability. These aspects of the decision may often be more significant than outright cost savings.

From the viewpoint of a software engineer or software architect, these decisions may seem remote. Nevertheless, the decision to move a service to a cloud is both technical and managerial. Some considerations require technical expertise to evaluate, such as network latency, bandwidth issues, failover and disaster recovery plans, and architectures. The IT department needs to be prepared to assist the business and financial sides of the house in evaluating the costs and significance of an outsourcing decision.

Management of Services Deployed on Clouds

Managing cloud services differs from on-premises services because a cloud service adds a third party, the cloud provider, to the management of the service. For example, the participants in an on-premises help-desk service are the end user and the help-desk staff who operate and administer the help desk.[19] The help-desk staff is responsible to their users for providing acceptable service. If the help desk is deployed on a cloud—SaaS, PaaS, or IaaS—the help-desk staff is still responsible for providing service to their consumers, but they are now dependent on the cloud provider for some aspects of the help-desk service. For example, in an IaaS deployment, if there is an outage in the provider datacenter, help-desk operations will be interrupted. See Figure 5-5.

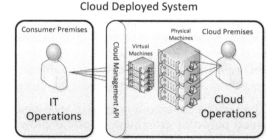

Figure 5-5. Managing an application deployed on an IaaS cloud adds another layer to management and transfers some responsibility to a third party

---

[19]This example posits a service in which the help-desk technicians are not outsourced but the help-desk software and storage are deployed on a cloud provider. The cloud service could be SaaS, PaaS, or IaaS depending on how much of the help-desk implementation is delegated to the cloud provider.

The picture in Figure 5-5 may be even more complex. The consumer may use performance and other management tools to monitor cloud-deployed application activity. These tools could run either on-premises or with the application on the cloud.

This is a management problem because the help desk is responsible to their users for delivering service, but the cause of interruption is in the hands of a third party, a situation that would not occur in an on-premises scenario where the entire service is provided by the same organization. When the deployment is on premises, there is a single management responsible for all aspects of the help-desk service. A cloud deployment requires coordination of the consumer management and the provider management. Therefore, a cloud deployment requires careful attention to the relationship with the third-party cloud provider. Often, the best practice is to designate a single point of contact between the cloud management and local management. The relationship manager is responsible for being familiar with the cloud provider's operations and the obligations in the relevant service contract. The contract between the cloud provider and the help desk is crucial because it sets down the obligations of the provider and consumer when an outage occurs. Providers often provide guidance for avoiding or minimizing outages that the staff must be aware of.

Service Contracts and Service Level Agreements

SLAs are usually part of a service contract. Usually, a service contract contains typical contractual elements such as the names of the entities to the contract, length of the contract, and renewal provisions. The SLA is part of the contract that specifies the service itself: the mutual obligations of the provider and consumer, exactly what the service is to deliver, the levels of service to be delivered, and the penalties and incentives for compliance and noncompliance to the agreed-upon service levels. The service levels themselves are usually metrics and thresholds that can be objectively determined. A service level agreement may also describe disaster recovery, auditability, inspection, security, and privacy provisions. Sometimes the SLA provides for periodic reevaluation of the SLA to adjust for changing conditions and requirements.

The service contract and service level agreement are crucial to any successful cloud public or community cloud deployments. Even purely internal deployments on private cloud get benefits for clearly describing the service and service levels in an explicit document.[20] They are the instruments with which the consumer is able to come to terms with the delegation of responsibility to a service provider.

---

[20]Internal SLAs are often called operating level agreements (OLAs).

The decision to deploy on a cloud is an important management decision, similar to outsourcing decisions. Although moving to a cloud is often a technical decision made in the IT department for temporary access to resources not available on the local premises, the decision should always be made with awareness of the managerial complications that can ensue and the service contract and SLA. If the cloud will support services that the IT department offers to other business units or externally, attention to the contract and SLA is even more important.

Service Models and Management

Cloud management challenges vary by service model. In one sense, they all face the same challenge (dealing with the third-party manager of the cloud), but what is managed by the third party varies with the service model. Consumers managing applications deployed on an IaaS cloud service delegate infrastructure management to the cloud provider but nothing else. This arrangement yields great flexibility to the consumer in what they deploy. In many cases, they are able to deploy exactly the same software on the cloud as they deploy on their premises. The inverse of this is that the consumer is left with the same software management tasks as they have on premises.

PaaS consumers sacrifice some of the flexibility of the IaaS model for a reduction in their share of software management tasks. Depending on what the PaaS provider offers, the consumer may no longer have to maintain databases, firewalls, web servers, load balancers, and other software utilities. Reduced responsibility for maintenance also brings with it some reduction in control of resources supplied by the PaaS provider. For example, the user of a database owned by the enterprise on their premises can decide for themselves which security patches to apply to the database and when to apply them. When a database is a PaaS service, the PaaS provider usually makes those decisions. In most cases, leaving those decisions to the PaaS provider is a convenience, but in some cases, the consumer may want or need more fine-grained control of a resource. This is a management trade-off that the consumer must be aware of.

SaaS consumers relinquish more control of the software they use to the SaaS provider. SaaS consumers must choose software offered by a SaaS provider and cannot develop their own modifications to the SaaS software. If their SaaS provider offers options for customization, these options are usually limited compared to traditional applications running on-premises or on IaaS or PaaS services.

In each case, the consumer offers a service to their own consumers by using the services of the cloud provider. The consumer reduces the risk, management commitment, and expertise required to offer the consumer's own service by delegating aspects of the implementation to the cloud provider. Consumers of cloud services lose some flexibility and control of the service they provide. The loss of control is often mitigated by a service contract and service level agreement. The consumer is often also willing to trade flexibility for the decrease in manpower and expertise needed to provide the service.

Conclusion

There are many benefits to using cloud applications and implementing on cloud services. But there are also many pitfalls. The benefits come in the form of increased efficiency, lowered costs, and features that would not be available without clouds. The pitfalls are a loss of control and a dependence on resources and third parties over whom the consumer has only limited control. To be safe, the consumer is obliged to balance the benefits and pitfalls. Often, with the aid of the basic tools of service management, the service contract, and the SLA, cloud services are satisfactory for both consumers and providers.

EXERCISES

1. Describe the three NIST service models.

2. Describe the four NIST deployment models.

3. What are some of the risks involved in a cloud deployment for a business? For an individual consumer?

4. What is the most important way that individual and enterprise consumers can protect themselves from a provider that fails to deliver a service?

Service Management

The Foundation

ITIL and Service Management

SUMMARY

Cloud deployments combine management innovation and technical innovation. They require network bandwidth and connectivity, software that will support flexible and scalable remote operation, and hardware designed for cloud datacenters. Cloud success depends on both technology and management to achieve its goals of technical efficiency and capacity as well as opening new potential for IT-based business. From the view of service management, cloud deployments and even private clouds are form of outsourcings. Clouds must be managed like outsourced services. ITIL guidance on outsourcing applies to clouds. Cloud deployments also require increased cooperation between technical and business specialists in several areas. Cloud deployments, especially SaaS deployments, have generated requirements for rapid incremental releases and have driven evolving software development methodologies that fit well with ITIL continual service improvement.

Information Technology Information Library (ITIL) and service management were introduced in Chapter 3. This chapter goes into some of the unique aspects of ITIL, service management, and cloud implementations and the criteria that often contribute to decisions about developing and deploying cloud services. This includes examining cloud implementations as outsourced services and the relationship between the ITIL service cycle and the development methodologies applied to cloud computing.

Cloud services are, almost by definition, outsourced services—services performed by an external entity. Even when an internal organization provides and manages a cloud, the relationship between the consumer and provider is a form of outsourcing because the consumer has handed over responsibility for the cloud service to the provider. Communications are usually simpler and more collegial when the consumer and provider are in the same organization, but the relationship is still an example of outsourcing. This chapter examines the nature of cloud outsourcing and the relationship between cloud consumer and provider.

Introduction

Chief information officers (CIOs)[1] and other IT executives are continually asked to make strategic decisions regarding the efficiency of the IT department and to balance costs against the quality and robustness of IT services. They must deliver increased IT functionality and contain IT costs. Sometimes they are fortunate enough to do both at the same time; at other times, functionality languishes and costs soar.

SUNK INVESTMENTS

A *sunk investment* is money that has been spent and cannot be recovered. A sunk investment cannot be withdrawn and reinvested somewhere else. Management can withdraw an investment that is not sunk and transfer it from one project to another. Salaries and wages are an example of a classic sunk investment; after they are paid, they cannot be withdrawn and used for another purpose. Money invested in physical IT infrastructure is sunk unless it can be sold at near or greater than its purchase price. For example, after IT purchases a server, the investment typically sinks quickly because little of the purchase price can be recovered by selling the used server.

Sunk investments can contribute to planning mistakes. Human nature tends to hold on to expensive projects with large sunk investments because humans often regret losing sunk investments more than they see value in change. What they may not realize is that whether a project is preserved or ended, the sunk investments are already lost. In IT, overvaluing sunk investments in infrastructure can contribute to wrong decisions. All other things being equal, hanging on to a sunk investment in on-premises infrastructure is a strategic mistake when an investment in cloud services will yield a greater return.

A sure way to guarantee the latter situation, low functionality at high cost, is an inflexible infrastructure that loses its value quickly. The IT department cannot readily repurpose an inflexible infrastructure to support new or enhanced functionality. This puts a drag on IT innovation, and when IT has no choice but to deliver increased functionality, it comes at a high cost in new infrastructure.

---

[1] I will use the term CIOs to represent all high-level IT decision makers, even though they may have a range of titles and shared responsibilities.

This is a bitter downside of the rapid growth of the capacity of computing technology and its relative decrease in cost. The other side of rapidly improving computing is that infrastructure ages fast and rapidly becomes a sunk investment. New functionality, designed to run on current hardware, always demands up-to-date equipment. PC gamers know that the latest games are no fun without the latest and fastest graphics. The same applies to the newest corporate functionality, and both gamers and CIOs are in a tough bind when the budget is limited.

CIOs have an option that gamers don't have: they can outsource.[2] Sometimes a decision to outsource is a way out of continual pressure to acquire newer technology by shifting responsibility for equipment to outsourcers. IT departments have always outsourced services when it makes economic sense.

Cloud computing is a form of outsourcing that can lessen the sting of sinking hardware investments and that can deliver other benefits to IT. Therefore, it is useful to examine outsourcing in general before examining cloud outsourcing. Much of what is unique about managing cloud services stems from its nature as outsourcing.

Outsourcing Services

Outsourcing is both popular and controversial. (See the following definition.) Offshore outsourcing is even more controversial. Outsourcing is often a type of creative destruction in which management replaces inefficient or outmoded internal capacity with services from an external provider.[3] Like all creative destruction, disruption is almost a given, and a perfect outcome is rare; however, careful outsourcing is often a sound long-term decision.

OUTSOURCING DEFINED
The essential characteristic of outsourcing is the involvement of an external provider. An external third-party service provider performs an outsourced service. The act of outsourcing transfers a service from an internal to external implementation or establishes a new service via an external provider. When the service provider is located outside national boundaries, the practice is sometimes called *offshoring*. However, services provided by offshore service providers are not always outsourced. In multinational organizations, the offshore provider may be part of the parent organization.

---

[2]This situation is changing for gamers. At least two systems, Nvidia Grid and Sony PlayStation Now, offer streaming games. Both have some hardware requirements, but they have reduced the requirements for computing and storage capacity on the local device.
[3]In many cases, especially for offshore outsourcing, the remedied inefficiency is cost. This has smudged the reputation of outsourcing, especially when quality is compromised.

Incentives

There are many incentives to delegate the performance of a service to a third party.

Cost

A commonly cited incentive is cost. When an organization uses a service only lightly, maintaining the service internally can be expensive because the service resources remain idle when the service is not used, or an outsourced service may be cheaper because the outsourcer is more efficient at performing the service. This can be because the outsourcer has achieved economies of scale or because they have developed greater expertise in delivering the service. Perhaps vigorous competition between outsourcers has reduced the price. In many cases, outsourcers take advantage of lower labor costs in certain areas. Often, an outsourced service price is temptingly low. However, before a final decision, consider carefully whether the outsourced service will fully replace the in-house service and supply the same quality of service. If the outsourced service does not, hidden costs may drive up the real cost significantly.

Cost-cutting is frequently cited as the reason for offshore outsourcing, and offshoring is often blamed for eliminating local jobs, but offshoring can also increase local jobs. Some companies are finding that offshore services offer an opportunity to expand local resources. A company is not a zero-sum game with a fixed pool of resources in which a gain for one player must cause a loss for another player. Instead, in a well-managed enterprise, allocating resources offshore increases the overall resource pool and opens opportunities that cause other groups to expand. For example, when a software company adds an offshore development team, the company may be able to combine offshore and local teams to deliver innovative and timely products and grow rather than shrink the local development team.

Flexibility

Cost is not the only factor in an outsourcing decision. An outsourced service can offer significant flexibility that an in-house service cannot supply. Growing and shrinking an outsourced service is usually quick and painless. An outsourcer that covers several time zones can offer extended hours that would be difficult to supply in-house at a single location. An outsourcer may be able to offer better coverage during peak times than an in-house organization with a fixed staff.

Focus

The decision to outsource can also be a decision to concentrate on skills and capacities that are core to the mission of the organization. An aeronautics company may decide that datacenter operations skills are not strategic skills in their industry. Instead, they want their IT department to concentrate on developing aeronautics-specific computing applications. Outsourcing datacenter operations can free IT resources to give them the competitive edge needed to be successful and therefore can justify the decision to outsource, even when the outsourced datacenter operation is more expensive.

Skills

Yet another justification for outsourcing appears when an enterprise must quickly ramp up a particular set of skills to meet some contingency. The enterprise may regard the skills as critical and therefore want to develop them internally, but the ramp-up time is too long to meet the contingency. Under those circumstances, they may decide to acquire the skills via outsourcing, at least temporarily until they can build up the skills internally.

For example, a retail company may need to start using big data techniques to analyze their customer buying records. These analysis skills have become mission critical for them in the current environment, and developing internal big data analysis skills are part of their strategic plan, but they need results immediately to compete. Therefore, they may conclude that outsourcing from a firm that specializes in retail big data analysis is tactically wise, even though it runs contrary to their longer-term strategy.

Risks

Outsourcing has risks. Although outsourcing often brings flexibility to an organization, one of the worst risks is loss of flexibility. This happens in two interrelated ways.

Lock-in and Dependence

Lock-in is a risk common to many third-party relationships. When a company finds itself in a position where it must purchase goods or services from a single vendor, it is locked in. It can no longer choose its vendor. If the company must use a product or service from a certain vendor or face a major redesign of its services, it has lost the flexibility to choose a more desirable vendor. When an enterprise cannot switch outsourcers without a major disruption, it has also lost its flexibility in vendor choice.

Dependence is another way to lose flexibility. A single vendor may not have the enterprise locked in, but the enterprise can still become so dependent on an outsourced service that it is constrained in its decisions. For example, the aeronautics company that decided to outsource its datacenter operations might decide that an application it developed requires specialized graphics hardware on servers in the datacenter. They may not find an outsourcer prepared to operate the graphics hardware. If the department has reached the point that it lacks the expertise and facilities to deploy and maintain the hardware itself, the options are few and costly. It must either redevelop its datacenter management talent or pay a premium to an outsourcer to supply the specialized service.

Organizations contemplating outsourcing often have to consider their own processes and infrastructure. For example, an outsourced service desk should use diagnostic tools that are compatible with the organization's own tools or waste time transferring and interpreting diagnostic data. Similarly, if the reports produced by the outsourced service do not fit in with the organization's reports and report distribution system, they must invest resources to train users and develop a distribution system.

Governance

Whenever another party enters a business relationship, the relationship becomes more complicated, and there are more opportunities for it to go awry. Governing an IT department is straightforward. Executive management sets policies and goals, managers guide people and processes according to the policies and goals, and employees reporting to the manager carry out the processes and roll out the products and services.

In this situation, accountability is clear. When executives set well-chosen goals and policies that result in profits and meeting other enterprise goals, boards and stockholders reward them. When managers permit policies to be broken or goals to go unmet, executives hold managers accountable. Managers hold their employees accountable for their duties. This simple system with clear lines of responsibility and accountability is relatively easy to govern. All the roles are members of the same organization and ultimately answerable to the same management. Tools like responsibility assignment (see the "Responsibility Assignment" sidebar) can be used to analyze roles in performing tasks.

RESPONSIBILITY ASSIGNMENT

Responsibility assignment matrices are useful in analyzing roles in service management and business in general. The goal is to identify the role of each person involved in a task.

- *Responsibility:* The person responsible for a task does the work to complete the task.

- *Accountability:* The single person accountable for a task approves the work to signify that it is completed satisfactorily and is liable to upper management for the results of the task.

- *Consult:* A consultant, usually a subject-matter expert and sometimes an external contractor, comments on a task before it is complete but usually is not a decision maker.

- *Informed:* Informed individuals receive reports after decisions are made but do not provide input to decisions.

Analyzing these roles in a task is often helpful in spotting bottlenecks and points of confusion in service delivery.[4]

When a service is outsourced, responsibility and accountability are not so simple. The service provider has managers who are accountable for the execution of the services delivered by the provider, but they are accountable to the service provider management. The external service provider is accountable to its own management, which has its own goals that seldom align exactly with the interests of the consumer of the outsourced service. When something goes wrong, there is no "single throat to choke," or an individual accountable for the service.

Consider the example of an outsourced service desk. Service is bad. The service desk ignores high-severity incidents disrupting a line of business. When the service desk is internal, the manager of the disrupted business would call the service desk manager. If a call did not remedy the situation, the next step would be a call to the service desk manager's manager, perhaps the chief information officer. If that didn't work, there is always the chief executive officer (CEO). At some point in the escalation, the service quality improves or there are adverse effects on careers.

The escalation follows a different path when the service desk is outsourced. The service desk manager is not in the company directory for business managers to call. Different organizations handle outsourcing differently, but a

---

[4]For more information on responsibility assignment, see the following: Michael Smith, James Erwin. "Role & Responsibility Charting (RACI)." https://pmicie.org/images/downloads/raci_r_web3_1.pdf. Accessed September, 2015.

hard-charging business manager would probably go directly to the CIO, and the CIO would have to sort out the situation. A CIO does not have anyone on his or her team directly responsible for the conduct of an outsourced service because that responsibility lies with the outsourced service provider, but the CIO probably does have someone who manages the service relationship. That person may have contacts in the outsource service provider and may be able to smooth over the problem, but the service relationship manager does not have the same kind of leverage with the outsourcer's manager as the internal business manager has over the internal service desk manager. The service relationship manager is a diplomat negotiating with a foreign entity, not a boss giving orders. If the problem represents a real clash of interests, the only recourse is to go to the service contract and service level agreements and enter into legal discussions.

In this environment, even simple issues can become complicated. If the service contract is not written carefully and the outsourcer is not eager to accommodate its consumers, trivial issues can become major annoyances. This represents an important risk in all forms of outsourcing: resolving misunderstandings and conflicts between the consumer and provider. It also depends upon a diligent inspection of the outsourcer's practices and reputation as well as a carefully prepared service contract and service level agreement before the relationship begins. Business relationships are seldom without issues. Without a clear and efficient method for resolving issues, blindly entering into an outsourcing agreement can be disastrous.

Diligent examination of outsourcers and the preparation of service contracts and service level agreements may seem remote from the responsibilities of the technical members of the IT department. Nevertheless, engineers will often be the first line in dealing with outsourcers. They have an interest in dealing with reliable and cooperative outsourcers with a solid contract that addresses technical relationships as well as business relationships. Service level agreements are a special point of engineering concern, particularly when the outsourced service is not directly exposed to the lines of business. When the IT department is accountable for a service that is performing poorly or unreliably because an outsourced service is misbehaving, the IT department is in a painful bind if its service level agreements do not allow IT to put pressure on the outsourcer. The bind is especially tight when the outsourcer's business manager is talking about profitable business agreements with the consuming business manager while the IT department is desperately trying to convince the business managers that the outsourced technology is at fault.

IT employees involved in outsourcing must develop some skills that they may not have had before. Researching outsourcer reputations, for example, is a long stretch from coding and writing specifications. It is usually the realm of corporate procurement negotiators. Nevertheless, the engineers of the IT department are sometimes the only people in the organization who can recognize inferior or questionable technical practices. In addition, determining appropriate metrics and thresholds for service level agreements is often a challenging technical problem and can determine both the cost and ultimate success of an outsourcing project.

Liability

Outsourcing can become a liability issue. In many cases, organizations are required by either regulation or business practice to retain end-to-end control of their business processes. Placing a portion of a process in the hands of an outsourcer does not alter the need for end-to-end control. Organizations outsourcing services must keep the need for control in mind, especially in the service contract and service level agreements.

The complex chain of responsibility in an outsourced service can become an issue for those concerned with due responsibility for the organization's assets and critical processes. When a department store uses an outsourcer to back up credit card and customer data, the department store remains responsible for the customer data. If a malefactor breaches the outsourcer's security, the department store, not the outsourcer, is answerable to their customers for damages. The provisions in the service contract will probably determine the liability of the outsourcer, and the outsourcer may or may not have the assets to compensate the department store and their customers. To avoid situations like this, an auditor may require that the outsourcer offer a bond or submit to additional controls in order to protect the department store's investors from damage.

Security

Security is another risk involved with outsourcing that is closely related to liability. If the service contract between the consumer and the outsourcer shifts all liability to the outsourcer, as unlikely as that may be, the consumer can still be harmed by a security breach. For example, the outsourced service provider may pay all the direct costs of a security breach, but a reputation for lax security may settle on the organization that outsourced the service. This topic will be treated in more detail when discussing security for outsourcing clouds.

Outsourcing Cloud

Outsourcing to clouds is a specialized form of outsourcing and shares many characteristics with outsourcing in general. The advantages and risks that come with outsourcing in general apply to cloud deployments on external providers, but clouds also have their own special advantages and risks.

Incentives

The incentives for entering into a cloud-outsourcing project are a superset of the incentives for outsourcing in general, but they have special technical aspects.

Cost Reduction

Like outsourcing in general, cost reduction is frequently cited as a reason to outsource services on clouds. Some of the ways in which clouds reduce costs have been discussed in previous chapters. Many of these are economies of scale similar to the gains from other forms of outsourcing, but there are gains that come from the technical nature of cloud. The scale and diverse loads of cloud datacenters help provide services that are resilient in the face of variations in load and datacenter faults. Consequently, clouds can supply reliable services while limiting expensive redundancy and under-utilization at a lower cost than a local installation that has to allocate extra equipment capacity to cope with occasional peak loads. Datacenters designed for energy efficiency produce greater computing capacity with less energy than smaller installations. Large datacenters can also locate close to energy sources. They can also be located and designed for efficient cooling. These all add up to substantial cost reductions.

Costs based on metered usage can also generate savings for cloud consumers that may not be available with other forms of outsourcing. Many forms of outsourcing help replace capital investment with operational expenses, which makes a service easier to manage financially. Usage-based costing adds to these benefits by aligning operational expenses to fluctuations in business.

Availability of Capacity

Outsourcing to the cloud provides opportunities to use technologies that require more computing capacity than an organization could obtain on its own. This is similar to a small local government unit that hires a professional economist to perform a strategic economic analysis. The organization does not have the resources to perform the analysis itself. Without the economist consultant, the organization would have to go without the analysis and expose itself to strategic blunders. In the case of cloud outsourcing, the critical resources are computing capacity for special projects.

Big data analysis is a good example of this in the cloud. Big data requires big computing resources, orders of magnitude larger than a small or medium business is likely to have. Even large enterprises seldom have the facilities to take advantage of big data. The data sources for big data analysis come in terabytes and petabytes, not the gigabytes that organizations are accustomed to managing. Rapid analysis of data of this magnitude requires thousands of computing processors. By using cloud resources, organizations of all sizes can obtain the capacity to perform big data analysis that they could not perform on their own equipment. These analyses can yield patterns and insights for many purposes including tailoring their services to customers that offer advantages over competitors who do not analyze. In this case, although the cost of cloud computing resources is less than on-premises resources, the need for the results rather than cost savings drives the decision.

Flexibility

Enterprises struggle with flexibility. Large and successful enterprises have a long string of products and services that have done well in their marketplace. However, times and environments change. In 1985, a stand-alone word processor that could perform basic editing and formatting functions was a killer application. Today, that product would compete against free products and well-established products that go far beyond basic word-processing functions. If the vendor of a 1985 word processor wanted to compete today, it would need to have the flexibility to add many features even to match the free open source offerings. An enterprise that is not able to respond positively to a changing environment struggles.

Small enterprises and startups face similar problems. They are looking at the future, the products that consumers will want a year or five years in the future. But crystal balls are murky. Every innovation and every social and political movement changes our vision of the future. Successful small enterprises roll with change and change their plans and goals as the perceived future changes.

Organizations competing in this changing environment retrain, reallocate, grow, and shrink their personnel frequently to keep up with change. However, their investment in physical infrastructure is not so easily changed. Both large and small enterprises are in a continual scramble to wring value from their sunk investments in depreciating hardware. Outsourcing to cloud computing offers a way out of this scramble. Instead of investing in rapidly sinking assets, cloud computing provides services that can scale up for business peaks and down for less active periods. This pay-as-you-go model can be very efficient, especially for smaller businesses with less capital.

Each service model affects the distribution of skills in the IT department differently. Outsourcing infrastructure following an IaaS model eliminates the need for skills in managing physical hardware, but it accentuates the need to manage applications running on virtual systems. These skills have some resemblances to physical hardware management, but they are also profoundly different. Instead of worrying about physical factors such as cabling and cooling, virtual system managers have to track images and configurations of virtual machines, which can change faster and with less authorization than physical systems. Patch management takes on new dimensions when patches to running both machines and their images must be managed. Instead of rushing out to the datacenter floor to replace a failing component, they must contact the cloud provider when signs of physical failure appear, which can be hard to detect in a virtual environment. Sometimes diplomacy has to replace technical skill. The total effort required to manage a cloud IaaS deployment will free physical hardware management skills for core activities, but some training may be required to deal with the virtual environment.

A PaaS deployment simplifies development and deployment by supplying development tools and utilities that the consumer does not have to install or maintain. This simplifies administration by shifting responsibility for these tools and utilities from the local staff to the cloud provider. This allows the consumer staff to focus on the unique aspects of the software needed for their enterprise.

SaaS takes this a step further and removes responsibility for the installation, maintenance, and administration of the SaaS-supplied software. This means that the local staff can concentrate on the process the application supports rather than managing the application.

The flexibility offered by cloud computing can be the difference between success and failure for an organization. It can move them out of the sunk hardware investment bind. Large organizations can avoid irrecoverable hardware investment. Smaller organizations avoid large outlays for computing assets. Cloud flexibility also often permits small organizations to operate with some of the efficiencies of a large organization without difficulties that come with size.

Risks

Like incentives to cloud outsourcing, the risks involved in cloud outsourcing are all similar to the risks of outsourcing in general, but the technical nature of cloud computing adds a layer of technical issues. Therefore, outsourced cloud deployments usually require more technical input than typical outsourcing agreements. Outsourcing to a cloud provider deals with a specific commodity: computing capacity, which is a technical resource that most enterprises use to solve business problems.[5] Unfortunately, business managers may misunderstand and over- or under-estimate its importance.

---

[5]Technical and scientific enterprises are the exception. They may use cloud resources for business, but they also use cloud resources on technical projects.

Technical Risks

Two kinds of risks are involved in outsourcing to cloud. The first involves the cloud environment. A crash or performance degradation of a cloud datacenter exemplifies this kind of hazard.

Another kind of hazard lies in cloud outsourcing agreements, which are often more technical and less business oriented than other outsourcing agreements. A traditional service desk outsourcing agreement has provisions such as hours of operation, length of call queues, issue resolution expectations, and so on, which are all easily understood by a business manager. Adoption of SaaS service desk software is different. The requirements for an outsourced service desk for the most part remain with the SaaS consumer. The local service desk agents determine the hours the service desk will open incidents. Keeping the call queue down depends on the number of local agents assigned, not the SaaS provider, and the speed and quality of incident resolution depends on agent knowledge and diligence.

Or so it seems. When the SaaS service is performing as expected, the local service desk department is responsible. But services do not always perform as expected. Servers crash. Patches can be misapplied. Configuration changes can be botched. When these unfortunate events occur, the service desk may be inaccessible during normal operating hours, call queues can lengthen, and incident resolution can fall or cease, through no fault of the local agents.

A robust cloud agreement should contain service level metrics, which may be difficult for business managers to translate into terms that affect their business. If the same service desk were to retain their service desk staff but subscribe to a SaaS service desk product, the service agreement would take into account the technical aspects of the outsourced software and hardware operations. If they do not receive adequate technical input, the metrics could be ignored or set too low to effectively protect business interests.

Security

All outsourcing, including cloud outsourcing, expands the security surface; that is, the points of security vulnerability increase. Adding an outsourcer brings all the points of vulnerability in the outsourcer's organization and infrastructure to the table in addition to the vulnerabilities of the outsourcing consumer. Expanding the security surface does not imply that an organization becomes less secure. It only means that the organization has new points that must be secured.

Sometimes, security itself is outsourced. A non-IT example of outsourcing security is hiring a commercial security service to supply guards at a company event. Hiring guards may increase security, but the company hiring the security service has extended its security surface to include the integrity of the guards from the service. If those guards are not prepared to do their job, the event might become less rather than more secure. In choosing security services, a prudent consumer seeks to avoid dangers from the extended security surface by choosing a reputable firm with well-trained and certified personnel.

Using outsourced cloud services is much the same. The security surface expands to the personnel, processes, and infrastructure of the cloud provider. The security surface may expand, but the level of security will increase if the cloud provider supplies well-secured services. It is the job of the cloud consumer to decide whether the services are secure.

Service Contracts and Service Level Agreements

In outsourcing services, the service contract and the service level agreement[6] are the most important documents for evaluating the safety and security of a service. Cloud services, SaaS especially, often do not have explicit service contracts or service level agreements. The cloud consumer must be cautious. Services used for some purposes will cause serious harm if they are unavailable, lose data, or allow unauthorized access. The extent of the harm depends on the business and the purpose. Services that are designed for casual noncritical use can get by without guarantees or contracts, but it can be dangerous to rely on them when their failure will cause damage.

Cloud backup services provide a good example. In some circumstances, losing data can be troublesome but not threatening. Losing the data on a personal computer used for recreation is annoying but scarcely an existential threat. On the other hand, authors losing their manuscript collection may result in both legal and financial trouble. The author must scrutinize a backup service carefully; a recreational user should too, but the need is not as great.

A number of reputable services provide secure and reliable backups. A consumer is tempted to think that these services will completely replace their local backups. This may be true, but some reputable cloud backup services do not fully replace similar on-premises services. These services synchronize on-premises files with files on cloud servers. The files are available on any computer connected to the Internet to anyone with the proper credentials and

---

[6]A service contract is a contract to deliver services and sets up the rules both parties will follow such as fees, billing schedules, and hours of operation, and it describes the service to be supplied. A service level agreement specifies thresholds for penalties and incentives for levels of service. The documents overlap, and sometimes a service contract will contain service level agreements, or vice versa. The combined documents should cover all significant aspects of the service. Terms of service are similar to the combined service contract and service-level agreement documents and are commonly used in click-through consumer web sites rather than service contracts and service level agreements, which are typically individually negotiated.

authorizations. These files are not dependent on the on-premises facilities. A disaster on the organization premises will not affect these files. Especially for home users, this may be better than a local backup that may be destroyed along with the computer in a home disaster.

Nevertheless, the service may not protect the files from a common cause of having to restore files from backup: files deleted by user mistake. Most users hit the Delete key at the wrong time more often than disks crash or tornados strike. On operating systems such as Windows, the trash receptacle is some protection, but sometimes users delete the trash permanently before they realize not all the content is trash. However, even when a file is deleted permanently, the file can still be restored from a recent local backup.

If there is no local backup and the synchronization backup service permanently deletes a file on the server when the user permanently deletes a file locally, the file is likely to be gone forever.

In addition, many consumers consider synchronized permanent deletion to be a desirable feature rather than a defect: if the service charges by the volume of data stored, permanently deleting files from the server avoids paying for storing unwanted data. In addition, permanent deletion is the ultimate privacy. However, if a consumer blindly assumes a cloud backup service can restore permanently deleted files like an on-premises backup, they are vulnerable to inadvertent loss.

To avoid unfortunate events like this, cloud service consumers have to make an effort to understand thoroughly the cloud service they are subscribing to and what the provider warrants. Above all, avoid assuming that a cloud service will provide the exact features and level of service of the on-premises version. Cloud services can be more secure and reliable than on-premises services, but they are also dangerous for the unwary.

Certification

An effective way for a cloud consumer to protect itself from a provider's vagaries is to look for provider certification. There are a number of forms of certification available. Not all are helpful to every consumer. Aspects of a cloud service that are critical to one consumer are not to another. A legal firm subscribing to a cloud e-mail service will probably be concerned about electronic discovery in which prompt and complete removal of documents designated for deletion is paramount. A healthcare firm is likely to be concerned about the Healthcare Insurance Portability and Accountability Act (HIPAA) privacy regulations. Certification satisfactory for a law firm may not be helpful to a healthcare organization, and vice versa.

Consumers have to be cautious with certification in several ways. International Organization for Standardization (ISO) 27001 is an important general service management standard that applies in many different circumstances. However, consumers have to be aware that ISO27001 certifies the processes that the cloud provider uses to establish security controls, not the security controls themselves. ISO27001 is an important standard and providers that have obtained ISO27001 certification have taken an important step toward security, but the security controls they have developed under ISO27001-compliant processes may not be the controls needed by any given consumer.[7] The consumer has to be aware of what has been certified as well as the certificate.

Another important certification is the Service Organization Controls (SOC) 1, 2, and 3 auditor's reports. SOC 1, 2, and 3 are guidance issued to auditors by the American Institute of Certified Public Accountants (AICPA) in its Statement on Standards for Attestation Engagements No. 16 (SSAE16). SSAE16 replaced SAS 70 in 2011.[8,9]

SOC 1 is roughly the equivalent of SAS-70. It does not mandate that specific controls be in place, only that the controls that are included in an audit report be satisfactorily auditable. It is up to the consumer's auditors to determine the effectiveness of the controls for the consumer's purposes. SOC 1 is useful to sophisticated service consumers who perform their own audits of the provider controls, but it is less useful to consumers who do not plan to execute their own audits.

SOC 2 and 3 are more specific and suited to the needs of less knowledgeable consumers with fewer resources for evaluating a provider. These reports address controls. The SOC 2 report was designed to be private and disclosed only to limited stakeholders. Nevertheless, a SOC 2 report is much more useful for consumers who do not plan their own audits.

The SOC 3 report was designed to be a public document and applies directly to cloud services. It can be posted on a web site and distributed freely. The SOC 3 does not report on the tests run or other details of the system, only the results of examinations of controls on security, availability, processing integrity, confidentiality, and privacy of services. A SOC 3 report is suitable for consumers who do not have the capacity or need to evaluate a provider's service in detail.

---

[7]For more information on ISO27001 and its companion standard, ISO27717, see my book *Cloud Standards* (also from Apress).

[8]SAS-70, Statement on Auditing Standards No. 70: Service Organizations, is an older service organization standard similar to SOC 1. For more detail on SAS 70, see my book *Cloud Standards* (also from Apress).

[9]AICPA. "Illustrative Type 2 SOC 2 Report with the Criteria in the Cloud Security Alliance (CSA) Cloud Controls Matrix (CCM)." April 2014. Accessed May 2014. https://www.aicpa.org/InterestAreas/FRC/AssuranceAdvisoryServices/DownloadableDocuments/SOC2_CSA_CCM_Report.pdf. This is a useful example of what an SOC 2 report could contain.

There are organizations that offer provider certification for specific purposes without the support of any legal or standards status. For example, there is no public standard for HIPAA compliance certification, but some organizations offer compliance certificates. These certificates can be useful, but the consumer must do their own due diligence on the value of the certificate.[10]

Identity and Access Management

Access and identity management (AIM) requires attention when outsourcing to cloud. Most organizations have robust AIM to control access to departmental and corporate IT systems.[11] The employee onboarding and offboarding process usually handles entering and removing employees from AIM. Since clouds are often new additions to the IT system, cloud access and authorization may not be included in corporate AIM.

A robust AIM collects all an employee's system privileges in one place. An employee's identity is established and verified following consistent corporate standards, and when all authorizations are kept in one place, there is less chance for inconsistent authorizations. When cloud access is not in AIM, someone has to manage a separate cloud access system and keep it aligned with corporate AIM, which often ends up as an error-prone manual task. When an employee changes jobs within the organization, someone or some process has to change both the corporate AIM and the cloud AIM. The solution to this challenge depends on circumstances. Occasionally, simple communication is adequate; the cloud administrator and the AIM manager keep in communication and keep the systems aligned.

In organizations of any size, a more sophisticated system is required. This will depend on the sophistication of the corporate AIM and the cloud. Security Assertion Markup Language (SAML)–based federation offers an elegant solution.[12] Using SAML, corporate, and cloud identities and authorizations appears interchangeable. An employee logged in to the corporate system is

---

[10]U.S Department of Health and Human Services. "What You Should Know About OCR HIPAA Privacy Rule Guidance Materials." Web site. Accessed May 2015. www.hhs.gov/ocr/privacy/hipaa/understanding/coveredentities/misleadingmarketing.html.

[11]Security best practice separates identity authentication from authorization. Users are authenticated when they supply proof of identity such as a correct password or personal characteristic such as a fingerprint or retinal scan. After authentication, users receive the authorizations they are assigned by the system. Some older systems do not separate authentication from authorization, and users must be given a separate login for each set of privileges they are given.

[12]Federated systems exchange information but remain distinct. SAML is a protocol for sharing access and authorization data between AIM systems.

also identified to the cloud system, and a person attempting to log in to the cloud system must be identified in the corporate system. SAML also supports sharing authorizations.

Unfortunately, the federation of corporate and cloud AIM is not always possible. Both the corporate and cloud systems must support some form of federation, which is not always available. Then a process or practice must support federation. Sometimes even that is difficult. When a department or an individual obtains cloud access without corporate involvement, the onus falls outside the IT department. Perhaps the worst possibility is that of an off-boarded employee who remains in the cloud AIM, giving a potentially disgruntled nonemployee access to corporate assets, which is a well-known security disaster scenario.

Iterative and Incremental Development and ITIL Service Management

The Deming Plan-Do-Check-Act cycle is the foundation of ITIL continual service improvement. Understanding the ITIL interpretation of the Deming cycle is the key to the practice of cloud service management. A robust service improves as it responds to the necessities of production and a changing environment.

Unfortunately, the ITIL approach sometimes appears to run counter to trends in development methodologies. Many developers look at the ITIL service management cycle and the division of service development into segmented stages with some skepticism. Superficially, and as it is too often practiced, service development appears to follow the waterfall development model that was once held up as the ideal development methodology but has been criticized for some time.[13]

This is a serious discrepancy. ITIL practices have driven the improvement of IT services for decades. At the same time, waterfall development methodologies have been identified as a cause of development failures. In place of the waterfall, more iterative and incremental methodologies (see the following definition) have become much more important, especially in cloud implementations. Continually updated SaaS implementations are often held up as examples of the iterative style of development. Large web commerce sites

---

[13]Craig Larman, Victor R. Basili. "Iterative and Incremental Development: A Brief History." IEEE Computer Society, Computer 36 (6). pp 47–56. www.craiglarman.com/wiki/ downloads/misc/history-of-iterative-larman-and-basili-ieee-computer.pdf. Accessed May 2014. Iterative and incremental development may actually predate waterfall, but waterfall development was held up as the ideal through the end of the 20th century.

are usually developed iteratively and incrementally. The difficulties in rolling out such sites as healthcare exchanges can be at least partially attributed to adherence to a waterfall model.

ITERATIVE AND INCREMENTAL DEVELOPMENT DEFINED

Beginning software classes teach a simple methodology: determine what the software is intended to do, consider ways in which code could perform the task and choose the best, write the code, test it, and hand in the assignment. This methodology works well for classroom exercises and not so well for large projects. An alternative method that scales well is to build the software a small part at a time, delivering a possibly incomplete but usable and defect-free product at regular intervals until the deliverable meets project goals. Each incomplete product represents an *increment*. The process used to develop each incomplete product is an *iteration*.

Nevertheless, the ITIL cycle and iterative development are based on similar principles, and they are reconcilable. Iterative and incremental approaches such as Agile development[14] are also based on the Deming cycle of repeated designing, testing, and improving. In other words, both iterative development and ITIL have the same foundation.

Waterfall Development

The name *waterfall* comes from projects organized into stages with barriers between each stage. Each waterfall project stage ends with a waterfall that marks a point of no return. When the project progresses from one stage to the next—"goes over the waterfall"—there is no going back. For better or for worse, the project team must now complete the next stage. When the project misses a deadline for a phase, managers must extend the delivery date or invest additional resources into the next phase of the project to make up the lost time. In an all too familiar failure scenario, the investment in each phase is fixed, and pats on the back and bonuses are handed out when a phase is on time and budget. To achieve this, problems are sometimes glossed over and

---

[14]The putative beginning for Agile was the Agile Manifesto formulated in 2001. See "The Agile Manifesto." Agile Alliance, 2001. www.agilealliance.org/the-alliance/the-agile-manifesto/. Accessed May 2014. Also see "The Twelve Principles of Agile Software." Agile Alliance, 2001. www.agilealliance.org/the-alliance/the-agile-manifesto/the-twelve-principles-of-agile-software/. Accessed May 2014. The Twelve Principles reveal more of the details of Agile methodology. However, Agile is based on many principles that were evident in the development community long before 2001.

passed on to the next phase.[15] The gap between plan and reality builds as each phase is marked complete. Eventually, the planned completion date slides by. At that point, a crisis is declared. Eventually, either the incomplete deliverables are accepted, more is invested to bring the project to true completion, or the project is abandoned.

A waterfall project follows a clear progression: analyze before specifying requirements; design only after requirements are locked down; don't write a line of code until the design is approved; no system tests until the unit tests are complete[16]; when the project passes system tests, roll out the entire project in a big bang.

All too frequently, the big bang is a bomb. The code is unstable, functionality is missing, and the cost overrun is staggering. Large government software projects traditionally followed a strict waterfall model, and the waterfall model still influences many projects. This has led to some notable apparent failures such as the 2013 rollout of online health insurance exchanges.[17] A disastrous big-bang rollout of a large project followed by a frenzy of activity to patch the failing software has been a common in the software industry.

Why does this happen? There are many reasons. Tossing problems down the waterfall is only one aspect of the problem. Software is complex, and the environment in which it operates is even more complex. Test beds seldom completely reproduce the environment in which a production service must operate, and differences between the real and test environments can let defects pass through that render a service unstable or unusable in production. The larger than expected volumes of users that bring down web sites during Super Bowl halftimes can be held up as an example of an inadequate test environment.[18] Software developers can misinterpret finely nuanced designs. Outright design flaws may appear only in hindsight. Requirements often change faster than software can be developed. The user base may be larger, smaller, or less well trained than the product was designed to support, or there may be unanticipated performance requirements or network issues.

There is a truism: software changes the requirements that the software was designed to meet. When automation eliminates one bottleneck, the next one appears. When automation eliminates one source of errors, it reveals a previously hidden source. Automating one process step brings to light a

---

[15]Programmers sometimes call this practice "tossing the dead rat over the fence."

[16]Unit tests evaluate individual modules. System tests evaluate groups of modules working together.

[17]I have no knowledge of the healthcare rollout other than what I read in the media. I am only an external observer.

[18]Under-estimating traffic volumes is endemic in the software industry. During every Super Bowl, a few web sites crash from the traffic generated by the ads. You can argue that these are dunderhead mistakes, but perhaps it is misguided modesty in estimating the popularity of a site.

weakness in another step that cannot handle the automated volume. A business manager may see that an automated voice recognition unit achieves its goal of expediting telephone call handling, but it alienates customers. In other words, a perfectly planned and executed waterfall software project may still fail because it changes its own requirements.

These problems, and others, with waterfall development models have been evident for a long time, and many development organizations have chosen to move away from a waterfall model. There are many alternative methodologies in use, but the one that has gotten the most attention recently is iterative and incremental Agile software development.

Agile Methodology

Agile takes apart the requirements-design-code-test-rollout sequence and turns it into what Agile calls *sprints*. A sprint is a short (usually a month or less) flurry of activity that addresses a few requirements and builds a deliverable that could be acceptable to a customer with that set of requirements. During the sprint, all the traditional participants—analysts, designers, coders, testers, onsite installers and trainers, and customers—work together to produce a product that may have limited functionality but is deliverable. Ideally, customers in a real production environment test the product of the sprint. In earlier sprints, the deliverable may not be placed into production, but customers and those close to the customer, not just quality assurance specialists, examine the results of each sprint.

Each sprint builds on previous sprints adding features and meeting requirements that were not addressed in the previous sprint. The work of the sprint itself may reveal new requirements and valuable potential features. Old requirements may be discovered to be irrelevant during a sprint. Designs change to meet the evolving circumstances, and the product is exposed to real environments as soon as possible. Reliability, functionality, and desirability of the product to real customers measure the progress of sprints. As the product becomes more complete and rich in function, it may be rolled out to more and more customers. When the project reaches completion, it is likely to be in use by a portion of the user base and ready to roll out to the entire user base, without the unpleasant surprises that come with a traditional big bang. In addition, this method of development fosters products that can be rolled out in phases by new customers to minimize the effects in their environments.

Hypothetical Iterative Rollout

A hypothetical iterative rollout might occur like this. The project is to develop an online life insurance sales site. The first public rollout might be a display-only web site that lists life insurance products and sends customers to agents on phones. In the second phase, the developers add a sign-on. Customers can now sign on and leave their phone numbers for agents to call them. In the next phase, customers can enter their own health information that agents use to price policies. The next phase might automatically price each policy based on the entered health information. In the final phase, the customer can complete the entire insurance purchase online. After a number of customers have purchased insurance smoothly and without issues, the site is widely announced with full publicity.

In the background, the development team steadily gains knowledge of the behavior of their product in increasingly complex circumstances. Instead of a waterfall, the process is iterative in which each phase, or sprint, executes all the phases of the old waterfall model. Before the site starts accepting substantial data from the customer, the developers know their sign-in works smoothly. Before the site begins using health information, the developers become familiar with the data that real customers enter. They check their ability to calculate prices accurately before they sell policies. When they complete the project, the final rollout is an anticlimax because the software has already proven itself in a real environment.

There are many variations on the iterative development theme. However, in one form or another, iterative development is widely used today. Large web commerce sites are usually built incrementally, feature by feature, and tested incrementally with segments of the customer base rather than rolling out the entire site at once.

ITIL Cycle

The Deming Plan-Do-Check-Act (PDCA) cycle is the foundation of ITIL continual service improvement. This cycle is the underpinning strategy for ITIL practices. Without the cycle, service management is a static set of rules that could not keep up with the rapid improvements in computing and infrastructure that characterizes IT today.

The ITIL interpretation of the Deming cycle is the key to the practice of service management in general and cloud service management in particular. Technology has improved at an ever-increasing rate, forcing IT change to accelerate proportionately. A robust service undergoing continual improvement responds to the necessities of production and changing environments. ITIL practices provide a systematic approach to establishing a robust policy of continual IT improvement.

ITIL has prescribed activities and processes for the phases in the ITIL cycle. In most ITIL implementations, humans, not software, execute most of the activities and processes of each phase. In these implementations, software may play a role, but the activity is primarily human. For example, in change management, a software-implemented configuration management database (CMDB) is usually required for ITIL change management, but it is a tool used by humans in a larger change management process, which plays a crucial role in service operations. The ITIL practice addresses a CMDB, but it is more concerned with the humans using the CMDB in change management, not the CMDB software. This is sometimes confusing to developers who are used to implementing designs in software rather than building software into a management practice.

If a service is established and placed into production in a single iteration of the ITIL cycle, ITIL looks like a waterfall model. When the ITIL cycle functions over a longer period, it becomes clear that the phases are iterative rather than a waterfall. The same applies to iterative development. If a project were required to be completed in a single Agile sprint, it would be difficult to distinguish the single iteration from waterfall development. However, such single-cycle projects violate both the spirit of ITIL and iterative development.

From a development standpoint, the ITIL cycle can be nearly invisible. Typically, software developers are called in during the ITIL transition phase, after both the strategy and design phases have completed. When the software project is complete (in other words, when it passes all the tests that were passed down from design and strategy) and all the test deployments are complete, the developers go on to another project and the service proceeds to the operations phase.

Developers see this as a waterfall followed by a big bang. The developers may feel that they have a set of immutable requirements thrown over a waterfall by the ITIL strategy and design phases. Development has only one chance to get the software and hardware right before final testing. When testing is satisfactorily completed, the project flows over another waterfall into operations. The only redeeming feature is that ITIL transition testing is extensive and involves test implementations; never mind the practical caution that testing is the first thing to go when projects lag.

This is not the way ITIL is supposed to work. Continual improvement assumes that improvement is always possible and the environment in which the service performs is always changing, requiring changes to the service. This applies to software as well as human-conducted processes. See Figure 6-1.

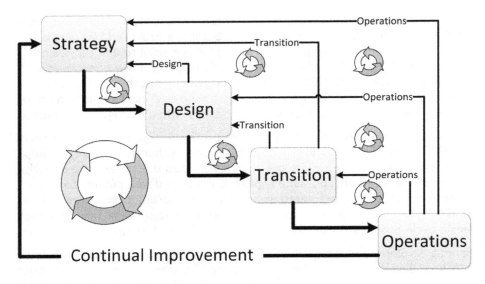

Figure 6-1. ITIL phases have nested cycles

Following best practices, each ITIL phase represents an overlapping team. Some members of the strategy team are likely to also participate in the design and transition teams, even the operations team. These teams do not disappear when a service moves to another phase. Although the size of these teams may ebb and flow with the needs of the organization, they all function simultaneously and are likely to contribute to a range of services. This persistence of teams is generally not characteristic of waterfall models in which teams tend to disband after their task is complete. Instead, ITIL works in cycles within cycles.

DevOps

DevOps, a portmanteau of "development" and "operations," is a development methodology, an organizational plan, and a collection of tools. It has arisen in response to demands for more rapid and reliable software development, especially software deployed on clouds. The purpose of DevOps is to speed the development cycle and make it more reliable while tailoring applications more closely to operational requirements. The foundation of DevOps lies in Agile principles that insist that all stakeholders be active in the development process. DevOps goes a step further and suggests that development and operations in an IT department should meld into a single group. Operations people should contribute to design, code, and testing, and developers should directly experience the challenges of operations.[19] The combined development and operations group concentrates on relatively small, incremental releases targeted on specific issues. The combined group produces these incremental releases and places them into production to a brisk cadence.

DevOps also involves tooling. Rapid releases are impossible without automated builds and testing. There is no extra time for assembling and disassembling test environments that emulate production, although realistic test environments are critical to software quality. With an assembled test bed, engineers should build effective tests for new features, not execute critical but tedious regression tests. There are commercial products for addressing all these tooling issues. CA's ca **Dev**Center portfolio is an example.[20]

Strategy

ITIL service strategy was discussed in Chapter 3. It is usually thought of as the first stage in the continual improvement cycle. The important tool of service strategy is the service portfolio, a master list of all the services the IT department offers, plans to offer, and has offered in the past. The service portfolio places all the information for developing an overall strategy into a single repository. It identifies all the stakeholders in a service and the requirements for the success of a service that provides an optimal solution for the entire organization. A service strategy addresses the full life cycle of a service from its inception to its eventual removal from operations.

The incentives and risks involved in cloud deployment are part of strategic decisions. Cloud deployment models—private, community, private, and hybrid—often are an important part of service strategy because they reflect high-level investment policy. Choice of service model (IaaS, PaaS, and SaaS) may be strategic, although they are more likely to be part of the service design.

Design

The ITIL service design phase can be confused with software design. Although service design can involve software design, the service design phase is more concerned with people and processes as much or more than software. During the service design phase, business managers, service managers, and other stakeholders translate strategy into a design to implement in the transition phase. Software design, in the sense of choosing code patterns and software

---

[19]This is an example of the time-honored principle that developers should "eat their own dog food." In other words, developers should have to use the software that they create. DevOps takes this a step further by suggesting that operations people should also experience the frustrations of developers.
[20]www.ca.com/us/devcenter.aspx

architecture, is usually left to the next phase, transition. For software, the output of the design phase describes what the software does, not how it should do it. The output may be a set of use cases or other forms of requirements that the software design must implement.

The design phase provides feedback to the previous strategy phase and, unlike a waterfall model, may initiate a change in strategy.

Transition

Transition is the phase in which services are implemented and put into production. This is the phase in which the software is developed, tested, and rolled out. Often, developers see only the ITIL transition phase in action. However, the transition phase offers feedback to both the design and strategic groups, continuing to hone strategies and designs as the service transitions from a design to a working service. This means that software designs may iterate all the way back to strategy as they are incrementally developed.

ITIL practices are often applied to services that affect the mission of the organization with large numbers of users relying on the service for critical activities. Failed rollouts for services like this can be costly. As a consequence, ITIL transition practices contain much guidance on how to test a service before putting it into operation. These tests include software, people, and process and range from software unit testing to testing user-training systems. The consequences of a failed test may be a software defect repair, a service design change, and even a strategy shift, and all of this may take place at the same time.

Operations

When a service has been fully transitioned into production, it enters the operation phase. ITIL has several concerns during operations. The goal is to keep the service working at peak efficiency while it meets the needs of the service consumers and efficiently meets enterprise goals. ITIL includes several functions for achieving this, including service desks, change management procedures, and application management. One of the most important functions is monitoring operations. The operations team is charged with monitoring the deployed process to determine whether it is meeting the goals and requirements laid out by the strategy and design teams. Operations works with the transition team to determine whether the service meets production requirements. The operations team often works with business teams to measure user satisfaction with the service. In this role as the monitor of production services, operations provides important input to the strategy team and completes the ITIL Deming cycle.

Continual Improvement

The continual improvement aspect of ITIL means the Deming PDCA cycle never ends. Services may be stable for long periods, but service managers must always be on the alert for changing requirements and opportunities for improvement. Iterative development is also a form of a Deming PDCA cycle. Each iteration is a repetition of the cycle. The iterative team plans the sprint. Developers, product managers, business managers, users, and other interested parties all participate. Next, in the Do stage, the team implements the software for the sprint. This includes code from previous sprints as well as new code. As the team members code, they operate the software and check its behavior against their goals, executing the Check phase. When they understand the behavior of what they have built, they act on their conclusions and begin a new cycle with planning for the next sprint, which may involve requirement and overall design changes as a result of the experience of the previous sprint.

ITIL and Iterative Development

The ITIL Service Strategy, Design, Transition, Operation cycle is not far from an iterative development cycle.

The ITIL cycle starts further back in the history of a project and stretches further into the future. Usually, certainly not always, iterative software projects start with a distinct end already determined, such as "build a new asset management system with these characteristics" or "create a SaaS version of this on-premises application." There were undoubtedly many hours of discussion and planning before the iterative project began. Business and technical leaders determined the feasibility and desirability of the project. Someone thought about how the project would combine with and integrate with existing technology. The finance department worked on budget and financing plans. Marketing had their say. This preproject planning is the content of the ITIL Service Strategy phase.

The ITIL cycle for a service ends only when the service ceases to operate, and even then, it lives as history in the service portfolio. Agile projects usually end when their goals are complete.

ITIL and iterative development combine well. In ITIL practices, developers, as subject-matter experts on the software used in a service, have a voice in each of the ITIL service lifecycle phases. However, since ITIL is concerned with services in a broad context that includes both people and processes as well as technology, software development is only one aspect of the service lifecycle, unlike development methodologies that touch lightly on the other aspects of a service but concentrate on software.

Iterative development and ITIL both are based on an improvement cycle, and both deal with a living cycle in which every stage contributes to every other stage and no stage disappears because its single job is done. Strict waterfall development, on the other hand, in its rigid stages, violates the spirit of ITIL, which is always prepared to respond to changing circumstances.

Developing cloud services can benefit from ITIL practices. ITIL practice recommends processes for gathering all the important input on developing a service and organizing the input into a usable form that supports a well-organized and responsive IT department. In addition, ITIL practices have clear feedback paths to support a continuous improvement cycle that goes beyond software development. Within ITIL practices, iterative software development is well supported.

ITIL practices are particularly important for cloud development because cloud computing is as much a business approach as a technological breakthrough. Technology and business must cooperate to make a cloud deployment successful both technically and for business. ITIL has a record of accomplishment for bringing business and technology together in a well-organized and sustainable way.

Conclusion

In some ways, cloud services are business as usual for service management. A cloud deployment outsources an aspect of IT that has not commonly been outsourced before. All the discipline that goes into managing any outsourced service is necessary for successfully managing a cloud service. However, cloud deployments have special requirements. Although they may look like a business agreement, they are also a highly technical shift and require technical input to be properly managed. Without technical input, service contracts and service level agreements may not adequately represent an organization's interests.

One way of ensuring that both business and technology are well represented is to follow ITIL service lifecycle practices along with an iterative and incremental development approach.

EXERCISES

1. What is the key difference between outsourcing in general and cloud outsourcing?

2. Discuss the dangers of click-through licensing in an enterprise environment.

3. Do certifications, such as SOC 3, guarantee that a cloud service will meet enterprise requirements for reliability and security? Why or why not?

4. Contrast waterfall development with iterative incremental development.

5. What are the four phases of the ITIL service life cycle?

6. How do the ITIL phases relate to iterative development?

The Edifice

Service Management Architecture

SUMMARY

This chapter describes two types of service management applications. The first type is an application that follows the source, collector, interpreter, and display architectural design pattern. A service knowledge management system (SKMS) is used as a detailed example. Most service management applications follow this pattern. The other type described is a policy or business process management application. This also follows the source, collector, interpreter, and display pattern, but it also has more complicated transactions that may require more complex interfaces. Cloud implementations both benefit and challenge implementations of both types.

This chapter describes the architectural considerations in building a service knowledge management system in an enterprise environment that combines cloud and on-premises architecture. Although an SKMS is interesting and valuable on its own, architecting an SKMS is an engineering project that exemplifies the challenges presented when building software to support cloud service management. This chapter explores service management architecture in a cloud environment using an SKMS as an example that ties together the entire service management superstructure.

Service Knowledge Management System

ITIL v3, published in 2007 and revised in 2011, added several new concepts to service management. One of those concepts was the service knowledge management system. The SKMS covers almost every aspect of IT and ITIL practices. It is also seldom, if ever, implemented with the full breadth described in the ITIL volumes.[1]

As you might guess, constructing SKMS architecture is of particular interest to architects because the SKMS connects all the critical pieces of software used in managing the IT service infrastructure and ITIL practice. Cloud implementations complicate the challenge because the IT service infrastructure is installed both on the enterprise premises and on clouds of all varieties; private, public, community and hybrid clouds all may appear in the service management infrastructure. In addition, the cloud services used for implementation can be of any variety; IaaS, PaaS, SaaS, Storage as a Service, Network as a Service, and all the other "as a Services" that have appeared can and are used in implementing service management. An enterprise with a firm grasp on the architecture for its SKMS also has faced the challenges of an architecture to support coordination of a collection of IT services.

This is distinctly not to say that building a software SKMS is the same as implementing ITIL or a service management practice. It is not. An organization is free to implement any or all ITIL practices. An SKMS ties together the service management practices and the software that supports them and is an ITIL practice itself, but software implementations are not required for ITIL practices; software makes implementing ITIL practices easier by helping tame the complexity and volume of services. However, even an SKMS ITIL practice could be implemented without software. In addition, an SKMS could be built to support an IT service system that avoids ITIL practices. The order in which practices are implemented is not set. One enterprise may choose to tie its SKMS tightly to existing ITIL practices. Others may choose to make an SKMS their first ITIL practice and use it to aid in operating and coordinating existing services that are not constructed following ITIL principles.

An SKMS need not be implemented with software. However, for organizations of any size, the volume of information and rate of change makes it difficult to implement the practices without some assistance from software. AXELOS, the current owner of ITIL, has a program for endorsing software that supports ITIL practices. The program works through licensed software assessors who review software submitted to them and determine whether the software possesses the features that the ITIL books require and supports ITIL practices and terminology.

---

[1]ITIL Service Transition. London: TSO, 2011. 181–195.

AXELOS-accredited assessors certify off-the-shelf software as supporting different ITIL practices, such as incident management, problem management, capacity management, event management, and so on.[2] An off-the-shelf package may be the best choice for most organizations, although an off-the-shelf SKMS may not be suitable for organizations with unique needs.

Here, I am not discussing building an SKMS to advocate taking on such a project. Building an SKMS illustrates most of the choices that must be made when planning any cloud service management software project. Since it is described in fair detail in the ITIL literature, it makes a good practical example of cloud service management development architecture.

SKMS Architecture

An SKMS brings together data from many sources that affects service management throughout its strategy, design, transition, and operation lifecycle, providing the information to support an effective continuous improvement Deming cycle. SKMS information is available and used at each stage of the service lifecycle. Information passes from one service management function to another via the SKMS. For example, the SKMS may collect and display information from capacity management tools. This information can help make day-to-day decisions in operations, scale testing during service transition, shape the design phase, and help determine long-term strategy.

The SKMS is a single collection point intended to synergistically combine information from different service management data sources. For example, an SKMS could combine data in service incidents with performance data to help determine appropriate service capacities.

The components of an SKMS can be located on a cloud or on the organization premises. From an architectural standpoint, the decision to deploy a given component on a cloud usually boils down to a few considerations. Clouds can provide greater compute and storage capacity than on-premises hardware. Clouds offer elasticity; in other words, clouds can provide increased capacity when loads go up. Clouds also are generally more accessible to users outside the corporate perimeter than on-premises installations. Whenever the need for any of these three capabilities appears, a cloud implementation may be the best choice.[3]

An SKMS has four architectural layers. A four-layer SKMS is similar to the classic Model-View-Controller (MVC) pattern long used in user interfaces. Like the MVC pattern, a four-layer SKMS separates the data sources from

---

[2]For the full list, see www.itil-officialsite.com/SoftwareScheme/EndorsedSoftwareTools/EndorsedSoftwareTools.asp. Accessed June 2014.
[3]These are architectural reasons for using a cloud. There are, of course, also business and administrative reasons, such as capitalization and amortization strategies.

business logic and data display. The SKMS layers separate the data sources from the consolidation and interpretation of the data, and the display of the interpreted data is isolated from the interpretation. When implemented, an SKMS can become quite complex, but its basic architecture is straightforward (Figure 7-1).

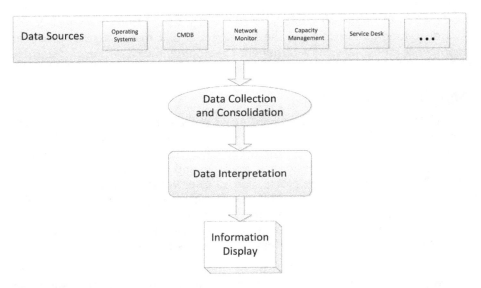

Figure 7-1. A basic SKMS architecture

Data Sources

A typical MVC architecture differs from an SKMS architecture in the multiplicity of data sources and the fact that many of these data sources will be legacy systems that may require special integration, which is the job of the data collection layer.

Enterprises follow many different road maps in evolving their service management practices. A "greenfield" implementation of a service management system, including an SKMS, built with all new components and infrastructure is ideal but rare in practice. Most service management practices are built up over time. Sometimes services are first manual and then automated gradually by inserting applications into the service process where they are most cost effective. Services that began as a paper system often turn into fully automated electronic systems through this evolution.

Usually, an automated management system also grows over time. For example, a growing printing business may begin with a trouble-ticketing system that is just 3-by-5 cards in a shoebox that the maintenance staff uses to keep track of equipment problems. As the organization grows, to handle the volume, the maintenance department replaces the shoebox with an issue-tracking database. To speed response times, software is added to open tickets. Gradually, a section of the maintenance department transforms itself into an IT department. Eventually, the trouble-ticketing system is merged with internal and external customer service, and what was a shoebox becomes the core of a complete service desk system. In real life, the ghost of that shoebox lives on in the names and choice of fields in service incident reports. Quite possibly, the custom software written long ago to instrument the original printing press (as per our example) may still be there, generating events when bearings overheat or when the press stops suddenly. This pattern of gradual evolution from manual to automated with older technology wrapped into newer technology is frequently seen in IT. Managers are often disinclined to replace software that works, even if the overall system has advanced. Consequently, IT departments often deal with software and platforms of many vintages.

Suboptimal components linger for many reasons. Often budget constraints block their replacement. Sometimes a poorly performing component lives on because it supplies functionality that the enterprise needs and new components do not replace. A range of platforms and a mixture of outsourced and in-house services, each with their own requirements, often increase the obstacles. These services and platforms often have constituencies that resist new architectures. In some cases, training costs for new software or hardware can exceed the benefits of the new infrastructure. Even when new software or hardware is clearly advantageous, organizational resistance to change can be hard to oppose. In practice, addressing only the most egregious problems and most desperate needs are often all a technologist can expect. Patience and perseverance generally triumphs but only on the long haul.

Consequently, an SKMS architect must often weave together legacy software and platforms with new software to consolidate and interpret data. The data source layer is often where the greatest difficulty occurs, but even the information display may sometimes have to be assembled from legacy components.

The data source layer corresponds roughly to the model in an MVC pattern, although the data structure of individual SKMS data sources can vary widely in complexity and sophistication. At one extreme, the model may be unstructured data that requires extensive processing to yield meaningful information, such as big data projects that extract significant patterns from unstructured documents. At another extreme, the model may be an object-oriented application that presents a complex object model, such as the model exposed by some service applications, through a well-structured and easily used web service. Somewhere in the middle, there are many structured relational databases with diverse schemas that can be queried with SQL or other standard query mechanisms. At the worst, there may be no practical API for a source, and the data model may be inconsistent and idiosyncratic, which can be the case for legacy technology that predates data and API structuring principles and transport design. Fortunately, there is usually a way around all these obstacles.

There are two major classes of data source from the viewpoint of the SKMS architect: those with and without APIs. A data source with an API has some intentional means of communicating with other programs rather than users. Applications with APIs are easier to work with. Fortunately, good software engineering practice is to provide APIs to almost all applications. With the rise of the Internet, best practice has been to provide not only an API but an API that is accessible through the web called a *web service*.

Unfortunately, there are still data sources in use that do not have APIs. Legacy components without APIs can usually be made to participate in the SKMS. The least automated and least satisfactory is the "yellow pad" method. A person physically goes to the source, copies a number from a gauge to a yellow pad, and goes back to their cubicle and enters the data into the SKMS. This method is slow, error-prone, and most likely expensive. However, when the number on that gauge is the key to a critical service's performance, changes infrequently, and cannot be acquired any other way, the effort may be worth the trouble. With the advent of the Internet of Things (IoT), instrumentation has become easier since the number of physical devices that are connected to the network is increasing.

Next up the scale is the venerable and universally excoriated practice of screen scraping. *Scraping* a screen means to convert data intended to be read by humans into data that can be used programmatically. Mainframe programs from the 1970s and 1980s often displayed data only onscreen and on paper; transferring data directly to other programs was often limited to transferring tapes. A screen scraper cobbles together an API, reading screen buffers and programmatically converting them to usable data structures using screen positions and searching for labels. Needless to say, the process is slow, difficult to program, and brittle. Minor screen changes can break the pattern and cause a complete and tedious rewrite of the scraping code. Nevertheless, it works. Screen scraping is a possibility when nothing more reliable and efficient is available, which may be the case for older mainframe systems. A form of screen scraping is also useful for extracting data from web interfaces by parsing the HTML. Conceivably, a SaaS application that offers no usable APIs could be cracked by some form of screen scraping.[4]

File sharing is next up the scale and superior to yellow pads and screen scrapers when it is available. Applications sometimes write their data to files. More sophisticated applications write to databases, now most often relational databases. Although these files and databases may not have been intended to be

---

[4]Tapping into the Domain Object Model (DOM) in the browser is usually more effective, but that is another subject entirely.

read by external programs, they often can be. This is a much more reliable and robust way of extracting data from a source, but it requires understanding of the internals of the application and may break if the application is updated.

Data sources with intentional APIs are much easier to work with. Applications designed before web services became popular rely on Transmission Control Protocol/Internet Protocol (TCP/IP)[5] or similar lower-level protocols that deal directly with the network. If a development team is prepared to work with the appropriate protocol stack, the major difficulty in tapping these applications for information is obtaining sufficient documentation. Unfortunately, the documentation for these APIs is often an internal technical manual or, worse, comments in code. Lacking documentation can be a nearly insurmountable obstacle.

When an application with an API based on a socket-level protocol, like TCP/IP, is deployed on a cloud, there can be difficulties in treating it as a data source. Communication between clouds is usually based on Hypertext Transfer Protocol (HTTP)–based APIs.[6] Administrators have good reason to suspect that direct TCP/IP communication with an entity outside the corporate perimeter is a security breach waiting to happen. Consequently, connecting to a data source using a low-level protocol is likely to have issues with firewalls and other security mechanisms. Usually, the firewall may have to open additional sockets, which administrators are loathe to do, as they should be. In high-security situations, changes or additional layers may have to be added to the architecture to avoid the extra open sockets. When Network Address Transformation (NAT) is present, and it is almost always used now, an additional layer that retains network addresses in some form may also have to be added to handle transformed addresses. These difficulties should not be underestimated, but they have the advantage of being relatively reliable and sustainable after they are in place.

Web-era applications are usually the easiest to deal with. They are likely to have HTTP-based APIs, which usually means REST or, to a lesser extent, SOAP-based[7] APIs. If the application and the API are even moderately well designed, these present relatively few difficulties for data collection. SOAP- and REST-based APIs are by far the easiest way to collect data from applications deployed on clouds.

---

[5] Marvin Waschke. *Cloud Standards.* New York: Apress, 2012. Pages 226–232 discuss TCP/IP.
[6] Marvin Waschke. *Cloud Standards.* New York: Apress, 2012. Pages 245–259 are a summary of the HTTP.
[7] SOAP once stood for Simple Object Access Protocol. SOAP has evolved to be not simple, not confined to object access, and not exactly a protocol. Therefore, the World Wide Web Consortium (W3C) SOAP working group declared SOAP no longer an acronym. REST stands for Representational State Transfer. Both these are discussed in more detail in the next section, "Data Collection and Consolidation."

In the ITIL SKMS practice, any entity that contributes to the service management lifecycle can be an SKMS source. That is a wide range of sources. In practice, the scope of SKMS data sources depends on the data an enterprise has available, the effort required to acquire the data for the SKMS, and the enterprise goals for the SKMS. Typically, an enterprise can prioritize critical services and issues. Those priorities then determine the scope of the SKMS data sources.

The data content also varies widely. For example, some organizations may want to include data from the operating systems of critical servers that run service software. This data could come from real-time queries or from events from the operating system. If near-real-time data is not needed, the information could come from operating system log files. Any of these methods can be useful. Operations is likely to find the more immediate data from a direct query useful in making on-the-spot decisions, but strategic decisions are likely to find trends extracted from logs more revealing.

Many organizations choose to concentrate on data closer to the services themselves rather than the infrastructure that supports the service, but the decision should always be driven by the enterprise goals for the SKMS. It is not an either-or decision. More data is better, but only if it is properly digested and interpreted. A wealth of data that is meaningfully combined, interpreted, and displayed is ideal. System monitoring facilities such as network monitors, security breach detection, and performance monitoring all are candidates as SKMS data sources.

At a minimum, most SKMSs include service portfolio systems; service desk incident, request, and problem management applications; configuration management databases; and change management records. Other sources, such as performance management, capacity management systems, asset management systems, and financial management may be used to focus on specific aspects of service management that are important to the enterprise. Practically, the investment needed to collect the data often helps decide which sources to include.

Data Collection and Consolidation

The SKMS collection layer brings the data from all the sources together. In a simple situation, the collection layer can be a pure pass-through, taking data from the data sources and passing it on to the upper layers without changing it in any way. The data sources and the data collection layers combined are the model in a Model-View-Controller (MVC) system. Unfortunately, data collection is often more complicated than a simple pass-through that homogenizes the individual application programming interfaces of the data sources into a single API that can be called by the upper layers. Usually, in an MVC, if there is more than one source of the data in the model, those sources are designed into the model rather than seen as separate data feeds. That is usually impractical for an SKMS because the data sources have their own structure that must be incorporated by the SKMS data collection layer, and the intention is to provide a window into service knowledge that may provide different views as IT services evolve. This usually involves something more complex than a simple pass-through.

The data collection layer must deliver data from all the data sources to the next layer up, the data interpretation layer, in a manner that the interpretation layer can use. The interpretation layer applies business logic to transform the collected data into meaningful business information. The collection layer may exist as a data warehouse or cache, or it may access the data sources directly. The collection layer may provide some data transformation. Translation to uniform measurement units is usual, and the data may have to be plugged into a common model.[8] There are many variations and combinations, but the architect must choose between caching data and querying for data.

A basic heuristic says caching consumes resources but improves performance; querying is more flexible and usually requires fewer computing and storage resources but may perform and scale poorly.

A data collection layer that passes queries for data on to the data sources, perhaps as SQL queries or using Open Data Protocol (OData),[9] can usually be constructed quickly. Using a protocol like OData, unanticipated requests for information may require no changes to the data collection layer, only a new query from the next layer up. However, this kind of data collection layer depends on the speed of the underlying data source and the transport of data from the source to the collection layer. This can be dishearteningly slow or erratic, and the SKMS architect has little control over the cause of the issues. It also may mask problems with differing data models.

An alternative is to construct a cache that is filled by the source on the source's schedule, which may be whenever the data is created or changes, or periodically at some appropriate interval. Using a cache, a query to the data collector depends on the speed of accessing the cache, not the performance of the data source. Usually, the cache will be much faster than the data source.

---

[8]More on this in a moment, but a simple example of a model problem is a financial asset application that differentiates between servers and desktops and a configuration management application that treats both as computers. If the data collector is simply a pass-through, the data interpretation may have three entities (servers, desktops, and computers) that are hard to interpret.

A cache gives the SKMS architect better control of performance, but the lunch is not free. There may be a lag between a value changing on the source and the value obtained from the cache, although a reasonably short lag is usually not important in SKMS. In addition, maintaining a consistent cache is often more difficult than it first appears. It often requires an in-depth knowledge of the inner workings of the data source. The cache itself requires resources, both in storage and computing capacity. Finally, when users request data not previously in the cache, the cache must support the new data. A simple and quickly built cache may require revision of the cache data layout to incorporate new data. If the cache code expects a fixed-data layout, coding may be required. In a dynamic organization, this can turn into a nightmare. That nightmare can be avoided with careful designs. Caches, often better called *data warehouses*, can be built to accommodate changing data schemas, but this can become a major project in itself.

The architecture of the data collection layer is often the most significant element in an overall SKMS design. There is no single best practice because it depends on the data sources, which vary from site to site.

In a greenfield implementation in which the architect can choose or build all the applications that contribute to service management, data sources can be chosen that have a uniform API for obtaining data. A protocol like OData is an excellent choice. The choice of OData also determines the transport used to transfer data from the source to the data collection layer because OData is generally considered a Representational State Transfer protocol, although it can be used in other contexts.

Other choices include SOAP,[10] which is connection oriented.[11] There are many SOAP toolkits, and many existing applications have SOAP interfaces. SOAP is also usually implemented over HTTP,[12] although, like REST, other transports are possible. In the past few years, REST has often been favored over SOAP because REST implementations have a simpler software stack. In theory, a REST interface can be used with nothing more than a simple command-line

---

[9]OData is a standard initially developed by Microsoft and now maintained by Organization for the Advancement of Structured Information Standards (OASIS). See https://www.oasis-open.org/committees/tc_home.php?wg_abbrev=odata. Accessed July 2014.

[10]SOAP once stood for Simple Object Access Protocol. As SOAP developed, it became neither simple nor primarily used for object access, so now SOAP officially is no longer an acronym. The protocol is now a World Wide Web Consortium (W3C) standard. See www.w3.org/TR/soap/. Accessed July 2014.

[11]See Marvin Waschke. *Cloud Standards*. New York: Apress, 2012, pp. 229–232, for some of the issues involved in connection-oriented and non-connection-oriented interaction.

[12]HTTP has drifted almost as far from its roots as SOAP. HTTP is now used in ways that do not much involve hypertext, passing everything from relational data to blocks of code.

tool like cURL.[13] In a powerful development environment, SOAP APIs are easy to write, but the hidden complexity of the SOAP stack can be an obstacle to debugging and maintenance.

SOAP's complexity also permits greater flexibility. REST servers do not retain client application state, which is not so important for SKMS but is important to other service management applications.[14] A call to a REST server depends only on the state of the server, not the state of the client. In other words, the server treats each call as independent and does not keep track of previous calls. Of course, if a call from a client changes the state of the application on the server, say by inserting a row into a database, the state change may affect the server's response to later calls, but that is the application state, not the server state. If, however, the client issues the identical GET commands repeatedly, the client will receive identical responses as long as the application state does not change. If the server were stateful, the server might keep track of the calls, and the client might get the first hundred rows, the next hundred rows, and so on, with each successive call.

The lack of server state makes writing REST servers somewhat simpler and more scalable. A REST server does have to contain code to manage client state, and it does not have to unwind the client call stack for error recovery, which makes REST servers easier to write and REST stacks lighter weight. The stateless REST servers are more easily load balanced because clients can easily switch between the servers. The flip side of these arguments is that REST clients may contain more code to keep the client state, and SOAP supports extended transactions, which can reduce the number of messages sent between the client and the server and are necessary in some cases. Avoiding excessive short exchanges between client and server instead of a few messages with more content can be important for performance over a network. In addition, developers trained in object-oriented programming often find SOAP transactions easier to understand when the complexity of the SOAP stack is hidden.

The distinctions between REST and SOAP become more significant when cloud implementations enter the picture. The "Cloud and Data Collection" section of this chapter discusses some of these challenges.

---

[13]cURL is a command-line client for Uniform Resource Locators (URLs) written in C and available on many platforms. On the command line, it is spelled `curl`. cURL sends and receives raw HTTP from a command line, and it is all that is needed to use REST, although for most purposes, more elaborate software is employed. Because it is simple and offers a transparent window into activity on the wire, cURL is useful for testing and debugging. For further information, see `http://curl.haxx.se/`. Accessed September 2015.

[14]Chapters 11 and 13 also discuss state.

When considering an SKMS data collection architecture, an SKMS architect should begin by asking what APIs are available for the data sources that will be incorporated in the SKMS. Asking what data sources might be employed in the future is also worthwhile. Although all APIs using a single protocol is ideal, building new APIs takes time and resources. Often a new API is impossible. For example, building a new API for an off-the-shelf proprietary application is completely infeasible in most cases. Even an open source or in-house application can present formidable obstacles to new API building.

As a consequence, the architect must, as usual, perform a balancing act by doing the minimum of work to make the data available and build a data collection layer that meets both performance and content requirements. Most often that ends up a conglomeration of data protocols and direct queries mixed with some form of data warehouse.

Figure 7-2 is an example of an SKMS data collection layer that combines proprietary, SOAP, REST, and REST OData protocols. The example also combines both data cached in a data warehouse and data that is queried directly from the data source. In the Figure 7-2 example, the Uniform Access Facade is shown using SOAP. SOAP will work as the data collection layer protocol, as will REST or many other protocols. Currently, REST would be theoretically favored in many IT departments. However, in an environment where SOAP or some other protocol is used frequently, it is often a good choice to stick with the protocol best known among the developers who will work with it.

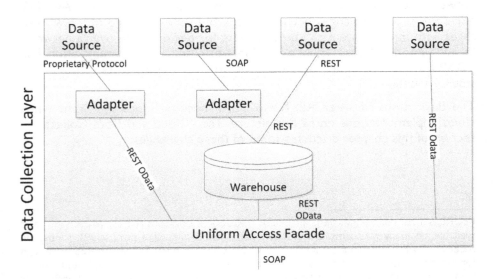

Figure 7-2. For an SKMS data collection layer that combines several protocols, direct querying and caching often is a good solution

The figure illustrates that much of the code required in data collection follows either the adapter or the facade pattern. The adapter pattern usually refers to code that translates one API protocol into another. A facade pattern usually describes an entity that provides a single unified interface to a number of sources. See Figure 7-3.

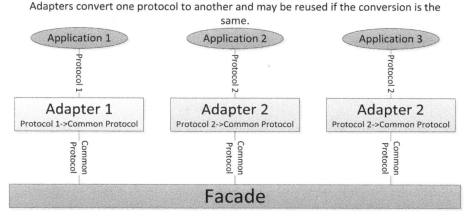

Adapters convert one protocol to another and may be reused if the conversion is the same.

Many applications behind a single façade interface.

Figure 7-3. Facades and adapters perform different functions

Most SKMSs have to address translating objects from one scheme to another. For example, one data source may have something called *storage* that models both internal and external disk drives that may be attached via a TCP/IP network or a Small Computer System Interface (SCSI) network.[15] Another data source may have separate direct attached storage (DAS), network attached storage (NAS), and storage area networks (SAN). Some code must bring this data together in a comprehensible fashion.

This vexing problem can become complicated. A basic strategy for dealing with the complexity is to choose a common model for data collection and translate all the data source models into a common model. This requires some advanced planning, but a common model is a scalable approach that makes adding data sources relatively easy.

---

[15]Marvin Waschke. *Cloud Standards*. New York: Apress, 2012. Pages 174–185. This book describes SCSI and various forms of network storage.

"Relatively" is a carefully chosen word. Adding a new data source can be easy, but it also can be maddeningly difficult, no matter how well-designed the data collection layer. If both the data model and the transport protocol are idiosyncratic, which happens all too often, developers are challenged to be smart and creative. However, it is always easier to add a data source to an established data collection layer based on a strong common model. Ad hoc model translation mechanisms without a common model are invariably fragile and difficult to understand and work with when a new source is added.

Some of these problems are addressed in dealing with configuration management databases (CMDBs),[16] and SKMS architects can sometimes leverage federated CMDBs. Information models such as the Distributed Management Task Force (DMTF) Common Information Model (CIM)[17] are also useful.

Adopting one of these general models as the standard for the facade can save work. CIM, for example, is already used in some IT management tools. If the data collection layer uses CIM as the model that is exposed in the façade, including management tools that use CIM in the SKMS is simplified because there is no translation between the source and the façade. A model that addresses services as well as infrastructure and software may be useful here.

Figure 7-4 shows data models in an SKMS data collection layer. In this example, a common model was chosen as the model behind the façade. The facade provides a uniform interface to other applications such as dashboards that will use the collected data. The data sources are in several forms, but they are all transformed so that they can be accessed through the uniform façade. A common model simplifies the facade and makes the system easier to modify by isolating conversions to the adapters and avoiding cross-model conversions. The example uses two data warehouses that are both addressed through the façade.

A system of adapters such as this may not need to be developed by each site. There are products, such as Teiid, an open source product, that provides software for much of this process.[18]

---

[16]The Distributed Management Task Force has published a standard that addresses some aspects of this problem. See http://dmtf.org/standards/cmdbf. Accessed July 2014.
[17]See http://dmtf.org/standards/cim. Accessed July 2014.
[18]For more on Teiid, see http://teiid.jboss.org/about/. Accessed September 2015.

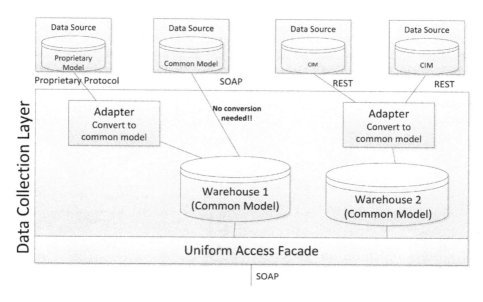

Figure 7-4. Using general data models strategically can reduce coding

Designing and building a scalable SKMS data collection layer is challenging because IT service management has developed gradually and coalesced from many independent applications. The data collection layer is where much of the difficulty surfaces.

Cloud and Data Collection

So far, this discussion has not mentioned cloud computing. Today, in many IT departments, service management is likely to consist of a mixture of applications that are deployed locally, deployed virtually on local servers that are not organized as a cloud, and deployed on public and private clouds. Although cloud acceptance has increased steadily since the concept's introduction, organizations are often hesitant to make radical and rapid changes to their infrastructures. CEOs and CFOs still fret over cloud security and governance. SKMS data collection layers will have to collect data from cloud and noncloud sources for at least the near future, although the number of noncloud sources are likely to decrease as time goes on. On-premises implementations may never completely disappear from systems with extraordinary security and secrecy requirements.

The architecture of a mixed local and cloud environment can be complex. Figure 7-5 is an example of a mixed environment. Several data sources are implemented on clouds; other data sources are implemented locally. In the example, the data collection layer is implemented on both cloud and local environments. The data collector uses a data warehouse implemented on a private IaaS cloud that was built by the enterprise, exists on the enterprise premises, and is administered as a cloud by enterprise IT personnel. Likely, a private cloud was chosen rather than a public cloud because the data in the SKMS warehouse is sensitive and management was unwilling to place it in a third party's hands.

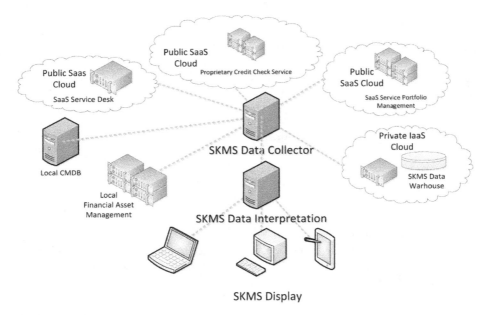

Figure 7-5. The topology of an SKMS in a mixed local and cloud environment can be complex

It is also likely that this private cloud evolved from a simple virtual environment on a cluster of servers that was originally deployed to run a number of applications utilizing the combined computing power of the cluster more efficiently.

These private clouds can be hard to distinguish from simple virtualization. The key difference is primarily administrative. A private cloud offers an on-demand environment, usually in the form of virtual machines and storage. The consumers of the on-demand environment configure and use it as they want, installing and running their applications as if it was their own physical infrastructure. The mechanism by which the consuming service is charged for the use of the infrastructure and the control the user is given over the infrastructure are important characteristics of clouds. There is no great value in making sharp distinctions, but whether an application is running in a virtual environment or a private cloud can make a difference for integrating an application as a data source for an SKMS.

A mixed environment like Figure 7-5 poses several challenges. SaaS integration depends on the extent of the APIs that the SaaS provider is willing to supply. Old-style, on-premises, enterprise applications often provide access to a rich array of data and events in the application. This has proven to be a mixed blessing: opening up application data and events widens the surface on which consumers interact with the application. This level of access can enable tailored customer implementations that exactly match enterprise needs. However, future development of an application with a wide surface must continue to support the exposed surface without changes or risk breaking backward compatibility with existing installations.[19] The wider the exposed surface, the harder to maintain complete backward compatibility. Without easy backward compatibility, the result is often customers who refuse to upgrade to new releases or difficult and brittle scripted upgrades that are expensive to build and test and often annoy customers. Over time, this can cripple the advancement of the application. Many SaaS providers have taken an opportunity to reduce this exposure by offering narrower APIs with less access to the internals of products. If the APIs are carefully chosen, this works well, but it can also make data collection for an SKMS difficult.

Issues with IaaS and PaaS cloud implementations are similar. Both are subject to the APIs of the applications running on the cloud. Most of these are HTTP-based REST or SOAP. However, older applications may have been ported directly to the cloud without changing their APIs. These may not be HTTP-based.

The cloud implementation itself may have data that must be collected for the SKMS. For example, a typical IaaS cloud charges consumers for the virtual machines that run on the cloud. These charges may be critical information for service management because they contribute to the cost of providing a service. The amount of cloud storage used, virtual network utilization, and other metrics all may be of value to the SKMS users. Therefore, the SKMS may be required to collect data from the cloud providers. Most providers may make this information available through some kind of web service. The DMTF Cloud Infrastructure Management Interface (CIMI) provides a REST API for accessing such metrics.[20] Proprietary APIs usually also provide similar APIs for accessing this sort of information.

---

[19]In this case, backward compatibility means that an SKMS data collector built to work with the API of an early release of an application should work equally well with a later release without modification to the collector. In addition, the information in the SKMS display from a later release should be as valuable as the information from an earlier release. The later requirement is often more difficult for an application builder to maintain than the former. The first requirement places constraints only on the form of the API. The latter requirement also places constraints on changes to the data structure of the application, which can seriously hold back the evolution of the application.
[20]See http://dmtf.org/standards/cmwg. Accessed July 2014.

Data Interpretation

The data collection layer is the workhorse of the SKMS, but the data interpretation layer is the business intelligence of the system. Data interpretation transforms raw data into information that can be used by the SKMS consumer. Data interpretation relies on the business rules and practices of the enterprise to give meaning to the data that is collected. Data interpretation can range from a simple pass-through of data values to an intense analysis of large amounts of structured and unstructured data. There are many possibilities: a data series can be examined for trends, big data–style analysis may reveal hidden relationships in seemingly unconnected data, or commonly used ratios such as mean time between failure (MTBF) can be calculated.

Perhaps the most important capability of an SKMS is to combine similar data from disparate sources. Such information might contribute to strategic and design decisions. An SKMS can make it possible to compare various aspects of productivity for different services. For example, an SKMS can normalize metrics for customer satisfaction for similar services and compare the services, judging them on their relative contributions to the enterprise reputation. The total cost of ownership for service assets used for similar purposes in different services can be compared, and better purchase strategies can be developed for the future.

The testing history and rollout issues in one service may be useful in planning transitions for another service. Combining with data from similar technical implementations can provide insight to operations personnel into overlaps and conflict in resource allocations that affect service delivery. Sharing service incidents from the service desk can yield clues to incipient weaknesses in similar services. Information in one service's solutions database can often be useful to other services with similar issues. The possible combinations and benefits grow as further data sources are added to the SKMS.

Bringing together information from different sources and synergistically combining them into insights that are greater than the sum of the parts is exactly why enterprises choose to build SKMSs. Combined information can be important for making strategic decisions and even low-level operational decisions that affect more than one service. These comparisons can be critical to strategic decisions for enhancing or replacing services.

Data interpretation depends upon a thorough understanding of the business. Without that understanding, the data from the collectors are facts that cannot be transformed into information useful to the enterprise. The business of the enterprise determines what is useful and what is not. The architecture of the data collection system must not hinder business input into the interpretation of the data. This is probably more of a documentation challenge than a technical challenge: the business side of the house must be able to understand exactly what the data is in order to decide how it is to be interpreted. The architect and developer must work closely with the business side in order to provide useful interpretation. This is often frustrating because neither understands the other well and may have little motivation to make the effort to understand.

Both sides must be patient and keep an open mind. It is hard to overemphasize the importance of mutual understanding in the interpretation layer. Without substantial understanding, the value of an SKMS will be limited to the business imagination of the developers of the system because the developers are the implementers. Without meaningful business input, the implementation can be a catastrophe because its information will not be of value to its business consumers who are likely to be the majority of users and the most influential.

Presentation

The two ingredients that make up a good SKMS display are convenience and understandability for its users. The lower levels (the data sources and the data interpretation and collection) are technical, unseen, unappreciated, largely unknown, and nonetheless essential.

No matter how well-designed, efficient, and maintainable the data collection and display layers, an SKMS without a good display will be a failure. Developers often assume that the SKMS display is only "eye-candy" and not necessary to the effective use of the SKMS. This has a grain of truth; a good SKMS cannot succeed without effective data collection and interpretation. A great display cannot compensate for inadequate data. The harmonious colors, elegant fonts, graphs, bubble charts, and dynamic screens are all useless without the right information to display. On the other hand, excellent data that is not presented as clear and useful information is equally useless.

An SKMS must be conveniently accessible. For an SKMS, display means more than the traditional liquid crystal or cathode ray tube monitor. There are more display media available today than in the past. An SKMS can make use of many different modes of display—some cutting-edge and others more traditional. Each has its place, and a well-designed SKMS display can use them all.

Paper reports, the oldest of computer displays, are still often favored for displaying long-term trends for planners and executives developing strategic policies and evaluating service portfolios. Traditional "fat client" displays in cubicles, on the racks in the data center, and on large displays in control rooms are important in some organizations. However, web browser–based displays, which are more device-independent, have largely replaced fat clients. Web apps and mobile apps on portable devices such as mobile phones and tablets offer real-time insight into service performance to roving managers and operators and untether employees for offsite work. The multiplicity of displays can be a temptation to poor presentation when developers and designers attempt to cut corners by not using the characteristics of displays to advantage. Displaying a PDF of a paper report unreadably on a mobile device and claiming to have a mobile app is an example of a misdirected rush to a new means of display.

An SKMS architect should plan for all of these types of displays. SKMS architecture does not differ from any other application that must display information to users. However, because the SKMS can often display information from legacy sources that do not have flexible user interface, the value of an SKMS increases when it provides a window into older sources whose information is harder to get to.

Service Workflow and Business Process Management

Not all service management applications fit the source, collector, interpreter, and display pattern. In addition to displaying information used for management, some service management applications manage business processes, enforcing and executing policies and actively managing objects that make up services.

Management and control are usually based on *events* and *alerts*. (See the following sidebar.)

ALERTS AND EVENTS

Following ITIL terminology, *events* are significant changes of the state of a system. Any change that affects the management of the system can be called an event. An event might occur when a file system reaches 80 percent capacity, or an event might be a periodic reading of CPU temperature or even a measurement of current inventory. An important aspect of events is that they indicate the state of the system at a specific time. Not all events indicate an actual or imminent malfunction. Some events indicate benign conditions that may be useful for management.

Event is occasionally used interchangeably with *alert*, but usually an alert is the notification that may be generated when an event occurs. Also, *alert* is often reserved for notifications that indicate an actual or imminent malfunction or situation that requires attention.

Service incident management is an example of event management. Many incident management applications, usually part of a service desk, automatically create incident reports based on policies or business rules and input from automated instrumentation of the virtual or physical infrastructure. Human sources and security systems also create and provide events for incident reports. The incident management application displays the information collected from users and automated agent, but it also automatically manages incidents, following policy rules to determine priority, assign technicians based on expertise and availability, escalate issues, and manage other aspects of the incident lifecycle. Policies may automatically close issues. Policy management, enforcement, and execution are often performed by a workload, workflow, or business process management component. Sometimes these policies are called *workflow policies* to distinguish them from other types of policies such as security policies; sometimes they are simply called *business rules*. Policy determines actions taken on the incident, and incident management applications have a more active role than collection, interpretation, and display applications.

Change management and other aspects of service desks such as problem and request management also enforce and execute policies. Other service management applications, such as financial asset, service portfolio, service-level agreement management, or service catalog may also include a business process management component.

These applications face all the challenges of an SKMS because they collect, interpret, and display information from data sources. They must integrate with different data sources with different architectures and different APIs or lack of APIs. And they confront differing data models that must be reconciled and rationalized. They gain the same advantages and disadvantages from cloud deployments.

Figure 7-6 represents a general architecture for a process control system. The architecture is actually similar to the SKMS architecture in Figure 7-1. Events are a special form of data, and they are consolidated just as data is collected and consolidated in an SKMS. Event consolidation is usually called *correlation*. The correlation function in event management attempts to identify events that stem from the same originating condition, often called the *root cause*. Sometimes that is easily done when a storm of events repeatedly contain the same information from the same source. Other times correlation reaches to the level of artificial intelligence and sophisticated data analysis when the linkage between events is subtle.

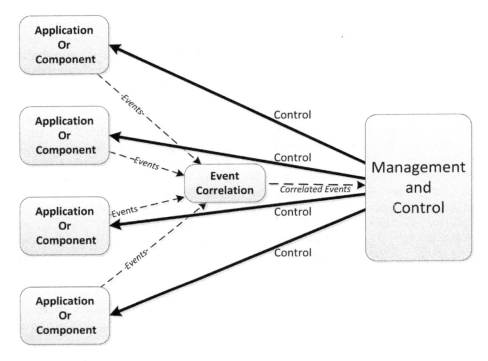

Figure 7-6. Service management and control service overview

Event correlation and data consolidation face some of the same challenge with different emphasis. SKMS tends to be challenged by reconciling different data models and repositories that refer to the same physical or virtual object. Event correlation has the same challenge, but usually the greatest challenge for event correlation is attaining a deep understanding of the dynamic relationships between events as they occur. For example, a rise in network traffic through a certain router may not be significant unless there is also an increase in the load on a certain server, which might indicate a denial-of-service attack on the server, rather than a general increase in activity. This level of inference goes far beyond the data in the event.

The most significant difference between Figure 7-1 and Figure 7-2 is the control arrows pointing back to the controlled application or component. An SKMS is a data collection mechanism that ties together data from many elements of the IT system. A system management application is a feedback loop that takes in event data and uses the data to exercise intelligent control of the managed applications and components.

The control is usually guided by management policies and rules. The management and control module must interpret incoming events and apply the policies and rules to the ongoing process. Sometimes this is a manual process performed by operators to view processed event data and use their experience and expertise to exercise the appropriate controls. In other cases, especially when instant reaction is required, the management and control module will respond automatically. An example is a system that automatically activates a fire control system when excess temperature is detected.

Unique management and control application challenges stem from the complex interaction that management requires. Often, control consists of a workflow rather than a single control message. In a workflow, the control activity may involve many steps, each one of which may generate its own events and require a change in the direction of the flow. All transactions in a "collect-and-display" application move data from the source to the destination. Either the source or destination may start the transaction. When the destination requests data, the transaction is a *pull*. When the source sends the data to the destination without a request, the transaction is a *push*. When executing a workflow, transactions are more complicated, involving more than a single push or pull step. Often, the managing application sends a request to a worker application and then waits for the worker to reply with a status on the effect of the request. These interactions can be complicated, especially when the system or network has elements of unpredictability such as a network that can slow down or even break. Management and control applications can be hypercritical as in our fire control system example.

The topology of a cloud implementation can critically affect control mechanisms, especially intricate control workflows. Interaction between public clouds and on-premises components are affected by the network that connects them. When the network is the Internet, the workflow must be designed to be resilient to slowdowns and interruptions. One way of addressing this issue is in the placement of components so that a network interruption can be compensated for with a component with an uninterrupted path, which may mean designing in redundancy and parallel processing. Often, parallel processing can serve a dual purpose of also improving scalability.

As much as possible, workflow transactions should be designed to be stateless and idempotent.[21] Even within a corporate network, mishaps sometimes occur, and the target of a message does not receive the request, the target never responds, or the sender dies before it gets its response. A stateless transaction can be repeated with the same effect each time, which makes recovery from interrupted transactions much easier. When some components of the architecture are on clouds, the likelihood of some kind of network interruption increases. Therefore, stateless transactions are even more important when clouds are present.

---

[21]Statelessness and idempotency are discussed in Chapter 13. An idempotent message can be repeated with the same effect as issuing it only once. Web applications that request that you click only once when submitting a transaction are not idempotent. The danger is that the second click will cause the transaction to be repeated.

When choosing between REST and SOAP, it is important to keep the statelessness of REST architectures in mind. It is also wise to remember that well-designed REST APIs have a stateless server, but sometimes the label REST is used loosely and API is not stateless. On the other hand, SOAP architectures can be designed to be stateless.

Sometimes designing a stateless transaction is simply not possible. A classic all-or-nothing accounting transaction that must complete or be completely reversed as if the transaction never happened is difficult to implement as a stateless transaction. If the instigator, and perhaps other players in the transaction, does not acknowledge the success of the transaction, the transaction must fail completely and return the server to the state before the transaction started. Recovering the prior state is difficult if the system must remain stateless. Usually, service management transactions are not as strict as accounting transactions, so statelessness is not as hard to achieve, but when stateful transactions are not avoidable, SOAP is connection oriented and will support stateful transactions. In that case, SOAP may be the best choice for APIs with the service management application.

Management of stateful transactions is the most difficult difference between source, collector, interpreter, and display patterns and applications that manage workflow and policy.

Although clouds raise the threat of more difficult recovery from network interruption, clouds may still be even more beneficial to workflow management applications than "collect-and-display" applications. Service desks, for example, are often in need of cloud elasticity. Like many other service management applications, service desk volumes reflect the volume of activity in the enterprise, which varies by season, account-closing dates, and even day of the week. Since a service desk is often a mission-critical service that is most needed during flurries of activity when volume is at its peak, a service desk application must be provisioned to perform well when it is heavily used, even though that may result in over-provisioning the vast majority of the time. Cloud elasticity makes over-provisioning unnecessary, if the application is designed to scale by increasing the number of virtual machines.

The accessibility offered by a cloud implementation is often the most important benefit of a cloud deployment when management and control applications are used widely, both inside and outside the enterprise.

Conclusion

Clouds can reduce up-front capital investments, make service management applications more accessible outside the organization perimeter, and increase flexibility and scalability, but they can also make integration more challenging and complicate governance and security. An SKMS is an information collection, interpretation, and display application that faces many integration challenges and is characteristic of many service management applications. Other applications, such as service desk or service catalog, implement policies and manage work-flows and business processes. These applications face additional challenges in a cloud environment, but they also gain similar benefits from cloud deployment.

EXERCISES

1. What is a service knowledge management system?

2. Describe the four architectural layers that make up an SKMS.

3. What is the general architectural pattern of an SKMS?

4. Describe another service management application that follows the same pattern as an SKMS.

5. Describe some of the challenges presented by legacy applications to implementing an SKMS.

6. List some challenges presented by cloud implementation of SKMS data sources.

7. List some advantages provided by cloud implementations.

8. Discuss some service management applications that do not follow the SKMS pattern.

Enterprise Integration

The Harder They Fall

Integration in the Enterprise

SUMMARY

As businesses grow, their IT system grows in three ways: the transaction volume increases as the business expands, the system becomes more geographically dispersed as the business enters new markets, and the system increases in complexity as additional processes are automated. Each of these aspects of growth involves many components and relationships in the IT system, and cloud implementations play an important role.

Effective enterprise integration depends on some fundamental concerns of enterprise architecture that make it possible to grow the enterprise in volume, geographic spread, and complexity without risking some of the issues that arise with growth.

Selecting the right off-the-shelf applications or designing and building in-house applications to meet the needs of a growing organization is challenging. Identifying the requirements of the organization, designing a solution, and rolling the solution out to users are difficult tasks. But there is another long-range challenge that continues after application selection or design and construction: integration. Integration challenges the IT department differently because it involves connecting and adapting existing components of the IT environment, which are tasks that require insight into working applications rather than building new ones. For most organizations, integration is as important as selecting and developing new components. Nevertheless, integration is often an afterthought that occurs after an application is installed and in production. Usually, attempting to add integration to a system that has not been designed to be integrated from the outset is expensive, and the result is often only marginally satisfactory. Perhaps worse, the cost of integration is easily under-estimated because the effort to connect applications looks small compared to the effort required to design and build the application's functionality. However, if suitable interfaces are not present, the cost of change can approach the initial cost of construction as components are rebuilt to accommodate proper interfaces.

Applications that work in isolation are rare; most serve the organization better when they are woven into the fabric of the system that make up the information technology of the enterprise. This fabric has expanded to include many aspects of an organization that were formerly not considered part of IT. Not too long ago, the heating, ventilation, and air-conditioning (HVAC) system was in the hands of the facilities department. The system was controlled remotely, first by pneumatic tubing, then by electricity. As controllers became more sophisticated, Ethernet interfaces were added. Ethernet is a bidirectional protocol. Consequently, the controllers could transmit information, such as temperature, as well as receive commands. To save costs, instead of an independent HVAC Ethernet network, the corporate network could be used. At that point, the IT department took on at least a portion of responsibility for the HVAC system.

Around 2000, the concept of the Internet of Things (IoT) began to appear. In its early stages, the IoT was associated with radio frequency identification (RFID) used for inventory control and the notion that computers could be supplied with content from things rather than humans.[1] The developments in HVAC fit into IoT well. At about the same time, the internal enterprise telecommunications network began to integrate into the corporate network. These developments extended the purview of the IT department beyond its earlier limitation to computing.

Enterprise Integration

Enterprise integration focuses on exchanging data and control between a wide range of elements involved in an enterprise. The most prominent among these elements are applications that run on computers that support the enterprise

---

[1]Kevin Ashton is usually attributed with coining the IoT phrase when he was working on automated inventory control for Proctor & Gamble. See www.rfidjournal.com/articles/view?4986. Accessed September 2015.

goals. Exchange with human systems and processes, mechanical processes, and various forms of instrumentation are also included. A critical aspect of integration is to identify and meet business drivers and requirements for integration.

Where does cloud computing fit into the enterprise integration challenge? The previous chapter discussed the architectural challenges involved in building an SKMS that ties together the service knowledge of an entire organization and how the features of an SKMS architecture can applied to other service management applications. The SKMS example reveals many aspects of the integration challenge. This chapter will go on to discuss enterprise integration more generally.

Challenges to Growing Businesses

As businesses grow, their IT needs follow a general pattern. Small systems start simple. When a business is small, its IT department may be only one person in operations who knows a little more about computers and has become the go-to person for computing problems. That person is probably not even called IT. There is no IT department and no formal IT system.

Most small businesses have an accounting system that is either a collection of spreadsheets or a desktop program. The finance department is a single accountant, with the entire accounting system at their desk. They make all entries themselves and maintain all the records. A business may also have specialized programs tailored to their business. For example, a law office may have a system for managing legal forms in their legal specialty. A construction firm may have a construction cost estimation programs tailored to the firm's type of construction. Other small firms might have specialized inventory programs.

Billing information from specialty systems can be entered manually into the accounting system, but as the volume of business increases, manual entry becomes an issue. The accountant's expensive time is taken up with data entry, the process is error prone, and the entries may not be timely. Either another person is delegated to data entry, or the systems can be integrated, which is often a better answer.

An integrated system quickly and accurately transfers data from specialty applications to the accounting system. After the initial cost, the ongoing costs are probably less than an additional employee. In addition, integration tends to be more scalable; the cost of running an integrated system increases only marginally as the volume of business increases. Depending on the architecture of the specialty applications and the accounting system, integration can be easy or can be difficult to the point that one or both of the systems must be replaced. In retail businesses, for example, the accounting system and the point-of-sale system are often integrated out of the box, but eventually, as a business grows, there are almost always new applications that are not integrated and need to be.

The previous example shows integration aiding in coping with increased business volume. Volume is not the only way business grows. Business IT grows along three axes: the volume of data and transactions processed by the system increases, the business spreads over a larger geographic area increasing the need for a geographically distributed system, and the system becomes more complex in its types of data and processing and interconnections between subsystems. In this chapter, these axes are called *volume, spread,* and *complexity*.

Not all businesses grow at the same rate along each axis. A business may concentrate on providing more locations that are convenient to their customers and charging premium prices for the improved service without increasing volume. Other businesses can increase volume without spreading geographically. Most growing enterprises find increasing complexity difficult to avoid.

Growth on each of these axes affects enterprise integration. Cloud deployments both complicate and simplify the development of integrated systems.

Volume

As an enterprise becomes more successful, it gets busier. The organization attracts more customers and clients, increases the amount of inventory to track, onboards[2] more employees to administer, and develops new lines of business to manage. All this results in more frequent and larger transactions of various types. Some are financial; others involve HR data on an expanding employee population, customer relations data on an expanding customer base, or larger and more varied inventories. The rise in transaction size, variety, and frequency generate one type of IT challenge that can be characterized as an increase in volume.

Applications

Volume forces applications to change. Employees can manage records in simple spreadsheets when the enterprise is small, and the spreadsheet lines of data and number of changes per day are measured in hundreds. As the enterprise grows, the volume of records becomes hard to manage in a spreadsheet. Changes and additions become too frequent to enter by hand, and the errors

---

[2]*Onboarding* is convenient jargon for the entire process of taking on a new member of an organization. It usually starts at hiring and includes orientation and training, providing necessary tools and facilities (such as a cubicle, chair, and computer), enrolling in human resources and payroll accounting programs, opening computer system accounts, establishing authentication and authorizations for security, and so on. In IT discussions, onboarding often focuses on establishing IT accounts and security. The reverse of onboarding is *off-boarding*.

from manual entry become a drag on the organization. The performance of simple homegrown databases begins to bog down, and the data design requires a professional's expertise to streamline data management.

Single-user spreadsheets, simple databases, and other applications become inadequate when the volume reaches the point that one person cannot manage the data. Enterprises typically replace these semi-manual processes with applications that support many simultaneous users. These applications use forms tailored to the tasks they perform. The forms discourage entry errors and have error-checking routines that increase accuracy. Databases replace simple files to manage increasing volumes of data and maintain data consistency and integrity. At some point, servers move from desktops and closets to a climate-controlled datacenter with conditioned power and backup generators where they are tended by trained IT staff.

Simple shared files are no longer adequate for managing data when data volume and number of users increase. Single-user applications are not concerned with colliding transactions when two or more users attempt to modify the same data at the same time. Supplying prompt and reliable data access to large numbers of users is a job that is usually delegated to commercial database management systems designed by specialists and running on dedicated hardware. The data and transaction models and structures, indexes, and physical data layout are designed and tuned by skilled database administrators.

Network

The IT network also expands as the enterprise volume expands. Instead of an externally connected router, a few simple switches, and some wiring to connect each desk, a large corporate network requires wiring plans and closets, firewalls, load balancers, perhaps several routers, many switches, and other facilities designed to support and optimize network high-volume usage within the enterprise.

Online customer sites are also challenged by volume increases. As the number of customers using the site increases, the enterprise has several new demands to face. Reliability becomes more important as the financial consequences of an interruption in service increase. The site must be prepared to support increasing volumes of transactions, which may be *bursty*, such that lower volumes are mixed with sudden bursts in activity that may be orders of magnitude greater than baseline activity.

Often, the bursts occur at exactly the time when performance is most critical—the performance of the web sites of advertisers during the Super Bowl, for example.

With increased volume, downtime increases in expense. In a small business, a failing system will affect a few employees and cause some delayed transactions. It's not a desirable situation, but it's not a catastrophe. However, when the business volume goes up, a down system affects more employees and customers. Failures become more expensive, and IT must begin to consider disaster recovery and design systems that keep working. Robust code that handles errors without ill effects, backup systems, and resilient systems that keep processing when a portion of the system fails all become more important as business volume increases.

Big Data

As business volume increases, the data generated by business transactions grows and becomes an asset in its own right. The data must be analyzed to gain value from it, but analysis of the volume of data businesses now collect presents new challenges. Data-intensive Internet enterprises like Google or Facebook generate daily data measured in terabytes and petabytes.[3] Just storing this data has spurred the development of new mass storage systems. The old tools of data analysis, mostly relational and object-oriented databases with associated reporting tools, are not adequate. New tools have been developed to handle the new volume of data.

Support

In addition to capacity to deal with increasing volumes of activity, supporting IT users becomes an issue as volume increases. With thousands of customers a day, every permutation of user error, incorrect entry, ambiguous prompt, and user confusion will occur regularly. The site must be prepared to support these customers. This raises the requirements for user interfaces. When a site has 500 users a day, it may be acceptable if 1 customer in 50 requires intervention from support. When volumes reach tens of thousands of customers per day, reducing the number of issues becomes critical. Careful design of user interfaces becomes crucial.

Increased volume and subsequent criticality of IT systems engenders a need for a sophisticated service desk. Not only must the service desk support the volume of user issues and support representatives necessary to respond to the issues, the service desk must be proactive, detecting and resolving issues before they are noticed by users. To resolve issues quickly, the desk must also have diagnostic tools and manage assignments and workloads to optimize both human and computing resources directed at a problem.

---

[3] A terabyte is a trillion bytes. A petabyte is a quadrillion bytes. A few years ago, the entire Library of Congress was estimated to contain 3 petabytes of information.

As lines of business increase, the number and types of applications also increase. Each service offered by the organization has its own set of automation requirements. A new product line may require an automatic credit check on purchases over a certain amount. Automated manufacturing equipment may be added that requires extensive external data storage. This not only increases the volume and diversity of services supplied by the IT department, but it also expands IT along other axes.

Security

IT security is also often a challenge as enterprise IT volume grows. With increases in volume, security usually becomes more granular, which increases the volume of processing. For a small organization, often three classes of users are sufficient: nonemployee, employee, and administrator. Nonemployees, such as customers and employees of other organizations with which the enterprise does business, typically have limited access. Employees usually have access to everything but critical systems, which are reserved for administrators. Simple security schemes like this work well for small organizations. However, as the enterprise grows, security becomes more segmented. Access is assigned by "need to know," and few need to know everything. One group of employees may have access to human resources data, others may have access to accounting information, others might have access to server configurations, and so on. Fine-grained segmentation like this requires processing that identifies users and their access rights, adding overhead to almost everything IT does. It is no longer sufficient to know who is using the system; the security system must also know what that user is authorized to do.

Enterprises with many customers and assets become targets for cybercriminals, further stressing the security system. The number of transactions that must pass increasingly complex security checks soars, but user patience does not increase proportionately, creating a demand for more efficient and tighter security.

Volume in Large and Small Enterprises

All of these challenges apply to any growing enterprise. As the enterprise grows, scale becomes a greater challenge. Management can no longer stroll around the floor asking questions and shaking hands to get a feel for the state of the business. Increasingly they must rely on reports and dashboards for an understanding of conditions. Instead of an accounting department of half a dozen trusted employees, large organizations may have hundreds, even thousands, of employees, each with different privileges, needing access to an integrated accounting system. Instead of a few applications that the IT architect must integrate with accounting, there may be hundreds of applications spread across hundreds of sites located around the globe. In addition, accounting may not be the only application needing integration. Supply chain management, inventory control, human resource management, and online business sites all have to be tied together.

A small organization that recognizes that these challenges grow as the enterprise grows and makes decision that will support rather than hinder growth will have a significant competitive advantage. A growing large enterprise is already caught up in these issues whether it realizes it or not.

Geographic Spread

Most businesses, as they grow, also expand to additional locations. They may have branch stores, regional sales offices, or remote manufacturing facilities. A law office may open a branch in another city but want to keep a single electronic document management system in the main office. A retail business may open branch stores with a single accounting system in the main store. Large enterprises expanding into new—often global—markets require new remote facilities, ranging from small sales offices to entire factory complexes. Geographic spread adds other factors to the integration challenge. Integrating with a remote system introduces unreliable networks, transmission delays, and new security vulnerabilities.

All networks are subject to accidents and events that may interrupt or interfere with transmission, some much more than others. An internal network within a single geographic site is usually more reliable than a wider area network. Global networks often depend on satellites and undersea cables. A private wide area network can be made more reliable than a public network. The Internet, with a wide range of known and unknown cooperating providers, can be the most perilous of all.

There are hosts of challenges when dealing with unreliable communications. Data transmission protocols are designed to minimize the effects of data delivery slowdowns, gaps, and cessations, but they do not eliminate these problems. When a data link goes down, transactions have to be rolled back. If the rollback is not done properly, data may become inconsistent or corrupt in unpredictable ways. Processes dependent on data from a remote site may halt, slow down, or become unstable. The remote site may suffer from the same conditions.

These situations can be mitigated. Data connections can be made more reliable, and redundant connections can be established. Applications can be designed to cope with vagaries in data transmission and avoid inconsistency and other deleterious effects. However, even with the most elaborate and careful preparation, sites must balance the needs for continuous availability and instantaneous data consistency. Said differently, if you want perfectly correct information from a remote site, you must be prepared to sometimes wait. If you must have data instantly and never have to wait, you must be prepared for data that occasionally will not be correct until the network catches up.[4]

Complexity

As businesses grow, their systems are likely to increase in complexity. A law firm may expand to different specialties and require systems for handling different forms and processes. A construction firm may also take on different specialties requiring additional systems such as computer-aided design and automated logistics planning. As the number of systems increases, integration is likely also to become more complex as more systems are wired together in different ways.

Complexity is a concept used in a number of disciplines. In some contexts, complexity has a precise meaning. In other contexts, it is descriptive term without precise meaning. Here, the complexity of enterprise IT systems is descriptive. The IT system of an enterprise can be seen as a single entity that provides services to the enterprise and its customers. This entity must be maintained and modified to meet changing business requirements. As the demands placed on the IT system increase, the interactions between each system component increase in number and variety. Connections between components increase. As these interactions and connections grow, the implications of any input or change to the system become more difficult to predict, and the system becomes more difficult to manage. The increased number and type of connections and interactions is what is meant by complexity here.

Some of the factors that contribute to enterprise IT complexity are the number of subsystems and applications, the number and types of relationships between the system, and the system dependencies and other state relationships between subsystems. Other contributors to complexity are the potential for influence on the activity of the system from its users and changes in system dependencies based on the activity of the system.

---

[4]See Marvin Waschke, *Cloud Standards*, Apress, 2012; pp 124-131 have a discussion of the Consistency, Availability, Partitioning (CAP) theorem and its implications for system communications. The CAP theorem asserts applications integrated over an unreliable network must balance data consistency with data availability. In other words, if completely accurate data must be available at every instant, the network must be perfect. If a perfect network is not available, consistency and availability must be balanced. Since perfect networks are only theoretically possible, availability and consistency are always a compromise. Most Internet applications settle on "eventual consistency," which places availability above consistency but guarantees that the data will eventually be consistent. Mobile devices with intermittent or varying connections exacerbate the need for eventual consistency.

Integration

Complexity and integration are linked. Integration is a cause of complexity. An enterprise IT system consisting of a single application with few inputs and outputs running in isolation may be internally complex, but the enterprise system is not. Two such applications running in isolation are also not complex. But when two applications are integrated, they no longer run in isolation. The two applications can and often do influence each other, and the complexity of the IT system increases.

Anyone who has administered systems is familiar with an increase in complexity. Two applications launched on the same server (even simple applications with few inputs and outputs, minor internal processing, and no interactions between the applications) eventually contend for system resources and make management more difficult. For example, the administrator may have to be careful not to start the two applications at the same time to avoid contention for startup resources. Even when there is no overt interaction, each additional application contributes to complexity. This simple example illustrates the increase in complexity as a system grows.

Coupling

Complexity is not the same as coupling, as most practitioners understand coupling. *Coupling* refers to the extent that components rely on the internal details of other components. In a well-designed system, internal changes will not impair other components as long as designated external interfaces are not affected. In a loosely coupled system, all interaction between components is through defined interfaces. Closely coupled components go beyond defined external interfaces and use characteristics of components that are not intentionally exposed. If a closely coupled component requires a modification, the effect of the modification on the relationship between the couple components is unpredictable without examining the code of both components. Closely coupled systems are usually the result of loosely defined external interfaces, or an architecture in which the boundaries between components are not well defined.

An example of close coupling is an application that uses the content of a file written by another application. If the format of the file is not publicly exposed and defined, the developers of the component that wrote the file will assume they are free to modify the structure and semantics of the file as they see fit and not worry about affecting other components. If a component is closely coupled, it may rely on the structure and semantics of the file. If the developers of the first component decide to modify the structure of the file, the second component is likely to fail.

Complexity is on a different level. A loosely coupled system can suffer from complexity, and a closely coupled system may not be excessively complex.

Even though the internals of each component remain private, a complex system may fail when each component is performing exactly as specified, but the content and frequency of inputs and outputs change. Complexity describes a situation where the output and input of applications are intricate, where the action of one application is dependent on inputs from several other applications.

Complexity addresses the nature of the exchanges of information between components. In a simple system, a change in the input to a component causes a predictable change in the output of a component receiving the output of the first component. In a complex system, a change in the input to the first component causes an output that is dependent on outputs from several other components. In simple situations, coders can rely on simple tables of possible inputs and outputs. However, most applications today are affected by more than simple input. Often the timing and sequence of inputs are factors. Also, the number and possible values of inputs can make preparation and evaluation of input and output tables impractical because the tables become intractably large. Typically, in complex situations, the performance of the system is predictable most of the time, but when the circumstances are extreme, the system may not perform predictably. Unfortunately, the extreme situations are often precisely when we hope that a system is rock-solid.

Support

Every time an application is integrated into an environment, more integration pathways are opened. Service desks are frequently an integration center because issue creation and response become more automated, as they must in a growing enterprise. Integration with the security system resets passwords. Integration with performance management generates automatic warnings at the service desk of slowing processes. Integration with the HR system puts a user in the service desk user-list automatically when the employee is hired. Often, each connection is made as a need arises and without consideration to an overall design.

As a system becomes more complex, detecting, diagnosing, and remediating issues become more difficult. For example, a service desk application may be designed to automatically generate a service desk incident document when the performance of a set of applications dips below a minimum level. Here's a trivial example of complexity: one of the instrumented applications begins to thrash, consuming resources at an unexpectedly high rate, but no longer passing tasks to a second application. The resource consumption of the second application drops because it is receiving zero requests from the failing application. Consequently, the idle second application and the thrashing first application average out to normal consumption. In isolation, neither high nor low resource usage indicates a problem in either application. To respond correctly, the integrated support system has to have logic that recognizes the dependency between the two applications. But this is questionable architecture because removing or changing either of the applications could require changes in the logic in the integrated support application. Good design can mitigate this kind of dependency, but designers must be aware of the potential problems.

Unpredictability

One of the worst consequences of complexity is unpredictability. When applications are connected, predicting and understanding the consequences of modifying one application can become difficult. The more complex the connections, the more difficult prediction becomes. The worst part is that the unpredicted effects of a change may appear remote from the change.

For example, when two applications are integrated, one application may receive data from the other, and the receiving application may have to wait for data from the other; in other words, one application may be starving the other application for data. Data starvation can be difficult to analyze and remediate. A complex application may have hundreds of threads, each spending most of its time waiting for data or events. Detecting the threads on the critical path at any given time is difficult. If the holdup is discovered, there are several solutions. One solution is to modify the first application to supply data more readily. This will solve the problem, but fixing a defect in one application by changing another application only masks the vulnerability of the second application. On a different day, the second application could fail because yet another element of the environment slows down. Another approach is to modify the receiving application to be resilient to data starvation. This is only one example of the ways in which applications may become coupled when they are integrated. These kinds of relationships contribute to the complexity of the system.

Proliferation and Brittle Systems

Unfortunately, some increase in complexity is inevitable. Relationships often are complex, and knowledge is required to handle the system well. This is part of the overhead of business expansion.

As the enterprise grows, integration becomes more complex. This complexity can become a business-crippling problem because complexity can make systems brittle. A brittle system will fail catastrophically when small, apparently inconsequential changes are made.

Expanding or changing a brittle system to meet new needs is likely to affect portions of the system that have only a tenuous relationship with the change. When a system is brittle, even the simplest fix or update can demand a high level of technical expertise, possibly detailed knowledge of the entire system, to avoid disaster. This consumes inordinate time and resources. The most skilled members of the development team are diverted from critical forward-looking projects and forced to deal with the simplest problems. This can result in a development team that is turned on its head: the best and most knowledgeable developers perform maintenance that ought to be simple, while challenging new projects are assigned to junior engineers, whose inexperience contributes to future complexity. As complexity increases, brittleness becomes harder to avoid. A small change in a component may cause a massive change in the behavior of the system.

Integration typically involves resource constraints as well as data constraints. Communication between applications is typically easier and faster when applications run on the same server. However, on the same server, one application can be starved for CPU due to the activity of the other application. Again, the system may have to be managed by load balancing or other means to avoid contention, which may have been preventable with better integration design.

The sophistication and internal complexity of applications is not so much a concern here. Complex applications may be involved, and they usually increase the integration challenge, but we are concerned here with the system: a group of applications with intertwined inputs and outputs. Understandably, when developers design an application, they tend to concentrate on the functionality of the application they are building and pay less attention to the external applications they may interact with. Designing external interfaces intentionally is usually the solution to this problem. Service Oriented Architecture (SOA) has put new emphasis on external interfaces, which has helped with integration complexity. However, the burgeoning of external interfaces helps only one aspect of the problem. Interfaces isolate the internal code of an application from integrated applications. However, this does not necessarily decrease the complexity of dependencies among applications.

Typically, integrators enter the scene long after the application is developed. When interfaces are clearly defined, their task is much easier, and many blunders of the past are circumvented. The problem of complex dependencies has to be addressed with a thorough understanding of what the applications do and how they interact in production.

Careful planning can ameliorate the effects of a growing system that encompasses expanding functionality.

ITIL and Complexity

When applications are designed to be integrated and the integrated system is designed as an integrated whole rather than a patchwork of applications, the resulting system is usually less complex, consequently more robust, and less brittle. ITIL practices begin with strategic planning of a coherent system that is tailored exactly to the business needs of the enterprise. With strong leadership that understands both business and technical challenges, the ITIL continual improvement cycle is effective in reducing complexity. However, the approach is dependent on leadership that can bring many different perspectives to the table and produce plans that satisfy all the stakeholders and yet retain a simple and vigorous architecture. Finding and empowering this kind of leadership is a formidable challenge.

Most organizations do not implement ITIL practices all at once. Most often, they implement a single practice or a single group of practices at a time. Many sites begin to adopt ITIL by implementing a service desk that follows ITIL practices. In many cases, implementing an ITIL service desk first has improved service levels and effectively proved the worth of ITIL practices in the organizations that adopt ITIL practices. However, single applications or groups of applications do not automatically help reduce system complexity.

The ITIL continual improvement pattern establishes a managed service portfolio with an infrastructure designed to support the entire portfolio instead of infrastructure to support individual services. This pattern has the potential to rationalize, simplify, and streamline integration. The pattern implies that the integration requirements of each component of the system will be examined and optimized at a high level.

Unfortunately, even where the value of a strategic plan is appreciated, there are obstacles. Advanced planning is often difficult in a fluid corporate world where business units are acquired, sold off, and merged. The IT system must change rapidly, incorporating new or different technology, replacing technology that has left with a departing business, and fusing together similar but not identical technologies. When time pressure is great, there often is little time or expertise to invest in designing a strategic portfolio with simplicity built into the infrastructure architecture.

Organizations that recognize the danger in growing complexity can act to reduce complexity or slow its rate of increase. One solution is to choose a single source for an integrated suite of products. This solution uses the engineering skills of the authors of the suite to help tame complexity and supplements the skills of the enterprise IT team.

An alternative approach is careful architecture by the enterprise IT team, developing a plan that avoids redundancy and unnecessary connections between applications while promoting consistency and reliability. This approach puts responsibility for a strong integration design on the enterprise IT team. Not all IT teams are willing or able to take on that responsibility, but the return is independence and flexibility. One element of this approach is to include clouds in the system design.

Often, the two approaches are different roads to the same end. A team that starts out aiming to plug carefully chosen products into their own architecture may find that they are consistently choosing products from a single vendor or a small group of vendors. A team that decides to leave responsibility to their vendors will usually find that there are aspects of their business that no vendor can help with and they have to come up with their own integration plan.

Cloud Systems

A cloud can be used in many ways to support integrated enterprise IT services. Stripped of all the business characteristics such as metered usage that go with external ownership, a cloud is a pool of computing resources, usually remote. These resources are in the form of computing machines, data storage units, and network facilities. Both computing and storage are usually virtual; cloud consumers do not interact directly with physical resources. Instead, the cloud provider offers an interface that acts like familiar operating systems and storage appliances such as disk drives. The simulation of the familiar environment is exact enough that consumers can run the applications they ran on their local premises on the cloud with few modifications.

The familiar patterns of cloud services (Infrastructure as a Service, Platform as a Service, and Software as a Service) offer ascending levels of abstraction to the consumer. Each level of abstraction presents a new set of benefits and challenges that apply to enterprise integration.

The initial impetus for a growing organization to begin to use cloud implementations is often to acquire computing capacity quickly and cheaply. This is especially true for technology-oriented organizations whose expansion is directly tied to expanding computing capacity. Using metered IaaS resources that can be expanded and contracted rapidly and easily, these companies can stretch their investors' dollars and advance quickly. These organizations are lucky: they do not have a legacy of systems that must be integrated into cloud expansion. Their choices will be relatively simple, and they have the luxury of building on a cloud platform with the potential to avoid many of the issues that IT has dealt with for years.

Advantages of Cloud for Integration

The three axes of enterprise IT growth described apply also to cloud implementations. Cloud-based applications, particularly SaaS applications, solve some integration issues for both large and small businesses. In fact, one of the issues facing large enterprises is the possibility of abandoning an integrated system that is the product of large sunk investments in both money and innovation over decades for an off-the-shelf service that solves integration issues easily and cheaply from the viewpoint of the end user.

Figure 8-1 depicts a traditional branch accounting system that is reminiscent of mainframe architectures and was typical in the early days of desktop accounting.

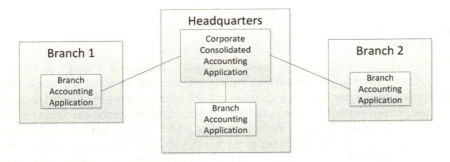

Figure 8-1. Traditional integrated accounting for branch offices

Each branch had its own accounting system. Headquarters also had its own accounting system with the same functionality as the branch systems. A corporate consolidated accounting system took input from each of the branch systems and produced combined statements that reflected the entire enterprise. Like mainframe systems that accumulated transactions through the day and then ran a batch job to post those transactions to the master record, these early distributed systems periodically updated corporate systems at headquarters. In its earliest form, the update might involve physically transporting a tape to the central system and returning a tape with updates on things like prices to be applied to a remote system. Later, the transmission was via a modem acoustically coupled to the telephone system. Eventually, these ad hoc methods were replaced by leased communication lines, private networks, and eventually public networks, such as the Internet. With faster data transport, batch updates evolved into transactional updates.

There are several problems with this approach. Managers in branch offices had to wait for the delivery of corporate reports to view their branch in the corporate context, comparing the performance of their branch with other branches and similar tasks. Infrequent updates of the corporate system meant that the corporate books were only periodically coordinated with dynamic situations. For maintenance, each branch required staff with the technical skills to administer and maintain the branch application. When a patch or update was needed, the patch or update had to be applied at each branch.

The cloud equivalent deploys a single copy of the application on a central cloud. End users access the application from their devices via HTTP, as illustrated in Figure 8-2. This is an improvement over Figure 8-1 Using a cloud, there is only one instance of the application to maintain, back up, and provide with disaster recovery and failover. Employees can use the application off the premises, and they can use a range of devices to access the application. In other words, employees are not tied to specific hardware or locations.

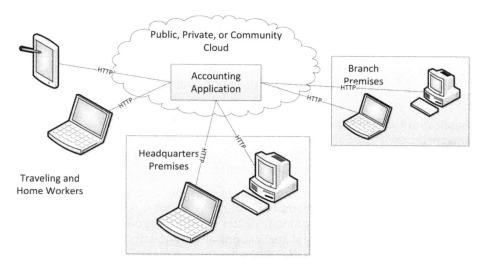

Figure 8-2. A cloud implementation of a distributed accounting system using HTTP for communication

NATIVE CLOUD APPLICATIONS
VS.
APPLICATIONS DEPLOYED ON A CLOUD

A native cloud application is designed and constructed to run in a cloud environment. Not all applications running on a cloud are native. Some are ported from a local physical environment to a virtual cloud environment that is likely to be remote. One of the attractions of an IaaS cloud is the possibility of porting to the cloud instead of building for the cloud and gaining the benefits of utility computing without investing in new applications and suffering the disruption exacted by new applications.

Native cloud applications have some important advantages over ported applications. They can be designed to scale well, recover from disasters more gracefully, and take advantage of cloud accessibility and distribution between cloud installations. They can also be designed to minimize some of the downsides of cloud deployment such as network unreliability and latency.

Cloud implementations usually use HTTP or HTTPS as the transport between the end user and the application. Consequently, large segments of the implementation are off-the-shelf, often open source, software. This decreases development costs and allows developers to concentrate on business logic rather than lower-level architecture.

The application can be supplied as a service from a third party. In that case, the service provider takes responsibility for maintaining the application in the cloud. The provider is usually responsible for maintenance, backup, disaster recovery, and failover. Maintenance usually includes updates and patches, and the provider takes responsibility for the performance of the application in the cloud.

Applications treated as a service do not necessarily involve a third party. An enterprise can build SaaS architecture in a private or public cloud, operate the application as a service to their employees, and gain many of the same advantages as SaaS applications from third parties.

Expanding the perimeter of the business presents one type of integration challenge that cloud implementations often ease, but a different set of challenges arise as the IT environment of the business becomes more complex, increasing both the number of applications and transaction volume that must be integrated into the fabric of the business.

For standard applications such as customer relationship management (CRM), human resources management, or service desk, there are SaaS applications available that will work well for them. All of these applications need to be integrated; onboarding a new employee into the HR SaaS application should not have to be repeated when the same employee has to open a service desk ticket. A new sales rep onboarded into the HR SaaS application should automatically appear as a sales rep in the CRM system.

Integrating these systems in a SaaS cloud is more dependent on the cloud SaaS vendor than installations on the local premises. Although integration of off-the-shelf software is dependent on the provisions made by the vendor for integration, the consumer still controls the environment in which the software runs.

The appearance of cloud-based systems has simplified many challenges for both smaller and larger businesses.

Small and medium businesses have especially benefitted from SaaS, which offers applications to small and medium businesses on affordable terms that are equal in complexity and power to those used by larger enterprises. Many of these SaaS applications are designed to meet enterprise integration requirements.

Nevertheless, even if a business chooses only to use SaaS, they still need to be aware of cloud integration challenges to plan their entire system well and choose the right products to include.

The previous chapter discussed a single type of integration: service management applications. Integrated IT is a bigger challenge: service management applications are only a subset of the total system, and the interchange of data and control in a complete IT system is more varied and complex. The SKMS system of the previous chapter is a data collection system; a few service management applications involve control as well as data, but service management is usually devoted to exposing data to service managers and planners. When we step beyond managing services and begin to concern ourselves with delivering services, we enter a more complex environment of integration.

Other chapters have discussed why enterprises need to be integrated. Even a novice wagon-master knows that the wagon train moves faster and farther when all the horses pull in the same direction, and every business manager knows that an enterprise at cross-purposes with itself is not likely to succeed for long. Integrating IT means establishing the communications paths that make IT services work together.

Building an Integrated Cloud

Building an integrated IT system begins with planning. In an ITIL environment, planning is the purview of Service Strategy and Service Design. The core of ITIL Service Strategy and Service Design is the service portfolio, which lists in detail all the internal and external services offered by the IT department. The service portfolio is oriented toward business decisions. It details how the services support lines of business and provides the information necessary for executive management to make business decisions about adding new services and decommissioning services that no longer serve a business purpose.

Top-Down Design

This information is useful as a starting point for designing a technical architecture that supports strategic business plans for IT services efficiently. The service portfolio usually will provide a framework that determines the volume, geographic spread, and complexity of the IT services. In many cases, the service portfolio either spells out or implies the integration requirements for the system. Integration is more easily simplified from the top-down view of the service portfolio than the bottom-up view built, while integration requirements are identified as they appear in production.

This top-down approach has clear advantages, but it can easily turn into a waterfall methodology in which barriers are erected between development and design. These barriers, which are erected with all good intention, prevent developers from responding to a changing IT environment.

Software architects should be aware of the possibility of slipping into a waterfall mode and act to avoid its barriers.

Software design is not like designing a bridge or a skyscraper. Software is infinitely malleable, even in its smallest details. A bridge designer is constrained to a few types of girder connectors because the connectors are manufactured and too expensive to build to order. The designer must choose among the connectors available that meet the engineering requirements, which are clearly understood and specified. These choices have to be made before the first girder is erected. After the choice is made, changes will be expensive and require a formal change order with several levels of approval.

The software designer also has prebuilt components in the form of software libraries and standard modules, but they are not as constraining as the component of a physical structure. Their strengths and limitations are not spelled out in tidy numeric tables. Software code is much more easily changed than a steel connector, and developers are often able to make substantial improvements with little effort by changing the details of designs. In addition, the product built from a software design is not as easy to project as the product of a bridge blueprint. Often, only after a software project has begun do some defects or deficiencies become clear. Not to take advantage of the opportunities to correct or improve the design when opportunities appear can result in projects that do not meet their promise.

Consequently, a pure top-down design is often problematic in software but still has important advantages. Balancing the two extremes is one of the key challenges to software architecture.

Planning

An integrated business system has both requirements that are specific to their business and requirements that are common to most systems. Business rules can be complex with many exceptions and special circumstances. They are also likely to change as a business evolves. Examples of business-specific requirements are the details of writing and tracking rental agreements in an equipment rental business where the business rules may differ for each type of equipment. Temporary special deals and negotiated agreements may be common, which make business rules not only complex but also dynamic. However, even an exceptionally atypical business will have architectural requirements for integration that they share with most other businesses.

Architectural Fundamentals for Integrated Systems

The fundamentals in this section specifically apply to the integration of applications and components into integrated IT systems. These fundamentals apply to clouds as well as systems installed on the premises. Architects are often challenged to combine systems on the premises. To this, they may have to add applications deployed on SaaS, PaaS, IaaS, and on-premises applications into a single system.

Each application in the system must communicate with other applications in such a way that data is available when and where it is needed

This is the basic tenet of integration. Data must be available where the business needs it. That may mean that the output of one application flows into another or that managing the system requires data from one (or several) to be available for management viewing. This requirement is fraught with difficulties. If there is no overall plan, the common tendency is to patch together connections between applications as needed in the easiest way available. When a connection to an additional application is needed, the easiest way to connect often changes. Consequently, a new communications channel is opened. Opening new channels invites complexity. This is especially bad where adding a new application adds its own complexity in addition to integration complexity.

A master plan can be helpful. A spoke-and-hub[5] or message-bus[6] design pattern for integration can provide the discipline to keep the number of data channels down and make data available where it is needed without a special code for each application.

A spoke-and-hub architecture has a central hub where all integration information is collected and distributed as needed to the integrated applications. A bus architecture has an information bus. Each application puts its information available for integration on the bus and may receive information from other applications off the bus. Both of these architectures are easier to understand than complex point-to-point integration. These architectures also make it easier to add new integrated applications without adding complexity. See Figure 8-3.

---

[5]For more discussion on spoke and hub architectures, see www.enterpriseintegration patterns.com/ramblings/03_hubandspoke.html. Accessed September 2015.

[6]For a detailed discussion of the message bus pattern, see Gregor Hohpe and Bobby Wolfe. *Enterprise Integration Patterns*. Boston: Addison-Wesley, 2004 (Kindle location 3386). Note that a message bus and an enterprise service bus (ESB) are not identical. An ESB provides access to services, frequently via SOAP web services. A message bus provides access to data and events, not necessarily services.

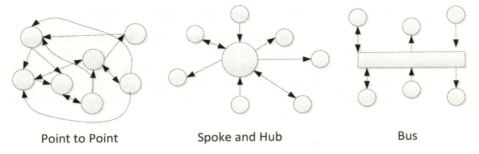

Point to Point   Spoke and Hub   Bus

Figure 8-3. Spoke-and-hub and bus architectures are easier to decipher than point-to-point architectures

Internal members of the organization and consumers of the organization's services must have access to integrated data and services

It is understood that integrated data should be available to the people and processes that want and need the information. Unfortunately, this often is not as easy as it ought to be. The data may be present and even flow from application to application. However, the data channels used by individual applications may not be accessible. For example, if two applications communicate via a hard-coded socket-to-socket link, tapping into the information flow between the applications will probably require substantial refactoring and possibly additional communications links. If the information flowing over the link is in a form that depends on implementation details of the connected applications, data interfaces may have to be redesigned to decouple the applications. Spoke-and-hub and bus architectures avoid this difficulty by providing a uniform communications channel that is designed for additional components or applications to tap into without disturbing individual applications or the fundamental architecture.

Integration should not open security holes

There is always a possibility that integration will reveal information or enable functionality that should not be accessible. The authors of an application are usually keenly aware of the security requirements for the data and functionality they manage and assume that data and functionality exposed for integration will be treated with the same awareness. However, the authors of an integrated application may be much less aware of the issues and inadvertently disclose information they should not.

An example of this can occur when a multi-application dashboard is added to a system. Usually a dashboard is designed so that the user can choose from a range of data to display from each application for a dashboard tailored exactly to their needs. However, not all users may be authorized to view all the data.

An ordinary user able to configure the dashboard to display private HR information, such as Social Security numbers, is a security breach. The dashboard becomes a backdoor into HR that circumvents the HR authorization system. The dashboard must be designed to display only data that all dashboard users are authorized to view, or the dashboard must be smart enough to check the user's authorization before displaying data.

Generally, a user who is denied access to some data or aspect of a service ordinarily should also be denied access to the same data or functionality through other integrated services. There may be exceptions to this principle when the integrated application has authorization rules that are allowed to override authorizations in other applications. Architects and developers should be aware of the potential for opening security holes and act to prevent them. A design that has a single security system that is called on to manage all authentication and authorization following manageable policies that reach to integrated data and activities will be much easier to manage than a design in which security is built into each application.

In addition, architects should be aware that an integrated application that handles sensitive integrated data must be protected from outside access as carefully as the originating application. Mobile apps provide a good example of this. Suppose a mobile app is planned for mortgage brokers to enable work outside the office. The mobile app is expected to integrate with corporate servers and provide a full range of data to the mobile broker. However, a mobile app usually emphasizes hassle-free access, not ironclad, security. If a developer does not make a special effort to secure the data and functionality provided by the app, the mobile app could invite devastating security breaches by exposing private data to anyone who happens to pick up the phone with the app installed.

User privacy required for business purposes or mandated by laws and regulations must not be violated by integration

Most systems, especially financial, medical, and systems that manage data from the European Union, must guarantee that access to data follows exacting privacy requirements. For example, regulations may require data to be encrypted as well as protected from unauthorized access. There may be special requirements for the disposal of data and other aspects of data management. Integration architects must note that an application that is integrated with a regulated application is also subject to regulation. The system must not only protect privacy under normal operations. It must also protect privacy from unintended or malicious access.

These requirements are best treated as guidelines to follow at all stages in developing the system. They have wide consequences for application design and implementation. For example, the security requirement may seem obvious, but implementing authentication and authorization uniformly across several applications can place detailed requirements on application design that reach deep into the workings of the code.

New features must be cheap and easy to integrate without affecting production services

Adding new applications and services is easy at the beginning but often becomes difficult and expensive as the system matures.

Point-to-point integration is often a seductive mistake. With only a few applications to manage, a quick integration (say reading a table in from another application to integrate the two applications) may be quick and easy. Convincing upper management to invest in a hub-and-spoke or bus architecture is a hard sell. The immediate return on the investment is low compared to the quick alternative.

If the enterprise continues to grow in volume, geographic spread, and complexity, as many successful enterprises do, eventually the system may become so cumbersome that adding or modifying an application is no longer easy and quick. Instead, it takes a master architect who understands the history of the system to tap into the application. The effects of the addition are often unpredictable, and making the addition may take weeks of tinkering to get the whole system working properly.

At this point, the enterprise must decide to pay the price of an architectural solution, which will be much higher than it was when the system was simple, or they must be content with the system as it stands.

The user experience, both internal and external, of the integrated system must aid rather than hinder growth in productivity

Perhaps this principle should be unstated, but it is occasionally ignored. Integration must improve the system. Systems can be improved in several ways. They can become more efficient by requiring fewer system resources to accomplish the same tasks. They can become more transparent by exposing data and functionality that can be used by functions such as audit and security. They can be made more reliable or easier to maintain. However, the most important way a system improves is by enabling greater productivity.

Any system that hinders productivity growth should be rethought and redesigned. This applies equally to integration. Integration can lead to displays of irrelevant information, may degrade performance, or may cause system unpredictability. These problems often arise when integration is pursued for its own sake. Integration must be justified by business requirements, not architectural elegance or because it is easy. When integration begins to hinder productivity, a review of the enterprise's approach to integration should be considered. Often this will be a job for an ITIL strategy team.

Architectural Fundamentals That Affect Integration

The fundamentals outlined in the previous section all apply specifically to enterprise integration. Other fundamentals apply to all IT systems that effective integrated systems also rely upon.

Avoid needless data duplication

This is an informal statement of a principle related to the relational database third normal form requirement. Third normal form requires all the data in a row is dependent only on the key and not depend on other elements of the row. Stated formally, third normal form may be confusing, but it is easily spotted in practice. When a column in a table has repeated data that could be placed in another table to avoid the repetition, the data is probably out of third normal form.

Following third normal form prevents inconsistencies between tables. Avoiding data duplication between applications prevents inconsistencies in a similar way. Figure 8-4 illustrates abstracting user phone extensions maintained in two applications to a single directory application. Abstracting the extension to the directory avoids the possibility that one application has the correct extension and the second application has an out-of-date extension. The correct extension need only be maintained in the directory application. By not duplicating the phone extension data in applications A1 and A2, this architecture both simplifies administration and avoids inconsistency in the integrated application.

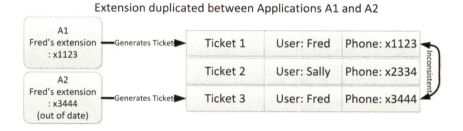

Figure 8-4. Avoiding duplicate data prevents inconsistencies

The principles for integration and relational databases are analogous, not identical, mainly because references such as embedded foreign keys are usually more quickly resolved in a database management system than between integrated applications. In Figure 8-4, the usernames, Fred and Sally, are the embedded foreign keys because they can be used to look up the phone extension.

Even in relational databases, schemas are sometimes denormalized in order to improve performance by accepting some consistency issues in return for decreased overhead with fewer lookups. For application integration, the performance issues can be much more severe because querying another application may be more resource intensive than a database lookup. Often application queries can increase rather than decrease complexity and brittleness in a system because they complicate the mesh of dependencies. In Figure 8-4, the duplicated phone extension introduces the possibility of inconsistent and incorrect extensions in tickets, but moving the extension to a directory application could slow down ticket creation because an additional remote call is necessary to get the extension to be included in the ticket.

There is no clear-cut answer to choosing when to duplicate data. Performance, accuracy, and complexity all have to evaluated and balanced as well as possible.[7] Often a caching scheme can help. In a hub-and-spoke architecture, caches can be part of the hub. Bus architecture can have a cache attached to the bus.

Scalable and elastic systems to handle varying workloads are required in most enterprises

This fundamental truth will be addressed more in Chapter 11 because elastic design is a basic virtualization and cloud characteristic. The favored method for building scalable systems today is to build parallel processes that can be scaled up and down by adding and subtracting processors and processes running on the processors. This is the basic principle behind large datacenters with thousands of computers running parallel processes.

---

[7]When storage was expensive, data duplication was avoided to save storage space. I cannot recall a single instance in my experience when a decision to deduplicate data solely to save storage space was a good decision. The code complexity and maintenance never justified the cost savings. Of course, the fact that the price of storage has decreased continuously for a long time has something to do with this, but not entirely. Infrastructure costs seldom exceed the cost of complexity. There are many good reasons for avoiding duplication, but saving storage is seldom one of them.

In distributed environments, including clouds, eventual consistency, discussed in note 4, puts a premium on availability over consistency but insists that the system eventually attain consistency. This applies to caches as well as data stores.

Unfortunately, integration and parallelization don't always get along well. A parallelized task can be no faster than its slowest thread. Consequently, a thread waiting for data from an external integrated process is likely to hold up the entire task. There are various ways to avoid this kind of situation. One method is to cache data from the external process so it is always instantly available to the task's threads. In a hub-and-spoke or bus integration architecture, caches can be built into the hub or the bus to buffer the effects of slower processes.

When designing an integrated system, data availability can be important for supporting acceptable performance levels as volume scales up. Although initial designs may not need facilities for high-speed availability, designs should allow for future requirements.

The system must be reliable. Outages must be brief and seldom, even in the midst of disaster

Integration and system reliability can be in opposition. The more integrated a system is, the more each component relies upon other components. Unless measures are taken to avoid it, the failure of one component may affect several others. Each of these may affect others, and eventually the entire system may stall. Alternate sources, system redundancy, strategic data caching, and awareness of availability versus consistency all can help increase reliability. It is also important to consider failover and disaster recovery. The key problem in failover is transferring state from the failing system to the failover system. An integration hub or bus can be designed to help with this by keeping clues to the integrated data available to the integrated processes at any time. This facility can also be useful in disaster recovery.

Maintenance must be minimal. Service outages for maintenance are not desirable

Software maintenance includes a wide range of activity and becomes more important as enterprises grow. One important aspect of maintenance is keeping up with software revisions. In a small business, replacing an application with a revision may be annoying, but it can usually be done without devastating effort. As enterprises grow and become more integrated, revisions can become more difficult. If the integration is not done through a documented interface, integration code often has to be rewritten and retested, which can be quite painful. Instead of running an install script that smoothly and silently replaces the previous version with no or only a short pause in production, someone has to design and write new code, create a test bed, and complete testing. Then, an error-prone manual installation of the new code threatens to further halt production. Large-scale integrated applications can take days to install and bring into full production if efficient upgrading is not given consideration in the fundamental architecture and each individual integration.

Parallelism provides a fundamental solution to maintenance issues. When several parallel processes are running, the whole system can be designed to keep running while individual processes are shut down for maintenance. This pattern can also be followed even when there is usually only one process. If an updated process and the production process can run at the same time and the production load transferred to the updated process, maintenance can proceed with minimal interruption.

Cloud Requirements

Cloud changes the business of IT significantly, but reliable integrated systems have the same basic requirements on the cloud as they have on the enterprise premises.

The fundamentals discussed in the previous two sections apply to applications and components running on the enterprise premises as well as clouds. The foundation for efficient and reliable traditional systems does not differ from the foundation for cloud-based systems.

Nevertheless, clouds have important special characteristics. Clouds are almost entirely virtual, and they are separated from the enterprise by network links, often over the Internet.

Virtual machines themselves run almost identically with their physical counterparts. However, because they are virtual, they can be added or removed from the system more easily and more rapidly than their physical equivalents. That means that the system, particularly the integration system, must be prepared to deal with a more dynamic environment. A physical system, which depends on hard-coded addresses to maintain connections between processes, is slow and annoying to change when reconfiguring the system, but it works. In a dynamic virtual environment, it can be a disaster. Consequently, message bus or spoke-and-hub patterns that manage dynamic addressing are even more important in cloud deployments.

Virtual systems can also be quickly reconfigured to be distributed to remote datacenters. This can be especially useful during failover and disaster recovery, but the movement may also introduce changes in latency between processes, and network reliability issues may appear, which the integration system may need to deal with.

Network performance and interruptions are more significant in cloud deployments. Generally, provisions for supporting availability and restoring data consistency after network issue must be more robust when a system is deployed on a cloud. Mobile devices maintain availability and eventual consistency by caching on the local device and then reconciling the cache with data in the cloud. The consistency and availability challenge on mobile devices is formidable because wireless connections to mobile devices are more vulnerable than conventional networks. However, as reliable as a network may be, in most cases applications are required to be available and consistency, must be restored after an interruption. Robust cloud-deployed systems must take this into consideration.

Conclusion

Although these requirements are diverse and complex, they are not impossible to meet. In fact, they are goals that have directed enterprise application design for a long time, and most design patterns used in enterprise applications are intended to support these requirements. Cloud implementations face all the problems of implementations limited to the enterprise premises. However, in some cases, some of the effort required for integration is taken on by the cloud provider. In other cases, the cloud architecture itself helps with good integration design. In all cases, sound integration depends on understanding the enterprise integration requirements and establishing an architecture that will support those requirements as the enterprise grows.

EXERCISES

1. Identify and describe an application that is not integrated and whose enterprise benefits would degrade if it were integrated into the enterprise information technology fabric. If you cannot think of any, explain why such an application is so difficult to find.

2. Describe the three ways that growing enterprises expand.

3. How does increasing volume affect an enterprise?

4. How does increasing geographic spread affect an enterprise?

5. Explain why increasing complexity is difficult for expanding enterprises to avoid.

6. Explain how integration can result in security holes.

The Contenders

Enterprise Integration Architectural Patterns

SUMMARY

This chapter is called "The Contenders" because it describes enterprise integration that does not rely on a cloud implementation. An enterprise that has chosen not to pursue cloud implementations can use the patterns and architectures described here. On the other hand, the patterns of this chapter are frequently used in cloud implementations, although modifications are sometimes needed.

The chapter focuses on three aspects of integration: data transmission, data routing, and data translation. These are the three basic requirements for integrating applications.

The preceding chapter described some of the guiding requirements on enterprise integration. This chapter describes some of the architectural patterns that implement these requirements. Software architects often describe systems with "design patterns." The contents of this chapter are best understood as design patterns.

Design Patterns

Design patterns are a common way of describing the principles underpinning software architecture and are a basic tool for planning software architecture. The method was originally created to express basic design components of dwellings and other structures, but the method applies well to software architecture.

A design pattern is a solution to a frequently occurring architectural problem. The pattern describes the problem and solution in a form that architects can use to identify recurring problems and implement common solutions in widely varying contexts. In software, design patterns are not tied to any programming language, operating system, or computing platform. The classic textbook of software design patterns is *Design Patterns: Elements of Reusable Object-Oriented Software* by Erich Gamma, Richard Helm, Ralph Johnson, and John Vlissides.[1]

Although the title of the classic text may suggest that design patterns are tied to object-oriented programming, they are, in fact, programming paradigm neutral. Objects may be the natural idiom for some design patterns, but most are equally applicable to other paradigms such as resource- or service-oriented programming.

Software design pattern books frequently use a set format, usually derived from the format used in the *Design Patterns* book and intended to make it easy for architects and developers to find and apply them to their work.

Enterprise IT architects have found the design pattern approach useful. The same enterprise architecture issues appear repeatedly, but enterprises vary widely, and other approaches to software reuse often are not sufficient. For example, code libraries for low-level programming constructs are efficient and widely used, saving millions of lines of code and promoting robust and efficient applications. Higher-level business libraries have been much less successful because business rules and conditions vary so widely. Business rules are often made up on the spot when business deals are negotiated. They address complex circumstances and business pressures. The resulting rules are often innovations that will not fit into established libraries. This wild variation can make business programming more difficult than other areas of software design.

Nevertheless, the same patterns and solutions recur on a high level, even in business. Reusable code often cannot address these recurring situations because the code may need to be radically different to address the specifics of innovative rules and complicated circumstances. However, these issues can be addressed with design patterns that describe solutions on a high level, which can be implemented with appropriate site-specific code. Developers can write appropriate code more quickly and with fewer defects by following guidance provided by patterns and solutions. Also, code that follows an established pattern is more easily and quickly understood by other programmers.

An example of a design pattern is a pattern to address idiosyncratic units of measure. Some businesses use units of measure that are not unique to their business. One business may group small parts in lots of 100. Other businesses group them on lots of a gross, 144. The obvious approach is to write code

---

[1]Eric Gamma, Richard Helm, Ralph Johnson, John Vlissides, *Design Patterns Elements of Reusable Object-Oriented Software*, New York: Addison-Wesley, 1994.

to deal with translation from a unit of 100 to another unit of a gross as they are needed to compare parts counted in gross to parts counted in hundreds. It is simple code and quickly written, often in the comparison function itself. However, a design pattern suggests a better approach: convert to a common unit and use only the common unit in code. Do all calculations and comparisons in the common unit. Experience has shown that this is a better approach because new units can be added without disturbing existing code. If a vendor, for whatever reason, decides to group parts into lots of 1,024 items, as computer engineers count bits on a memory chip, all that is necessary is to add a 1,024 conversion to and from the common unit. The rest of the code will then work properly with the new vendor.

This conversion design pattern can be implemented in any programming language on any platform. The pattern applies whenever incompatible units are used for quantities that must be combined. The discussion in the previous chapter on transforming disparate data sources to a single common model instead of transformations between each model is an example of this pattern. In fact, this design pattern is one of the keys to extensible integration.

A number of design patterns are useful in creating an integrated implementation of an IT system. Here I will discuss integration patterns on a higher level, focusing on the interaction between architectural design and business. The foundation for this focus is the design patterns that can be used to implement the interactions. There are excellent sources on software design patterns that are helpful to developers, but here I will be not be so concerned with implementation and more concerned how the patterns relate to business requirements.[2]

Integration Patterns

Small and uncomplicated systems integrate easily, but as an organization expands, simplicity evaporates. When the number of data sources to integrate goes up, integration may seem to get turned on its head. Patterns that were simple to implement become nightmares. Patterns that seemed to be complex wastes of time begin to beckon like oases in a desert.

---

[2]There are a number of excellent references on design patterns for enterprise and cloud applications. Martin Fowler, "Patterns of Enterprise Application Architecture," New York: Addison-Wesley, 2003, is an excellent starting point. Gregor Hohpe and Bobby Wolfe, *Enterprise Integration Patterns Designing, Building, and Deploying Messaging Solutions*, New York: Addison-Wesley, 2004, takes off where Fowler leaves off. Bill Wilder, *Cloud Architecture Patterns*, O'Reilly: Cambridge, 2012, carries design patterns into the cloud era. Although *Cloud Architecture Patterns* draws on Microsoft Azure for examples, it is much more than an Azure handbook.

The applications in some large enterprises can almost document the history of computing. Some mainframe applications may be decades old. The authors of some applications may have written in mainframe-era FORTRAN, COBOL, and PL/I. Distributed applications that are more recent are likely to be written in C, C++, C#, or Java. Application architectures also often combine Service-Oriented Architecture (SOA) based on SOAP or REST, open source J2EE applications, proprietary integration architectures and tools, and other home-grown or standard architectures. Applications themselves can consist of code written by the IT department (often with the authors long gone); others are off-the-shelf products, perhaps several releases out-of-date, and some are bespoke applications from external vendors. In extreme cases, the source code for old production applications can be lost or exist only in difficult-to-follow assembly language.

This mélange of applications contributes to the complexity that grows as organizations grow. Criticism is easy, but most organizations grow in this way for good reason. Separating the structure of the IT infrastructure and the organizational structure is difficult. Lines of business grow according to the laws of economics and commerce, not hardware and software architecture. Business units want software tailored perfectly to their own needs and maintained to meet their schedules and requirements. Business units clamor for divergent requirements that actually point to the same application, but recognizing this can be nearly impossible for both executive management and the IT department. At the time, separate systems, perhaps built in radically different ways, may seem to be the best solution. And of course, the adage "If it ain't broke, don't fix it" is always attractive, especially to those who do not or cannot anticipate the catastrophes waiting ahead. The long-term implication is chaos, but at every step, the decisions seem like the right thing to do.

The implementation of enterprise integration faces three fundamental technical challenges. Data must be transmitted from application to application. The data must be delivered to the applications that need it. Receivers must understand the data they receive. Often, data must be transformed into a form usable by the receiver. If data does not flow correctly and understandably, integration does not exist.

Data Transmission

The basis for any form of application integration is interapplication data transmission. The methods available to architects have increased with the expansion of technology. As the IT expands and the level of integration increases, different methods become appropriate.

Data Serialization

Data serialization is the process of transforming data structures into a form that can be stored or transmitted over a communications link. Serialization is a part in all data transmission. There are many possible formats for data transition. Wikipedia lists almost 30 well-known serialization formats.[3] When proprietary and one-off programmer-written formats are included, the number must stretch into the thousands. The large number of formats is one of the challenges to integration.

One way to serialize data is to dump data structures exactly as they are laid out in memory into a byte stream and store it in a file or transmit it over a communications link. This is efficient: the dump is fast, the data is represented compactly, and little code is needed. However, memory dumps are seldom suitable for integration because the receiving application must know the exact, byte-for-byte structure of the transmitted data in order to use it. The byte-for-byte structure is dependent on the application data structure, the programming language used in the application, and the memory conventions of the hardware the application was running on. Even minor code changes to the dumping application can change the data structure. A change in the code standard or compiler can break the integration. Moving from one type of hardware processor to another can also break communications. The problems arising from this level of coupling are seldom offset by the speed and efficiency of a memory dump and load back into an identical data structure, but when speed is paramount, it may be the best choice.

Standard and commonly used formats, such as comma-separated values (CSV), Extensible Markup Language (XML), and JavaScript Object Notation (JSON), are an important step forward. These formats do not depend on implementation details or hardware. They all can be parsed using standard parsers. All three have rules for structuring data that do not depend on the internals of the sending or receiving application.

CSV is simple, both to parse and to write, but it conveys the least information. CSV requires each unit of data, datum if you will, to be written out in plain text and each separated from the next with a comma. CSV format does not say anything about content of the datum, except for some rules for handling commas that are in the datum and are not datum separators. Data type, format, and semantics are not touched.[4] For the reading application to use the

---

[3]Wikipedia. "Comparison of data serialization formats." February 8, 2015. http://en.wikipedia.org/wiki/Comparison_of_data_serialization_formats.
[4]CSV is mostly an informal standard. There is an Internet Engineering Task Force (IETF) request for comment, RFC 4180, http://tools.ietf.org/html/rfc4180, but it is informational, not a recommendation. CSV is so common and so simple that most developers don't think about standards for CSV.

data, there must be metadata that describes the data. Often with CSV, there is no attempt to formalize the metadata. Typical older applications bury the metadata in engineering notes or it is passed along as verbal lore.

XML took an important step beyond CSV and CSV-like conventions. The XML authors attempted to develop a self-describing data format. Whether they succeeded or not is a matter of perspective.

Figure 9-1 shows clearly one advantage of CSV: it is more compact than XML. The CSV order uses 2 lines and 49 characters; the XML uses 18 lines and 297 characters.

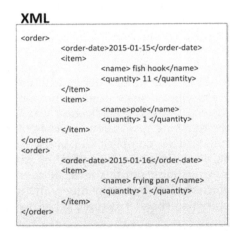

CSV

```
011515, fish hook,11, pole, 1
011615, frying pan,1
```

XML

```
<order>
        <order-date>2015-01-15</order-date>
        <item>
                <name> fish hook</name>
                <quantity> 11 </quantity>
        </item>
        <item>
                <name>pole</name>
                <quantity> 1 </quantity>
        </item>
</order>
<order>
        <order-date>2015-01-16</order-date>
        <item>
                <name> frying pan </name>
                <quantity> 1 </quantity>
        </item>
</order>
```

Figure 9-1. CSV is more compact than XML

Formatting the XML for human readability emphasizes the volume of the XML message, but it also highlights some of the advantages of XML. The XML, although somewhat redundant with end and beginning tags, conveys more information than CSV.

The XML tags show that the document is a list of orders and clarifies the meaning of each field. The first field in the CSV record could be a date, but it could also be a serial number or some other value. In the XML, it is unambiguously a date.

Furthermore, CSV is limited in the data structures it can convey. In this example, the lines of the order repeat: "fish hook" and "pole" are both items. There is no clue in the CSV file itself of the repeating fields. In fact, expressing repeating fields in this way is common, but it is a stretch. Most generic CSV parsers will be confused, and RFC 4180 does not mention the practice. If an application must have a structure more complex than a simple flat file, CSV is usually inadequate.

XML has few limitations on the complexity of the data structures it can express. With the addition of an XML schema (a formal grammar describing the hierarchy, type, and cardinality of each element in the XML document), an XML document can be automatically checked for validity, verifying both structure and data types. For instance, in Figure 9-1, if the order-date were not a date in an acceptable format or the quantity not a numerical type, the validator would reject the file. Where sophisticated security is necessary, a tight XML schema and validation can prevent some kinds of attacks.

The sophistication of XML is also its most important defect. It is relatively hard to learn and interpret; XML Schema more so. Many developers are impatient with the finicky verbiage required to write XML and complicated schema rules. Nonetheless, XML and XML Schema have been widely accepted in web services and SOA.

JSON is similar to XML and based on JavaScript. It is more compact and simpler than XML but not as expressive, a compromise between simple CSV and complex XML. JSON has supplanted XML in areas where simplicity is more important than support for more complex data structures. Also, there was, at least until recently, more standard tooling available for working with XML than JSON, but that is in flux.

However, neither XML nor JSON solves the semantic problem. Standard XML and JSON parsers have eliminated custom parsers for each application that passes data, but that is not all that is needed for integration. In Figure 9-1, "order" may seem clear, but a purchase order and a product order must be accounted for differently. Without some agreement on the exact meaning of the XML tags, they are only approximate and can be misinterpreted. Without additional information, often called metadata, the file cannot be properly interpreted and processed. Sometimes the metadata is expressed in formal documents, but the metadata is also often communicated casually. Casual communication could be as simple as a phone conversation between developers. Casual communication works, but it depends on human memory and note taking and breaks down as a system grows.

XML and JSON are not only used for formatting shared files. In fact, they are probably more used for messaging than anywhere else.[5]

---

[5]XML, JSON, and Yet Another Markup Language (YAML). All perform similar roles. XML is the oldest and expressive but complex and relatively hard to work with. It is used in many enterprise systems and has an extensive array of tooling for parsing, generation, validation, and translation. However, XML is not as popular as it once was. JSON is easy to understand and works naturally with JavaScript. Simplicity has made JSON the language of choice for many new applications, especially those based on REST. YAML is relatively new. It has the same basic syntax as JSON, but it has features that fill in many of the deficiencies of JSON versus XML. YAML may be the compromise of the future.

Data Transformation

Data cannot always be consumed directly by receivers. A classic example is big-endian versus little-endian byte orders. Processors in the Intel x86 family store the most significant byte of a word in the highest address. Processors derived from the IBM mainframe architectures generally store the most significant byte of a word in the lowest address. For data from a big-endian system to be understood correctly on a little-endian system, the data must be transformed from big-endian to little-endian. Without transformation, the letters in a string of text are garbled from one processor architecture to another. Numeric representations and calculations are also mixed up. Until the data is transformed, it cannot be processed.

When integrating systems, transforming between big-endian and little-endian is usually a minor issue because the transformation is often built into hardware. In addition, the transformation is well-known, and a simple algorithm will perform the transformation correctly.

When transferring data and events between applications, transformation is much more difficult. It depends on the form the data is in at the source and the form expected at the target. It may involve semantics: one application may refer to a network interface controller (NIC), while another might call the same thing an Ethernet port. The transformation engine must be able to perform translations like this. Sometimes applications use different units to express the same value. In other cases, two applications may deal with the same virtual or physical object but refer to them in a different way; for example, one application may have a name for the object that identifies it, while another application may use a machine-readable serial number or some other designation. These and more issues have to be resolved in data transformation.

File Sharing

File sharing is generally easy to implement, and the coupling between the sender and receiver is loose. This is especially for files formatted with XML or JSON because parsing is standard, although semantic metadata is still an issue. In addition, the sender and receiver can write and read at any time. They do not depend on either being active, and as long as the format and metadata are clear, neither needs to understand anything of the other's inner-workings.

File sharing is the probably the oldest form of integration. With a few exceptions for simple embedded controllers, all operating systems support some form of files: real or virtual contiguous sequences of bytes that are durable and later retrievable. The life cycle of a file is independent of applications that write or read the file. A file may continue to exist after the application that wrote it has terminated and may exist before an application that reads it has started. An application may write a file that another reads.

These are important properties for integration. An application that is sending data through a file does not need to know anything about the receiver of the data. The receiver also does not need to know about the application that wrote the file, although it must understand the layout of the file on some level. It has to be able to parse the file, that is, to break the file up into individual units of data as the sending application intended, and it must understand the semantics of the data.[6] For example, if the producing program intended a data element to be a 4-byte string designating a user account code, the consuming program must not interpret it as a 32-bit integer containing a market closing price.

File sharing is used as a method of integration more often than it may appear. For example, when users download apps, they are participating in a form of file sharing. A file written in the development environment of the author is transferred to the device. Next, software on the device runs to install the app and prepare it for use. The downloaded file, or some portion of it, remains on the device and is executed when the app runs. This form of file sharing works because the data is extremely "bursty"—one large burst on the initial download and then an occasional patch or update usually separated by days or weeks. File sharing handles this kind of integration between the author's development platform and devices well. Notice, however, that file sharing would absorb unacceptable bandwidth if updates occurred every minute. Other methods are better for activity that is more granular. For example, most apps have a separate communications channel for the app content that is faster and more continuous than file sharing.

Speed is a disadvantage to file sharing. Files are slow to read and write, and they are usually written and read only at relatively long intervals. Thus, file sharing is unsuitable for data that changes faster than a file can be written and read. File sharing is perfectly adequate for a financial application that, when the markets close, writes a file that is read by several other applications to prepare reports for the next morning. But a performance monitoring application that requires hundreds of samples a second and expects up to the second accuracy cannot rely on file sharing to collect data.

Another problem with file sharing is sometimes called *impedance mismatch*. When data from a slow application is combined with a faster application, stale information can be combined with fresh information yielding poor performance or misinformation. Attempting to combine data from a slow-paced financial application with a fast-moving performance monitor might be confusing. Combining up-to-the second performance measures with data that could be as much as 24 hours old could present a distorted picture.

---

[6]Simple file locking is an extreme example of file sharing. The application locking the file or the operating system writes a file with the same name but a different extension as the file to be locked. This extra file signals other applications that the file is not to be touched until the lock file disappears. The existence of the file conveys the essential information. The file is empty or the contents are irrelevant in the simplest case.

For example, the cost of performance at one time of day could appear different than another even though they are the same because financial data gets less accurate as it ages. Therefore, integrators need to be cautious when combining data transfers of different speeds and frequency. This kind of mismatch can occur with any communications method, but the mismatch occurs commonly when the source is an older application that writes files rather than uses a more rapid communications method and the receiver is a more streamlined application.

Database Sharing

When relational databases were new, an enterprise with a single normalized relational database[7] shared by all applications represented the holy grail of integration. It is no longer held in such esteem.

Such a system would have no data duplication, and all data would be equally accessible to all enterprise applications. Using database transaction–enforcement tools, the data would always be consistent. A single version of the data would be available to all applications at the same time. In theory, a clear corporate data dictionary and schema would make application design simple. Maintaining a single database should be easier than maintaining a database for each application.

Disadvantages

Shared databases are excellent in concept but hard to realize. The shared database strategy requires a comprehensive and deep agreement between groups in the enterprise on data formats and semantics. In practice, agreement on the contents and structure of a simple table such as a list of employees can require months of negotiation. In the end, no one is completely satisfied. Within months, the most dissatisfied are likely to start their own tracking in a spreadsheet or personal database. There is a good chance a department's hand-tailored private data store will work better for them than the generic corporate data. The department will then be patted on the back for their improved performance, and the enterprise is on a slippery path back to individual data silos.

After the arduous and politically prickly task of designing such a database is done, new problems arise. If the enterprise is large, database administrators often have difficulty tuning the performance of a database implementation

---

[7]Relational database normalization is a difficult subject. A fully normalized database contains no duplicated information, and each row in the database is independent following rules derived from relational algebra. Replacing good database design with rote normalization can lead to poor performance and complex schemas. Consequently, database normalization is not as well thought of as it was in the past.

that serves many different applications. Different applications use the tables differently; an index design and a page size that improve performance for one application may degrade performance for another. Reaching a compromise that satisfies all the consumers is often difficult.

When multiple applications are sharing data, the opportunities for lock contention increase.[8] In a heavily used transactional database, lock contention is often a significant performance issue. In less-complex and less-used databases, the classic write starvation problem is usually minor. Write starvation occurs when the opportunity to get a write lock is prevented for long periods by read lock holders. The write lock is on hold until all read locks are released. On heavily used databases, write starvation can be a substantial issue. When a table is used in a different way by different applications, write starvation becomes more frequent.

If the database mechanics challenges are met, maintenance and update can still be an issue. The downside of data consistency is close coupling. A common database can be a vicious form of close coupling between applications. Changing a common table (the user table is a good example again) requires the agreement of every application that uses the table. Sometimes adding a new column can be relatively painless, but something such as changing a string length can cause a calamitous series of hidden defects and, in some circumstances, security flaws.

Changes affecting several development groups are seldom politically acceptable. The requirement often has to be addressed with a kluge or workaround. Good design seldom wins over political expediency. When a change is carried out that requires a number of applications to examine or modify code, all the applications are held hostage by the last application to complete the change, which wreaks havoc with scheduling.

The shared database architecture for enterprise integration is elegant but is unfortunately unwieldy in practice, especially in enterprises that have a heterogeneous collection of applications and development groups that follow different coding and design practices.

Common database projects were frequent in the past. Unfortunately, many have failed or were eventually abandoned. In general, they have been replaced by federated approaches that preserve individual databases but maintain active lines of communication. When requirements are cohesive and coordinated and all the parties work exceptionally well together, a shared database can be

---

[8]Transactional database locking is complex, and several methods exist. For this simplified discussion, read locks block changes but not views, and write locks block both changing and viewing. A write lock cannot be taken when a read lock is in place. A row lock may be either a read or write lock and locks a single row. A table lock is like a row lock but locks an entire table. A database lock locks all tables. Some databases can hold only a limited number of locks of any kind. Locks are promoted to reduce the total number of locks.

an excellent solution. Even under those circumstances, business events such as mergers and acquisitions can be difficult to cope with. The upshot is that this strategy usually does not work in the long term and is difficult to implement well in the short term.

The approach works best where a relatively small group of applications share a common semantic and structural view of the data. Under these circumstances, a shared database can be an excellent architectural choice.

Messaging

IP-based messaging is the form of process communication that is used frequently today. Messages transmit data streams, events, and control from application to application, sometimes directly and often via an intermediary queue.

File and database sharing are fundamentally similar. Both push and pull data from a persistent repository. In each case, data is inserted or extracted from a repository. When the repository is a database, the interface is usually through a data access language such as Structured Query Language (SQL). When the repository is a file system, the interfaces are usually composed of operating-system read and write functions and a formatting and parsing facility. Communication takes place through the repository, and the connected applications never have to communicate directly.

Messaging is different. In its fundamental form, no repository is required. One application sends a message directly to another. The receiver reads the message immediately. The messaging pattern does not require storing the message at either end. Both the sender and the receiver can persistently store the message content, but there is no requirement, and storage is incidental to the pattern.

The message pattern has both advantages and disadvantages. It is flexible, fast, and scales up well. A robust messaging application implementation can handle massive quantities of data. Messaging systems can be loosely coupled. Well-designed messaging architectures permit applications to be added and removed easily.

A fundamental shortcoming of messaging is that pure messaging is unreliable without additional mechanisms. If the receiving application is not prepared to receive the message, the message is lost. The link between applications may fail. The message may be garbled in transmission. Neither the sending nor receiving application is likely to know of message failures. In practice, messaging is almost never implemented without infrastructure to manage its reliability. Messaging is still the communications method of choice for most recent applications but almost never without some form of support for greater reliability.

Today, file sharing often takes place via messaging in which entire files or segments of files are transferred via a messaging system. Applications communicate with shared databases via messaging. The same messaging mechanism that transmits messages from network node to network node will also transmit messages between processes running on the same node, giving the design great flexibility in distributing processes. Often, commercially available messaging services can be used. These are often reliable and efficient.

Basic TCP/IP and UDP/IP Communication

Transmission Control Protocol (TCP) and Internet Protocol (IP) combine into the most common messaging protocol in use on the Internet. IP is the addressing function that directs data packets from one source to another. The familiar "example.com" is an IP address translated into a human-readable form. TCP is a protocol that guarantees that data will arrive in the order sent and free of transmission errors.

TCP and IP are two layers in the stack of software that supports the Internet. Since they are usually often used together, TCP/IP has almost fused into a single word. TCP/IP is implemented on almost every hardware platform and on all devices connected to the Internet.

User Datagram Protocol (UDP) over IP is less common than TCP/IP but still important. TCP provides reliable messaging service, but reliability adds overhead, which can reduce performance. UDP does not guarantee either error-free transmission or that data will arrive in the order sent. Therefore, UDP is less reliable, but it is faster. In some situations, such as streaming data, UDP's performance outweighs its unreliability.[9]

Synchronous vs. Asynchronous

Interprocess messaging is divided into synchronous messages and asynchronous messages. Both are used frequently, and both are useful in the right place. Synchrony and asynchrony are independent of protocol, although they are usually implemented on TCP/IP.

Synchronous Messaging

Synchronous messages are something like a telephone service. The caller speaks (sends a message) and waits for a reply. If the wait is too long, the caller hangs up and may or may not call again later. This method has pros and

---

[9]It's worth noting that implementing checks and responses in the communicating applications can render an unreliable protocol such as UDP reliable. Sometimes this is an effective tactic.

cons. The caller always knows the exact state of the communication. If they are calling to shut down their television cable service, they know the service is properly shut down when the service representative tells them it has been shut down.

Instant certainty that the service has ended may be important to some customers, but other customers might choose some uncertainty in return for avoiding a wait, especially when the service center is busy and the wait is long. Sending an e-mail is an alternative to calling. E-mail is a form of asynchronous messaging. The sender writes a message, presses the send button, and goes on to other business, occasionally checking their inbox for a reply to the e-mail. This is not as immediate and simple as a phone call, but the sender probably will get more work done.

A common form of synchronous messaging is the remote procedure call (RPC). An RPC looks similar to an ordinary function call, but a separate process, usually running on a remote machine, executes the body of the function. An ordinary function executes within the calling process. The program calls a function and gets back a reply, often a status. If the status is successful, the code moves on to the next step; if it is not successful, execution shifts to some sort of error handling. Within the calling code, function execution is just another step in the program, no different from executing an assignment or a line of computation. However, executing an RPC can take time—lots of time. From the viewpoint of a user of an interactive application, the program may go into suspended animation while it waits for the RPC to return.

RPCs are not the only form of synchronous messaging, but all synchronous messaging is challenged to deal with server processes that may be slow or have other problems. There are solutions. For example, the local part of the RPC may return with an error if the remote part does not reply within a time limit. A time limit, with many variations including automatic retries, helps, but waiting for the time limit and retries is still annoying. When there is no user interaction, the waiting usually shows up as performance degradation.

Waiting may or may not be acceptable. Users are accustomed to pausing for a few seconds when the cursor turns to an hourglass, but more than a few seconds calls for special handling with progress bars, expected completion times, and all the other ploys that have been devised to convince users to remain patient.

Synchronous messaging can be especially annoying when working with remote applications or servers. Network latency, the time it takes to communicate with the application running remotely, is always present and can be substantial. Networks are inherently unreliable, and there is always a risk that messages will be lost or impossible to deliver. Often, remote applications provide complex services that may take many steps and require remote interactions and long-running computation. If the application were deployed locally, the interaction might be broken into steps, but when network latency and unreliability intrude on each step, minimizing the number of steps is often advisable. This means that a calculation in one long running step is faster than breaking it into smaller steps with better user feedback. In this case and others, asynchronous messaging may be a better alternative.

Synchronous messaging is usually much easier to code and understand than asynchronous messaging. When the pauses that usually accompany a synchronous interface are negligible or not an issue, a synchronous interface may be a simple solution. Another case where synchronous messaging plays an important role is in real-time applications in which actions must be performed in a limited time. In real time, it is often better to abandon a synchronous call than to go on to another activity while waiting for an asynchronous reply. For instance, when streaming audio or video, it can be better to abandon an effort to get data, replace the missing data with an approximation, and move on. The approximation is a compromise, but it is better than a gap.

Asynchronous Messaging

Asynchronous messaging is an alternative to synchronous messaging. The sender of an asynchronous message does not wait for a reply. The sender hands off the message to the messaging subsystem, and the sender proceeds to its next task. The sender does not get their information sooner, but they, or the application, are able to move on to other processing instead of being blocked.

"Fire-and-forget" is a simple way to use asynchronous messaging. The message system fires off a message, hoping it will reach its target and succeed but not caring if the message reached its target or executed successfully. The code calling the message system does not wait for a reply. If this is acceptable, it can be fast and efficient. A classic regular postal service works this way. Mail is dropped into a mailbox without waiting for a confirmation. If the receiving post office cannot process the mail, it may be eventually returned to the sender, but return-to-sender mechanism is not expected to be prompt or reliable. If a postal service user wants to be sure their mail is received, the user upgrades to registered mail. E-mail is also largely a fire-and-forget service.[10]

Fire-and-forget is efficient and easy to implement, but situations may require a more sophisticated strategy. However, in software, less is often more. A fire-and-forget takes fewer resources and is usually executed more quickly than other strategies. For example, a fire-and-forget strategy is appropriate when messages are sent regularly and a missed or out-of-order message is not a significant error. This can be the case for event management systems.

---

[10]Under the covers, the message exchanges between e-mail servers are more complicated than "fire and forget," but after the user clicks the send button, the e-mail is out of their control.

Other asynchronous strategies include callbacks. When the sender's message contains an address of some kind where a reply message can be sent and trigger some code, the address is called a *callback*. Using a callback strategy, the sender sends a request with a callback address. For example, a client might send a request to a storage server to load several gigabytes of data into storage from a local address. This may take several hours. When the load is complete, the storage server sends back a message to the sender's callback address confirming the load and containing security credentials for the client to use when accessing the data. Code on the client side then processes this information and stores the credential for future use.

The callback strategy for asynchronous messaging is extensively used and can be powerful, but it is usually more complex to implement than may appear. When the remote system sends a message to the callback, the callback code begins to execute. Callback execution may be in an interrupt or in another thread. The callback code must be designed to be thread-safe or re-entrant if the results of the callback are to be processed in the context of the original message. For example, in the previous storage example, the data may have been stored for a single user. If the user is to get the credentials to access the stored data, the callback code must be aware of the user associated with the original message. The sender could include a user ID in the original message to be returned with the callback message, but that is not always possible. If the callback is designed to have access to the context of the sender of the message, the context will tell the callback which user gets the credentials. If several callback messages can start the same callback code, care must be taken to match the message to the correct context.

This can be complicated, and errors can be difficult to detect and fix. For some developers, the transition from straight-line coding to interrupt-driven code is difficult. In interrupt-driven code, execution is not from line to line; instead, execution may shift to another code block as external events occur.

Synchronous and asynchronous messaging are patterns for building effective communications systems, and TCP/IP is the protocol most of these communications systems are based on. However, there are higher levels of reliability that should be addressed by an enterprise integration system.

Assured Delivery

A reliable messaging service such as TCP/IP is not enough to support reliable integration. TCP/IP guarantees that data will be delivered in the order in which it was sent, and the content will be unchanged. It does not guarantee to the sending application that the data was received, nor does it guarantee to the receiving application that it has not missed messages that it was supposed to receive.

The limitations of TCP/IP are limitations imposed by its level in the data transmission stack. For successful messaging, the problem must be addressed on a higher level. A classic example is a production machine controller that sends out a critical warning message to a service desk that will automatically generate an issue. TCP/IP guarantees that the information will be delivered accurately, but what happens if the service desk receiver is down when the message is delivered? The message is lost, the issue is not generated, and a catastrophic failure ensues, which could have been prevented if the issue were written. The failing machine could keep resending the message until the service desk sends an acknowledgment, but a simple controller may not be able to accept an acknowledgment or resend and may even have failed itself. Alternatively, a messaging service could queue messages until the receiver was ready to receive them. By delegating assured delivery to the message service, the system becomes less coupled because the service desk does not need code to send an acknowledgment tailored to the receiver nor does the sending application have to manage sending the message to match the service desk requirements.

Messaging services frequently have assured delivery options. A robust messaging service with assured delivery options is often the most scalable and reliable choice for integration messaging.

Data Routing

Data must not only be transmitted efficiently but must also be routed to the correct recipients. One form of routing involves inspecting the contents of messages and determining the recipient from the content. Another common routing activity is to reduce a swarm of identical, similar, or logically related messages to a single message. Sometimes messages are discarded when they are not useful. In other cases, messages may be broken up into chunks that are of interest to different recipients. In some messaging architectures, all messages are directed to all recipients, and processing logic in the recipient filters the input down to the messages the recipient can use. This arrangement has the advantage that the logic to determine the recipient's input is with the recipient, not spread through the routing system; however, it increases the traffic into the recipient. A combination of complex routing and intelligent recipients is an interesting compromise.

No matter how simple or complex the routing, when using TCP/IP to transmit data, the sender must know the IP address of the receiver or the domain name of receiver and resolve the name via the Domain Name System (DNS).

Hard-Coded Addresses

The simplest way to access a receiver's address is to hard-code the address directly into the sender's communications stack. This certainly works, but it has drawbacks. Changing the receiver involves code changes. If the sender's code is compiled, the code has to be recompiled. Even if the code is interpreted rather than compiled, good practice requires the code changes be recorded into the software configuration system. Many sites will require at least a partial rebuild of the system to ensure consistency with the configuration whenever the content of the software configuration changes. In addition, the new software must be tested, and there is always the risk of failure, taking you back to square one. This is a lot of work and risk for a simple change.

Despite the drawbacks, hard-coded addresses are a simple solution for a small system that does not change often. Hard-coding generally implies a point-to-point system where routing and addresses never change. With only a few integrated applications, this system can be adequate. There is an added requirement that IP addresses do not change. This puts a constraint on changing the hardware, but where software and hardware seldom change, the simplicity of hard-coding may outweigh its inflexibility. Larger and more dynamic IT installations have to develop systems that are more easily changed.

Configuration Mapping Files

A simple solution is to provide a configuration-mapping file that each application reads. The file can map a single sender to each of its receivers, or the file can contain mappings between several senders and their receivers. When a sending application is ready to send to a receiver, it resorts to information from the configuration-mapping file to find the correct IP address.

A configuration-mapping file avoids the pain and risk of hard-coding, but it still has limitations. Keeping configuration files up-to-date can be an issue, especially when the system is distributed over many network nodes. In that case, when the configuration changes, files on several hosts may have to change. This is an added administration burden and an opportunity for a failure. Placing mappings for more than one sender into one file that maps senders to their receivers reduces the number of mapping files to maintain, but a single file means sending applications that use the file must have similar code to read the mapping file, which may not be possible with legacy and third-party applications. In a large and heterogeneous system, the mixture of multi-application configuration files, single-application configuration files, hard-coding, and other mechanisms can become an error-prone tangle. Forgotten configuration files can be a nagging problem for system administrators. Avoiding them is sometimes a significant achievement.

In addition, to avoid the overhead of repeatedly reading the same file, applications often are coded to read configuration files into memory at startup. In that case, some means must exist to cause the configuration files to be reloaded when they change. Sometimes a brute-force stop and restart is enough, but often the refresh must occur without pausing production.

The file refresh and reload issue can be addressed in several ways. One approach is to deal with configuration files in the same way that patches and updates are managed by Windows or Linux. These operating systems have code installed that responds to files that are downloaded from central repositories. The installed code manages the updates and patches, making required settings and signaling applications to reload or the system to reboot. These approaches are effective, but they are also major engineering efforts and may be outside the scope of an IT department to develop for their own system. Also, configuration changes can be relatively slow. This may be an issue when systems change dynamically in a virtualized system. In a virtual system, the sources and targets for integration messages can undergo constant and rapid change. Continually changing and redistributing files can become impractical.

Publication-Subscription

Other approaches have different advantages. One of the most common integration routing architectures is called *publication-subscription* (or *pub/sub*).

Pub/sub is modeled after a magazine clearinghouse that distributes several different magazines. When the customer initiates a subscription with the clearinghouse, they choose the magazines they want from the magazines the clearinghouse offers. The customer contacts the clearinghouse, not the individual magazines. Extending the metaphor, a magazine that has joined the clearinghouse does not deal directly with subscribers. The clearinghouse takes care of the overhead of directing the magazines to the right customers, and the customer deals only with the clearinghouse, not each individual magazine. Thus, magazine publishers don't need to know the addresses of their customers, and the customer does not need to know the addresses of the magazines. Both publisher and subscriber need to know only the single address of the clearinghouse.

Pub/sub message routing works similarly. Usually, a broker process acts as the clearinghouse.[11] Applications register with the broker, offering messages to which may be subscribed to and subscribing to messages that interest them.

---

[11] A separate broker process may not be necessary. The broker function can be distributed if there is a means to distribute all the subscription to each integrated application, and each application has code to use the subscription information. This avoids the broker becoming a bottleneck. Alternatives include broker clones that distribute the load.

The details of the registering with a broker can be challenging. In a simple form, an application simply registers its address and a unique identifier for each type of message it has to send by sending a registration message to the broker at a known address. Subscribing applications register their address and the messages they want to receive. The subscribers must know the identifiers of the types of message they want to receive. They must also know how to process the associated type of message. In this simple scenario, applications must still know some details of the senders and their messages in order to use the messages, but address management is left to the broker. The only address the applications need to know is the address of the broker.

Pub/sub is occasionally criticized for semantically coupling senders and receivers. Ideally, decoupled applications should be able to register for messages without knowing anything about the source of the message, and the senders of messages should not have to consider their receivers. This scenario is attractive: applications could register with the pub/sub broker and immediately begin receiving all the relevant messages, and other applications would begin to receive relevant messages from the new application. Ideally, when an application adds, removes, or updates services, the system would automatically adjust to the new situation. Unfortunately, this scenario is more aspirational than real.

However, the aspirations are approachable. For example, consider MIME types as they are used with HTTP. MIME types, also called Internet media types, were developed to describe data content of files attached to e-mail and are often associated with a file extension. MIME types are registered with the Internet Assigned Numbers Authority (IANA), the same authority that manages domain names and IP addresses. Using the IANA registry, anyone can see an authoritative definition of the type.

MIME types appear in the headers of HTTP packets. The MIME type tells the receiver of an HTTP packet about the format of the payload of the HTTP packet it receives. MIME types make it possible for web browsers to know to parse an HTML document as HTML rather than some other format like pure text.

MIME types vary widely. Some are general, and an application can expect almost anything in the content, such as an HTML type, which is fine for browsers displaying HTML. As HTTP has grown to be used for more than exchanging documents and has become a protocol for exchanging information between applications, MIME types have become useful for specifying finer-grained types.

In some ways, the World Wide Web[12] is an ideal application integration system. Individuals and web sites that know nothing about each other use published MIME types and a standard message format and protocol to exchange information. This is close to complete decoupling of receiver and sender and represents one pattern for decoupled pub/sub integration. The pattern has two essential elements: a shared protocol like HTTP and public message types.

Although setting up a pub/sub broker requires investment, it is scalable and more easily reconfigurable. The broker can be either the hub of a spoke and hub system or a component on a message bus. For many sites, hooking applications up to a broker is a major accomplishment and a great improvement because it shifts address management to a central broker that is relatively easily managed. The applications still may be semantically coupled, but using standards like MIME types reduces coupling.

Sites that go further with public message types and high-level standard protocols may gain even greater benefits. SOA is a step toward easier integration because they are standard architectures, protocols, and published message types.

Data Translation

If everyone spoke the same language, communication would be easier, though perhaps not as rich. However, supporters of universal languages such as Esperanto and Interlingua argue for the value of a neutral language more or less easily understood by everyone. A similar situation occurs in enterprise application integration. There are the equivalents of international languages; Distributed Management Task Force Common Information Model[13] is one example that is widely acknowledged.

As long as an application communicates with a small group of other applications whose developers and administrators are all familiar with the messages and models of the entire group, this works. However, as new applications are added to the mix and personnel changes, fewer and fewer technicians are prepared to understand communications between the applications.

At that point, the value of a fully decoupled sender and receiver architecture becomes evident. Unfortunately, the pub/sub system described earlier may be impossible to implement under time and budget constraints.

---

[12]Strictly speaking, the World Wide Web is a sprawling information system that runs on the Internet. The Internet is the interconnected mass of networks that enables widespread communication. The components of the World Wide Web include browsers such as Internet Explorer, Firefox, and Chrome; HTTP servers like Apache and Internet Information Services (IIS); and a myriad of web sites.

[13]See www.dmtf.org/standards/cim.

This leads to data translation. A data translator takes a message generated by one application and translates it into a form usable by another application. The translation can translate formats. For example, a translator may transform a file in CSV form to XML. The translation can be complex, changing terminology, performing calculations, and executing business logic to convert data prepared for one purpose into a form suitable for a different purpose.

At its extreme, each pair of applications may need a special data translator, leading to a situation, which should be familiar to readers by now, where the number of translators increases exponentially with the addition of each new application. Even with a pub/sub system that manages application addresses and message types, each application may need an array of translators to deal with each message type it receives. The application may not know where the message is coming from, but it still must know how to decipher the message.

There are models that can help with translation. Consider that an international language like Esperanto can still be useful when only a few speakers use it. In a room full of people who speak different languages, a few Esperanto speakers can act as mediators. If one of the Esperanto speakers speaks language A and another Esperanto speaker speaks language B, the A speakers and B speakers can communicate via the two Esperanto speakers.

Chapter 7 discussed the CA Unified Service Model and its use as an intermediary between data sources and targets. This approach can be generalized in an integration model. Instead of building a data translator for each application pair, each data source converts its data to the agreed-upon "Esperanto" form. Each data receiver builds a translator from Esperanto to its native internal form. This plan eliminates the unique translators for each pair of applications.

This pattern isolates the individual applications from the universal model, which reduces the amount of reworking of each application in order to participate in the integration system.

There are also some downsides. The central model has to be comprehensive enough to serve the needs of all applications, which is not an easy accomplishment. If the model is not comprehensive enough, someone has to build a one-off specialized translator or the model has to expand. Deciding which route to take is delicate. A one-off translator may be the best solution if the requirements are truly unique. There is little point in expanding an entire model for a one-time event. On the other hand, one-time events are often not as unique as they were initially thought to be.

Conclusion

Designing data transmission, transformation, routing, and translation systems requires knowledge of the IT domain and the content of the applications in the domain as well as the technical advantages of various integration patterns and how to implement the patterns in hardware and software.

This is no small challenge. Hardware and software alternatives rise and fall in prominence continually. Enterprises that can accurately predict what their business will be doing five years from now are rare. The big picture is only one thing that an architect designing an integration system must understand. What will be the direction of application design in the domain of the enterprise? What kind of automation will new lines of business require? How will automation change in current lines of business? There are probably no answers to any of these questions, only better or worse guesses. That is no reason for an architect not to try. Architects are more likely to be right if they guess the future and guess wrong than they are to be right if they flail in the dark.

EXERCISES

1. Identify and describe an application that is not integrated and whose enterprise benefits would degrade if it were integrated into the enterprise information technology fabric. If you cannot think of any, explain why such an application is so difficult to find.

2. Describe "design patterns" and explain why they are important to enterprise IT architecture.

3. Describe the difference between synchronous and asynchronous communication and the implications for cloud application design.

4. What is meant by file sharing? What are its strengths and weaknesses?

5. Shared databases are not as popular as they once were. Discuss their strengths and weaknesses.

6. Why is data translation necessary for integration?

Virtualization

Not in Kansas

Virtualization Challenges

SUMMARY

Virtualization is a computer technology with a long history that has bloomed in recent years. Originally developed to support multitasking on mainframes, virtualization is the foundation for cloud computing today and contributes to the flexibility, reliability, and ease of use of computing today. Before the technology could become as common as it is now, it had to be applied to the workhorse of distributed computing, the x86 architecture. When that was accomplished, virtual systems spread rapidly in datacenters around the world and led to the next phase: cloud computing.

This chapter discusses some of the ways virtualization is used, how it is implemented, and some of the challenges it presents.

Virtualization is not as familiar to the public as cloud computing, but most cloud enterprises are based upon virtualized computing environments. *Virtualization*, as the term is used here, decouples software from hardware. In a virtual environment, applications interact with an environment simulated by software instead of interacting directly with the hardware. Virtual platforms support virtual machines (VMs) that interact with a hypervisor or a virtual machine monitor (VMM). Usually, a VMM monitors a single VM, while a hypervisor manages a number of VMMs. A VM usually consists of an OS, called a *guest OS*. Guest OSs are usually unmodified OSs that run on physical machines and support programs on a VM in the same way they support programs on a physical machine. In some cases, the guest OS is modified to run on another OS. This is called *paravirtualization*. See Figure 10-1.

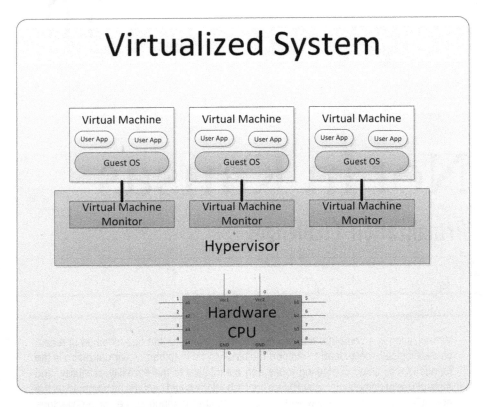

Figure 10-1. A typical virtual system consists of virtual machines, a hypervisor, and the physical device

In 1974, Gerald Popek and Robert Goldberg described the requirements for a virtual machine system.[1] Their definition still is used. Their first requirement is that a program running on a virtual system should act identically to the same program running directly on physical hardware, except for differences caused by resource availability or timing dependencies. Second, for efficiency, the virtual system must run a substantial portion of the virtual program's instructions directly on the physical processor. Third, a virtual program can access only those resources that are allocated to it, such as memory or storage, but under certain circumstances, the hypervisor can take back control of resources already allocated. These requirements are still considered fundamental for virtualization.

---

[1]Gerald Popek and Robert Goldberg. "Formal Requirements for Virtualization of Third Generation Architectures." Communications of the ACM, July 1974, Volume 17, Number 7. Accessed March 2015. www.cs.nyu.edu/courses/fall14/CSCI-GA.3033-010/popek-goldberg.pdf.

A virtualized system is not the same as a multi-user operating system, which is implemented on a different level. Multi-user system users sign on to a single computer running a single operating system. The multi-user operating system apportions resources among users. In a virtualized environment, a hypervisor allocates resources to each VM and its guest OS. The allocation is to a guest OS, not to a user of the VM. Early virtualized environments, such as IBM CP/CMS, were invented to support multiple users on the same computer as a more easily implemented alternative to multi-user operating systems. Today, most operating systems are multi-user, but with portable and readily available computers in many sizes and shapes, most individual users run their own instance of the OS on a personal physical device.

Why Virtualize?

Virtualization can be a great convenience and, perhaps surprisingly, increase the efficiency of a physical system. Although virtualization platforms are surprisingly efficient, the virtualization mechanism adds overhead to the system, particularly when the context switches and the operating environment of one VM are switched out and another takes its place. However, it is exactly these context switches that offer greater efficiency because they free and reallocate resources instead of hoarding them where they are less useful.

The only physical existence of a VM is an image file that can be launched on a virtualization platform. A running VM may have been modified and no longer match the image from which it was launched. An image may be a bare-bones OS, waiting to be launched by a virtualization platform and installed with applications by the user, but an image also can be fully installed and configured with software. Although managing image files has some difficulties, the effort required to physically reconfigure and reconnect is much greater.

Safe and Efficient Use of Resources

One of the basic benefits of virtualization comes from deploying several applications on separate VMs instead of deploying the applications on a single physical device. VMs can share the resources of a single physical device without the danger of undesirable interaction. The allocation of resources is left to the hypervisor. The VMs still cannot consume more resources than the physical device has available, but independent VMs can share resources more safely than applications contending for resources on a single OS on a physical machine.

Several VMs make better use of physical resources if the workloads running on each VM are staggered in timing. Instead of sizing the physical machine to support all VMs with peak workloads simultaneously, the machine can be sized for the maximum combined workload, which can be considerably lower if workload peaks never coincide. If the physical machine is sized for the maximum combined workload, the machine will operate closer to its maximum capacity more of the time.

Simplification of Installation

A frequent example of a more complex VM image is a *LAMP stack*. A LAMP stack VM is a fully configured application server with a Linux OS, an Apache HTTP server, a MySQL relational database manager, and the Perl, PHP, or Python programming language completely installed and ready to start up. A developer can launch a LAMP stack image in minutes and begin developing web applications using the generic stack, instead of spending hours installing and configuring each component. Installing complex software quickly and easily as preconfigured images saves time and ensures that the installation is correct every time. Consequently, preconfigured VMs can be deployed without special expertise from the IT department after the first image is created. In addition, complex and tricky installations can often be deployed as simply as less complex installations.

Maintenance

Operating systems running on emulated virtual hardware can be maintained independent of the hardware. An operating system running on a VM can be patched, updated, and even halted and rebooted without interfering with the operation of the physical hardware and other VMs. Each application can have an operating system at the exact patch level and set of installed features the application needs for efficient operation. When the VM must be taken down for maintaining an application, the work can be done at the best time for the application, not during a maintenance window that is a compromise between the needs of all the applications running on the physical hardware. For applications that need little maintenance, uptime increases because they do not have to stop for maintenance windows needed by other applications. Applications that need more maintenance do not have to delay needed work to accommodate the community.

Clustering

A clustered system is a group of physical servers that are linked in such a way that applications running on the cluster can move from physical server to physical server to optimize their delivery of services. This is usually done using a hypervisor that can move virtual machines from physical machine to physical machine.

Applications running on clusters can make better use of available computing capacity, especially if peak usage periods of the applications running on the cluster do not intersect. When applications need extra capacity to service their users, they are allocated more resources from spare capacity left by idling applications, or additional servers are added to the cluster. The additional servers may be removed from the cluster and used for other purposes when the demand decreases. The overall result is that the IT system can deliver better performance more efficiently.

One of the reasons for excess capacity is the need for isolation. Servers are often available that have the capacity to run two separate applications, but there is danger that one application will interfere with the other in some way, such as depleting some OS resource such as file handles or sockets. In a purely physical environment, the only sure way to prevent two applications from interfering with each other is to install them on separate servers. Virtualization isolates applications by installing them in separate VMs on the same physical machine or cluster of physical machines.

Clustering is valuable when physical servers require maintenance. VMs can be moved off a server needing maintenance and onto other servers in the cluster and moved back when the maintenance is done, and the work is complete without ever interrupting the service.

Clustering is also valuable for failover. When a server or group of servers in a cluster is impaired or halted, the applications on the cluster may drop in performance, but they continue to service users. If the servers in a group are geographically dispersed, the cluster can move processing from one geographic location to another, providing protection from disasters such as fires or floods.

Flexibility

A virtualization platform can support operating systems that are not supported directly on the physical hardware. For example, a VM running a Windows operating system can be launched quickly on a physical Linux machine using Kernel-based Virtual Machine (KVM) or other virtualization software.[2] Then new VMs with Linux and non-Linux operating systems can be installed without the effort of installing a new operating system on the physical machine, offering great flexibility in supporting applications designed for different operating systems. This strategy is also a way of safely testing new applications that

---

[2]Most Linux distributions come with KVM installed. Other virtualization software available for Linux includes VirtualBox Open Source Edition from Oracle and VM Workstation from VMware. VirtualBox and VM Workstation also run on Windows. Microsoft Hyper-V runs on Windows.

might harm the system on which they are installed. In addition, multiple VMs can run simultaneously on a single computer; sometimes many instances of a single OS (and, in other cases, different OSs) may be used for different VMs. For example, a single computer might run five separate VMs to support five simultaneous users, each a differently configured operating system as if they were the only user of the system.

Snapshots

Most virtualization platforms support some form of *snapshotting*, which is writing an image of a VM to a file that holds the state of the VM at the instant of the snapshot. A developer working on an application can take a snapshot of a work in progress and quickly reproduce a running version of the application at that point. The snapshot could then be archived, handed over to quality assurance for testing, or simply moved to another physical machine for further work.

Virtual Desktops

Virtualization also supports *virtual desktops*, which have several valuable characteristics. A virtual desktop is usually a VM image that contains the entire environment of an end user, as if it was running on a private physical PC. The desktop images are stored on a powerful central server that is capable of running several desktop images at one time. When a user wants to use their virtual desktop, they log in to any computer on the enterprise network and request their virtual desktop. Their desktop is started for them, and they are now in their familiar environment with all their files and applications. Employees who travel from office to office can get their desktops in remote offices without trouble. The computing devices users log in to need to have the capacity to support their desktop activity since that occurs on a powerful central server. This also makes it easy for employees to switch easily and seamlessly from desktop to laptop to tablet to smartphone. When users end their session, the central server takes a snapshot and stores the image for the next time the users want their desktops.

Clouds

There will be much more said about clouds and virtualization later, but clouds must instantly supply computing capacity to their consumers in a readily usable form. Without virtualization, this is effectively impossible. Therefore, it is hard to imagine clouds without virtualization.

Implementation of Virtual Platforms

The software that is used to emulate hardware and manage virtual systems is usually called a *virtual platform*. These can be implemented in various ways.

X86 Rings

The x86 central processing unit (CPU) architecture, which is the basis for most modern computers, was long thought to be impossible to virtualize because it did not support instructions deemed necessary for virtualization. In the late 1990s, software techniques were developed to circumvent the hardware deficiency. Later the x86 architecture was extended to support virtualization. An understanding of some aspects of x86 architecture is needed to understand current virtualization.

Hardware instruction restrictions are called *rings* in the x86 architecture. In a conventional system with a conventional OS running on a physical machine, rings isolate the user from critical instructions, memory locations, and input and output ports that could cause mayhem for the system. The rings prevent user processes from activities such as halting system processes, overwriting critical system descriptor tables in memory, and promiscuously accessing external resources.

The inner ring, "ring 0," is the most privileged and permits all the instructions the hardware CPU supports. Ring 0 is usually reserved for the operating system kernel that controls direct access to the hardware. If an ordinary program wants access to hardware resources, it must make a request to the kernel, which will execute the request for authorized processes. Most processors offer several rings, intended to support finer-grained instruction access. However, operating systems almost always use only the inner ring 0 and the outermost ring in order to support the lowest common denominator among processors.

Supporting fewer rings can be a performance issue. Making a call to request execution by a lower-level ring can exact a performance toll because a request to the kernel can be slow. If low-level device drivers operate at ring 1, the drivers can execute some instructions that a less privileged process would have to go to the OS for execution. If the privileged low-level device driver makes fewer slow kernel requests through the OS, execution will be faster. Assigning higher-level drivers to ring 2, and so on, reduces the number of system calls. The more rings used, the fewer kernel requests and the better the performance.[3]

---

[3]Kernel request performance has improved since Intel added the SYSENTER instruction and AMD added the SYSCALL instruction to speed up system calls. John Gulbransen has written a good description of SYSENTER and SYSCALL. John Gulbransen, "System call optimization with the SYSENTER instruction." `www.summitsoftconsulting.com/syscallopts.htm`. Accessed March 12, 2015.

However, performance is better only if programs operating in a privileged ring make use of the privileged instructions available to them. If the program ignores the privileged instructions available in their ring and makes kernel requests through OS calls instead, the program gets no benefit from the instructions available to its ring, but the program will operate in outer rings that do not have access to the privileged instructions as well as its inner ring. The potential increase in performance will not be significant if the system does not make extensive use of the privilege-enhanced drivers. A process will always run correctly in a more privileged ring than it was written for, but a program written for a more privileged ring will not run in a less privileged ring.

Using more rings performs better, but coding is more complex because each ring has a different set of permitted instructions and the code is compatible only with processors that support the additional rings. Therefore, most current operating systems make use of only two rings: ring 0 for the kernel and the outer ring for everything else. This division corresponds to "supervisor" and "user" mode that is often implemented in non-x86 CPUs. Supervisor and "user" modes are commonly used when talking about hardware process privileges.

When discussing hypervisor design, some terms are useful. *Safe instructions* are hardware instructions that will not violate virtualization rules, as defined by Popek and Goldberg. *Unsafe instructions*, as one might expect, are instructions that could be used to violate virtualization. *Privileged instructions* are instructions that are allowed to be executed only in supervisor mode. On some CPU architectures, all unsafe instructions are privileged instructions. Others allow some unsafe instructions to be executed in user mode. The x86 processor, in particular, was not originally designed to protect all unsafe instructions.

There are several different approaches to virtualization, but they all rely on the distinction between supervisor and user modes and the variations possible with additional rings.

Hypervisors

Hypervisors, also called *virtual machine monitors* (VMMs), replace direct interaction of the OS with the hardware. Direct interaction with hardware is often software writing or reading a value to or from a memory location that is an input or output register in hardware rather than a location in general-purpose memory. Instead of storing the data for future use, like general memory, interacting with a hardware register communicates with a hardware component internal or external to the core computer. Placing a value into the register could, for example, send the contents of a block of memory to a hard disk drive or cause the hard disk to deposit a block of data into a region of memory. In a virtualized system, the software reads and writes to the same designated memory location, but the value does not go directly to the hardware. Instead, a layer of software, called a hypervisor or VMM, handles the interaction with the memory location. The hypervisor may relay data to and from a physical hard drive, or it may do something completely different such as simulating the hard drive with random access memory or transmitting the data to a virtual storage device. Whatever the hypervisor does, it provides the same service as a direct call to the hardware. Ideally, the software running on a hypervisor cannot distinguish the hypervisor from the physical machine.

Hypervisors fall into three types: trap-and-emulate, binary translation, and paravirtualization.

Hardware-Assisted Trap-and-Emulate

Trap-and-emulate is the oldest, some would say classic, virtualization method. Trap-and-emulate was used in the earliest IBM virtual environments. In principle, trap-and-emulate is simple. A VM with its guest OS operates in user mode. Therefore, the guest OS is allowed to execute user mode instructions directly on the CPU. If a guest OS attempts to execute a supervisor mode instruction, a trap is issued, and control is switched to the hypervisor. The hypervisor examines the instruction. If the instruction is safe, the hypervisor passes it on to the CPU for execution. If the instruction is not safe, the hypervisor replaces the unsafe instruction with a safe emulated instruction and only then passes it on to the CPU. Unsafe instructions are instructions that could allow a VM to access the resources not allocated to it by the hypervisor or to cause other threats for the orderly operation of VMs. See Figure 10-2.

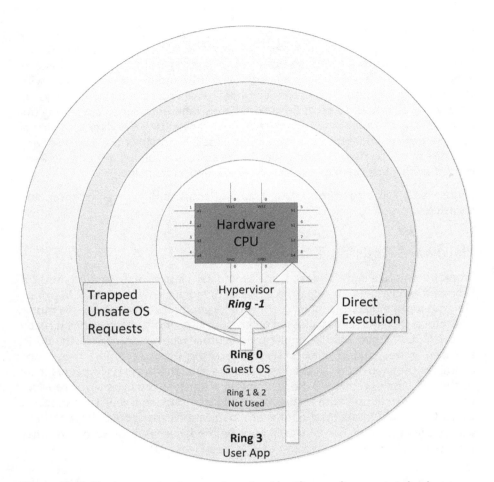

Figure 10-2. Hardware-assisted trap-and-emulate identifies unsafe requests in hardware

Trap-and-emulate is a relatively simple and efficient implementation of virtualization. Since most instructions in programs are executable in user mode, most programs execute almost entirely directly on the CPU, and VM performance on trap-and-emulate platforms is almost equal to direct performance.

However, trap-and-emulate implementations are not always possible. Traps occur when a user mode process attempts to execute a supervisor mode instruction. For trap-and-emulate to work, all unsafe instructions must trap. In other words, all user mode instructions must be safe, and all unsafe instructions must be reserved for supervisor mode.

Binary Translation

Binary translation was the first method to achieve complete virtualization on the x86 CPU architecture. A binary translation hypervisor scans code for unsafe instructions and replaces them with safe instruction. See Figure 10-3. Scanning and translating are performed by software. It does not depend on hardware to trap unsafe instructions like trap-and-emulate virtualization platforms.

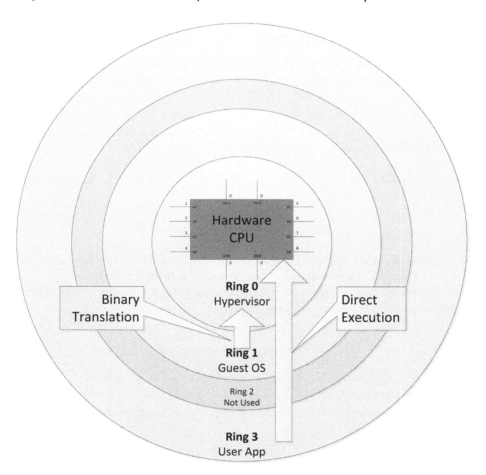

Figure 10-3. Binary translation identifies unsafe requests and translates them in software

Translation can occur on demand as the code executes or on entire programs prior to execution.

If the hypervisor had to scan every line of code and translate it, performance for binary translation would probably be poor. However, depending on what a program does, little code ordinarily has to be scanned. As in trap-and-emulate, most user code does not require unsafe instructions. User programs seldom speak directly to hard drives or send arbitrary binary commands to printers. Therefore, most user code can execute directly on the CPU. Consequently, translation is infrequent, and binary translation can perform well.

Also, because it is implemented in software, nested virtualization is possible. Several VMs could be launched as guests on another VM with their own hypervisor running on the guest OS of the first VM.

Unfortunately, x86 CPU rings were not designed for safe virtualization. Until recently, x86 processors did not assign all the instructions needed for safe virtualization to supervisor mode. Consequently, a classic trap-and-emulate hypervisor for x86 that could not be circumvented was impossible. Both Intel and AMD have added new instructions that now make trapping unsafe instructions possible.

Paravirtualization

Paravirtual systems use modified OSs and device drivers for virtualization. The modified OS communicates directly with the hypervisor via APIs instead of trapping or translating unsafe instructions. See Figure 10-4. In theory, paravirtualization yields better VM performance.

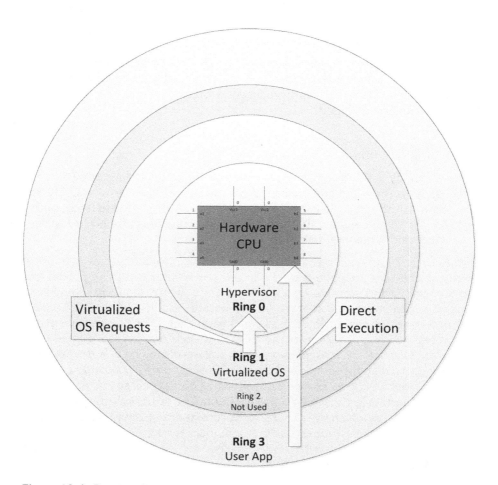

Figure 10-4. Paravirtualization uses modified OSs

Guest OSs must be modified to run on a paravirtual hypervisor. For open source OSs like Linux, this is relatively easy. For closed OSs like Windows, the OS can be modified in effect with an appropriate set of device drivers that interact with the hypervisor.

Paravirtualization is often used in combination with other virtualization schemes. A guest OS may be modified to be virtualization aware and run faster than an unmodified OS on an appropriate hardware assisted trap-and-emulate hypervisor.

Alternate Forms of Virtualization

Not all virtualization techniques fit the classic Popeck and Goldberg definition. Some rely on hardware features that support virtualization that is similar to the classic form. Others rely on a different approach to sharing resources. All approach can be combined.

Logical Domains

Logical domains (LDoms)[4] is a virtualization platform developed by Sun Microsystems (now Oracle) for its SPARC multiprocessor hardware.[5] LDoms has some of the same characteristics as other virtual platforms and confers some of the same benefits, although it does not quite correspond to the classic Popeck and Goldberg definition.

The LDoms hypervisor manages the distribution of processes over multiple virtual processors supported by the processor architecture. The processors share memory and storage. An administrator configures domains, designating processors, memory, and storage to a separate instance of an OS. Domain resources are not shared. Processes running on each OS instance have exclusive access to the resources of the OSs, as if each domain were a separate computer. Like software running on a VM, software running in a domain sees itself running on an independent computer. Process performance in a domain degrades from resource starvation only when the processes in the domain deplete the resources allotted to the partition. This is unlike other virtualization platforms on which VMs share resources and a VM may be affected by other VMs gobbling resources. Because a domain is a hardware configuration, software failures and some hardware failures are physically unable to affect software running on other partitions.

This is both a strength and a weakness. The computing capacity of a domain is stable. As long as resources remain allocated, they are stable and will not disappear from events or loads outside the domain. Mission-critical applications can rely on the resources of the domain. This is important when reliable performance is the most important consideration. On other virtualization platforms, heavy loads on one group of VMs can deplete system resources for other VMs. Consequently, performance may be unpredictable.

---

[4]Officially called "Oracle VM Server for SPARC."
[5]SPARC is an acronym for Scalable Processor ARChitecture introduced by Sun in 1987. The architecture uses a reduced instruction set. Subsequently Sun established SPARC International Inc., a nonprofit member-owned organization to promote and release SPARC as a royalty-free, open architecture. SPARC has been adopted for a number on non-Sun computers. See http://sparc.org/. Accessed September 2015. The SPARC architecture supports the appearance of many processors dynamically assigned to processes. Oracle acquired Sun in 2010. Oracle has continued to develop SPARC.

However, the stability of domains presents some of its own issues that are similar to those of a dedicated server. If domains cannot be changed dynamically, the administrator has to allocate more resources to the domain than the application needs under normal load to guarantee critical application performance during peak periods. This leads to waste of resources under less than peak loading just as it does on an over-provisioned dedicated physical server.

Dynamic reallocation of domains mitigates this situation. A software domain hypervisor dynamically allocates partitions, or domains. The hypervisor can or contract these domains without stopping running processes. Resources can be reallocated dynamically to provide more capacity to a domain that needs them during peak loads. Like VMs, the hypervisor can create and release domains at will. The hypervisor differs from typical virtualization systems because each domain is supported by independent unshared hardware, which the hypervisor can create, expand, and contract.

Containers: Virtualization by Resource Restriction

Containers are an older technology that has gained attention and revitalized in the last few years. Containers are not implemented with virtualization, but they achieve similar goals and are therefore closely associated with virtual systems. They also can be combined with more conventional virtual systems effectively. Since containers are often lighter weight, require less overhead, and are more easily managed than a full-fledged VM, they are often a technology of choice.

Unlike VMs, containers do not insert a virtualization layer. Instead, the container isolates processes and resources hosted on an OS running on an underlying system. The underlying system may be virtual or physical. Processes isolated in a container are similar to a process running in a VM.

UNIX and UNIX-like operating systems have supported a form of containers since version 7 was released by Bell Labs in 1979. The basis for this form of virtualization is the `chroot` command with which administrators can change the root directory of a running process and its children. In UNIX-like systems, changing the root directory of a process changes the operating environment of the process. By switching to a properly constructed alternate root hierarchy, the process is in a so-called "jail" in which its access to resources is strictly controlled. In effect, the process has its own version of the parent operating system. The separation is not as strict as VMs on other virtualization platforms because a privileged user on the parent system has complete access to the resources of the guest system and a privileged user on the guest system has some low-level access to system resources, such as the ability to create and mount file systems.[6]

---

[6]The Linux container technology discussed here is not Kernel Virtual Machine (KVM), which is a technology for supporting true VMs. Using KVM, a Linux installation acts as a hypervisor for virtual Linux machines.

Simple chroot-based process isolation is still used on UNIX and Linux today for some purposes such as isolation of unstable software for testing. It can be used to run 32-bit software on 64-bit hardware, and it can be used to run older software on newer releases of the OS. Process isolation is almost weightless compared to other virtualization platforms because it does not have the overhead of a hypervisor intensively scrutinizing and controlling low-level instructions. It is also used to isolate processes into a safe sandbox or other special environment for testing.

Over the last decade, process isolation based on the Linux kernel has progressed rapidly. Features have been added for substantially greater control over the resources a process or group of processes can access. Docker[7] is an open source product for creating, deploying, and maintaining containers. A group of partners that includes Amazon Web Services, IBM, and Microsoft supports Docker. Recently, a project has begun to establish an open standard for containers. Docker has donated its code to this project, which has been established under the Linux Foundation. The project has a wide range of support.[8] Microsoft has developed container technology for the Windows Server operating system.[9]

Virtualization and Security

Virtual environments are inherently neither more nor less secure than physical environments, but a virtual environment requires developers and architects to consider the special characteristics of a virtual environment. The challenges to security in a virtual environment resemble integration challenges.

The foundation of most computer security is a hierarchy of privilege zones that restrict access to control and assets. Outsiders have less control and access to less important assets than insiders, managers have access to more important assets and more control that employees, and highly privileged system administrators and executives have access to everything. Each of these sets of privileges constitutes a zone. In practice, zones can be much more granular than a simple four-layer hierarchy.

On a more concrete level, within computer systems only processes have access privileges, which are usually derived from the authorizations granted to the authenticated owner of the process. Ultimately, the processor instructions

---

[7]For more information on Docker, see https://www.docker.com/. Accessed September 2015.

[8]For more information, see https://www.opencontainers.org/pressrelease/. Accessed September 2015.

[9]For more information on Windows containers, see https://msdn.microsoft.com/en-us/virtualization/windowscontainers/about/about_overview?f=255&MSPPError=-2147217396. Accessed September 2015.

available to a process determine what the process can do. Computer systems control instruction execution on many levels. Lowest-level restrictions are enforced in the hardware.

Security practically deals with administration and enforcement of zones, but on the lowest level, the only form of control is through access to processor instructions and their targets. Nevertheless, control over individual hardware instructions is distant from security as we ordinarily understand it. Much of the time, security deals with assets, mostly data stored on disks such as critical management reports and customer records. It also deals with control of processes such as starting and stopping mission-critical production processes, security systems themselves, and so on.

Security code usually checks the identity of the process owner and determines what the owner is authorized to do. Ultimately, all security depends on restricting access to hardware and instructions. The rules put in place by the processor are the final arbiters of security. These checks cannot be changed or circumvented without executing commands that are accessible only from supervisor mode. Thus, the security function controls the high-level functions that a process is authorized to perform. Most of the security code will be ordinary user mode instructions, but privileged instructions protect the security code. Hacking into a computer system usually involves an effort to gain access to privileged instructions that will permit the hacker to circumvent normal security.[10]

Hypervisor Vulnerability

Virtualization complicates security because security is no longer dealing with a physical computer. One of the consequences of a virtual architecture is the attack surface of the system has increased. The attack surface is the collected aspects of the system exposed to external manipulation. In a typical, nonvirtual system, the attack surface consists of the external interfaces of the hardware, the operating system, and the applications on the system. We are all familiar with the patches and updates that are applied to our computing devices all the time. Many of these patches are designed to close up inadvertent opportunities for unauthorized access to system privileges. These fixes can be sorted out into operating system fixes and application fixes. A virtual system adds a new kind of fix: hypervisor updates and patches.

In other words, the hypervisor is a new attack surface with new opportunities for intrusion. The greatest fear on a physical system is that a malefactor could slide into supervisor mode and take complete control of the system. If a malefactor were to gain ring -1 control of a hypervisor, many VMs would be available for takeover. In addition, the hypervisor runs at the highest level of privilege and

---

[10]Sadly, some hacking exploits require only user-level access, but the most potentially devastating involve supervisor mode.

therefore has access to the entire physical machine. Although there have not been many exploits against hypervisors, the potential for damage is great. In a single stroke, a successful attack will compromise many applications.

If a VM could reach the hypervisor, only one VM with poor security could compromise an entire system. Suppose enterprise accounting VMs and marketing VMs were configured to run on the same hypervisor. Further suppose that the hypervisor has an undiscovered flaw that would allow VMs access to the hypervisor. This scenario could happen. As diligent as developers and testers are, flaws make their way into all software. Hypervisors are not an exception.

Accounting systems usually carefully follow best security practices, but marketing is often more freewheeling and more likely to have security gaps. If a hacker were to break into a marketing application and tap into the hypervisor via the previously unknown flaw, the accounting application would be open to the malefactor. No matter how secure one application is, it is still as weak as the weakest VM running on the hypervisor. This raises the chilling possibility that a malicious party on a public cloud could use a hypervisor flaw to attack other cloud users.

VM Mobility

Hypervisor vulnerability is not the only complication added by virtualization. The ability to move VMs from physical host to physical host and rapidly launch new VMs also complicates security. A simple example is two servers, one in a secure data center and the other on an employee desk in an open office. Suppose the virtual system is configured to overflow to the second server when the first server reaches a threshold. When the first server passes the threshold and new VMs begin to launch on the desktop, the security environment changes rapidly from a physically secured environment to an unsecured environment.

This example is simple and the problem is easily identified, but breaches like this can be subtle and harder to detect when access privileges are more complex. For instance, the overflow server might be secured in the datacenter, but at some time, access may have been granted to an outside consultant who is outside the scope of control of the enterprise. The challenge increases as the rules governing the movement of VMs become more complex.

Proliferation of VMs

The ease with which anyone can launch a VM can also lead to security issues. When installing and launching an application on a physical device takes hours or days of effort from technical staff, there are opportunities for evaluating the security of the application. The staff is likely to have an installation procedure that includes a security check, giving the department security experts a chance to evaluate the application and suggest modifications and incorporate the new installation into their security controls.

It takes little more than an image file to launch a virtual machine with a complete installation of an application. The technical bar for launching is low. Consequently, someone with little knowledge of the implications can launch a virtual machine with a full application stack with unpredictable security consequences. To deal with this proliferation, the security team has to set and enforce new guidelines, which may be difficult to enforce. The situation resembles the early days of distributed computing when zealous employees installed applications indiscriminately without regard for enterprise strategy or security.

Virtual Networking

Networking in a virtual system presents other security issues. The foundation of traditional network security is to create a secure perimeter around the corporate network. This model is no longer effective in many situations. Mobile devices, such as smartphones, tablets, and laptops, allow employees to work from outside corporate facilities. Readily available broadband connections make working remotely easy and efficient. Cloud implementations have moved key services off-site. The traditional perimeter barely exists. The response has been greater use of encryption and attention to monitoring all network traffic, watching traffic as it crosses not only the perimeter but inside the perimeter as well.

Security teams no longer assume that malicious activity will always be visible as an intrusion. Network intrusion prevention tools monitor all enterprise network traffic for suspicious patterns and signatures. Monitoring takes place through both hardware appliances and software installed on hosts.

Virtual networks can be invisible to intrusion monitoring because virtual network traffic, traffic between VMs, takes place through virtual software switches running on the physical virtualization host and usually does not flow over the physical network. Although it is possible to monitor the virtual network, detection will not happen if the security team is not aware of the potential blind spot.

Conclusion

The separation of physical hardware and logical software is akin to the evolution from single-cell to multicelled organisms. Single cells are limited by the physics of the cell. They can scale up only so far; their organization is limited by the chemistry of a drop of fluid surrounded by a semi-permeable membrane. They are largely confined to a living surrounded by water.

At some point, cells began to join into multicellular organisms and transcend the limits of a solitary cell. Each cell in a multicellular organism contains DNA that is a detailed blueprint for a 90-foot blue whale or a 7-ton elephant, for example. Cells manufacture all the chemicals and control all the actions that bring these gigantic animals to life, but they are microscopic and unable to live on their own. Organized cells work together; they are not limited by the physical limitations of their cellular existence and are freed to develop into the diverse ecosystem we know today.

Computing when limited to a single physical machine is similarly limited. A physical computer is scalable only to a certain point like a single cell. All computing is binary arithmetic performed in sequence. Like a single cell, the sequences of binary arithmetic performed by a physical computer can be wonderfully complex and achieve many things, but a physical computer is limited by the physics of a processor and motherboard.

Virtualization frees the dependence of computing on that individual physical machine. It allows machines to work together to support processes that spread across many machines and shift to other machines as needed, just as single cells have transcended their own physical limitations.

We have seen large-scale computing projects begin to change the world we live in. Social media require massive virtualized systems to handle their millions of participants. Climatologists and meteorologist refining our understanding of climate and weather use enormous and complex computer models that require massive virtual systems to model and predict the actions of the atmosphere.

Where virtualization will go from here is unknown but sure to be amazing.

EXERCISES

1. Describe the three characteristics of virtualization according to Popek and Goldberg.

2. Virtualization increases computing overhead, but it can also increase system efficiency. Explain.

3. Why do OSs that use more rings potentially perform better than systems that use only the inner and outer rings?

4. Give some reasons why an OS designer may choose to use only two rings.

5. What is the difference between trap-and-emulate virtualization and binary translation virtualization?

6. What are the advantages and disadvantages of paravirtualization?

7. Why are hypervisor security breaches potentially serious?

8. What are some of the areas that security teams must be aware of when dealing with virtualized systems?

Splendid Isolation

Virtual Architecture in Practice

SUMMARY

Virtualization separates hardware from software. The opportunities presented by this separation are startling. Long ago, engineers conceived virtualization as a tool for supporting multiple users on a single computer. A side effect of this separation was the possibility of providing significantly different and separate environments for each user. Eventually, virtualization came to support a rich environment for entire ecosystems of applications and services and became the foundation for cloud computing.

Another method of supporting multiple users on a single computer was developed at about the same time as virtualization. This method, referred to as *containers*, separated users by restricting their resources and access without providing a virtual machine for each user. This method has also proven useful.

This chapter describes some of the usages that make virtualization powerful.

This chapter is about virtualization usage. Developers and architects should not expect to implement all of these practices. Some will be implemented in third-party platforms and not by the users of the platform. Virtualization and clouds present opportunities for redesigning and building a new infrastructure for enterprise technology. These opportunities are also challenges that require expertise and foresight.

Whenever stepping into a new and large IT project like one involving shifting to or using a virtual platform for the first time, there is a decision: accept a third-party facility or build it yourself. Both alternatives have advantages and pitfalls. This is particularly true for virtualization projects. Virtualization is an active area of innovation. New products appear every year, and products are transformed and disappear as companies are acquired, merged, and close their doors. The ferment and churn make the "build or buy" decision more difficult. New and innovative products are tempting, but their future may be hard to predict. Building for yourself offers stability but has other issues.

An application or component developed in-house depends on the talent and resources of the enterprise to build, and even when the enterprise employs contractors for construction, the enterprise still must use in-house talent and resources for maintenance. Often, these projects support enterprise goals but are not central to core mission-critical objectives. Consequently, in-house applications or components are a continual drain on the core mission. Any application or component used by most businesses and organizations is likely to be available from a third party. This is especially true of technology such as virtualization, which has captured a great deal of interest. The enterprise should consider these products carefully before deciding to build in-house.

Architects and senior managers often forget that the cost of maintaining a service is frequently more expensive over the lifetime of the service than the cost of the initial build. Virtualized noncore basic applications, such as service desk and customer relations management, are good examples. These applications are likely to serve for many years. The cumulative cost of maintaining these applications is a good reason for avoiding developing these facilities independently and preserving enterprise development resources for areas that are exclusively in the enterprise's core goals and competence.

There are several other factors to consider in deciding to build in-house. Many developers prefer to "roll their own,"[1] for the sheer pleasure of completing a challenging project. That is not a good reason for using enterprise development resources, but some circumstances may still warrant building in-house. One good reason is to avoid dependence on a third party for mission-critical technology. When the long-term viability of the third-party supplier is questionable or there is fear that a competitor may acquire the supplier, an IT team may be compelled to avoid the threat of an unsupported or hostile technology by building the technology themselves despite all cautions. In other cases, intellectual property or licensing issues may make using a third-party product undesirable. Applications built on virtual platforms can easily fall into the category of mission-critical technology. Enterprises may want to build virtual platforms and applications over which they retain complete control.

---

[1] This is a developer's phrase for coding for yourself rather than using a standard library, an off-the-shelf component, and so on.

When a technology is mission critical but far from the enterprise core competency, an open source product supported by an industry consortium can be an excellent alternative. A strong consortium offers long-term stability and guards the technology from acquisition and control by a hostile competitor.

When a gap analysis reveals that a third-party technology only approximates the needs of the enterprise, there may be another good reason to build in-house. However, this situation requires scrutiny. Gaps can be in the eye of the beholder. Every enterprise thinks they are special, and most are, but that does not mean that every detail of their architecture will be different.

Third-party products are often more capable than they appear through the eyes of someone infatuated with the uniqueness of their situation. Second and third looks may inspire more ingenuity. Often, technologists discover that a third-party product can meet their special needs when they are prompted to revisit the problem.

Enterprises are often cautioned not to go beyond their core competency. This is good advice. Many organizations have regretted ignoring it, but there are exceptions. When an exception begins to appear desirable, it is time to double down on scrutiny. When a group decides to step outside its core competency, misjudgment is easy. But it can be the right decision. Virtualization technology differs from on-premises development in ways that many strategists, managers, and developers will find unfamiliar and beyond their core competency. They may venture into noncore areas without understanding the consequences.

This chapter examines some of the unique virtualization practices that a site should consider and use in evaluating decisions about whether to buy or build, which products to consider, and the architecture of the components the site decides to build for themselves.

Virtualized Integration

Virtualization separates the process from the hardware it runs on. Like security, traditional integration assumes that processes are tied to physical hardware.

The fundamental pattern for deploying virtual machines and reconfiguring virtual machines (VMs) causes issues for integration. When a physical server does not have the capacity to support a service, the service is often moved to another physical server with more resources available for the service. The second server could have a faster processor, have more cores, or simply be less heavily loaded than the first processor. A human operator working from a virtual infrastructure management interface may make the decision to move the service, or an automated process that detects overloaded physical devices may shift processing to less loaded devices. Moving processes is one of the basic activities of a clustered virtual system in which several physical machines support a collection of processes.

Figure 11-1 shows the response when the system determines that service A must be moved from physical server 1 to physical server 2. The first step is to quiesce[2] VM1 and take a snapshot, a file that contains everything in the memory and registers of the VM. The second virtual machine, VM2, is then started on the second physical server using the snapshot of VM1. Quiescing a VM stops all action, so the snapshot is an accurate picture without inconsistent images of moving parts. At this point, VM2 is an exact image of VM1, running service A. The final step is to direct consumers of the service to VM2 and possibly shut down VM1.[3]

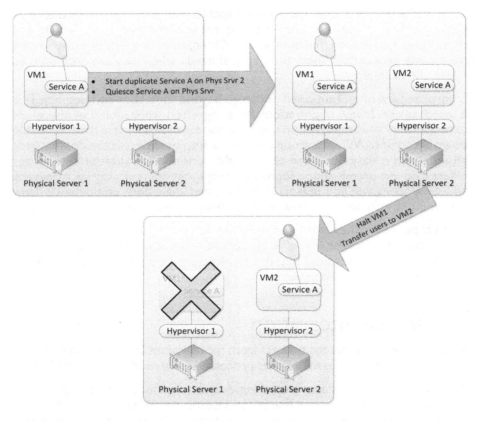

Figure 11-1. Virtualized systems often move virtual services from physical server to physical server

---

[2]*Quiesce* means to become still or cease activity.
[3]Some virtualization products streamline the movement from server to server using proprietary technology to take a snapshot of memory and quiescing the original VM when the snapshot is stable. The rest of the process is the same, but it is automated so there is no human latency.

This scenario works well when the environment is uniform, the service is stateless, and the service transactions are granular, but it begins to break down when the situation becomes more complex.

Environment

First, consider the environment. If physical server 1 and physical server 2 are the same architecture and hypervisor 1 and hypervisor 2 are from the same vendor, there is no problem. If the physical servers are different architectures or are running different OSs (say Linux and Windows), there may not be problem as long the hypervisor supports both physical server configurations. However, when hypervisor 1 and hypervisor 2 are different, problems are almost certain to appear. Although hypervisor vendors have been working toward compatibility, there are still challenges. Hypervisor vendors compete on features. Unique features are by nature incompatible. Coding to the lowest common denominator is a solution for hypervisor interoperability but is seldom desirable. Open Virtual Format (OVF) is helpful, but even OVF is not as simple as one would hope because of incompatible hypervisor features.

Stateless Services

Stateless services make scenarios like this much easier to manage. When a service is stateless, previous calls by a consumer to the service do not affect future calls.

For example, a request to the National Oceanic and Atmospheric Administration (NOAA) web service is stateless. A request for the current temperature in Blue Earth, Minnesota, will be unaffected by a previous request for the temperature in Bellingham, Washington. A stateless service is much easier for a provider to code and manage, although it can be more work for the consumer. A stateful service would allow the consumer to declare that Bellingham, Washington, will be the location for future requests and follow the declaration with requests for temperature, rainfall, and humidity on various dates without mentioning that the request is for Bellingham. When consumers shift their interest to Blue Earth, they could send a request to change their state from "location=Bellingham" to "location=Blue Earth" and repeat their queries exactly and get results for Blue Earth. A practice like this lends itself easily to writing scripts that return all the information for a location by specifying a single parameter. This becomes more significant as the data delivered or the actions performed by the service become more complex. It can become difficult to put together requests that contain all the information necessary to make the next stateless request in a sequence.

To a certain extent, stateful and stateless are a trade-off. In a stateful interchange, the server must retain information about the state of the sequence of transactions. In a stateless interchange, the client usually has to keep similar information. In the big picture, clients are in a better position to keep the state because a client has only its own state to track. A server with many clients has many states to track.

When a component or the network fails, a stateless interchange can recover easily. The client repeats its request. When a stateful interchange fails, recovery is more difficult. The server has to reconstruct the state prior to the last interchange, often by replaying the client's messages. This involves tricky logic and a log of previous messages.

This issue is particularly important when VMs are stopped, started, and moved from hypervisor to hypervisor, as in Figure 11-1. When a stateless service is quiesced to clear its queues, snapshotted, and stopped, and then the snapshot is restarted, the service is ready for activity. Transactions interrupted in mid-flight (that is, sent by the client but not received by the server) need to be repeated by the client only when no reply is received.

Stateful servers have a somewhat different problem. Stateful servers must track their clients and their states. If the server clears its client state table when the service is quiesced, the client must start over on their transaction, which means they will have to unwind their stack to find their starting state. But clients ordinarily don't need to keep a record of transactions, and it is quite likely that they will not be able to recover. Architects and developers usually can meet or circumvent stateful server challenges, but the service becomes more arduous to develop and maintain.[4]

Stateless processes are also important for scalability. A task divided into many stateless subtasks can be run in an arbitrary number of parallel processes to scale up the volume of data processed by the service. If subprocesses can be restarted without regard to state, the system is more resilient to errors and runs faster.

Service Granularity

Granular services perform poorly over high-latency networks, but a more granular service will transition more smoothly from one hypervisor to another. A highly granular service is a service that interacts in small steps.

---

[4]The scenario described here is not the migration of processes from one physical device or hypervisor to another. The memory snapshots used for migration hold state, and the state is reproduced in the target VM. For state recovery to become an issue during migration, something would have to happen to interrupt the migration and cause the snapshot to be damaged or lost. This is not impossible but unlikely.

This is good and bad. It is good because an interruption in a highly granular service will cause only a small amount of backtracking. On the other hand, highly granular services are chatty; they send a message, get a message, send a message, and get a message with only a little data processing in between. A less granular service sends fewer messages to accomplish the same activity with less latency.

Typically, each message requires two traverses of the network: one request and one reply. A service that uses two messages for an activity will require four traverses. A service that uses six messages will require twelve traverses. See Figure 11-2. Since each traverse of the network takes roughly the same time, a service that uses two messages will expend only a third of the latency of a service that uses six messages. Unless a service is highly compute intensive, network latency is usually the lion's share of service response time.

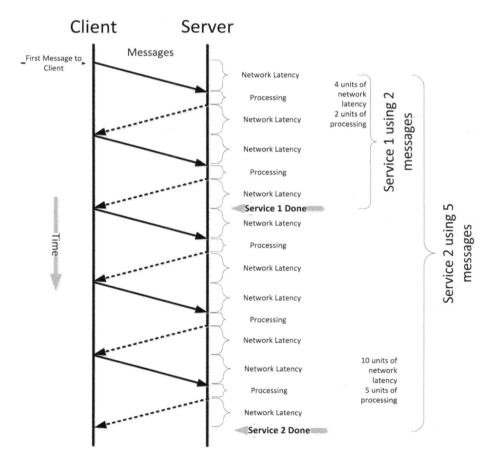

Figure 11-2. Network latency slows highly granular services

If the network is fast, as it usually is on a virtual network or a LAN, latency may be too small to matter. The difference between one-tenth and three-tenths of a millisecond latency may be negligible. However, a more granular service may be able to transfer from one hypervisor to another much more quickly than a less granular service, and that difference could be significant.

Many variables are involved. Message latency varies considerably depending on the environment. When the client is many routers and switches away from the server, latency is usually large. In an internal network, it's not so large. Some services lend themselves well to high granularity; others are awkward without large transactions.

The biggest disadvantage of low granularity is lack of control. Compare a food-ordering service that lets you enter a dish and immediately sends back the price for the item and the total for the meal. As you add dishes, the total keeps current. It's easy to decide when you have met your per diem for lunch. A less granular service might give you the total only after you have selected your entire meal and you have to start over if you go over. The first method may be more convenient, but the second method will take less time on a slow network. The best decision often requires both testing and educated guesses.

Another aspect of granularity is *microservices*. As opposed to granular services that act in many small steps, microservices are services that provide single-purpose generic functionality that can be combined into a larger service. This philosophy harks back to the early days of UNIX, which was based on many small functions that could be composed into complex applications. UNIX typically ran on a single processor, minimizing the latency between function calls. Often, reliable and efficient applications could be built quickly by stringing together stock functions in a script that controlled the logic.

Microservices can be used to quickly build reliable applications just like UNIX functions. The significant difference is the addition of the network into the system. Microservices are subject to the same latency issues as granular services, and decisions must be made on the same basis.

Addressing in Virtualized Environments

Addressing is another issue when dealing with the VM moving scenario in Figure 11-1. Unless special provision is made, VM2 will have a different Medium Access Control (MAC) address[5] and a different IP address from VM1. Most

---

[5]Medium Access Control (MAC) addresses are globally unique strings that are assigned when hardware is manufactured. The global uniqueness of MAC addresses is a fundamental assumption of computer networking. When VMs are not exposed outside the virtualized space, MAC addresses can be assigned and changed by the hypervisor, which follows its own rules. When a VM can communicate with the outside, MAC addresses must be assigned more carefully.

hypervisors can start a VM with a static MAC and IP addresses that will remain the same when the VM is stopped and restarted, but the addresses are lost when the VM is deleted rather than stopped.

MAC addresses of physical devices are determined when a physical device is manufactured. Its MAC address is burned in a chip and cannot be changed. Virtual devices have MAC addresses assigned. This adds complexity to managing virtual devices.

In Chapter 9, tracking and managing process addresses was a major topic. Virtualization increases this challenge because virtual network addresses are more fluid than physical addresses. Until virtualization became popular, an IP address in a distributed system referred to a physical device connected to a network. Routers and switches direct packets to devices, not processes. Identifying processes on a server is dependent on the IP address of the server, which in turn is connected to the MAC address of the device.

In theory, running on a virtualized system is seamless: whether physical or virtualized hardware, everything works the same. Moving from one physical server to another physical server and hypervisor should not affect operation of the service. For an isolated VM, this principle generally holds, but when VMs communicate with other VMs on the same hypervisor or with VMs on a different hypervisor or a physical host, special provisions need to be made.

A traditional integration challenge is to make integrated application addressing and routing as flexible and reliable as possible, but behind the efforts to meet this challenge, there usually lurks an assumption that addresses will be in some sense constant and change slowly.

Virtualization invalidates many assumptions that traditional integration relies upon. An unsophisticated integration assumes that two communicating processes will be stationary; the process addresses can be hard-coded into application code, and the processes will always be able to exchange information. Integrations that are more sophisticated do not assume that addresses will never change, but they do assume that every address change will accompany a configuration change that will track changing addresses. When the address of a communicating process changes, the code of the processes will not need to change, but a configuration file or something similar will change.[6]

---

[6]One way of accomplishing this is with a reverse proxy. A reverse proxy acts as a front end with an address that does not change. The proxy keeps track of the real location of services and forwards the message to the real target. When the target replies, it sends the message to the reverse proxy, which then passes the message on to the originator. This is similar to Network Address Translation described in the next section.

Network Address Translation

Network Address Translation (NAT) often helps in this situation. NAT is usually implemented on a router or a switch, and it is used to map one IP address space into another. NAT can be either "one-to-one" or "one-to-many." One-to-one NAT maps an address in one space to a single address in another space. It used to be used as part of bridges between networks with incompatible addresses, such as IP and mainframe networks. This use is not so important now because IP addresses are almost universal. Another use of one-to-one NAT is to continue to use old addresses after a network has been physically reconfigured. The real addresses follow the physical configuration of the network. The old addresses are translated by NAT to the new addresses so the old addresses can continue to be used.

One-to-many NAT maps a single address to many addresses and is used for different purposes than one-to-one NAT. Most one-to-many NATs map a single publicly exposed IP to many private hosts. See Figure 11-3. A home wireless router is a typical example. The router has a public IP address assigned by the Internet service provider. Within the local wireless LAN, individual PCs, laptops, tablets, and phones are assigned private IP addresses that are not routable on the public network.

When a device within the private network directs a request to an address outside the network, the request goes to the NAT router, which appears to be an ordinary external gateway. The packets sent by the internal device have the device's private IP address as the source and the public address of the target as the destination address. The NAT switches the internal source address to an external public address assigned from the NAT's address pool and records the internal and external addresses in a binding table. Then the NAT sends the packet to the public network, where it finds its way to its destination. The destination device has no clue that the packet has passed through a NAT. If the destination device replies, it will place the source address of the incoming packet into the destination address of the outgoing packet and place its own address into the source address of the outgoing packet. When the packet arrives back at the NAT, the NAT will replace the destination address with the value in its binding table that matches the incoming destination address. At this point, the destination address is the private internal address of the originating device, which will receive the packet. Thus, the internal private address of the device never appears on the public network. One-to-many NAT used in this fashion is so common now that it is usually what is meant by NAT.

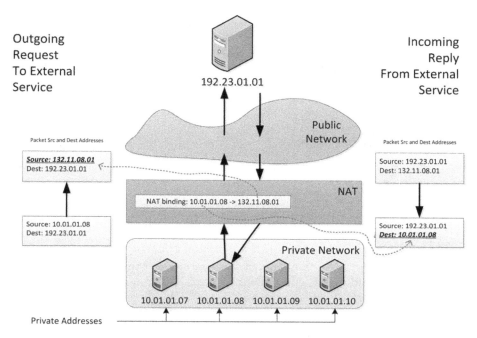

Figure 11-3. One-to-many NAT permits sites to have many internal addresses without using public addresses

Under the typical one-to-many NAT practice, all traffic coming into the private network must be a reply to a previous outgoing request from inside the network. This is acceptable for typical users because typical computer users do not offer services for public access. In fact, NAT is often considered useful for security since it discourages intrusion from outside.[7] Nevertheless, some applications require a public address. Any application that acts as a server to other devices on the public network or communicates with peers on the public network requires a public address. For home networks, games are the most common applications that require public addresses. Applications that require a public address in order to act as a server on the public network are more common in enterprises. Most NAT implementations have provisions to support a limited number of devices with public addresses.

NAT is a "shim" technology. A NAT device can be put in place between a public and private network without disturbing processing on either its input or output side. This makes NAT easy to deploy. There are a number of criticisms of NAT as an easy but incomplete or short-term solution. For example,

---

[7]Be cautious. The security benefits of NAT are a side effect, not part of its design. It is irrelevant to most common exploits. No one should ever assume that because NAT is in place, their network is safe.

one important use of NAT is to combat depletion of the IPv4 address space. IPv6 is a long-term solution with benefits beyond an expanded address space. However, critics point out that NAT has taken away the urgency to convert to IPv6, which is holding up improvement of the Internet. Other critics are concerned that NAT violates a basic principle of the Internet: every device has a unique identity characterized by its network address.

NAT and Virtual Systems

NAT can be an important tool for managing virtual systems. Using NAT, hypervisors can assign private addresses to VMs without regard for the requirements of the public network, which could be onerous, given the short lives and constant churn of VMs in many environments. These VMs are still able to communicate externally, although they cannot act as servers to the outside world.

VMs managed by a NAT implementation can move from physical server to physical server and be assigned new addresses. As long as the NAT implementation is aware of the change and keeps its binding tables updated, the outside world will not be aware of the shifts. When a VM with a public address changes private address, only the NAT binding table that binds the internal to the external address must be changed.

Scaling

Most successful services scale well. Scaling well means that the capacity of the service easily and smoothly changes to match the load placed on the service. Most services eventually need to scale up. Loads get larger as a successful enterprise expands and the service must scale up. Often, services also need to scale down, shrinking when the need for the service declines during off-hours or off-seasons. Scaling down is often a prudent use of resources. The strengths of virtual implementations are especially well-suited to scaling, and virtual implementations can be designed to scale exceptionally well.

There are two fundamental approaches to scaling: vertical and horizontal.

Vertical Scaling

Vertically scaling a service means replacing one computer with a computer that has more capacity or enhancing an existing computer using methods such as adding a faster or more efficient processor, increasing the speed and capacity of the data bus, and providing faster memory or storage. See Figure 11-4.

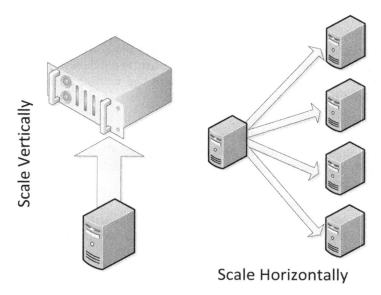

Figure 11-4. Vertical scaling replaces a computer with one of greater capacity to scale up. Horizontal scaling adds several computers of similar capacity to scale up

Vertical scaling is limited by the availability of more powerful hardware. Vertical scaling is typically easier than horizontal scaling because software usually changes little, or not at all, when higher-capacity hardware is put in place. When a site that already has top-of-line high-capacity hardware needs to scale up, a crisis occurs. Unless higher-capacity hardware can be found, the site has few alternatives. They can set up another identical system and move some of their clients to the new system. This solution works, but when the service is based on sharing between clients, this may be rather awkward to implement satisfactorily. Another possibility is to redesign the service to scale horizontally. This is often the best solution, but it is seldom easy.

Horizontal Scaling

Horizontal scaling increases the capacity of a service by adding computers, (often called *nodes*), each performing the same task. The common alternative to horizontal scaling is vertical scaling.

Converting a service from vertical to horizontal scaling is difficult because horizontal scaling usually requires a more complex and carefully planned design than a vertically scalable service. Fundamentally, a monolithic vertically scalable application may be complex, but it simply executes a request from beginning to end. A horizontally scalable application decomposes a request into segments that can be executed in parallel. These tasks are then distributed among available processing nodes. At some point, or several points, individual tasks may have to merge to exchange data or to deliver the result to the client. In addition, there probably needs to be code for picking up execution when a processing node fails since economical horizontal scaling usually assumes that hardware will use redundancy to achieve reliability. All of this is support for the logic of the task itself, which must be implemented in the decomposed segments.

Developing horizontally scalable services generally requires more coordination between developers and development teams, more experienced developers, and a more sophisticated development group. Consequently, developing horizontally scalable applications is usually substantially more expensive than vertically scalable applications.

There are several critically important advantages to horizontal scalability. The first is that horizontal scaling does not have the kind of limit that vertical scaling faces. In theory, a horizontally scalable service just keeps adding processing nodes to match the load on the service. There are limits to horizontal scalability that come from the necessity of maintaining coordination of the processing nodes, but those are far higher than vertical scaling limits.

Another advantage to horizontal scaling is that a production service can scale up or down easily. A vertically scaling service cannot scale down unless spare resources can be diverted to another service when they are not needed. Scaling up a vertically scaling service involves a hardware change that often disrupts production.

Horizontal scaling is suited well to virtual systems. Adding VMs to a virtual system to scale up a service is a simple process. When the virtual system is on a cloud, scaling up in this way may even be transparent to the enterprise owning the service. When properly designed, the service can be robust enough to failover transparently when a disaster strikes. The issues discussed earlier relating to Figure 11-1 are usually dealt with in the design of the service and present fewer problems than appear in vertically scalable designs. Vertical scaling can be a problem for virtually implemented services; the capacity of VMs supported by a hypervisor is often limited. Most virtual systems focus on many small VMs rather than a few large virtual devices.

Horizontally scaling services can often easily take advantage of automatic scaling, often called *elastic scaling,* available on many public clouds. When this feature is available, new VMs are automatically launched when threshold conditions are met and shut down when use declines.

Failover and Performance

Failover and performance may seem like an odd juxtaposition. Failover is the ability for a service to withstand a component or equipment failure or other disaster without interrupting the service by shifting to other equipment or facilities or using redundant resources. Performance is quite different. A service that performs according to specifications responds with appropriate speed to all queries. Failover and performance may seem disconnected, but when designing virtual applications, they are in opposition. Without careful design, a service that fails over well may not perform well.

The Open Virtual Format standard has useful terminology. OVF refers to affinity and availability. *Affinity* relates to performance, and *availability* ties to reliability and failover. They are two principles used for choosing where to locate virtual machines. When two VMs are located with a preference for affinity, they are located as close as possible. *Close* can mean various things in OVF terms, but the fundamental idea is that close VMs communicate quickly and less close VMs have greater communication latency. *Availability* is an opposing locating principle. VMs that are located for availability are as distant as possible. Like affinity, availability can have various meanings, but VMs that are more distant will be less affected by failures in the proximity of the other VM. In general, VMs with high availability will not have high affinity. See Figure 11-5.

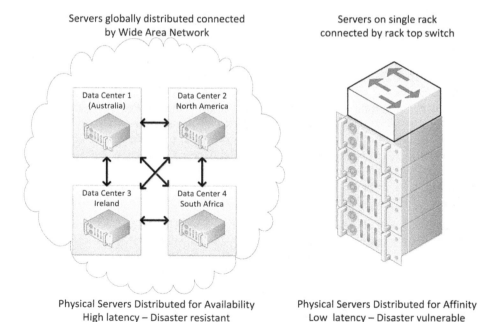

Servers globally distributed connected by Wide Area Network

Servers on single rack connected by rack top switch

Data Center 1 (Australia)

Data Center 2 North America

Data Center 3 Ireland

Data Center 4 South Africa

Physical Servers Distributed for Availability
High latency – Disaster resistant

Physical Servers Distributed for Affinity
Low latency – Disaster vulnerable

Figure 11-5. *Availability and affinity are two ways of distributing physical servers*

Some examples will help understanding. Suppose a service must perform well. The application design might call for horizontally scaling processes to run on up to eight VMs on four physical servers available. If those VMs were designated to run with affinity, they might be located on a single rack in the datacenter with inter-server communication through a single rack-top switch connecting the devices on the rack. This configuration supports fast communication. However, if a fire were to break out close to the rack and the sprinkler system turned on, every server on the rack could go down simultaneously and recovery could take hours.

On the other hand, if the service were deployed with availability, each VM might be deployed in widely separated, even globally separated, datacenters. A failure, such as a fire, in one datacenter would be a minor blip as processing transferred to a remote and unaffected VM. However, the cost of this level of reliability would be performance because communication between the services' VMs would almost certainly involve several switches and routers, resulting in much greater latency than the VMs all located on the same rack.

This presents a basic trade-off. A highly reliable system requires more resources to perform well. A highly performant system requires additional resources to be reliable.

The trade-off is often surmountable, but it requires analysis of the available resources and the nature of the consumers of the service. For example, if consumers are divided geographically, between Australia and North America, for example, one group of servers could support Australia, and another could support North America. Each of the groups can be organized for affinity—close together for optimum performance. If a disaster occurs in Australia, the Australian consumers could failover to North America. Performance would drop for the Australian customers because of greater network latency, but service would not be interrupted. In many cases, this will be an acceptable compromise. Often, the segmentation of the consumer base will not be so clear-cut; in North America, East Coast and West Coast segments are common, but it is difficult to decide which segment is right for consumers in Denver.

Virtualization makes these issues easier to cope with because shuffling VMs is easier than moving physical servers, which typically involves re-cabling and manual reconfiguration. Starting a VM on a different hypervisor is much simpler and can probably be accomplished from a single console.

Open Virtual Format

Open Virtual Format (OVF) is a standard that is supported by major hypervisors. It is a packaging format standard for virtual systems. An OVF package contains the images that a hypervisor will deploy and a descriptor that describes how the images fit together. OVF packages can be large. The standard does not limit the number of virtual machines that may be part of the package. The descriptor is hierarchical, and the standard places no limits on the complexity of the hierarchy. The virtualization platform determines those limits.

Packaging Format

OVF is a virtual system packaging standard. It's easy to get confused on exactly what that means. A packaging standard is not a management standard, and it is not a software stack. The OVF standard tells you how to put together a set of files that clearly and unambiguously defines a virtual system. An OVF package usually has system images of the virtual machines that will make up the virtual machines in the package. A package also contains a descriptor that describes virtual configurations that will support the images in the packages and how the entire system should be networked and distributed for reliability and performance. Finally, there are security manifests that make it hard to create an unauthorized version of the package that is not exactly what the author intended.

A packaging format is not designed to manage the systems it deploys. Expecting it to do that would be like trying to manage applications deployed on a Windows platform from the Control Panel's Uninstall a Program page. There are other interfaces for managing applications. The OVF standard also does not specify the software that does the actual installation. Instead, it is designed as a format to be used by many virtualization platforms.

The OVF package consists of several files. See Figure 11-6. The only required file is the descriptor, which is written in XML and contains the description of the system that the virtualization platform uses for deployment. The manifest and certificate are optional, but when present, they provide assurance that the contents of the package have not been tampered with and are from a certified source. The image files are images of the objects the virtualization platform will install. The formats of image files are not specified beyond requiring that they follow a publicly available format. The packager and the user must determine that the virtualization platform will accept the format. Resource files are additional resources to be installed in the package. These are often installable images of applications. The files in an OVF package can be compiled into a single file using a Portable Operating System Interface (POSIX) tape archive (tar) format or can be left as individual files.

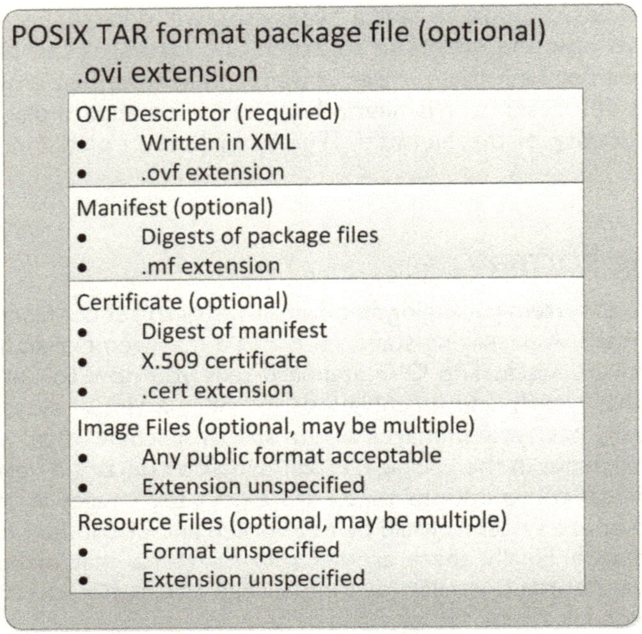

```
POSIX TAR format package file (optional)
.ovi extension

    OVF Descriptor (required)
    •     Written in XML
    •     .ovf extension

    Manifest (optional)
    •     Digests of package files
    •     .mf extension

    Certificate (optional)
    •     Digest of manifest
    •     X.509 certificate
    •     .cert extension

    Image Files (optional, may be multiple)
    •     Any public format acceptable
    •     Extension unspecified

    Resource Files (optional, may be multiple)
    •     Format unspecified
    •     Extension unspecified
```

Figure 11-6. An OVF package consists of several files

Interoperability

OVF is closely tied to the virtualization platforms on which OVF packages are deployed. The Distributed Management Task Force (DMTF) OVF working group has members from most significant hypervisor vendors and many significant users of virtualized environments.[8] Consequently, an OVF package can be written for almost any virtualization platform following the same OVF standard. The standard is not limited to the common features shared between the platform vendors. If that were the goal, all OVF packages would be interoperable; that is, a single OVF package would run equally well on many different platforms, but because platform features vary widely, the capabilities of the package would necessarily be limited to the lowest common denominator among virtualization platforms. In fact, interoperable OVF packages can be written, but they seldom are because most OVF users want to exploit the unique features of the platform they are using.

---

[8]See http://dmtf.org/standards/ovf for further information on the OVF standard.

An OVF Use Case

Here is an example of an OVF package that is not interoperable between virtualization platforms but is still valuable.

Consider a simple physical system; let's say it's a LAMP stack (Linux, Apache, MySQL, and Perl, Python, or PHP) that requires at least two servers, one for an HTTP server and the other for a database. Suppose QA uses this LAMP stack system repeatedly. If QA wants to go virtual, an OVF package for this LAMP stack implementation is simple. After the package is written, instead of redeploying the system piece by piece each time QA needs a new instance, QA hands the OVF package to their virtualization platform, and it deploys the system as specified, exactly the same, every time. This saves QA team time and equipment because they perform tests that need a basic LAMP stack every few weeks. When the test is over, they remove the LAMP stack implementation and use the physical resources for other tests. When QA needs the LAMP stack implementation again, they pass the OVF package to the virtualization platform to deploy it, and they have a fresh installation in minutes with no error-prone manual configuration.

Of course, a developer could do all this with a script, but in most similar environments, formats and tools have supplanted scripts. Linux application deployments are an example. Decades ago, developers wrote shell scripts for deploying complex applications, but now most applications use standard tools and formats such as installation tools and .deb files on Debian distributions and .rpm files and tools on other Linux distributions. .deb files correspond closely to OVF packages. Scripts still play a role, but the overall control of the installation comes from the installation tool. On Windows, .bat files have been replaced with tools like InstallShield. The results are increased reliability and ease of development and maintenance.

OVF provides similar advantages. With an OVF package, authors don't have to untangle idiosyncratic logic to understand and extend packages. They don't have to invent new spokes for a script's wheel, and they can exchange packages with other authors written in a common language.

An International Standard

OVF has significant visibility as a national and international standard. OVF has been through a rigorous review by a national standards body (ANSI) and an international standards body (ISO/IEC). The next revision of Twitter may not depend on OVF, but many services are more reliable and perform better because they have an OVF package or two in the background. Hot prototypes may not depend on OVF, but solid production services depend on reliable and consistent components, which is exactly why OVF exists.

Every builder of IT services that run on a cloud or in a virtual environment should know what OVF can do for them and consider using it. OVF is a stable standard, accepted in the international standards community and not just the body that published it (DMTF), and it makes products easier to write and maintain.[9]

Conclusion

Virtualized systems are fluid. They can change quickly in response to changing workloads and physical conditions. But fluidity also generates challenges. Processes are no longer barnacles attached to a physical server; they are movable but only with planning and effort. In a virtual environment, processes are more like fish that flit freely from node to node in the form of images that can be stopped on one device and immediately reappear on another.

Traditional networking relies on addresses that are assigned to physical devices with an assumption that address changes will be a rare event. But with virtual devices appearing and disappearing, addressing becomes a challenge.

In a virtual environment, the natural means of scaling up is to increase the number of virtual machines processing the workload. In a nonvirtual environment, the scaling up is often via increasing the capacity of the physical machine, which means many applications must be redesigned to scale horizontally rather than vertically.

The opportunities for failover and performance optimization are different in a virtual environment. This requires rethinking the physical distribution of the environment.

Finally, taking full advantage of virtualization requires a means of conveniently packaging and deploying complex systems so they can easily be replicated and managed.

The next stage in the progress to cloud service management is use of clouds, which are largely impossible without virtual systems but add new dimensions to virtualization.

EXERCISES

1. Distinguish stateless and stateful services.

2. How does service granularity affect service performance?

3. Distinguish between vertical and horizontal scaling.

4. What is the role of NAT in virtual systems?

5. What is the purpose of OVF?

---

[9]OVF is supported by most major hypervisor manufacturers, including IBM, VMware, Microsoft, Oracle, and Citrix.

Clouds

Slipping the Surly Bonds

Cloud Architecture Practices

SUMMARY

Cloud implementation is not easy. The hype says moving implementations from the premises to a remote cloud is an instant cure for many IT ills. The hype is true, but only for some implementers. Frequently, the problem is a basic misunderstanding of the nature of cloud implementation. It is both a business pattern and a technology. Cloud computing opens up business possibilities and new combinations and scales of technology, but unless business and technology work together, the results will most likely be disappointing. In addition, cloud computing is best when it supports whole systems of services. A service can be implemented on a cloud independently, but usually the greatest benefits will not be realized until several services work in a synergistic cloud implementation. Strategic planning, as ITIL best practices advocate, promotes long-term cooperative strategizing, which can help guarantee cloud success.

This chapter emphasizes the business side of cloud implementation, pointing out areas where business participation is especially important.

Cloud is a tremendous success; look at the trade press, the literature published by vendors offering cloud-related products, or the general press. In many ways, this declaration of triumph is true. Cloud vendors enjoy increasing revenues and stock prices. It seems that "cloud" is on everyone's lips.

Cloud implementations are enabling many organizations to slip away from the surly bonds of inflexible on-premises implementations.

But there is a dark underside to cloud implementations. Many have outright failed. Others have stalled in a morass of unmet expectations and disappointment. Yet others succeed only in lip service: an organization may implement a cloud project that has only marginal success, but the organization still may hold it up proudly as an innovative implementation of forward thinking and woe to anyone who says different.

These symptoms are shared with the early adaptation of most innovative technologies. Whenever a technology captures the interest and imagination of management and the public, there are bound to be occasions when organizations chase the phantom of a technological solution rather than address the real obstacles to progress.

Cloud Failures

Cloud solutions are open to a double punch: the cloud concept is both business and technical. Both the CFO and the CIO have an interest in cloud implementations. CFOs see a new business model in which IT costs show up on a monthly invoice based on transparent resource consumption. In a crisis, the CFO hopes to be able restrain the cloud service and reduce the monthly invoices.

The investment in on-premises computing is in depreciating technical assets that rapidly become obsolete and unrecoverable. Consequently, these costs are difficult or impossible to control. Once the investment is made, there is no going back. CFOs become excited at the possibility of dialing down IT equipment costs during business slowdowns and dialing them up when situations improve. There is a shining light for a future where the total cost of delivering services will decrease.

CIOs see greater flexibility for modifying existing services and introducing new services. Services that scale up and down automatically in response to demand are a solution that IT has wanted for decades. Technologists are tantalized by the prospect of developing services based on the instant availability of seemingly unlimited computing and storage capacity.

The CFO and CIO, as well as the CEO, are easily enthralled with visions of praise and gratitude from their boards and stockholders because they are reaping the benefit of the attractive new cloud concept that everyone is talking about. Even the name, *cloud*, conveys romance and vision, unlike "service-oriented architecture" or "distributed systems" that suggest someone with thick glasses and a pocket protector working nights.

But these benefits may not appear as expected or on schedule. Long-term contracts, startup costs, and opportunity costs all complicate the vision. Modifying existing applications for cloud deployment can be more difficult and time-consuming than expected, especially when development is unfamiliar with cloud. Worst of all, poor planning or faulty technical implementation can result in services that have to be redesigned and rebuilt after the cloud implementation is up and running. When these headwinds become too great for executive management to stand, the deflation of expectations is punishing.

In this atmosphere of over-expectation and minimal understanding, projects can start for the wrong reasons with inadequate or inappropriate strategic and tactical planning. Success, not failure, is surprising.

The problem is especially vexing because both the business and technical sides of the enterprise have expectations, and both must cooperate to achieve success. If the business side sees cloud computing as a cost-cutting measure with minor technical requirements or the technical side sees cloud as a technical effort that will save the business a bundle without similar investment from the business, success is difficult.

Cloud success requires full participation by both business managers and technologists. For example, a business manager may propose to move to a cloud an in-house application that fluctuates broadly in resource consumption. The manager is hoping to take advantage of usage-based billing to reduce costs during slow periods. Without the help of the technologists, the business manager may not realize that the application has a monolithic architecture that cannot scale by adding virtual machines. Therefore, it must be redesigned to scale horizontally if substantial cost reductions are to be gained from usage-based billing. The business manager will not be able to make an informed decision without a technical estimate of the cost of building in horizontal scaling, which could be minor or prohibitive, depending on the construction of the application. A proposal from the technical side may not take into consideration business requirements. For instance, they may propose moving an application to a cloud without being aware that the application is subject to auditing requirements that could not be met on the cloud. If this is not discovered until an objection is raised on the audit, the results could be disastrous.

Business Failures

Many of these issues stem from lack of planning and expectation setting. Cloud implementations transform capital investments into operational expenses over time, but that shift may be hard to detect because most of the time, current asset investments continue to support existing services or they have already been written off. Consequently, the immediate effect of deploying a cloud service is to increase operational expenses without a corresponding decrease in capital investment. There may be a decrease in capital investment, but it is a sum not spent, and it will not appear on either a revenue statement or a balance sheet. A cloud deployment may generate real cost savings, but only comparisons between real project costs and projected costs will show the savings. In real life, comparisons of real costs to projected costs can be unconvincing because they depend too much on the judgment of whoever made the projections.

Usage-based costing is a sword that cuts both ways. The traditional up-front investment in technology, hardware and software, offers some assurance of predictable costs. Usage-based costing may be predictable over a longer term, but monthly costs may vary unpredictably. When combined with inevitable startup costs, the early-days bill for a cloud deployment can be startling.

The arguments for cloud implementations can be divided into business and technical arguments. On the business side, organizations expect reduced costs from usage-based costing and a shift from capital investments to operational expenses. They also expect an overall decrease in costs from more efficient use of resources, and they expect a decrease in IT expenses as internal IT costs are shifted to external cloud providers that are expected to provide similar services at lower cost.

Cloud Business Success

The risk of failure for cloud projects can be significantly reduced with strategic planning and thoughtful assessment of the potential benefits of the implementations. Cost-based arguments for cloud are real, and they grab attention, but, like most good things, they are no slam-dunk and may take time to achieve. However, cloud architectures provide business benefits that are more likely to offer immediate satisfaction than cost arguments. For example, scaling up and down automatically is a cloud feature that is frequently highlighted as a cost benefit. However, the superior user experience from the responsively scaling may be a substantially larger benefit. By strategically planning and emphasizing for these benefits, a cloud project becomes more likely to succeed early.

Cloud Strategic Planning

Without strategic planning, all projects are hit or miss. Formally, a strategy is a plan to move from one state to another by achieving certain objectives while considering the wider context within which the plan is executed. In other words, to plan strategically, an organization must know where it is, where it wants to go, what it wants to achieve, its peers, its competitors, its dependencies, and its obligations. All strategy involves some prediction of the future, which is always subject to error. However, prediction based on a full knowledge of present conditions is much more reliable than prediction without accurate knowledge of the starting point. Gathering the knowledge required for strategizing is often more difficult than forming the strategy.

Strategy differs from design. A design resolves a challenge that is defined by requirements and constraints. Strategy determines the requirements and constraints. Without a strategy, a design has no exterior direction. However, designs are the concrete means of implementing strategies.

A strategy moves an organization from one state to the next. The starting state could be, for example, success in a certain market. The end state could be continuing success. If the aims of the strategy are higher, the end state could be success in several related markets or creating an entirely new market. Identifying the desired end state is the greatest challenge in strategizing. Achieving the chosen end state will require many designs and subordinate plans, but the goals of these designs and plans derive from the strategy.

Organizations do not exist in a vacuum. They have competitors, partners, obligations, and dependencies that can defeat the strategy. An organization is unlikely to excel in a market without a strategy that does not recognize the capabilities of competitors. A strategy of datacenter expansion is likely to fail if it does not consider the cost of energy. An effective strategy must consider many sorts of questions: How will the organization obtain needed resources? How will it ward off competition? How will it foster the innovation needed to achieve its goals? Strategy encompasses all these considerations.

The designs constructed to implement a strategy must also consider the strategy's environment. For example, dominating a particular market may be a strategy. A design that proposes a product identical to a competitor may be inadequate because the strategy calls for a product that is much better than its competitor.

Gathering the knowledge needed for a good strategy is difficult because it involves many sources, including board resources and the highest levels of executive management. Often, forming a strategy is a trickle-down affair. The board determines a few fundamental high-level goals and principles. Executive management adds detail and color, and division and department heads work out the practical implications of the strategy.

The top-down approach is sometimes limited by incomplete knowledge of the enterprise environment that could be supplied by employees lower on the enterprise ladder. Progression through management layers can push aside historical and environmental context and practical limitations.

ITIL practices suggest some tools that help avoid these limitations when dealing with IT services. The basic ITIL strategy tool is the service portfolio. The service portfolio is a master catalog of IT services.[1] It includes services that are no longer in production, services in production, and planned services. The portfolio records the goals and expectations for each service, life-cycle status, who is responsible for the service, the service's customers, its dependencies, the plans for the service, and other relevant information. Taken altogether, the service portfolio contains the strategy for IT services in the organization.

The ITIL service portfolio is a business document because its primary purpose is to describe services as parts of an overall business plan for IT services. The portfolio typically contains only references to detailed technical designs and descriptions of the implementation of the services. Nevertheless, the service portfolio is important for technical planning. The portfolio shows the business relationships between services, which ones reveal information flows, the relative importance of services, which services are expected to decline in use and withdrawn from operations, which services will expand and scale up, and a host of other details of the life cycle of services.

The broad service portfolio view of IT services encourages building services and components that will have a long and useful life. Information from the portfolio can have immediate practical implications. A service nearing withdrawal is not a good candidate for redesign for scalability. A service slated to evolve into new business models is an excellent candidate for moving business logic to an easily modified separate module instead of hard-coding new layers of logic into a monolithic application.

Cloud implementation strategy potentially affects every aspect of IT services. A cloud implementation is often a new approach to managing costs and investments. Without a master plan like a service portfolio, decisions are likely to be shortsighted and inconsistent. Choosing the order in which services or service support components will move to a cloud is a fundamental decision that architects make in the early stages of an implementation. Many factors influence that choice. Services subject to heavy regulatory constraints may never be implemented on a public cloud. Services with globally distributed consumers may be ideal candidates, as would be services that have to scale up and down easily. A current and complete service portfolio makes prioritizing much easier with information on the role and plans for all services in one place.

---

[1] ITIL also defines a "service catalog." A service catalog helps manage services in production. It is not for managing services strategically. An ITIL service catalog does not contain services that have been removed from production or not in production yet. There is another concept of a service catalog that is an interactive application that employees use to order or modify services. This kind of catalog is often closely tied to the ITIL service catalog. Occasionally, ITIL service catalogs are implemented as part of service portfolios since there is some overlap in information in the two components.

Other aspects of a cloud implementation work best when guided by a strategic view of IT services that is part of an overall strategy for the enterprise. For example, failover and disaster recovery are aided by a strategy that identifies the priority of services for business activities. A portfolio that indicated service dependencies is also important for planning recovery. Understanding expansion plans are important for designing for scalability.

Too often, without a service portfolio, there is no comprehensive view of IT services. Cloud architects are forced to interview departmental managers and monitor service usage to determine the relative importance and relationships between services. This kind of research may always be necessary, but a comprehensive portfolio greatly increases the probability of a good design.

Cloud Business Strategies

The concepts in this section are primarily business considerations that affect technical implementations. One of the biggest mistakes that can be made in establishing a cloud architecture is to ignore or under-use the business advantages of the cloud.

Design for Flexibility

Virtual systems are flexible, but cloud deployments can be designed to be even more flexible. In fact, a cloud project that does not increase the flexibility of the organization should be reevaluated. Flexibility is crucial for enterprises in the rapidly changing 21st century. The structure and direction of businesses change daily. Video rental stores are gone. Who buys music on CDs today? Cab companies don't own cabs anymore. Businesses that continue to succeed are flexible.

What do we mean by flexibility? Flexible services are easy to change. They may be closely tailored to the needs of a particular line of business, but they are also designed with generic components that can be reused to support other lines of business. They are also designed with the assumption that the environment and the business may change in the future. The more flexible a service is, the fewer resources are required to modify the service to serve a new purpose.

Flexibility does not appear automatically when a cloud implementation is chosen. Ultimately, it is a business decision to invest in the foundation to support flexibility and support the guidance supplied by business to IT architects and designers. The technologists must understand how business is expected to evolve and where flexibility is needed.

The basic architecture of cloud, a hidden physical system that appears to support a limitless number of lightweight VMs, is ideal for generic service components that can be stopped, started, and reconnected at will. Instead of endless estimates of loads and reconfiguring machines and clusters, tailoring a service to a new line of business potentially becomes a gap analysis to determine new service components needed and how to reconfigure existing components. In the end, a service for a new line of business rolls out.

Reusable components are one of the foundations of flexible services that can support changing requirements and environments. With reusable components, services can molded to fit new circumstances by putting the components together in different ways like building bricks. However, reusability is not as easy to build in as it might appear. All too often, when the time comes to reuse the component, it comes close to the requirements, but the gap is wide enough to force some recoding. If this happens repeatedly without considering the overall architecture, the component is no longer generic and becomes a collection of disconnected bits of code specific to a number of services. This kind of component often becomes difficult to understand and maintain.

Reusable and enduring generic components stem from a cooperative effort between business and technology. Frequently, a poor component incorporates details that do not transfer beyond its initial tasks because the component design did not properly isolate the changing features from the static features. An analysis performed jointly by business and technology can determine which aspects of the component are likely to stay the same as a business evolves. Both business and technology contribute to identifying the appropriate level of generality, and both are needed for a system that can evolve smoothly and quickly over the long term.

Another aspect of flexibility is scalability. A cloud service should gracefully respond without interruptions or dips in performance when consumer demand suddenly increases or decreases. When service consumption decreases, consumption of computing resources should also decrease. The increase or decrease in service consumption could be the result of the unpredicted success or failure in business, such as an overwhelming response to a Super Bowl television spot; the discovery of a new use for the service; or the expansion or contraction of the business environment caused by fluctuations in the global economy.

Autoscaling is an example of an *autonomic service*, a service that can respond to its environment and manage itself. An application that adds additional VMs in response to increasing load is autonomic. Scaling is not the only possible autonomic response. Any process that responds to changes in its environment can be considered autonomic. For instance, streaming services can be designed to change the streaming rate in response to the quality of the network connection. Autonomic services have great potential for increasing the manageability of large systems such as those deployed on clouds.

One of the annoying aspects of typical traditional systems is that their cost seldom tracks to consumption of the service. If an e-mail system is designed to support 10,000 messages an hour, traditionally the cost will be the same when business slumps and traffic drops to one message an hour. In a well-designed cloud system, some of the system overhead will be inelastic (staff costs and amortized design and software development costs, network infrastructure for communicating with the cloud, and so on), but a substantial portion of the cost that would ordinarily go for on-premises equipment and the staff to keep it running will drop in proportion to usage. This elasticity will be important to any enterprise in the long term.

Geographic flexibility is also important. For some businesses, penetrating markets in new geographical areas is critical. Where and when a new market will appear is often unpredictable. Rapidly deploying services to these new markets often determines the success or failure of the venture. Cloud implementations can be geographically agnostic: a service designed for geographic flexibility on the right cloud can perform identically and equally well in Canberra, Indianapolis, and Munich.

The process described here is idealized. Services for new business opportunities are not trivial to design. There is no substitute for vision and insight. Nevertheless, cloud computing removes many physical obstacles to flexibility.

Working together with the IT department, an organization can plan a cloud deployment that offers great flexibility. However, flexibility is wasted if the business does not use it. One of the most effective ways of taking advantage of a well-designed system is to follow the ITIL Service Strategy best practices that were discussed in Chapter 3. The fundamental tool of ITIL Service Strategy is the service portfolio, which catalogs all the services of the enterprise, including quiescent historical services, production services, and planned services. Enterprise strategists, usually senior people from both the technical and business sides of the organization, can use the flexibility of cloud deployment to advance the entire portfolio, not just a single department, line of business, or technology.[2] Services that are planned and deployed as part of a portfolio designed to support the enterprise effectively can take advantage the flexibility and agility that a well-designed cloud deployment will provide.

---

[2]It's worth noting that a rigorously applied service portfolio approach is an effective tool for preventing application sprawl and departmental computing silos, which can be a danger as cloud computing becomes more ubiquitous. Launching a private copy of an application or subscribing to an SaaS service is so easy and quick, small groups can quickly build a stack of applications that isolates them from the rest of the enterprise. This can lead to many of the abuses that appeared in the early days of distributed computing.

Plan for "Bring Your Own Device" (BYOD)

Mobile devices—laptops, smartphones, and tablets—have become a way of life in the workplace. Although mobile devices are not inherently tied to cloud deployments, many mobile apps interact with applications on clouds. An enterprise mobile app combined with an enterprise cloud can be a powerful combination.

The ubiquity of mobile devices has driven major changes in the architecture and security of the enterprise. These changes have been intertwined in many cases with increasing use of cloud services. We've pointed out several times before that the old model of enterprise systems was a fortress with impregnable walls with a small number of armored entrances. Employees entered the physical enterprise through cipher and card locks. Security guards scanned for valid authorization badges. The enterprise network was inaccessible outside the building. Access to the Internet was strictly limited through proxy servers. All devices attached to the enterprise network were usually owned by the enterprise with tight controls over their configuration and contents.

Applications were built assuming they were protected by the enterprise outer wall. Developers assumed that their main security concern was preventing ordinary users from sneaking system administrator privileges and they could concentrate on easy and open access to applications from users inside the wall. The wall guaranteed that the user had at least lowest common denominator authorization. Users within the wall could be assumed to be using hardware controlled and sanitized by the IT department.

This has all changed for many organizations. The perimeter has expanded or even dissolved. Some employees work from home. They may be working with strategic documents that must be kept secret. Others are seldom in one place for long, working from their mobile devices wherever fancy takes them yet still accessing strategic or critical information. HR workers may have access on their mobile devices to confidential information that may invoke legal action if it is exposed. Salespeople on the road have full access to order tracking, inventories, and product literature including documents that require nondisclosure agreements. Senior executives have access to the most critical and confidential information both inside and outside the office and while traveling, perhaps to countries with significantly different rules on information practices.

BYOD practices often mean that employees may purchase their own devices and mingle their data with enterprise data on the same device. In some circumstances, there is a risk that the enterprise may become responsible for the safety of personal as well as enterprise data. These devices may be highly insecure, and they can be lost or stolen. In addition, these devices may have limited resources. Architects cannot assume that these devices meet some corporate minimum standard. Many issues must be addressed though management policies rather than technically, but a technical solution that cannot be ignored or intentionally violated is usually preferable.

Security issues aside, a roving user base has different performance and reliability issues that stem from using an external network for communication.

Cloud-based systems already face many of these problems. Cloud deployments are, almost by definition, remote implementations that are accessed from outside the sphere of control of the cloud provider. Self-implemented private clouds may be an exception, although many private clouds are constructed following the same principles as public or community clouds. When private cloud are deployed on the enterprise premises, they are not inherently remote like public clouds usually are. However, on-premises private clouds can be constructed outside the corporate network. This may be done when the private cloud is intended to be accessible in the same way a public cloud is accessible.

Cloud deployment gives the enterprise architect some help in designing a system that will effectively support BYOD, but only if BYOD requirements are kept it mind. For example, a cloud application that is designed to be distributed between geographically remote cloud datacenters may help maintain performance for far-roving mobile devices as well as provide failover sites that can respond to regional failures. Mobile apps are well suited for interacting with remote cloud implementations, especially if they have built-in provisions for temporary communications outages.

BYOD security is often implemented using encryption. Encrypting critical data is generally a good policy in cloud implementation. Since the data is in the hands of a third party, even with the strictest personnel policies, the data is accessible via administrative mistakes or rogue employees. Although the possibility is remote, encryption provides some protection against such unauthorized access. By building applications that encrypt all data as an optimized part of the fundamental design, data in the cloud and data on mobile devices are both less accessible to outsiders.

Strategists and architects are often tempted to take existing applications and perform a minimal port to an IaaS or PaaS cloud. They are likely to be disappointed because the benefits they gain from the cloud implementation may not compare well to the experience of peers who make better use of cloud characteristics. Enterprises have an opportunity to respond to both the challenges of BYOD and the demands for agility and efficiency with a cloud deployment, but only if using the advantages of the cloud.

Designs and Business Plans for Usage Based Costing

Perhaps one of the most disappointing aspects of cloud computing is the failure of some businesses to reap the promised savings from usage-based charging for computing resources. There are several reasons for the difficulty. Perhaps the easiest to explain is the ease with which additional resources are obtained. When a new VM can be launched in minutes with little or no strategic authorization, there is little constraint on overusing resources, and usage-based costs go up. This is often called VM *sprawl*.

It is also easy to forget that an application that is not designed to take advantage of usage-based cost may cost as much to run idle as it does to run at peak capacity. One of the most important financial goals for cloud computing is to couple business activity to computing costs. If the cost of IT does not go down as business decreases, it is fixed overhead that will eventually become onerous. Cloud computing promises to allow the cost of IT to decrease when the business it supports declines.

Applications designed to scale vertically rather than horizontally typically do not respond to a decrease in demand by reducing the number of VMs in use. Cloud costs are typically calculated on the number of VMs running. In other words, shutting down a line of business or curtailing production in other ways will not decrease the cost of running the application.

Storage is less of a problem. Storage costs are usually calculated on the quantity of data stored and the frequency of access. Most applications will not write or read as much data when usage decreases, which causes storage costs decrease as usage decreases. Generally, the elastic nature of cloud storage implies that applications can write without regard for exceeding physical storage limits in a cloud environment.

Even when applications are designed to increase or decrease resource consumption as usage changes, the enterprise may not take advantage of these changes. Often this is the result of the absence of a comprehensive cloud strategy that combines technology and business strategy. For example, suppose the enterprise uses an SaaS-based document processing service and back charges each business unit a fixed amount for the service. The fixed back charge may be an artifact from a previous era when the enterprise purchased a site license with unlimited usage. If the back charge policy is not changed, the business units will see the service as free and have no incentive to use it prudently.

A different type of example is SaaS customer relations management (CRM). An on-premises CRM system is typically a fixed cost no matter what the usage. Unlike document processing, many businesses will experience an increase in CRM usage when business goes down because the sales department increases its use of CRM to find customers ready to spend. The increased cost of the SaaS CRM could be a nasty surprise if business plans assume that the cost of CRM will remain constant as it typically does when the solution is on-premises.

Benefits from use-based compute and storage pricing can be substantial, but they are not automatic, and the strategies to realize benefits are both business and technical.

Prepare for the Transition from On-Premises to Cloud Deployment

The transition from on-premises to cloud-based services is not trivial. Even when the transition involves only deploying existing applications on an IaaS cloud with minimal porting, the organization will change.

Simply porting an application to IaaS minimizes transition. The change is similar to moving from one operating system to another. The IT technicians who administer the application have the most to learn and the most significant changes to make, but the rest of the organization will experience a few changes. They may see changes in the performance of the ported application— perhaps improvements, perhaps degradation, and most likely a mix. Support may change also. The service desk may have to learn to distinguish between issues that can be solved by the local team and issues that have to be solved by the cloud provider, and the user will have to change their expectations for the speed of resolutions. Change on this scale is easy to cope with, but it may not be the best strategy. Avoiding change minimizes disruption, but it also can minimize the benefits of a cloud implementation.

Cloud transitions that minimize change may not require extensive transition and training plans, and they may not involve changes in staffing. However, by avoiding changes to the business, they also minimize the potential benefit to the organization. In addition, even minimal changes can be more disruptive than expected. Transition planners should never forget that moving to cloud computing is a business change as well as a technical change. Part of the transition often involves training for business managers on the possibilities for management offered by the cloud implementation.

When substantial service changes may be required, ITIL provides detailed guidance for transition to new or modified services that can be useful in cloud transitions. Transition in ITIL practice is not an isolated event. Transition begins long before technology is deployed. It starts with strategy and design that identifies the goals of new services, who will implement the service, who will operate the service, and who will be the consumers of the service. Early on, an assessment begins to determine what will be needed from each of these groups for a smooth and successful deployment.

Transition from on-premises to cloud services may be more difficult than other transitions. ITIL practice points out that a change in a service often requires a shift in responsibilities.[3] This applies to movement to the cloud as much as a transition on the enterprise premises. The transition is not only

---

[3]Stuart Rance. ITIL Service Transition. The Stationery Office. 2011. Page 203. The service transition volume goes into detail on shifting responsibilities.

to new applications. The transition also requires understanding of new cost models and external dependencies. These changes can result in displacements of established relationships within the organization.

Data Strategy

The cloud offers new opportunities for storing and using data. Cloud data costs are dramatically lower than the costs of storage and access when many of the basic applications that run businesses were written. Some applications go all the way back to the mainframe era when bulk data storage meant tape drives. Tapes, compared to disks, are slow, both to record and to access data. Although tape is by no means dead, large datacenters now tend to use disk technologies for long-term storage. The slowness and difficulty in accessing tape archives often limited the value of this stored data.

Cloud vendors often offer tiered storage. At the top of the tier, using specialized hardware such as solid-state drives, access is very fast, but the cost is relatively high. At the lowest tier, cost is moderate, but retrieval may take minutes instead of milliseconds. Even top-tier fast data storage is cheap compared to the systems of a decade ago.

Cloud implementations offer the opportunity to store much more data than in the past. In addition, many more transactions run through computer systems, increasing the volume of data to be stored. Mobile devices with global positioning systems have added a whole new type of data that can be collected and stored. Innovations in data processing (Big Data) have made available ways to analyze and use unstructured data, unlike not too long ago when usable information could be extracted only from data stored in hierarchical and relational databases.

Cloud data strategy should take into account these changes. Applications can write more to storage and use new data management techniques to handle the increased volume. This stored data may eventually become a long-term asset for the organization. In general, cloud storage costs are less than storing locally. Consequently, enterprises can store more, especially because new analysis practices can increase the value of stored data.

Understanding Cloud Providers

A cloud provider, or at least a public cloud provider, is a third party. The priorities of the provider are never identical to the priorities of the cloud consumer. Cloud consumers must recognize this fact. Whether the consumer negotiated their service level agreements (SLAs)[4] and contract with their cloud provider or the provider dictated them to the consumer, a successful cloud implementation is impossible if consumers do not thoroughly understand their SLAs and contract. The consumer's implementation must accommodate the provisions of their SLAs and contract. The provider may not automatically report SLA violations to the consumer. The consumer may have to detect and report violations to the provider and request payment of penalties. If there are misunderstandings, the consumer must take an informed stance to hold their own in discussions.

Prepare for Provider Outages

A provider may consider a one-hour outage for a limited number of consumers to be a minor glitch, but when that outage causes a gap in sales during a peak selling period, it may be a major issue to an online retailer. The cloud provider calculates its liability under its SLAs and gives a collective shrug because the loss is manageable. On the other hand, after collecting the SLA penalty from the provider, the retailer still might go out of business.

Most public clouds are reliable, but reliability is a relative term. Even the most reliable cloud service will eventually have some failures. The probability of a failure on any given day may be miniscule; the probability of a failure some time in a year is much higher. Over a longer period, some outage becomes almost a certainty.

The extent of preparation for outages will depend on many interrelated factors. The first of these is the criticality of the uninterrupted delivery of the service. Other factors include the availability of alternative sources for the service, the robustness of the provider's operations team, and the adequacy of the SLA and service contract for compensating losses from an outage.

A service that could go down for several hours or even days with little effect on the cloud consumer's business does not need much preparation for a provider outage. The plan may be as simple as a procedure for escalating service outage issues to the person who manages relations with the provider.

When the service is critical, the plans must be more complex. Long before the service goes into production, the service manager should make some critical calculations. In the event of an outage, what portion of the real damages will be compensated by the SLA penalties? Are those penalties certain to be applied? Some SLA agreements have provisions that limit SLAs to certain

---

[4]SLAs may be part of a service contract or a separate business document. SLAs spell out penalties and incentives for levels of delivery of services. An example SLA is "For every minute of service outage over 99.9 percent service uptime per month, the consumer will receive $1,000 in credit."

configurations or circumstances. When a multiday outage starts tearing into the enterprise bottom line is not the time to learn that a service is not eligible for outage compensation because it does not meet configuration requirements. For example, implementations that are not distributed over geographically separate datacenters within the provider's cloud may have a weaker SLA than implementations that follow the provider's specifications. It is usually the cloud consumer's responsibility to see that the implementation is distributed properly, even though the cost may increase.

Managers of critical services should have some plans made for an outage. The first step is to know exactly how to inform the provider of the outage and get their assessment of the severity and likely duration of the outage. Contact with the provider could be direct communication by the service manager, or it could be through the IT department. The IT department may have failover or recovery procedures that they can put into effect. Second, the manager should have an escalation plan within the organization. Who needs to know about the outage? Transparency is often a good policy. Finally, the manager should have a "Plan B" for failures that go beyond the expected. For example, point-of-sale registers may be designed to operate when the cloud is unavailable, but when an unexplained defect or situation shuts down point-of-sale registers, Plan B may be to give cashiers pads and paper to record sales, rather than close the store.

Some outages can be avoided by taking advantage of failover facilities of the cloud and transition smoothly to other facilities. Traditional applications that are ported directly to a cloud environment may not distribute well to remote datacenters. Cloud business planning may need to assess this possibility and require the necessary technical changes, which may be considerable.

The cloud consumer should always assume that outages are possible. SLAs and contracts can compensate for this eventuality, but the compensation is often only partial when the full effects of the outage are considered. Damage to the reputation of the cloud consumer's business is one such effect. Technical solutions are often costly, but business requirements may outweigh the cost.

Prepare for Security Breaches

Provider security breaches are similar to provider service outages. They are not supposed to occur, but they do, and when they do, the consumer must be prepared.

A cloud implementation, in terms of business, can be breached in two ways: via the cloud provider and via the cloud consumer's code or the consumer's interface. Breaches via the consumer's own code or interface are similar to security breaches that occur with on-premises applications.

Consumer Security

Applications running on clouds have vulnerabilities somewhat different from on-premises applications, but many of the weaknesses are the same. The consumer is responsible for any breaches that occur, just as they are responsible for on-premises breaches.[5] Cloud consumers should take all the precautions that on-premises systems take. This includes instructing personnel on best password practices, avoiding using the same password to access critical data and functionality, appropriate use of encryption both of stored data and inter-process communication, secure system partitions, network traffic analysis, firewalls, and traditional anti-malware software.

Although some vulnerability is unavoidable, consumers are largely as vulnerable as they allow themselves to be. Security is not free. It is expensive and inconvenient. For enterprises with valuable assets online, such as thousands or millions of credit cards, the justifiable cost and inconvenience of security is very high. Enterprises with less vulnerable value may see less justification. However, they should be aware that value might not be apparent until it goes out the door.

Prevention is usually not enough, particularly for enterprises with large assets online. Despite every precaution, security breaches may still occur. Rogue employees, stolen laptops and phones, or a clever phishing expedition and a second of inattention can all compromise the most carefully secured system. Security should not stop at system compromises. Plans and procedures should be in place to control damage and identify the intruders as quickly as possible.

Provider Security

None of the previous precautions is unique to cloud implementations. They represent good security practices for all systems. Cloud implementations do present special security challenges. Other than private clouds, cloud providers are third parties. Systems running in a cloud datacenter are as secure as the physical datacenter and its personnel. The cloud consumer has no direct control. The datacenter does not belong to them, and the datacenter personnel are not consumer employees. The consumer must rely on the cloud provider to enforce the integrity of the facilities and their personnel.

---

[5]SaaS and PaaS can be more complicated. For instance, if a malefactor breaches an application by taking advantage of a defect in the SaaS application or a component supplied by the PaaS provider, the breach will ordinarily be the responsibility of the provider. However, if, for example, the malefactor phishes credentials to get into the application, it is the consumer's responsibility. In any case, the consumer should always read their SLA carefully. The SLA determines who is responsible for what, and that could be surprising.

This is a contractual, not a technical, issue. The vulnerabilities of the consumer are for the most part determined by the levels of security the provider has contracted to provide. This may include physical security of the cloud datacenter, secure communications between datacenters, background checks on personnel, bonding, liability insurance, and so on.

Some of the most insidious cloud security threats involve cross-communication between consumers. One example is the possibility of a defective hypervisor that allows ordinary users to execute privileged commands that allow one consumer's virtual machines to access virtual machines launched by other consumers. A similar scenario might allow two consumers who share the same storage disk to access each other's data.

Another scenario posits an illegal organization that stores data on a public cloud. The authorities could confiscate the miscreant's data and in doing so confiscate the data of lawful consumers stored on the same disk. The lawful consumers would be left with disruption and delay.

The cloud consumer relies on contracts and the reputation of the cloud provider to avoid the kind of scenarios depicted. Consumers with critical data and processes may want to obtain guarantees that their activities run on dedicated processors and their data is stored on dedicated storage devices. They should look carefully at SLAs and determine what portion of the real costs of security failures will be compensated by the SLAs and take steps in proportion to their appetite for risk.

Many organizations may choose to require their providers to have some form of certification. ISO 20001[6] certification and certificates from the American Institute of Certified Public Accountants (AICPA)[7] are both prominent. These standards were discussed in Chapter 6. Although provider certification offers protection, cloud consumers should always be wary. Certification is "one-size-fits-all"; it addresses most of the vulnerabilities of most cloud deployments. However, organizations vary widely, and certification does not address every vulnerability of every consumer. The consumer is responsible for identifying areas where the standard does not protect their organization.

Know Provider Backup Procedures

It is tempting to believe that using IaaS or PaaS will relieve IT administrators of all their responsibilities, but that is nowhere near true. Although the cloud provider takes over physical administration, the consumer still is responsible for keeping the software deployed on the platform running properly. That can

---

[6]See www.iso.org/iso/catalogue_detail?csnumber=51986. Accessed September 2015.
[7]See www.aicpa.org/Pages/default.aspx. Accessed September 2015.

involve applying patches, overseeing automated load balancing, and performing any maintenance or administrative procedures that involve hands-on intervention. SaaS deployments are an exception. The provider takes responsibility for both hardware and software administration and maintenance. This is one of the attractions of SaaS.

Backup is sometimes a gray area. It is hard to imagine a cloud provider that would not keep their system backed up, and consumers may be tempted to rely on the provider's backup system. There are some circumstances when this is a reasonable approach. For example, when a consumer subscribes to a storage service, it is reasonable to expect the provider will restore the data if it is lost or damaged. However, that is not certain unless assurance is included in the service contract or SLA.

Data that is in process is more difficult. For example, an application that writes a file or storage in a virtual system is not necessarily writing to persistent storage. Consequently, the concept of "data in flight" may be considerably expanded in a cloud deployment.

Cloud consumers may find it expedient to perform their own backups of critical data. Cloud provider backups are usually intended for disaster recovery. These backups will not help a user who inadvertently deletes or overwrites a file and wants it restored. There are cloud services that address this problem, but they are SaaS backup services for users, not for enterprise failover.

Prepare New Financial Reporting Structure

Usage-based costing of cloud IT resources presents many advantages for managing IT investments in services, but only if the enterprise can make use of them. In a cloud implementation, one of the primary managerial documents should be a monthly report on charges for cloud computing. That report, at its simplest, consists of a single lump sum that rises and falls with the seasons and the business climate. This is the equivalent of running a retail business with a total cost of sales but no breakdown of where the cost went.

Most cloud providers offer the instrumentation and reports necessary for breaking down costs, but making use of the data requires some advanced planning and cooperation between business management and IT. Business management probably wants to see the cloud cost per service delivered by IT and possibly a breakdown by business unit consuming the service.

The problem is that the cloud provider is aware of the virtual machines running, the data moving on virtual networks, and the data being stored, but it has no insight into the services the cloud consumer has implemented on the cloud or how the consumer is using these services. Consequently, the IT department is responsible for implementing ways of breaking down usage.

Usually, this is not difficult. Providers offer ways of distinguishing services, but the IT department has to use the facilities provided. More importantly, business management has to make clear the data that should appear on reports and how it should be broken down. Making these plans early could prevent expensive missteps in implementing the cloud deployment and enable more effective business management of cloud services.

Conclusion

Cloud implementations are a joint effort between business management and IT because cloud computing is a much a business pattern as a technical innovation. If either IT or business management does not participate in a cloud implementation, failure or compromise is a real possibility.

Too often, a cloud implementation starts with enthusiasm from either the IT department or the business management, neither having a clear idea of the level of participation needed for success. Sometimes, a notion appears that an existing application can be quickly ported to a cloud environment and the organization will realize great benefits. This may be true occasionally, but more often, it is not.

This chapter has examined the business side of cloud implementation, pointing out areas where business must pay special attention to the implementation to aid in success.

EXERCISES

1. Why is cloud computing both a business and a technical concept?

2. Describe ITIL strategic planning. What is a service portfolio? Distinguish it from a service catalog.

3. Why is flexibility important? What can business management contribute to construction of a flexible cloud deployment?

4. How should a service manager prepare for a cloud service outage?

5. How do service contracts and SLAs affect cloud deployments?

13

Tricky Business

Cloud Implementation Practices

SUMMARY

This chapter is about the technical side of cloud applications. It discusses implementing applications and services that are to be deployed on clouds. The chapter emphasizes Infrastructure as a Service (IaaS) implementations, although much of the material applies also to Platform as a Service (PaaS) implementations. The approach is high-level, discussing architecture rather than code strategies. The strategies also apply to building Software as a Service (SaaS) applications for cloud deployment but not specific strategies, such as multitenancy, for SaaS. In addition, public clouds are assumed. Private and community implementers will also benefit from the material here, although their implementations may be somewhat simpler.

Any IT project requires collaboration between IT technologists and business management. Every project carries some risk. Cloud projects often generate more risk because the technology is new and the business model is unfamiliar. The previous chapter discussed the business aspects of cloud projects. This chapter will discuss the technical side of cloud projects.

Business and technical requirements are related closely. Both business and technology have to work together to deliver an implementation that meets expectations. Often cloud projects do not focus on new functionality. Instead, they are expected to reduce the cost of delivering the service, increase reliability and maintainability, and streamline on-premises operations and administration. Success requires some purely business initiatives, as discussed in the previous chapter, but the technical side also has to take steps to achieve these goals. Too often, moving an existing service to a cloud is seen as a *port,*[1] similar to a port from one operating system to another. That is only partially true. Most applications built to run on-premises are not designed with cloud features in mind. They probably will port with some changes here and there in network addressing, firewalls, and perhaps strengthening security to cope with more exposed communication with the cloud. However, the resulting cost savings are likely to be less than expected, and other anticipated benefits may not materialize.

The solution is to make the investment necessary to revamp the on-premises service to one that takes advantage of the cloud or to propose a stepwise approach that will add anticipated benefits slowly over time. Both of these paths can easily become expensive. Rebuilding an application to work well on a cloud is seldom trivial. A gradual approach may have less up-front cost, but the total cost may be more. Managing and designing stepwise development is often more challenging than rebuilding from the beginning. There is no easy answer, but the pitfalls are fewer and less deep when all the parties are aware of the trade-offs.

The upside is that the techniques of cloud computing are not new. Most of them are long-standing best practices for enterprise service design that are now being applied in a new way. An application built or revised recently to follow best practices for scalability, performance, security, and accessibility is likely to transition easily to a cloud environment without excessive redesign or rewriting; this is less so for older applications.

Cloud Implementations and Technical Success

A successful cloud implementation above all must meet business requirements. The challenge to the developer is to confirm that business requirements are met before correcting the issues becomes irredeemably expensive. Some issues can be self-correcting; if business representatives become aware that a requirement is not met, they often put up such a squawk that the gap is quickly filled. Unfortunately, this does not happen as frequently as one would hope. It may be counterintuitive, but the more often the business side of the house raises issues, the more likely the project is to succeed, provided both business and IT approach the issues in a spirit of cooperation rather than antagonism.

Gaps cannot be identified if the requirements are not articulated clearly, especially to the business managers themselves. They sometimes are not aware of the reasons for a move to a cloud implementation and recognize the issue only after the project is complete. Or the project may be developed in

---

[1]Porting software means to modify a piece of software to execute in a different environment. Ported software's operation is expected to be identical to its operation in the old environment. Usually, porting changes as little of the original code as possible.

isolation without a robust feedback loop between business and development functions. Also, the business benefits from a cloud implementation are not easily tested until after the project is deployed, which may lead to skepticism. Agile development methodology is especially helpful here. One of the basic tenets of Agile development is a sturdy feedback loop between developers and customers from beginning to end of a project. Agile development also encourages many small incremental releases that can be examined by the stakeholders and tested as they are released. For most cloud implementations, there are two customers: the consumers of the services implemented on the cloud and the business owners of the service. Success depends on a thorough mutual understanding among all parties. The previous chapter attacked these challenges from the view of the manager.

Basic Cloud Application Requirements

A successful cloud must be maintainable. It must have a convenient mechanism for applying patches and upgrades without interrupting production. When defects crop up, the system should degrade gracefully. Systems should reduce features and output rather than crashing, never corrupt or destroy data, issue helpful error messages, and write extensive internal logs for maintainers to trace the root cause of the problem. Designers must be aware that cloud-based virtual systems may require methods that are not the same as on-premises applications. For example, patching virtual machines present problems that do not exist on-premises nonvirtual applications.

When possible, processes should be tunable; that is, the operating parameters of a system can be changed to match the circumstances of the workload. For example, systems are usually conservative about starting and stopping new virtual machines in response to fluctuating workloads. Starting and stopping virtual machines is slow and consumes system resources. Therefore, adjusting their number too quickly can cause the system to waste resources by responding to minor fluctuations in the load. However, in some situations, a more liberal policy of starting new processes quickly provides superior performance and justifies the use of resources. If an administrator can adjust the starting and stopping of parameters, the process can be tuned to the workload with superior results. The use of containers provides further opportunities for tuning. Since several containers can run on the same VM, new containers can be launched without the overhead of a full VM launch.

It's often said that the only constant in business is change. A cloud system ought to be built as flexibly as possible to ensure that it can be modified and reused in the future as the business and technical environments change. It also must scale both up and down and meet basic security requirements and the special requirements of the business.

Cloud applications usually depend on networks more than on-premises applications. Therefore, cloud applications should be built with the network in mind. For example, backups and failover are likely to involve the network. Designers must assume all components, especially the network, may be unreliable.

Finally, the system must be usable. Visual displays should not be difficult to interpret or use. Consumers should have convenient access to the data they need, and the appearance should be aesthetically pleasing. In addition, displays should be easily ported to new display devices, perhaps smartwatches or other wearable computing devices.

These characteristics mark any successful system, not just a cloud system. In cloud implementations, these characteristics make successful systems both easier and more difficult to implement.

CLOUD APPLICATION IMPERATIVES

- *Maintainable*: Include maintainability features, such as supporting patching without interrupting production.

- *Tunable*: Design applications for adjustment to workloads and the environment without patching or rebuilding.

- *Flexible*: Support easy modification to conform to changing business conditions and environment.

- *Network aware and fault-tolerant*: Design applications to tolerate unreliable networks and components that may fail.

- *Usable*: Provide customers with convenient and effective access to the system.

Cloud Implementation Principles

Cloud configurations can be changed quickly without the costs and delays associated with purchasing, leasing, and re-cabling physical servers. Additional virtual servers can be launched with a few keyboard strokes instead of waiting for the hardware to be delivered from a supplier or warehouse and installing it in the datacenter. Unlike physical assets, cloud implementations can be scaled up and down quickly and easily because the changes are all in the software, not in the physical hardware. From the cloud consumer's view, virtual assets are reconfigured in software, but on the provider's level, physical computing resources are acquired and relinquished. This activity can be carried out almost entirely automatically but only if the consumer's applications running in the implementation are designed to reconfigure and scale well in a virtual environment. Other advantages to cloud implementations, such as resilience, are similar, but only when the consumer's implementation is designed to use cloud facilities efficiently. Developers should be aware of a number of concepts for building cloud applications that deliver on the cloud's promise.

Avoid Monoliths

In the early stages of computing, all programs were single, stand-alone entities, now often called *monoliths* or *monolithic applications*. A monolith is an application in which all functionality is built into a single self-contained process. When a monolith is up and running, it does not depend on any processes other than the operating system. All the code for the application is coded, compiled, and linked into a single entity. This approach worked well on mainframes, and some mainframe programs are still monoliths.

A monolith is the most natural architecture for an application. When developers begin with a set of requirements and start writing code without much thought to the overall system or its behavior in production, chances are good that a single large component, a monolith, will be the result. How the system will scale, how it will be maintained, how will it behave when a defect appears, and how it will support a large geographic area will all be afterthoughts.

If there is more than a single developer, the code of a monolith may be separated into libraries and code modules to clarify the organization of the code and make it easier for developers to code simultaneously, but the executable runtime module will still be linked together into a single runnable entity. Programs like this can be well-designed and efficient, but they seldom have characteristics that take advantage of the strengths of cloud deployment.

A monolith usually scales up vertically by running on higher-capacity processors at increased processing cycles per second, with faster data buses, more and faster random access memory, and faster input and output.[2] It can scale down by running on a smaller processor with fewer resources. This is often the only alternative because the monolith is not designed to increase capacity by adding new processes to divide the load.

---

[2]The terms *CPU*, *processor*, and *core* are similar and often used interchangeably, and meanings have shifted with the progress of hardware. However, they are not strictly the same. *Central processing unit* (CPU) traditionally has referred to a collection of chips and other components that process instructions and data. These consist of arithmetic and logic evaluation, instruction fetching, interrupt handling, and input and output. All these components eventually shrank to a single chip called a *CPU* or a *processor*. As chips became denser, more and more functionality crowded onto single chips. Eventually, additional arithmetic and logic evaluation units, *cores*, appeared on single CPU chips. These cores are not full CPUs because they share functionality with other cores on the same chip, but they have many of the capabilities of a complete CPU. Servers often have several processor chips each with multiple cores. Mobile devices are usually limited to a single processor chip that may have many cores. Sometimes the word *processor* refers to the entire processing capability of a virtual or physical computer, which may include several processing chips with multiple cores. You should be aware that the terms are used loosely.

Scaling up and down by varying the size of the virtual machine to another is seldom practical. Moving to different CPUs is easier in a cloud environment than a physical environment, but both scaling up and scaling down monoliths tends to be disruptive because monoliths are seldom designed with starting, stopping, and transferring workloads in mind. Users may have to restart transactions that are interrupted before they complete. If the monolith is not built with well-designed threads, the application may not gain much capacity when moved to a virtual machine with more cores rather than greater clock speed and a faster bus. Unless the application underwent testing with multicore systems with scaled-up loads that drove the threading hard, hidden defects are hard to avoid in the complex code that monoliths often exhibit.

There are some benefits from a multicore processor that do not require well-designed threads that are derived from parallel processing in the operating system and compilers that can produce parallel code automatically, but many applications, especially older applications, do not gain much capacity from multicore processing. This is unfortunate because cloud providers tend to provide more cores and processors than faster CPUs and buses in their larger virtual machines. This reflects the fact that most cloud providers build their datacenters from many identical and relatively simple generic computers rather than larger and large servers. In addition, chip manufacturers now usually increase the capacity of their chips by adding cores.

Applications that use more than one process can be distributed over multiple CPUs and cores to take greater advantage of the added capacity.

Further, a single monolithic process can be difficult to maintain in a high-production environment. It is difficult to make a single process degrade gracefully. Most often, when a fault occurs, the entire service crashes. Keeping a single process running when part of it is no longer functioning is not impossible but difficult.

An application that consists of several asynchronously communicating processes is more difficult to code, but degradation is easily managed and scaling is much simpler. At its simplest, when a process fails, processes sending messages to a failing process begin to queue messages, waiting for the failed process to begin to receive messages. Processes that expect messages to wait, presumably will do useful work until the messages arrive. If the failing process is not restored, eventually the system will probably stop, but there is time to put up informative error messages, repair, or restart the failed process before damage is done.

There are many elaborations and variations on this pattern. In the best scenarios, the faulty process is automatically restarted or redundant processes simply take over for the weak sister.

Threads can increase the resiliency of a monolith because the failure of a thread will not halt the process, but there are trade-offs. Threads, especially when indiscriminately used without due regard for reentrancy, increase the complexity of a system and multiply opportunities for defects. In addition, a thread is not isolated from the overall process. When the process fails or degrades, all threads fail or degrade. Generally, threads can make some aspects of a system, such as asynchronous messaging, easier to code, but an application that uses multiple processes can be more resilient.

Applications that use more than one process are also often easier to maintain because processes can be stopped and replaced with patched versions without bringing down the whole application. A typical action performed while maintaining a process is to stop the process, apply patches, and restart the process.

A further refinement on multiprocess applications is multiple parallel processes. Parallel processes do the same thing. Instead of sending all requests of a given type to the same process, the request can be sent to any number of processes. This can be done in a simple round-robin that distributes messages without regard to the load on the receiving process. Another possibility is distribution to the process with the shortest input queue. More sophisticated algorithms are also used. Applications like this are well-suited to a virtual cloud environment. They scale up and down by adding or removing virtual machines. For an application that consists of a number of parallel processes on virtual machines, all doing the same thing, patches that require shutting the process down can be performed without interrupting production. The virtual machines are patched one at a time, keeping the others running to support the production workload. Each virtual machine is shut down and patched and then restarted. Patching this way is frequently scripted and automated.

Using these techniques, rolling releases become attractive. A *rolling release* updates an application or system in increments rather than massive installations that replace the entire application. A rolling release introduces change gradually and aligns with the small and frequent releases of the Agile methodology and DevOps practice.

Horizontal Scalability

Horizontal scalability is not a new concept in this book, but developers must realize how crucial horizontal scaling is to building robust cloud applications. Without horizontal scaling, many of the technical and business advantages of cloud computing are compromised. Without horizontal scalability, as discussed earlier, automated up and down scaling is difficult. Costs are likely to stay constant as usage declines, and performance is likely to degrade as usage increases.

As desirable as horizontally scalable services are, they are more complex to build than vertically scalable services. A fundamental example is based on the common architecture in which a web server receives Hypertext Transmission Protocol (HTTP) messages from remote processes, usually either browsers or mobile apps.[3] There may be multiple web servers, as in Figure 13-1. A load balancer distributes connections among the web servers. The web server breaks the message down and passes subrequests to the message to the application server. A load balancer distributes messages among the application servers. If the remote processes are stateless (in other words, the reply to the request does not depend on state from previous requests stored on the server), the load balancer for the application servers can pass the message to any available application server. If the requests sent to the application server have state, the load balancer must maintain connections between each application server and the end consumers it is supporting. On both the web server level and the application server level in this example, the number of servers can be extended automatically by management processes built into the cloud.

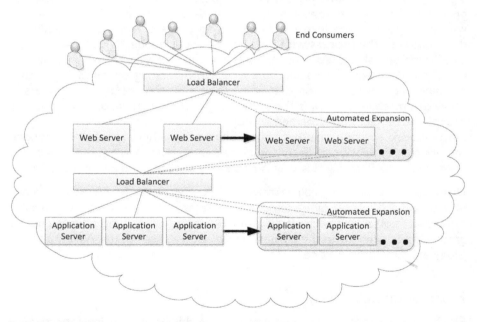

Figure 13-1. A service designed to scale horizontally often scales on more than one level

---

[3]An *HTTP server* is a more precise name for a server that receives and replies to HTTP. A web server could, conceivably, be based on a non-HTTP protocol, but that happens rarely, if ever.

Stateless Services

Services that do not rely on state are easier to build, are usually more reliable, and scale better. At the same time, they usually require more planning for performance and usability. If application server processes are not stateless, information on what has happened in previous transactions with the application must be preserved. This can be accomplished in several ways. One way is for the application server to store a record of previous transactions with the end user. The load balancer must also keep track in some way of which application server was used to service which users. The requests from the same user go to the application server, and the application server holds the state of the interaction with the user. This method requires that a client session always reattach to the same server. A much better approach allows a client to attach to any server. A central repository for state that all the servers can access supports clients reattaching to any server. A central repository can increase robustness but adds another component to build and maintain and another potential source of latency.

HTTP is designed to be stateless. HTTP does not require that a server ever keep track of previous messages from a sender. For example, when basic authentication is used, the user must send a valid username and password with each message. If the server does maintain an authenticated state between pages, it is done over HTTP without relying on the protocol to support the state.

Compared to a stateless service, a stateful service is complicated. The store of state information has to be managed. When transactions complete normally, problems may be few, but that is not nearly adequate for a production service. Devices overheat. Disks fail. Browsers crash. Users click the wrong button or are distracted and walk away. Administrators make mistakes. Especially in cloud implementations, network connections fail or time out. When a transaction is interrupted, the server must decide when to kill the transaction, how much of the transaction to roll out, and what to do with store of state information—delete it all, save some, leave it intact, or reconstruct the transaction from the log when the user returns. Each alternative is appropriate in some situations. To gain the information necessary to decide, the state store must be examined, and the state of the transaction must be determined. After evaluating the state, action choices depend on the business use of the application as well as software engineering. Developers cringe at coding for these situations because unwinding those state stacks often lead to surprising and anomalous situations that are seldom addressed in the specifications. Developers, and often the quality assurance team, are left to muddle through to a solution that is often an unsatisfactory and uninformed compromise. Pickles like this are not unique to unwinding the transactions stack, but stateless servers remove one source of the issues.

Business and technology are always mutually dependent and require mutual understanding. Stateless services are one way of relaxing that binding. In the case of horizontal scaling, maintaining stateless where possible eases the job of software designers and, at the same time, makes the design of the application more transparent to the users.

Sometimes stateless transactions are not possible, but when they are possible, they result in more robust and reliable systems.

Service-Oriented Architecture

Service-oriented architecture (SOA) is an elegant and efficient way to build applications that works well in cloud computing. Many large enterprises have invested heavily in SOA. An SOA designer decomposes applications into a hierarchy of services. All services and subservices have their own addressable APIs. When a service is needed, its API is called, and the implementation of the service responds. A service implementation may be shared between several services, or services can be implemented independently. Applications are constructed by combining and composing services.

Several architectural concepts are closely related to SOA and more suited to smaller installations. The fundamental concept is to decompose architectures into granular services and objects that can be accessed independently. Access is built on web services. *Microservices* emphasize granular services. *Resource-oriented architecture* (ROA) focuses on granular access to application resource objects.

SOAP and Representational State Transfer (REST)

Two types of SOA interfaces are common: REST and SOAP.[4] Both interfaces usually use HTTP as their transport protocol, although both are transport protocol independent and can be used with other protocols. SOAP implementation stacks are readily available, but some developers find them overly complex and irksome. REST interfaces do not require an elaborate software stack, but the REST architecture is based on document exchange on the World Wide Web. Consequently, supporting some applications, such as transactional applications that involve interaction with several data services, can be more difficult with REST. SOAP interfaces are likely to be found inside

---

[4] SOAP used to be an acronym for Simple Object Access Protocol, but the SOAP authors came to realize that the protocol is for service messaging that often does not involve objects. Also, although the committee did not mention it, most developers say SOAP is far from simple. To avoid misconceptions, the committee declared that SOAP is just a name, not an acronym. For more details, see http://lists.w3.org/Archives/Public/xmlp-comments/2005Sep/0002.html. Accessed June 2015.

enterprise implementations, while REST is more prevalent in widely accessible Internet applications. Often applications combine REST and SOAP, using REST for browser to web server activity and SOAP in the back end.

Occasionally the SOAP and REST advocates seem to be armed camps in opposition. Each side has its strength. The SOAP stack is complex, but developers can install it as a black box and not worry about its inner workings. However, tuning and debugging a service when the stack is a black box can be difficult. REST does away with stack complexity, but complexity re-appears when applications are not easily expressed in the REST model.

The decision to go with REST or SOAP frequently depends on the familiarity of the development team with the two approaches. A team that is expert with SOAP and comfortable with its stack will produce a more robust application with SOAP. A REST team can produce a more compact and performant application building on REST. Neither is likely to do well with an unfamiliar technology.

SOAP and REST have many significant differences, but a major difference is that REST is stateless; SOAP is stateful. In addition, SOAP is a protocol that can be used with many architectures. REST, on the other hand, is an architecture that enables a protocol. Stateless SOAP-based services are possible, and it is possible to implement the equivalent of a stateful service with REST.

SOA in the Cloud

Whether based on SOAP or REST, SOA, along with microservices and ROA, is well suited to cloud implementations. Applications implemented with SOA typically can be made to scale well in a cloud with load-balanced parallel service implementations. An application that exposes SOA services as its public interface can be used by browsers and other graphic interfaces such as mobile apps. In addition, such an application can be used by "headless" processes such as those used in the Internet of Things. The "mix-and-match" style of SOA also promotes flexibility and rapid development of services created from new groupings of existing services.[5] SOA also contributes to ease of enterprise integration by providing SOA interfaces as a natural means of connecting enterprise applications.

Figure 13-2 illustrates an SOA cloud implementation of two applications that share services. The upper application, A, is highly scalable with both web servers and application servers automatically replicated as the load increases. On the SOA service level, services 1 and 3 are replicated and

---

[5]The Internet of Things (IoT) refers to the appearance of things, such as heating and ventilation controls or security cameras, on the network. Many people project rapid growth in the IoT in the next few years and the integration of the IoT with traditional applications.

load balanced. Services 2 and 4 are not, probably because they are not likely to cause performance issues. Perhaps the services are infrequently used or they are lightweight and execute rapidly.

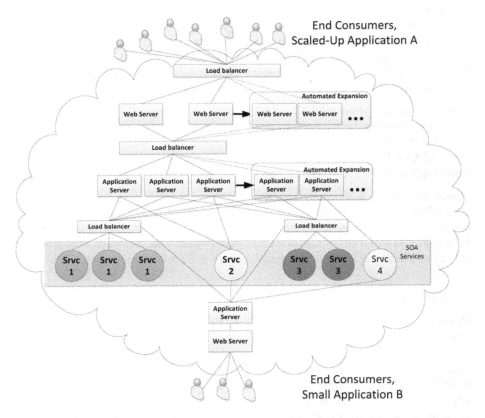

Figure 13-2. An SOA architecture decomposes business functions into services that can be used by more than one application

Application B is not designed to scale, except when necessary to cope with application A's load. Notice that the B application server goes through the load balancers for services 1 and 3. This means that loads coming from application B are in the same pool of loads as those coming from application A. If the B loads were to go directly to one of the instances of service 1 or 3, the instance of the service used by B could be overwhelmed by loads from A. By going through the load balancer, B loads are always directed to the optimum service instance.

Asynchrony and Responsiveness Principles

Asynchronous communication is a type of message protocol that has been discussed before in these pages. However, asynchronous communication is a cornerstone of all efficient cloud applications. Without asynchrony, processes are held in lockstep. If a process must stop processing and wait for a reply, such as calling a function from a statically linked library, the calling process is blocked by the called process until it is complete. Asynchronous messaging deals with this problem. The cost of avoiding blocking is the overhead of callback and wait mechanisms. Usually, this is an acceptable trade-off.

Synchronous dependency can be acceptable in a low-volume environment where communication is not subject to variations in network latency and bandwidth and variable loads on different parts of the system. In a low-volume system, a synchronous wait typically results in a pause for one user, which is undesirable but tolerable. In a high-volume system, the same wait will stop many users, which can easily become intolerable. Public clouds that rely on the Internet are always subject to network variations, which can be slowdowns or flat-out interruptions. A synchronous wait caused by a network failure can bring an application to a halt. Wireless connections add another element of variability.

Asynchronous communication is usually used in conjunction with message queuing in basic web application architecture. A browser sends an HTTP request to an HTTP server[6] running on a cloud, which calls an application layer to perform an operation. If the browser waits synchronously for a reply from the server, the user may end up staring at an hourglass while the browser waits for a reply from a busy application server. A much more suitable approach is to use asynchronous messaging with queuing. Operating in this manner, the users send their requests, and the HTTP server immediately replies, acknowledging that the message has been received but nothing more. The HTTP server passes the message to the application server queue. The message stays in the queue until the application server is ready to process it. When the message is processed, the application server sends a message back to the HTTP server. The HTTP server then passes the message to the user.

Handling the message queue has complications. If, for example, the application server fails before the incoming message is properly processed, the request should remain on the queue to be picked up by the next available application server. Commercial queue-handling products devote substantial effort to resolving complex queue handling issues.

---

[6]An HTTP server is also a web server. Here, when HTTP is important in the discussion, I use the term *HTTP server*. When HTTP fades into the background, I use the more common term, *web server*. An Internet web server that does not use HTTP is possible, but it would not work with most of the World Wide Web.

Idempotency and Message Handling

An idempotent message can be repeated arbitrarily, and the effect is as if the message was delivered only once. A simple request for information is idempotent. The request can be repeated many times, but the result will not change. A less trivial example is an update to a relational database row. A simple update is idempotent. If the same row is updated and then updated again with the same values, the row will be the same as if it had been updated only once. On the other hand, a request that updates a numeric value using a database-stored subroutine to increment and update the value is not idempotent. With each repeated request, the value increases. Several requests are not the equivalent of one request.

Idempotent commands are easier to manage than nonidempotent commands. In the user interface, consumers are inclined to push a button repeatedly if the interface does not respond immediately with an acknowledgment. Warning messages cautioning users to wait after issuing a nonidempotent request are easily ignored or confused. Asking the user to compensate for a weakness in the interface courts user errors, especially when the interface is used continually by thousands of users.

More important for cloud applications, idempotent commands are much easier to manage internally when communications are interrupted or delayed.

If a command is not idempotent, it may be impossible to determine whether a command should be repeated. For example, a user issues a nonidempotent message to place an order; that is, repeating the request will generate two order records. The browser begins to wait for an acknowledgment. An accidental partitioning of the network blocks communication between the browser and the server. If the block occurred before the server received the message to place the order, the order request must be repeated. If the break occurred after the server received the order but before the acknowledgment was sent, the order request must not be repeated.

This dilemma for the browser and the end user is more difficult than a problematic message. The problem can be remediated, but the solution usually involves sorting out message sequences on both the browser and the server. Rolling back transactions may require complex logic. These solutions are best avoided if possible.

An idempotent order request is easier to manage. No harm is done if the browser or end user repeats the request until an acknowledgment arrives.

In the simplest case, using the idempotent HTTP PUT method rather than the nonidempotent POST is all that is necessary for idempotence. However, simply changing POST to PUT is seldom all that is necessary. A PUT targets a specific object. If the object does not exist, the server must create it with the values in the PUT body. If the object exists, the server must replace the object with the values in the PUT body. Calling the same PUT repeatedly has no effect because the contents of the PUT body do not change and the target object does not change.

POST is different. Usually, a POST targets a process that processes the POST body. The process may create a new object, modify an existing object, or do other actions. The effect of sending the same POST repeatedly depends on the process. If the process is to increment a value, the value will be nonidempotently incremented again. If the process does the equivalent of a PUT, the POST is idempotent. When a process must be involved, it can be designed to be idempotent. For example, an increment process can use data in the HTTP header to determine whether the POST is a repeat and not increment on subsequent calls.

Idempotency can be important to horizontally scalable cloud installations. These systems are dependent on communications between processes that are distributed over multiple interconnected nodes. Although many of these nodes may be within a single datacenter and less likely to fail than networks that depend on remote routers and communication links, they are nonetheless subject to accidental partitions, such as a connector pulled out of its socket when a technician trips over a cable. If requests are idempotent, recovering from a network failure is simply repeating the request. With load-balancing code to route the repeated request to an alternate node, the application is resilient to this kind of system fault. For large-scale, critical production applications, resiliency to network failures is extremely important, and time devoted to designing idempotency into interprocess communication can provide substantial return on the investment.

Consistency, Availability, and Network Partitions

One of the basic principles of distributed system design is the impossibility of a distributed system in which the data on every node is always consistent, the system is always available, and the system is never affected by network failures. The Consistency, Availability, and Network Partitions (CAP) principle asserts that only two of the three properties can be maintained at any one time. Since network partitions (failures in which one part of the network becomes isolated from the rest) are unavoidable in practice on the Internet, designers must always choose between consistency and availability.[7]

The ideal for data transactions is Atomicity, Consistency, Isolation, Durability (ACID). Without going into the details of ACID, it is an ideal that the CAP theorem shows is an unattainable goal in a distributed system that relies on an unreliable network. A basic challenge to cloud computing, and any other network dependent distributed system, is to cope with the reality of CAP.

---

[7]For a full discussion of CAP, see Marvin Waschke, *Cloud Standards*. Apress, 2012, pp. 124–131.

Although a cloud implementation could occasionally be deployed on a single node and therefore not be distributed, cloud designers always have to assume that CAP applies. The choice between availability and consistency may be more subtle than it first appears.

Usually, it is an important business decision. Consistency is often thought of in conjunction with accounting. The accounts must always be consistent. However, most people have real-world experience with deposits, especially large deposits, that do not appear in their account until several hours—even days—after the deposit was made. Financial institutions often build latency into their systems to vet for mistakes and fraud. Instant consistency is not so important to them. This is the case for many systems.

On the other hand, availability may appear to be less important. A site that is unavailable for a short time may not seem to be important. But ask a large online retailer about sales sites that are unavailable. They may say that every minute of downtime costs them many dollars in sales.

The balance between consistency and availability is critical to many businesses. When shifting from an on-premises application where network failure within the enterprise perimeter is rare to a cloud implementation that is more exposed to network failure, cloud architects have to keep the consistency-availability trade-off in mind. They must also realize that the terms of the trade-off are critical to business, not just engineering. Most of the time, an adequate solution is a guarantee that, like the check that eventually shows up in your account, the system will eventually become consistent and availability will not be compromised to attain consistency.

Containers

Containers are an alternative to hypervisor-based virtualization that has gathered attention and favor recently. The concept behind containers was discussed in Chapter 11. Containers can be considerably smaller than a corresponding virtual machine image because they contain only the application, not the virtual machine that runs the application. When a container is launched, the operating system rather than the hypervisor manages processing and prevents mutual interference between containers.

The fundamental container abstraction is an application that can easily be deployed into an identical environment on a number of machines. In contrast, virtual machines are abstract machines on which applications are pre-installed. The abstract machine with the installed application can then be deployed identically many times. Applications deployed in containers and applications on virtual machines can be spun up with identical configurations and operating environments, but the two operate on different layers. Awareness of this distinction is important when deciding whether a container or a virtual machine will be more appropriate for a cloud deployment.

There are advantages to containers over virtual machines. Containers are lighter weight than virtual machines. A container usually has a much smaller disk footprint than a virtual machine because it uses more functionality from the underlying operating system. Using containers, fewer of the computing cycles of the underlying hardware are consigned to overhead, so more containers can be run on the same processor. This is because some operating system functionality is shared between containers running on the same node. In addition, lightweight containers usually start up faster than virtual machines.

On the downside, a holder of root privilege on the underlying operating system has access to the contents of the container, unlike a virtual machine, which can be made inaccessible without credentials for the specific virtual machine. This can be an issue in high-security and mission-critical scenarios. In addition, tooling and management facilities for hypervisor-based systems are more available, and expertise in developing and managing is well-established, although this situation is rapidly changing with increased interest in containers.

Containers are not an all-or-nothing choice. A container can be launched on a virtual machine. The combination of containers and virtual machines on hybrid Linux and Windows platforms may prove to be the most viable architecture in the future.[8]

Plan for New Interfaces

The appearance of handheld devices, smartphones, and tablets has transformed enterprise computing in many ways, and the change promises to continue. Wearable computers (such as wrist monitors and other wearable devices) and the Internet of Things are adding new devices such as security and utility controllers to enterprise networks, and they all promise to place new demands on enterprise IT services.

These are new interfaces to computing systems. Mobile computing has changed the enterprise perimeter, and you can expect new devices to change perimeters unpredictably. Already, mechanical control systems attached to the enterprise network have become a vector for malicious exploits. Mobile apps have driven new ways in which employees and customers communicate with enterprise systems. Cloud-deployed applications are often the back end to these interfaces. Back ends tend to remain stable longer than front-end interfaces. Cloud architects and designers should plan for front-end change.

---

[8]Docker is the most mentioned container project today. It is an open source Linux-based project that is supported by a company named Docker. See https://www.docker.com/, accessed July 2015. A widely supported group has formed to write an operating system and platform–independent standard for containers. See www.infoworld.com/article/2938638/application-virtualization/docker-donates-its-container-specs-for-opc-open-standard.html, accessed July 2015.

That means carefully thinking through the separation between the functionality of the service and the presentation of the service. Because I do not know what these transformations will require, specific recommendations are difficult. However, the principle of separation of presentation and functionality (which made it possible for a back end to weather the change from thick to thin clients and from thin web clients to mobile apps) has a good chance to aid in the transformations to come.

Store Freely

Storage used to be expensive. Now it's relatively cheap. In several decades of building and designing enterprise applications, one observation has been consistently true: every decision made to reduce the volume of data stored or to store data more compactly at the expense of losing information or decreasing the ease and speed of access eventually turns into a blunder. That observation is not a license to waste capacity by storing identical data repeatedly or bloating files with gigabytes of nulls from memory dumps. However, cloud storage is much cheaper now than storage has ever has been. In addition, the techniques for manipulating and analyzing large quantities of data have evolved to the point that masses of data have become assets instead of burdens. The value of data has increased in direct proportion to the capacity to store it and analyze it efficiently. Masses of data that would have been on a list for purging a decade ago have become enterprise treasures.

Therefore, architects should not skimp on storing additional data in the form of more detailed logs, storing records that might have been treated as temporary before, and storing data incidental to transactions. Predicting what will become important as the analysis proceeds is difficult, but decreasing costs have made it more practical to err on the side of storing more, not less.

The cloud is the perfect place to take advantage of masses of data because big data analysis requires monumental computing capacity, but only for a relatively short time, and it works best with expanding numbers of parallel processes, which are exactly suited to a cloud architecture. This is another argument for storing data freely.

Conclusion

Building efficient cloud applications that will contribute enduring value to the enterprise is not easy. Cloud implementations can be more efficient and perform better than on-premises applications, but only if good practices are followed. Some of these practices, such as horizontal scalability, SOA, microservices, and ROA may be unfamiliar, but they are easier to implement in a cloud environment where they are the expected architecture.

Most important, by following healthy cloud-oriented architectural practices, applications that deliver on the promises of cloud are possible.

EXERCISES

1. Name three basic cloud application requirements.

2. What is a monolithic application? Explain why it may not be suitable for cloud deployment.

3. Differentiate between SOAP and REST. Which is more suitable for cloud deployments?

4. What are containers?

Fish nor Fowl

Mixed Architectures

SUMMARY

The most realistic scenario in large enterprises is a mixture of legacy on-premises applications, cloud IaaS or PaaS applications, and SaaS applications. All these applications are likely to need some level of integration with the rest.

Architectures that mix on-premises and cloud applications are likely to be present in enterprise IT for years to come. Many enterprises have successful applications deployed on their premises that are effective and efficient. As long as the investment in these applications continues to return sound economic value, the applications are not likely to be replaced by cloud deployments. In addition, security and regulatory compliance requirements make some applications difficult to move from the premises. Security threatens to be an issue for some time to come. Aside from the hesitance to entrust third parties with critical data and processes, cloud technology is relatively new. Experience has shown that immature technologies are more susceptible to security breaches than more mature technologies. This drives some skepticism of the safety of cloud deployments for critical components.

MIXED CLOUD ARCHITECTURES

The term *hybrid cloud* is often used with almost the same meaning as *mixed architectures* is used in this book. The National Institute of Standards and Technologies defines a hybrid cloud as a combination of several clouds, which may be private, community, or public.[1] A common example is a private cloud designed to expand into a public cloud when extra capacity is needed. The definition has drifted and sometimes includes on-premises applications. In this book, a mixed architecture or environment refers to an architecture that includes traditional on-premises applications along with clouds. The clouds may be private, community, or public, and applications may be implemented on IaaS or PaaS clouds or may be SaaS. In most cases, cloud and on-premises implementations are integrated in a mixed architecture, although mixed architectures without integration are possible.

Some applications are not likely ever to be moved to the cloud. Security and regulatory issues aside, some applications will be deemed so critical to the corporate mission that they cannot be entrusted to a third-party cloud. Some of these issues are solved by private clouds, which are built exclusively for a single enterprise, but private ownership of a cloud does not convey all the business and technical benefits of a third-party cloud deployment.

Given the business and technical advantages of cloud deployment and the equally potent arguments for avoiding clouds, mixed environments are inevitable.

If the applications in a mixed architecture operated independently, without communicating with each other, the mixed environment architect's life would be easy. Cloud applications deployed on the cloud would not contend for resources with applications deployed in the local datacenter, which would make planning the on-premises datacenter a bit easier. If cloud applications communicated only with their end users, network concerns about latency and bandwidth communicating between cloud and premises and cloud-to-cloud would not exist. Connectivity issues would be greatly simplified. The architect's task would only be to decide which applications to replace with SaaS, which to rebuild or port to IaaS or PaaS, and which to leave in the on-premises datacenter.

---

[1] See http://csrc.nist.gov/publications/nistpubs/800-145/SP800-145.pdf, accessed August 1, 2015.

Mixed Integration

However, as you have seen in earlier chapters, enterprises without integration are unlikely because integrated applications deliver increased value to the enterprise. Integration is always important, but it may be made more important by the cloud. SaaS applications provide an example. As more enterprises move to a limited number of popular SaaS offerings for some types of application, the software in use tends to become uniform. Consequently, the service delivered to enterprise customers also becomes more of a commodity that yields little competitive advantage.

Consider a popular SaaS customer relationship management (CRM) application. The SaaS application is popular because it meets many business needs. The installation effort is minor, the product is well designed, and it is easy for the sales force to learn. Each organization using the application is a tenant of a single multitenant application. In other words, the features for each organization are fundamentally identical, perhaps with a few customizations. The responsiveness of the sales division and the range and content of customer services become essentially the same. This places the organizations using the multitenant application on a level playing field.

In business, level playing fields are desirable only when the field is tilted against you. As soon as the field is level, good business requires you to strive to tilt the field in your favor. Integrating an SaaS application into an organization's superior IT environment may well be the competitive advantage the organization needs.

When the enterprise integrates with the SaaS CRM system, the business can gain advantage from the design of the entire IT system, not just the commoditized CRM system. For example, an enterprise with a comprehensive supply-chain management system could integrate with the order inquiry module of the CRM SaaS application. When the customer calls about an order, the integration would provide the CRM analyst with exact information on the status of the order in the production line. Armed with this information, the analyst is prepared to present an accurate, up-to-the-minute status to the customer. If competitors do not have this information from their own environment integrated into their CRM application, they cannot offer their customers the same level of service as a more integrated enterprise. They are at a significant disadvantage, and the level playing field has tilted toward the integrated enterprise.

Skipping integration between on-premises and cloud-based applications is unlikely to be a realistic possibility. Bridging the premises and the cloud is likely to offer some of the most critical links in the entire integrated system because applications that require on-premises installation are often mission-critical applications that the entire enterprise depends on in some way. That dependency is expressed as a need to know the state of the on-premises application by many other applications in the system. Mixed integration supplies that need.

For example, a manufacturer may have a highly sophisticated process control system that is tailored exactly to an organization's facilities and processes. It is the main driver of an efficient and profitable business. Deploying this control application on a cloud would simply not work. The controls work in real time. A network breakdown between a cloud-deployed control application and the physical process could be catastrophic, destroying facilities and threatening lives. In addition, the application represents trade secrets that management is unlikely to allow to leave the premises. But at the same time, data from this critical application also controls much of the rest of the business and must be integrated with the other applications that run the enterprise, both on and off the cloud.

For example, the supply chain system uses flow data from the control system to determine when to order raw materials and predict product availability for filling orders. Management keeps a careful eye on data from the process to plan for future expansion or contraction of the business. Customer resource management relies on the same data to predict to customers when their orders are likely to be filled. Some of this functionality may effectively be deployed on clouds; other functionality will remain on the premises but eventually migrate when it must be replaced or substantially rebuilt. Integration between the process control system and other applications is essential if the organization is to work as a coordinated whole. If a cloud-based application cannot be integrated with the on-premises core system, the application must be kept on-premises where it can be integrated, even though a cloud implementation might be cheaper and better.

The Internet of Things (IoT) also adds to the importance of mixed environment integration. Heating, ventilation, and air conditioning (HVAC) systems have become part of the Internet of Things for many enterprises. For example, controllers embedded in HVAC components become part of the Internet of Things and appear as nodes on the corporate network and may be exposed to the Internet. HVAC engineers can monitor and control the system over the corporate network or the Internet. This presents creative opportunities. A datacenter HVAC could be integrated with the load management system in the datacenter. Since increasing or decreasing loads raise and lower cooling demands, the HVAC system could respond before the temperature actually changes as loads vary, resulting in more precise temperature control and perhaps decreased cooling costs. Similarly, an integrated physical security system might transfer critical resources to a remote cloud site when designated barriers are physically breached, preventing physical tampering with the resources. Since the embedded controllers are located with the equipment they control, they will always be on-premises while the applications that use data from the controllers and manage the equipment may be cheaper and more efficient in a cloud implementation, requiring cloud-to-premises integration.

As long as the environment remains mixed, mixed integration will be crucial to enterprise success.

Challenges of Mixed Integration

Integration in a mixed cloud and on-premises environment has all the challenges of integrating in a traditional on-premises environment, but the addition of cloud implementations erects some barriers of its own.

Figure 14-1 represents a hypothetical mixed architecture site. Two SaaS applications reside on their respective vendor's clouds. They are each integrated with several on-premises applications and two applications that are hosted on public clouds. In addition, the two SaaS applications are integrated. One public cloud application is deployed on IaaS. This application could have been developed by the site and deployed on the cloud, or it could be a traditional off-the-shelf application that the site has deployed on IaaS. There is also an application deployed on PaaS using a platform supplied by the public cloud vendor. The deployment of each of these applications presents unique challenges for integration.

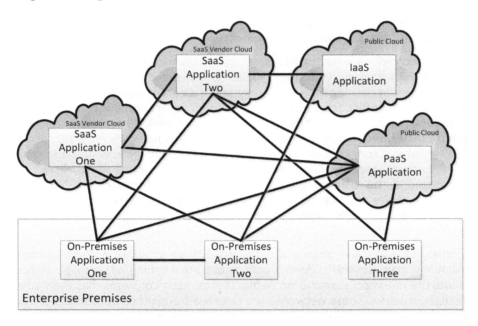

Figure 14-1. The point-to-point integration of SaaS, IaaS, PaaS, and on-premises applications can be complex and frustrating

Figure 14-1 shows the integration connections as solid lines. A point-to-point integration would implement each solid line as a real connection over a physical or virtual network. If the entire system were on-premises, all these connections would flow through the physical network. In a mixed system, connections between on-premises applications (On-Premises Application One and On-Premises Application Two in Figure 14-1) would still travel on the physical network. Applications in the cloud would use combinations of virtual and physical networks.

Virtual Networks

The current challenge in integration in mixed environments is to manage the network connections within clouds, between clouds, and between the premises and off-premises clouds. A virtual network is a network that is not based on physical connections between physical devices. Virtual networks can be divided between networks that are superimposed on physical networks and networks that are implemented via a hypervisor and may exist on a single physical device. Superimposed virtual networks include virtual private networks (VPNs), which identify nodes on a physical network as elements in a virtual network accessible only to members of the VPN. Network Address Translation (NAT) is another type of superimposed network established by managing IP addresses. Hypervisor-based virtual networks often include virtual network devices such as virtual switches.

Virtual networks are among the least mature technologies in cloud engineering, but the integration of cloud applications depends upon them. A single virtual machine running on a cloud only needs a connection to the Internet to perform useful work for a consumer. When an application consists of several interconnected virtual machines, some sort of network is required to connect the machines and manage the communication. This network must be part of the virtual environment. Sometimes, the virtual machines may all be running on the same hardware processor. In that case, the virtual network will be supported by the memory and data bus of the processor machine. When the virtual machines are running on different machines, the virtual network must be implemented in the hypervisor run on the physical network of the cloud provider.

Virtual networks are often a key to securing an application. When virtual machines from several different consumers are running on a single virtual cloud, the common scenario on public clouds, each consumer has their own virtual networks. These networks are shielded from other consumers. If that shielding were to break down and consumers were to have access to each other's networks, it would be a severe security breach. The requirement for separation may extend to virtual infrastructure within the same enterprise. A single organization may require groups of virtual machines to be isolated from other groups, say accounting and engineering groups. This can be accomplished with separate virtual networks.

Mixed environment integration also depends on virtual networks to support secure integration between virtual machines running on clouds by controlling security appliances such as firewalls and encryption of information in transit. The configuration of virtual networks also can be a critical factor in the performance and capacity of systems in mixed environment by controlling factors such as quality of service (QoS) and bandwidth.

Software-Defined Networks

Software-defined networks (SDNs) are a related technology that increases the speed and efficiency with which complicated networks can be configured. Traffic in networks is controlled by switches that have control and data planes. The control plane determines how each packet is directed and expedited through the network. The data plane carries out the control plane's instructions. Software-defined networking supplies an abstract management interface that administrators and developers access to control the network. This management interface acts as the control plane for the network and enables rapid complex reconfiguration of both virtual and physical networks. The combination of hypervisor-defined virtual networks and SDN promises to be powerful. The hypervisor and SDN switches can work together to bridge the gap between physical and virtual networks.

Software-defined networking is currently a rapidly developing area that promises to make implementation of all cloud integration, including mixed environments, easier.

Bus and Hub-and-Spoke Architectures

Point-to-point integration is relatively cheap and quick to implement in simple systems, but eventually it can generate considerable redundant code and confusion. A system of the complexity of Figure 14-1 can become a nightmare to troubleshoot and maintain.

Figure 14-2 is the same system as Figure 14-1, redrawn with an integration bus. A bus architecture simplifies the integration diagram, but it requires more up-front development and may not begin to deliver value until later in the evolution of the enterprise when the number of integrated applications has increased.

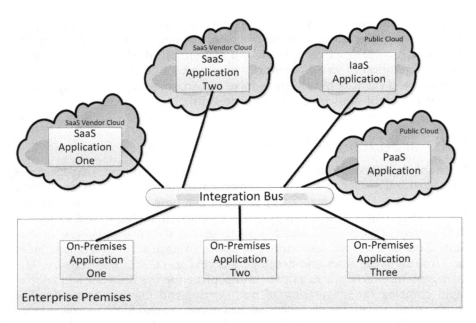

Figure 14-2. The same system as Figure 14-1. A bus architecture simplifies the integration diagram

Hub-and-spoke integration designs are similar to bus designs. Figure 14-3 shows a spoke-and-hub design for the same system as Figures 14-2 and 14-1. Both reduce the number of connections between applications and simplify adding new applications. The primary difference between the two is that a hub-and-spoke architecture tends to place more intelligence in the hub. In a hub-and-spoke architecture, the hub usually decides which messages are sent down the spokes. In a bus architecture, each client examines the messages on the bus and chooses those of interest. There are advantages and disadvantages to either approach, and many implementations combine the two in different ways. Earlier chapters discussed these two integration architectures in more detail. Both have many strong points, and commercial versions of both are available.

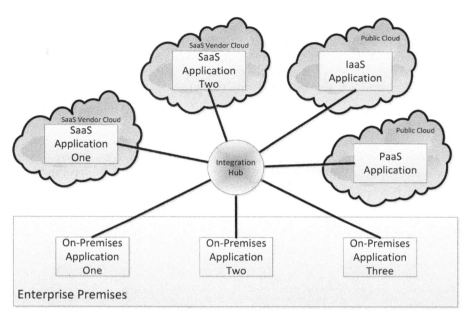

Figure 14-3. Hub-and-spoke integration is similar to bus integration

An integration architecture that avoids the unwieldiness of point-to-point integration is especially important in a complex mixed environment, because in a mixed environment, integration is likely to use a variety of interfaces that may be difficult to manage, especially when they involve proprietary third-party code.

The difficulty of the integration challenge increases with every application that is added to the system. Whether an added application is hosted on-premises or on a cloud, connections have to be added from the new application to each integrated application. When the connections are through proprietary interfaces (as is often the case for SaaS applications) and over virtual networks that may be managed differently from cloud to cloud, a clear and easily understood centralized topology is important. In addition, point-to-point integration often means that adapter code has to be written for both ends of every connection. Either a bus or a hub cuts down the amount of redundant adapter code. Adding new applications becomes much easier, and the resulting system is easier to understand and maintain. In the beginning, there is a substantial investment.

This presents a dilemma. Stakeholders like immediate return on their investment, which argues for starting with a point-to-point system and migrating to a bus or hub architecture later. However, implementing a central architecture from the beginning when there are only a few applications to integrate is by far the most efficient way to implement a centralized system. Site-built applications can be designed to interoperate off the shelf with the bus or hub, and SaaS applications can be chosen for their ease in connecting to the bus. Building a bus or hub later usually entails designing around existing heterogeneous applications, which is possible but usually is more difficult and likely to involve undesirable compromises in the design.

Some thought has to go into deciding whether an integration bus or hub should be deployed on-premises or on a cloud. The bus is a critical component. Its failure potentially shuts down all communications between applications in the system. This argues for placing the hub on-premises with failover either on a cloud or in a remote location. An on-premises hub is under the direct control of enterprise staff, and it may be more convenient to configure the hub on-premises rather than remotely. However, the topology of the system may offer greater bandwidth and network reliability if the hub is deployed on the cloud. See Figure 14-4.

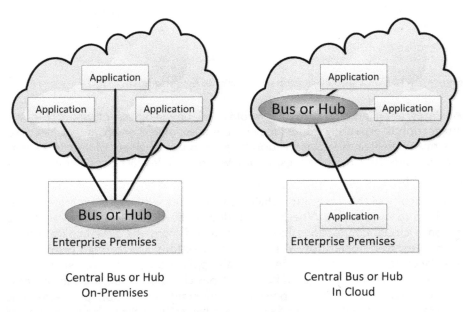

Figure 14-4. Two different integration distribution schemes

Small, Medium, and Large Enterprises

The challenges of integration in a mixed environment hit the smallest organization as well as the largest. In many ways, small organizations benefit more from cloud implementations than larger organizations because they have a "green field" for development. Larger organizations usually have a legacy of applications. In many cases, larger organizations have built their business around their applications. Moving those applications to a cloud may be impossible, even though keeping the applications on the premises is no longer practical. At that point, the enterprise must buy or build a cloud replacement that will integrate both to other applications on the cloud and to applications left on-premises. Smaller organizations can avoid these hazards by considering cloud implementation in their plans immediately.

Application training in larger organizations can be an expensive issue because application changes may require retraining of hundreds of employees, and the training period may stretch into months of reduced productivity. Therefore, large organizations often place a premium on user interfaces that minimize change. This can be a problem if the switch is from a fat client (desktop-based interface) to a thin client (browser-based interface) because thin clients use a different interaction pattern than most fat clients. Although the trend has been to provide browser-based interfaces for all applications, there still many on-premises applications with fat clients that present problems when they are moved to the cloud.

The biggest challenge to large enterprises in a mixed environment is dealing with legacy applications that do not have modern integration interfaces like web services. An example is a legacy application that offers exit routines.[2] Integration of these applications is often hard to understand, especially when the original authors are not available. Enhancing or extending the integration to applications deployed on the cloud often require sophisticated code and extensive quality assurance testing. Although exit routines may be a worst-case scenario, many site-built integrations are similarly challenging.

Although large organizations are likely to have the resources to move on-premises applications to cloud deployment and the scale of their IT investment may provide ample financial incentive for the move, they are likely to encounter more technical difficulties than smaller organizations.

Smaller organizations usually don't have legacy problems. They can base their choices on the cost and functionality of applications. Therefore, cloud deployments often are a smaller organization's choice. The low investment in hardware is usually attractive, and the functionality is often far beyond the minimal level of automation the organization is used to. Out-of-the-box integration facilities will often satisfy their needs.

---

[2]*Exit routines* are routines that are coded by the users of an application and linked into the application. They offer a tricky path to integration that tends to expose the internals of the application and result in an inflexible relationship between the integrated applications. They are more commonly used in customizing the kernels of operating systems such as Linux. Installing a new application on Linux occasionally involves relinking the kernel with new or additional code. Applications that offer exit routines frequently need to be relinked when the application is upgraded. Although they are tricky, they are also flexible and powerful, amounting to a do-it-yourself programming interface. The right exit routines can make adding a web service to a legacy application possible, even relatively easy, but some routines seem impossible to work with.

In addition, smaller enterprises may have fewer problems with regulations and security. Private enterprises typically do not have the compliance issue of publicly held corporations. Although security is usually as important for both small and large organizations, smaller-scale organizations often do not need the sophisticated security management that enterprises with thousands of employees require. In addition, applications are built now with interfaces for standardized security management, which is much easier to deal with than legacy applications from the pre-Internet days when IT security meant a cipher lock on the computer room.

Choosing Which Applications to Deploy on the Cloud

Everyone knows that some applications are not likely ever to be deployed on a cloud. Security and regulatory compliance were two considerations discussed frequently in earlier chapters.

Some applications are especially well-suited to cloud deployment. Perhaps the most important technical characteristic of clouds is their flexibility. An organization can deploy one or a thousand virtual machines on a sufficiently large cloud with almost equal ease. Configuring machines for a special purpose is also easy. Instead of thumbing through catalogs or talking to sales representatives to find compatible equipment and then having to bolt and cable up the hardware, virtual machines can be configured and launched in minutes. The cloud provider takes responsibility for assembling the right physical equipment, which will probably be a small partition of much larger equipment in the provider's datacenter.

Load Variations and Scaling

Which applications require that kind of flexibility? Any application whose load varies widely is a good candidate. An application that needs fifty servers at midday and only two at midnight can use this flexibility well. Similarly, an application that needs fifty servers in the last week of the month and two for the other three weeks is also a candidate. It is not surprising that some of the most successful SaaS applications, such as customer relations management or service desk, fall into this category. Retail web sites also fit the category. In fact, much of the cloud concept was developed to respond to load variations at large retail sites.[3]

---

[3]Amazon is the retail site that inspired much cloud development. Amazon's cloud offerings are solutions developed by Amazon to cope with its own difficulty standing up systems to respond to its growing system loads. For some background on Amazon's development, see www.zdnet.com/article/how-amazon-exposed-its-guts-the-history-of-awss-ec2/. Accessed July 28, 2015.

Changing Machine Configurations

Projects that require many different machine configurations are also good candidates. Consider the machine configurations depicted as radar charts in Figures 14-5 and 14-6. Each of the configurations is designed to support applications with specific needs. A cloud provider typically offers several VM sizes. An extra-small VM might have a single CPU and less than a gigabyte of memory; an extra-large VM might have four CPUs and 7GB of memory. For example, the storage configuration may be appropriate for a database server. Sometimes these basic configurations are combined. A database server may also need a high-performance CPU for rapid processing of retrieved data. When using physical hardware on-premises, adding a bank of RAID disks or an additional CPU will require time-consuming and expensive physical hardware reconfiguration such as connecting cables and reconfiguring racks. In a cloud deployment, these configurations can be changed rapidly in software.

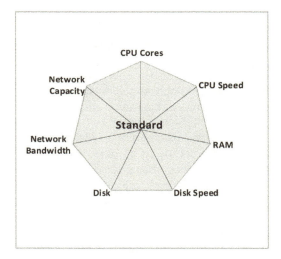

Figure 14-5. A standard, multipurpose machine has moderate capacity and roughly equivalent CPU, network, and storage capabilities

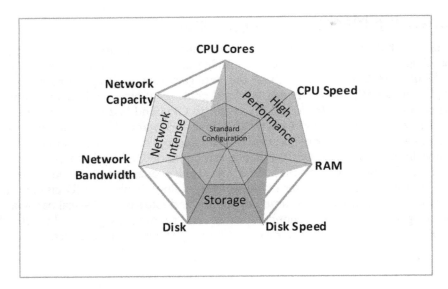

Figure 14-6. Specialized machines have extended capacities adapting them to special purposes

Both are associated with development. Developers often need to change hardware while coding to achieve maximum efficiency. Coding and compiling ordinarily do not require a high-end server, but unit testing of the compiled code may require much more capacity. The capacity and type of the required resources vary with the unit testing to be performed. Usually, developers are assigned to a multipurpose device with adequate resources to run the code they write. If they are developing on the cloud, their options increase, and they can tailor their configuration to the job at hand. Costs are decreased because they are not using more capacity than their work requires. The work speeds up and quality improves with proper unit testing. Sometimes, the availability of cloud hardware makes unit tests possible that would have to be deferred to the system test phase. A truism of software development is that the earlier an issue can be discovered, the better and cheaper the fix.

Cloud configuration flexibility is also beneficial during system test. Quality assurance engineers used to tear their hair trying to put together test environments that resembled the user environment. Many defects have been put into production that could have been identified and fixed during system testing if the quality assurance team had an adequate test bed. Cloud test beds reduce cost because they can be stood up and taken down quickly, and the organization is charged only for the time the test bed was deployed.

Compute-Intense Applications

The cloud is ideal for big problems that require intensive computation and extraordinary storage capacity. A retailer may analyze years of purchasing data from millions of customers to identify buying patterns. The retailer uses the analysis to tailor sales and marketing plans. A structural design firm may use high-capacity computing to plot stresses in a machine part on a highly granular scale to design a critical structural part that is both strong and light weight. In both cases, using cloud computing capacity lets organizations achieve results that used to be possible only using enormously expensive supercomputers.

Cloud implementations offer the opportunity for even smaller organizations to utilize large-scale computing. In the past, only the largest businesses or governmental organizations were able to construct and maintain supercomputers. The hardware costs, facilities, energy supply, and cooling capacity were prohibitively expensive for any but the deepest pockets.

Cloud implementations have brought down the cost of high-capacity computing in two ways. The large public cloud providers have built datacenters and networks of datacenters that are larger than any that preceded them. By relying on relatively low-cost modules that are replicated many times, they have driven down hardware costs. In addition, they have been innovative in situating and designing datacenters to maximize cooling and energy efficiency.

The second way cloud computing has reduced the cost of high-capacity computing is by permitting users to purchase only the capacity they need for the time that they use it. When an organization has a problem that can best be solved by using a very high-capacity system for a relatively short time, they can deploy it on a cloud, run the system for as long as it takes to solve the problem, and then stand down the system. Unlike an on-premises system, the cost of the solution is only for the computing capacity actually used, not the total cost of acquiring and setting up the hardware.

A project that uses a large quantity of cloud resources for a short time may be the lowest hanging of the cloud fruits, if an organization is in a position to use it. Such a project hangs low because it does not involve a potentially risky replacement of an existing on-premises service and will not be expected to be continued or maintained in the future. The resources used depend on the project. Project to evaluate an intricate model, such as those used for scientific predictions, probably will require extensive CPU and memory. Large IoT projects could require high speed and volume input and output. Large-scale data analysis may require extensive storage. The decision to undertake the project usually assumes a cloud implementation because the project can be undertaken only on the cloud. The deciding factors are usually the potential return on the investment and the level of expertise in the organization for undertaking the project. If the expertise is adequate and the return on the investment justifies the effort, the organization will likely see its way to undertake the project.

A short-term high-capacity project is not likely to require extensive integration. These projects are usually batch jobs that start with a large and complex data set and progress to the end without additional interactive input. A project such as this often requires expertise in big data techniques such as map-reduce programming and statistical analysis. If the right expertise is available, a project like this could be a starting point for developing the technical expertise in working with cloud deployments that may lead to deploying more applications on an IaaS or PaaS cloud in a mixed environment.

SaaS Mixed Integration

SaaS can be a great opportunity for organizations of all sizes. Ease of installation and maintenance can free up valuable personnel and improve the user experience. Installing and operating a SaaS application requires the absolute minimum of technical skill. For this reason, it is an easy first step to cloud-based IT. In many cases, SaaS licensing and decreased administration will reduce the total cost of ownership of the application. SaaS applications are usually easily accessible outside the enterprise perimeter. Successful SaaS products are well-designed with appropriate features and are easy to use.

Regardless of the reality, some decision makers may oppose moving applications out of the enterprise perimeter and relinquishing local IT control of applications. In some cases, government regulations, auditing rules, or other constraints may require hosting the applications on the premises. Other times, there may be a deep-seated prejudice against moving off-premises.

There are also reasons not to embrace SaaS for all applications. Although vendors make provision for customizing their SaaS applications, some organizations may require more customization than the SaaS application will support. This often occurs when the application has to fit into a highly technical environment, such as an industrial facility, like a pulp mill or power plant, with special requirements for record keeping or instrumentation.

SaaS also usually involves links that traverse the Internet. These links can present special problems. When the application must be available in locations where Internet access is difficult (for example, at remote power transmission stations in the Alaskan arctic), the bandwidth available may not support SaaS applications. In other cases, the volume of data transferred may be no problem over InfiniBand or Gigabit Ethernet in the datacenter, but the volume is just too much to transfer over the Internet without an unacceptable delay.

An unfortunate aspect of Internet communication is unpredictable latency. Disasters such as cables severed in a construction accident and transoceanic cables attacked by sharks[4] can affect bandwidth and latency. Everyday variations in latency that occur when a wireless user moves from provider to provider or latency increases because of traffic increases can all present performance issues and sometimes errors from undetected race conditions.[5] In Figure 14-7, the Internet intervenes three times in the SaaS implementation, effectively tripling the unpredictability of the application.

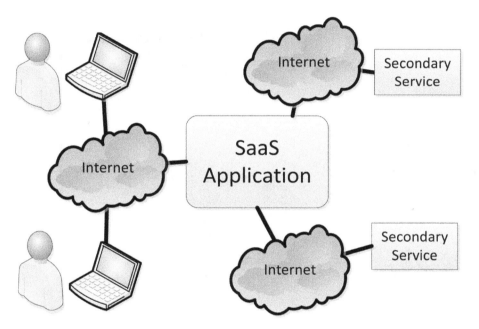

Figure 14-7. *SaaS adds Internet links to the network supporting the application that may behave differently from traffic within a datacenter*

The ease with which SaaS applications are integrated is largely dependent on the facilities provided by the SaaS vendor and the facilities that are already present in the environment. Most vendors provide some kind of a web service

---

[4]Google has reinforced the shielding on some undersea fiber-optic cables to prevent damage from shark bites. See www.theguardian.com/technology/2014/aug/14/google-undersea-fibre-optic-cables-shark-attacks, accessed August 5, 2015.
[5]A *race condition* is an error that occurs because messages arrive in an unpredicted order. Usually, this occurs when messages always come in the same order in the development lab, and the developer assumes this is stable activity. If quality assurance testing does not happen to generate an environment that brings out the race condition, the error may not be caught until the application moves to production. Undetected race conditions can appear when a stable on-premises application is moved to a cloud.

programming interface, usually SOAP- or REST-based. Figure 14-8 illustrates a typical SaaS integration pattern. The SaaS application is deployed on the SaaS vendor's cloud. Users of the SaaS application interact with the SaaS application via HTTP and a browser. The SaaS application also interacts with an integrated application. The integrated application is deployed on another cloud or on the enterprise premises. Both the integrated application and the SaaS application expose a web service–based programming interface. Frequently, both SOAP and REST messages are supported by the SaaS application.

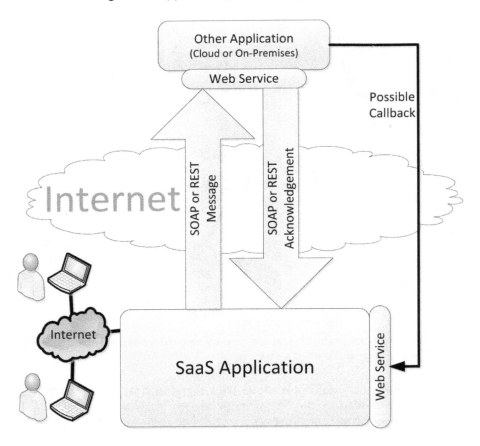

Figure 14-8. A typical SaaS application integration scenario using web services

Figure 14-8 is somewhat deceptive in its simplicity. The scheme is well-engineered, representing current best practices. However, there are circumstances where such a scheme can be difficult or impossible to work with, especially in a mixed environment. For an integration between the SaaS application and the enterprise application, the SaaS application needs to have a web service that will transmit the data or event needed by the organization's application. For example, for an SaaS internal service desk, the enterprise could want the SaaS application to request the language preference of the user from the enterprise human relations (HR) system instead of using a preference stored in the SaaS application. This is a reasonable requirement if the HR system is the system of record for language preferences, as it often is. The SaaS application must send a message to the HR system indicating a new interaction has started that needs a language preference. Then the SaaS application web service must accept a callback message containing the language preference from HR. This integration will work only if the SaaS application has the capacity to send the appropriate message to the HR web service and the capacity to receive the callback from HR and use the language preference delivered in the callback. The message sending and receiving capabilities are present in Figure 14-8, but that does not mean the application behind the interfaces can produce the required message when needed or act on the callback from the integrated application.

Organizations have widely varying integration requirements. If the SaaS application integration services open too wide, they risk not being able to change their own code because they have revealed too much to their customers. On the other hand, if the SaaS application's integration interface is too narrow, the interface cuts out too many customers whose integration requirements are not met.

Enterprises often assume that their requirements are simple and common to all business; this assumption is often invalid and results in disappointment. Users must be aware that although integration facilities are there, it does not guarantee that the facility will meet their needs. Often this problem is worse when the organization attempts to integrate legacy applications with SaaS applications that replace older on-premises applications. Designers may assume that a longstanding integration between the older applications will be easily reproduced with the modern web services provided by the SaaS application. It is possible that it will. But it is also possible that it won't.

IaaS and PaaS Challenges

IaaS and PaaS tempt organizations to take an easy way into cloud deployment and port their existing applications onto a cloud rather than redesign the application for cloud deployment. That strategy has worked for some organizations but not for all. The reasons for porting failures were discussed in detail in Chapter 13.

Assuming that applications have been successfully redesigned or ported to the cloud, integration in a mixed environment can have some special challenges. These challenges are approximately the same for IaaS and PaaS. A PaaS provider may supply useful components that can make building the applications much easier. Databases, HTTP servers, and message buses are good examples.

Depending on what the platform vendor offers, integration may also be easier when the enterprise can rely on carefully designed and well-tested prebuilt components such as SOAP and REST stacks.

A key to understanding the problems when integrating with a virtual machine is to understand that a file on a virtual machine is not persistent in the same way that a file is persistent on a physical machine. If an application uses the old style of integration in which one application writes a file and the other application reads it, several unexpected things can happen because the files do not behave like files on physical machines.

The files are part of the image of the virtual machine, kept in the memory of the underlying physical machine; unless special measures are taken to preserve the file, it will disappear when the memory goes away. If a virtual machine is stopped and then restarted from an image, its files will be the files in the image, not the files that were written before the virtual machine was stopped. One reason for stopping a virtual machine is for update. Often the update is accomplished by replacing the old image with one developed in the lab. Synchronizing the file that was last written with the file on the updated image adds an extra layer of complexity to shutting down and starting a virtual machine. Since most virtual machines will not need this treatment, the integrated application becomes an annoying special case.

Modern applications usually store the state of an application in a database that is separate from the application. When an application restarts, it takes its state from the database, not files in its environment. Occasionally, a C++ or Java program will persist an object by writing an image of the object to a local file. If these persisted objects are used in integration, they present the same issues.

Conclusion

Computing devices do not communicate well when the communication is through a human intermediary. When devices communicate directly, the data flows faster and more accurately than any human can ever move information.

Removing humans from communication links does not eliminate the human element from enterprise management; instead, humans are freed to do what they do best: evaluate, envision, plan, identify opportunity, and a host of other activities that require uniquely human capacities. The humans in a completely integrated system have the data needed, as well as the data that they may not know they need yet, delivered nearly instantaneously in exactly the form they request. This data is a sound basis for informed decisions and planning.

Compare this integrated scenario with the enterprise of a few decades ago. Technicians copied data from terminal screens and gauges to make management decisions. The information was transferred as fast as a pen could write and a technician could walk across a shop floor. It takes minutes, not milliseconds. However, only exceptional individuals never make transcription mistakes. Therefore, the data was not only late but also unreliable.

Integration replaces poor-quality data with better-quality data and offers the opportunity to combine and analyze data from different sources in useful ways. Integration also supports integrated control, especially when the Internet of Things enters the system. As devices and sensors are attached to the enterprise network and the Internet, the possibilities for integrated monitoring and control multiply. When the system is distributed over the enterprise premises and cloud deployments, integration increases in both importance and complexity.

However, the transition from on-premises to the cloud, with a few exceptions, is gradual. Some applications are not likely ever to be moved to a cloud implementation. Consequently, developers will face integrating between on-premises and cloud applications for a long time to come.

EXERCISES

1. Why are some applications unlikely to be moved to a cloud?

2. How does regulatory compliance affect cloud applications?

3. How do bus and hub-and-spoke integration architectures simplify mixed architecture implementations?

4. Do web services always support required integrations? Why?

Conclusion

Cloud Practices

Cloud computing is a revolution, a revolution built on high-speed, high-capacity global networks for communication and virtualization technology for flexibility. Network speed and capacity makes possible the separation of computing resources and resource consumers. Virtualization provides the flexibility to offer consumers the exact computing capacity they need within protected boundaries on shared hardware.

The result has been the appearance of huge datacenters holding massed computing resources that were once inconceivable. These resources are usually what "the cloud" means. In many cases, new cloud services do not duplicate existing services provided by computers distributed among consumers and enterprise IT departments. Online purchases from Amazon, instant information from Google, virtual communities on Facebook, and streaming movies on Netflix are all services that can exist only when supported by a cloud. The highly portable devices that have become so popular for personal computing—smartphones, tablets, and laptops—are all tied to the cloud, and they also have become dependent upon cloud computing as the availability of cloud-based services has increased.

Cloud business patterns are also disruptive because the cloud is more than a technology. It also is a way of managing and financing IT.

Prior to the cloud, most computers were owned and operated by enterprises whose business was not computers. These companies manufactured cars and airplanes; they sold insurance and offered banking services. They delivered freight and sold equipment in small and large towns and a myriad of other lines of business. Only a comparatively few computer-owning businesses manufactured computers, developed software, or provided computer services as a business. For most, their IT department and computing hardware were costs they could not avoid because their business depended on IT.

Enterprises always have had the option of delegating their IT to outsourcers, but that is not a viable solution for many enterprises because their dependence on IT is so profound they are uncomfortable with entrusting their IT to a third party. Cloud implementations are a form of outsourcing that is sort of middle ground. An organization can step out of the role of owner and custodian of IT equipment yet retain control and responsibility for IT services they implement on clouds.

The possibility of outsourcing to cloud providers drives basic changes in IT departments. Depending on the type of cloud service—IaaS, PaaS, or SaaS—different types of expertise and tasks are delegated to the provider. This delegation results in significant changes in the organization of the IT department. Costing for cloud services is largely based on metered usage; on-premises IT is typically based on staff time and investment in hardware. Since staff and investment do not correlate well with IT usage, cloud computing offers better alignment between costs and revenue.

Cloud implementations are fundamentally outsourced relationships. Consequently, contracts and service level agreements affect cloud implementations much more than they affect on-premises implementations. Expertise in writing, interpreting, and managing contracts takes on greater significance for IT as cloud usage increases. In cloud implementations, contracts can affect system reliability, capacity, performance, security, costs, and many other aspects of enterprise IT.

Cloud computing also opens up the possibility of improved IT services, new services, business innovations, even new lines of business, but to take full advantage of the technical and business advantages of cloud implementations, cloud projects often require a different approach to planning and design.

Unlike most innovations in IT, the cloud is as much a business innovation as a technical innovation. This implies that business and technology must work, and technology must work in tandem to realize the promise of the cloud.

Cloud implementations require cooperation between the business and technical sides of the enterprise. Service management best practices, such as ITIL, are directed toward effective cooperation between both technology experts and business managers and the design and construction of systems that are both technically efficient and supportive of enterprise business goals.

ITIL service management is based on the Deming cycle for continual improvement: plan, do, check, and act.[1] ITIL adapts the Deming cycle to IT with its own set of equivalent steps: strategy, design, transition, operation.

---

[1]See Chapter 6 for a detailed description of the Deming cycle and Agile development.

Many enterprise IT projects have suffered from a misinterpretation of the Deming cycle. They isolate activities in each stage in the cycle into independent steps that start with a set of inputs, transform the inputs into a set of outputs, assign each stage to successive teams, and evaluate each team on the speed and precision with which they execute their transformation within the narrow constraints of their assigned activity. This describes the waterfall development methodology. Deming himself argued against this approach. He interpreted each stage in his cycle as part of a process that ultimately leads to a satisfied customer. Stages must interact to achieve the goal of customer satisfaction, and no stage is complete until the customer is satisfied.[2] Figure 6-1 in Chapter 6 expresses this concept.

A well-planned and executed cloud implementation follows the ITIL phases with continuous feedback and interaction between each stage, not in rigidly isolated and independent steps. The deliverables from each step are still required, but the other stages in the cycle interact as the project progresses. The process is a continuous loop that improves stakeholder satisfaction in an evolving environment.

Many readers will recognize flexible progress toward customer satisfaction as a characteristic of Agile development. Chapter 6 discussed Agile development methodology and ITIL. The approach suggested there follows Deming's lead in treating the stages in the cycle as occurring more or less simultaneously, interacting with all the others. The combination of the Deming's interpretation of Deming cycle and Agile development provides a powerful tool for addressing the dual technology–business nature of cloud implementation.

The rest of this chapter will cover the steps in the ITIL cycle applied to the cloud.

Strategy

Strategy should be the beginning point of any substantial cloud implementation, including the adoption of a SaaS application specifically requested by a business division. Each stage in the ITIL process is important, but strategy occupies a special place. A cloud project must fit into the business and technical strategy of the enterprise. The project strategy must establish a clear expected outcome that will support business goals, align with existing technical infrastructure, and take advantage of the unique strengths of cloud implementation.

---

[2]See Paul Deming, *Out of Crisis*. Cambridge, Massachusetts: MIT Press. 2000. Pages 88–90 express his views of the cycle.

A strategy that meets these criteria must have attention on the executive level, perhaps the CEO and the board, because the consequences are often enterprise-wide. A cloud project can have profound effects on governance, finance, and sometimes the entire direction of the enterprise. Conventional technology can often deeply affect the enterprise, but cloud computing is likely to have wider effects because it is both a technical innovation and a business innovation. Even when a cloud application is identical in every functional detail to an existing on-premises application, moving to the cloud can have financial and organizational implications because the ownership and costing model will change.

If the financial/business managers do not understand these implications, their planning can be compromised and lead to issues that better planning would have averted. Understanding these implications may present a technical dimension that will require help from the IT department. For example, if the cost per month of running an application depends on CPU loading rather than lease payments on equipment, a financial planner cannot rely on his knowledge of lease agreements to project future costs. Instead, costs depend upon future process loads more than favorable or unfavorable equipment leases. Projecting those loads requires technical advice. In addition, he may have to consult other business experts because the cloud loads may depend on business projections, which were not relevant when cost did not depend on load. From the beginning, all the enterprise players must understand the strategy as the project progresses. This requires executive-level support and approval.

These are some key items in the strategy stage:

- Determine a strategy for serving the customers, clients, patrons, or other stakeholders in the enterprise. IT is just one part of this strategy. Typically, this strategy will be a product of enterprise planning.

- The strategy should delineate the parts of the service strategy that this project is intended to implement, including the strategic requirements and constraints on the project.

- If an IT service portfolio does not exist, establish one. An IT service portfolio is an executive-level document that describes each service supplied by IT. Minimally, the portfolio describes the functionality and value of each service, who manages it, who uses it, the service costs, and when it went into production. If the service has an expected termination date, that should appear also. The portfolio is the basic tool for viewing the scope and depth of IT activity and determining how a cloud service fits into the fabric of the IT environment.

- The strategy will not necessarily mention a cloud implementation. Later phases may indicate that a cloud implementation will best meet strategic demands. When a cloud implementation does appear in the strategy, the strategic reasons for the choice are important. If, for example, implementing in the cloud to reduce costs during business lulls is part of the strategy, the strategic deliverables should state it.

- A new cloud project must align with the strategy and coordinate with the services in the IT service portfolio, identifying new services to be developed, old services to be replaced or eliminated, and existing services to be used.

- The strategy should discuss high-level demand for the services supplied by the cloud project. Required capacities are derived from these demands.

- Concern over governance and management consequences, such as personnel changes, new auditing procedures, and security issues, should appear.

- Financial implications (including funding plans for developing the project) and where returns are expected are important to the strategy. Some discussion of cloud providers may appear in strategy but should focus on the strategically significant characteristics of potential providers.

Strategies change as business environments change. They may also change in response to technological changes that alter the finances of a project or open business possibilities that were not available in the past.

ITIL Design, Transition, and Operations

ITIL distinguishes a design stage, a transition stage, and an operations stage. In the design stage, the high-level goals and requirements in the project charter developed by the strategy team are transformed into concrete plans that direct the implementation of the project. The transition phase consists of implementing and placing the project into production. Much of the transition phase is devoted to testing the new project, training personnel, and adopting the project into production.

Design, transition, and operations are especially interdependent. Separating design from development and testing can have painful consequences. A project built to support a discarded strategy or a project that fails to meet production requirements are both bad, but a design that cannot be built or a development that does not meet requirements because the design was misunderstood is egregious. A design that does not keep up with changing operational requirements is even worse. Discovering that a project is of minimal use to customers after the development is complete is a tragedy. A fact of both business and technology is that environments always evolve and requirements change. A perfectly executed project that meets only old and irrelevant requirements has little value. Hence, design, transition, and operation must always be a mutually interactive effort. Nevertheless, the teams representing each of these stages have special concerns.

Design

The design team translates strategic goals and requirements into a design that will achieve the goals and meet the requirements. In theory, a design describes what to do but not how to do it. In practice, what and how often blend because what often implies a how. For example, a design may specify a communication protocol that is connection oriented and guarantees packets will be delivered in the order sent. The designer probably chose those characteristics because they are met by available protocols, and the design was probably built around the assumption that an available protocol would be used. In fact, a design that requires a new protocol would probably be unwise without an overwhelming reason for inventing a new protocol because a new protocol has wide implications for development, testing, and support. Something as potentially expensive as a new protocol should be justified by both design requirements and consultation with the developers who will be assigned to implement it. Their implementation plan may affect the performance, reliability, and long-term maintainability of the service as well as the cost. These considerations may even require revisiting the strategic plan. Although returning to strategy may seem calamitous, it is better done early in design, not after a deleterious service is delivered to consumers. This is another example of the interdependence of the phases.

The following are some specifics of cloud design:

- Designs must support the functionality described in the strategic plan. This may involve indicating which processes will be implemented on a cloud, which will be traditional on-premises processes, plans for bursting to or between clouds, and requirements for communication between all components.

- Business considerations beyond functionality, such as metering usage and assigning costs to business divisions, should be addressed in the design.

- Design for manageability and limited complexity.

- Designs should indicate which applications should be supplied as SaaS. Choosing between IaaS and PaaS can be left to the transition team, but a SaaS decision should be made in design. Strategy may dictate SaaS also.

- The design should describe the functionality, inputs, and outputs for each process. The human interactions and the business requirements for each process are part of this description. Consideration should be given to the distribution requirements of processes including network limitations, data consistency, disaster recovery, and failover.

- The scalability requirements and expectations should appear in the design. Direct special attention toward horizontal scalability, cloud elasticity, and the possibility of expansion and contraction between clouds.

- Geographic distribution influences reliability and performance of processes and data availability. The design should include these aspects.

- The design should include integration requirements and an integration architecture. It should also specify how existing integration architectures are to be included in the design.

- The design should spell out availability, capacity, performance, and security requirements. Note that the availability specification includes enterprise requirements that indicate the risks and dangers involved in process failure or degradation. Disaster recovery and failover requirements also appear here. Security requirements may have broad implications for the design and must address process access as well as at-rest and in-transit data security. Service level requirements and service contract requirements that derive from the strategy or design should appear.

Transition

From the developer's point of view, transition is where the work is done. During the transition phase, developers translate the design into working code. The quality assurance team tests the code. A training team prepares training materials such as manuals, online and offline classes, and online help. The training team also trains the trainers on the new service in preparation for instructing the users who will work with the new software and services.

A rollout plan provides for the orderly transfer of the new service into production. Eventually, the operations team receives responsibility for the new service.

Neither Deming, Agile development, or current DevOps practice advocate a practice that executes the transition phase as a discrete series of steps. They all suggest that the transition phase, as well as all other ITIL phases, should be a collection of simultaneous and interactive processes. See Chapter 6 for a more detailed discussion of Agile, DevOps, and ITIL. The testing team must be familiar with the enterprise strategy, the design, and the implementation to assure that tests exercise the important and vulnerable aspects of the service rather than dwelling on easily tested minor issues. A test that trips up development with a different interpretation of the design is a pointless waste of time. Both development and testing must agree on the design from the beginning. Development must work with the testing team to build in instrumentation that will verify that the code is behaving properly. Trainers often have profound insight into user requirements and interaction with existing services. This insight should inform design, development, and testing. The operations team and the consumers of the service are the ultimate judges of the system and should be involved from the beginning. The simplest and most effective way of achieving these goals is Agile-style incremental development that is released to all the players for examination, testing, and feedback.

Here are some considerations for the transition phase:

- All the players must keep the strategy and design documents in mind. An issue discovered during coding, testing, training, or rollout planning may require redesign or even reconsideration of strategy. Addressing the issue immediately will be more efficient than dealing with it after the project is in production.

- When scalability is an issue, assure that the scalability built into the product aligns with the scalability goals in the strategy and design. When cloud elasticity or bursting from cloud to cloud is anticipated, be aware of the requirements of the cloud platforms you intend to deploy on.

- Choose the right form of virtualization for the job. Containers use the underlying physical hardware more efficiently and are easily portable but are less inherently secure than virtual machines and may not have all the needed functionality. Make the choice carefully, although current trends are to use more containers.

- When development must decide between an IaaS and PaaS platform, consider the strategic direction of the enterprise as well as development needs. Outsourcing the ownership and maintenance of utilities to the PaaS provider should align with enterprise strategy. Also, consider governance issues such as ownership of data, auditability, and security.

- Base decisions on storage on anticipated volume of data and need for rapid access. Also, consider cost and governance issues such as ownership of data, auditability, and security.

- Messaging and event strategies are vital to the long-term success of integrated systems. Make decisions based on the entire system. Consistency is often more advantageous than a collection of messaging systems tailored to individual processes. Consistent use of a commercial or in-house messaging bus or hub may be a good long-term decision.

- The development group must work with service management to craft service level agreements and service contracts that will meet strategic and design requirements. Development must include instrumentation that will detect service violations.

- Testing should begin as early as possible. Even paper designs can be tested against requirements. When functionality is delivered to customers in small increments, the customer's comments become part of the testing process.

- Training groups should prepare users for the cloud experience, including new support expectations, such as continuous delivery that enhances services continually instead of incrementally by releases.

Operations

The operations team should participate in or be aware of every stage of a cloud project. The operations team will be held accountable for a successful cloud project longer than any other group in the ITIL cycle. The work of the preceding teams will be lost if operations cannot successfully deliver the planned services. Therefore, the previous stages should make every effort possible to assure that operations will be happy with the results. The only group more important than operations is the consumers. The previous phases are obliged to pay attention to the concerns of operations at all times. Even the strategy team must pay some attention to operational requirements such as provision for adequate facilities and network connections for operating the anticipated services.

At the same time, the operations team is obligated to provide useful feedback to the strategic, design, and transition teams. Without feedback from operations, the Deming cycle is incomplete. Not only must the operations team manage the delivery of services, they must also monitor the success of the service so that the service can continually improve.

The operations team should do the following:

- Maintain a service desk. The purpose of the service desk is not just to expedite the resolution of operational issues. It must also record and classify issues for improvement of the system, including "out-of-band" requests that might indicate gaps in the service portfolio.

- Collect resource consumption and performance data.

- Detect and report to service managers on service level violations.

- Work with cloud provider to take full advantage of cloud features such as failover and elasticity.

- Provide continual feedback to the transition, design, and strategic teams on all aspects of the performance, reliability, and acceptability of the deployed services.

Summing Up

Service management is always a cycle, not a single project. The business of services is never complete because business environments always change. Sometimes the change comes from the outside in the form of new customer demands, the availability of new resources, or new regulations. Competitors rise and disappear. Leaders revise strategy based on new external environments, the experience of operations, and the vision of business to come. Design and transition follow strategic direction and inject real experience into strategy. Operations absorbs the results of design and transition and delivers services to consumers whose reaction drives strategy.

From the standpoint of service management, cloud implementations are a form of outsourcing made possible by high-bandwidth networks and virtual systems. They can shift the expense of IT from capital investment to operational expense. The cost of cloud-implemented services can track more closely to business demands than on-premises services. Clouds can provide extensive capacity at low cost, which offers technological opportunities that would otherwise be unavailable. Scaling on demand is a basic property of cloud architectures. Scaling on demand is critical to the online business world that must respond to consumer demand that varies unpredictably. Clouds also enable services that are available anywhere, such as music services and document sharing.

Like all technology, cloud implementations can be done well or not so well. The rules for building cloud implementations are not greatly different from conventional projects, but the expectations from a cloud implementation are justifiably high, and the consequences of a design that does not consider the unique characteristics of clouds can be onerous. Successful enterprise cloud projects require a systematic approach to implementation following established principles of service management.

Index

A

Access and identity management (AIM), 153

Amazon Web Services (AWS), 6

Apple iOS, 94, 97

Apple iPhone, 84

Application programming
interfaces (APIs), 98

Atomicity, consistency, isolation,
durability (ACID), 325

B

Bring your own device (BYOD), 83, 99, 300

Business and IT architecture
architectural divide, 41
cloud and enterprise architecture, 40
definition, 38
fragmentation, 40
full-duplex, 40
subunits, 39

Business rules, 185

Business strategy, 72

C

Capability maturity model (CMM), 65

Capital expenditures (CAPEX), 76, 116

Cascading style sheets (CSS) screens, 95

Cellular vs. Wi-Fi, 85

Central Computer and Telecommunications
Agency (CCTA), 67

Central processing unit (CPU), 49

Change management, 185

Cloud computing
advanced equipment and technology, 26
advantages
connectivity, 117
financial, 116
individual consumers, 114
larger organizations, 114
scale, 115
smaller organizations, 113
specialization, 115
AWS, 6
big data, 7
bursting, 112
consumer cloud service
applications, 125
storage, 123
deployment models
advantages, 110
community cloud, 112
disadvantages, 110
hybrid cloud, 112
private cloud, 111
public cloud, 110
enterprises
individual consumers, 126
providers, 127
Facebook, 6
implementation (see Cloud
implementation)
improved IT services, 354
Industrial Age, 8
Information Age (see Information Age)
management
business cloud users, 128
cloud deployed system, 131–132
IaaS consumer, 133
individual consumers, 127

Cloud computing (*cont.*)
    on-premises help-desk
      service, 131
    outsourcing, 129
    PaaS consumers, 133
    SaaS consumers, 133
    service provider, 129, 131
    service providers, 130
    SLA, 132–133
  NIST definition, 106
  revolution built, 353
  risks and obstacles
    auditability, 120–121
    independence, lack of, 121
    performance and outages, 122
    privacy and security, 119
  service models
    Backup as a Service, 110
    IaaS, 108
    IT as a Service, 110
    Network as a Service, 110
    PaaS, 108
    SaaS, 109
    specializations/extensions, 107
  services
    costing for, 354
    type of, 354
  Technological Age, 9
  technical innovation and business
    innovation, 356
  timeshare customers, 25
Cloud bursting, 112
Cloud implementation
  asynchronous communication
    CAP, 325
    containers, 326
    high-volume system, 323
    HTTP server, 323
    idempotent message, 324
    interfaces planning, 327
    process, 323
    storage, 328
  business failures, 293
  business success
    backup, 308
    BYOD, 300
    consumer security, 307
    data strategy, 304

    financial reporting structure, 309
    flexibility, 297
    on-premises, 303
    provider outages, 305
    provider security, 307
    strategic planning, 294
    usage based costing, 301
  cloud failures, 292
  contracts and service level
    agreements, 354
  gradual approach, 312
  ITIL (see Information technology
    information library (ITIL))
  monoliths (see Monolithic applications)
  port, 312
  technical success, 312–313
Cloud infrastructure management
    interface (CIMI), 111, 181
Cloud security, 101
Comma-separated values (CSV), 227–228
Commodity, 43
Common-cause variation, 68
Common information model (CIM), 178
Community cloud, 112
Compiled clients, 91
Computer-aided design (CAD), 39
Computer-aided manufacturing (CAM), 39
Computing hardware, 55
Configuration management
    databases (CMDBs), 178
Consistency, availability, and network
    partitions (CAP), 325
Customer relationship management
    (CRM), 54, 129, 210, 302, 333

D
Data transmission
  database sharing, 232
  data serialization
    byte-for-byte structure, 227
    CSV, 227–228
    JSON, 229
    metadata, 229
    XML, 228–229

file sharing, 230
messaging
    advantages and
        disadvantages, 234
    assured delivery, 238
    asynchronous messaging, 237
    SQL, 234
    synchronous messages, 235
    TCP and IP, 235
transformation, 230

Deming cycle, 69

Direct attached storage (DAS), 177

Direct costs, 76

Distributed Management Task Force
    (DMTF), 111, 178, 286

Domain name service (DNS), 48

E

Enterprise applications, 97

Enterprise architects, 102

Enterprise integration
    businesses growth, 195
    business units, 226
    cloud computing, 195
    cloud systems
        branch application, 208
        computing and storage, 207
        CRM system, 210
        HTTP/HTTPS, 208–210
        initial impetus, 207
        native cloud application, 209
        off-the-shelf service, 207
        perimeter, 210
        SaaS, 210–211
        service provider, 210
        SKMS system, 211
    complexity
        construction firm, 201
        coupling, 202
        ITIL, 205
        IT system, 201
        proliferation and brittle
            systems, 204
        startup resources, 202
        supporting, 203
        unpredictability, 204

data routing
    configuration-mapping file, 240
    hard-coded addresses, 240
    publication-subscription, 241
data translation, 243
data transmission (see Data
    transmission)
design and construction, 193
design patterns, 223
distributed applications, 226
geographic spread, 200
HVAC system, 194
planning
    availability vs. consistency, 219
    bus architecture, 213–214
    cloud requirements, 220
    data duplication, 217
    features, 216
    laws and regulations, 215
    maintenance, 219
    mobile app, 215
    multi-application dashboard, 214
    organization and consumers, 214
    point-to-point integration, 213–214
    scalable and elastic systems, 218
    spoke-and-hub architecture, 213–214
    user experience, 216
top-down design, 211
volume
    applications, 196
    Big Data, 198
    customers and clients, 196
    large and small
        enterprises, 199
    network, 197
    security system, 199
    supporting, 198

Event correlation, 186

Extensible Markup Language (XML), 227–228

F

Fat clients, 91

File synchronization and sharing
    services, 125

Financial management, 76

Fixed costs, 77

4G LTE, 85

G

Google Android, 94

Google Docs, 87

H

Healthcare Insurance Portability and Accountability Act (HIPAA), 151

Heating, ventilation, and air conditioning (HVAC) system, 194, 334

HTML5, 98

Hybrid apps, 96

Hybrid cloud, 332

Hypertext transfer protocol (HTTP) servers, 91, 171

I, J

Indirect costs, 76

Industrial Age, 8

Information Age
  distributed computing
    client–server system, 15
    hub-and-spoke, 14
    scalable system, 16
    software performance, 15
  distributed system integration, 17
  economists and historians, 10
  impact of
    BYOD, 23
    economists changes, 18
    exponential growth, 19
    instrumental and incremental changes, 18
    IoT, 24
    Moore's law, 19
    social networks, 22
  mainframe, 11
  timesharing, 13

Information technology information library (ITIL), 137
  Deming cycle, 354–355
  design
    availability specification, 359
    business considerations, 358
    communication protocol, 358
    disaster recovery and failover requirements, 359
    distribution requirements, 359
    functionality, 358
    geographic distribution, 359
    high-level goals and requirements, 357
    human interactions and business requirements, 359
    integration architecture, 359
    integration requirements, 359
    manageability and limited complexity, 359
    SaaS, 359
    scalability requirements and expectations, 359
    security requirements, 359
    service contract requirements, 359
    service level requirements, 359
  operations, 361
  strategy, 355
    enterprise planning, 356
    executive-level document, 356
    financial implications, 357
    governance and management consequences, 357
    high-level demand, 357
    new cloud project, 357
    service strategy, 356
  transition, 357, 359

Information technology infrastructure library (ITIL), 59

Infrastructure as a Service (IaaS), 53, 108

Insurance companies, 41

Integrated development environments (IDEs), 54, 97

Integration
  application integration, 33
  best practices and established technology, 28
  data integration, 31
  data redundancy, 31
  definition, 30
  enterprise-wide reporting and dashboards, 30

International Telecommunications Union (ITU), 85

Internet Assigned Numbers
 Authority (IANA), 242
Internet of Things (IoT), 24, 334
Internet Protocol (IP), 235
Internet service provider (ISP), 48
iPad, 84
ITIL service management
 Agile methodology, 157
 Deming cycle, 154
 DevOps
  continual improvement, 163
  design, 161
  operation phase, 162
  strategy, 161
  transition phase, 162
 iterative development, 163
 PDCA cycle, 158
 waterfall development, 155
IT service management (ITSM). See Service
 management

K

Kernel-based Virtual Machine (KVM), 253

L

Local area network (LAN), 85
Logical domains (LDoms), 262
Long-term evolution (LTE), 85

M

Mean time between failure (MTBF), 182
Microservices, 276
Microsoft Office 360, 118, 125, 126
Microsoft operations framework (MOF), 65
Microsoft Windows Phone/Windows 8, 94
Mixed architectures
 business and technical advantages, 332
 cloud deployment
  compute-intense applications, 345
  load variations and scaling, 342
  machine configurations, 343
 connectivity issues, 332
 hybrid cloud, 332
 integration

bus architecture, 337–338
 cloud-deployed control
  application, 334
 CRM application, 333
 disadvantage, 333
 hub-and-spoke integration, 338–339
 HVAC systems, 334
 IaaS and PaaS, 349
 IaaS application, 335
 IoT, 334
 mission-critical applications, 333
 on-premises and cloud-based
  applications, 333, 335
 on-premises hub, 340
 PaaS application, 335
 SaaS application, 333, 335, 346
 SDN, 337
 sophisticated process, 334
 virtual networks, 336
 larger organizations, 340–341
 security and regulatory issues, 332
 smaller organizations, 340–341
Mobile devices
 BYOD, 99
  enterprise architects, 102
  pre-BYOD-and-cloud IT
   management, 100
 cloud and mobile devices, 98
 computing security, 89
 definition, 84
 DOS and Windows, 86
 Moore's law, 89
 NOAA weather stations, 87
 privacy and reliability, 89
 programming
  hybrid apps, 95
  native apps, 93
  web apps, 90, 96
 stand-alone computing, 88
 traditional word processors, 86
 word processing program, 86
Mobile device, 84
Model-view-controller (MVC) system, 172
Monolithic applications
 CPUs, 316
 elaborations and variations, 316
 higher-capacity processors, 315
 horizontal scalability, 317

Monolithic applications (*cont.*)
  multicore processor, 316
  parallel processes, 317
  rolling release, 317
  single developer, 315
  SOA
    APIs, 320
    microservices, 320
    REST and SOAP, 320–321
    ROA, 320
    share services, 322
  stateless services, 319
  threads, 317
Moore's law, 19, 89

N

National Institute of Standards and
    Technology (NIST)
  cloud service models, 53–54
  definition, 106
  deployment models
    advantages, 110
    community cloud, 112
    disadvantages, 110
    private cloud, 111
    public cloud, 110
  service models
    Backup as a Service, 110
    IaaS, 108
    IT as a Service, 110
    Network as a Service, 110
    PaaS, 108
    SaaS, 109
    specializations/extensions, 107
National Oceanic and Atmospheric
    Administration (NOAA), 87, 273
Native apps, 93
Network address transformation (NAT), 171
Network address translation (NAT), 278, 336
Network attached storage (NAS), 177

O

Ohm's law, 47
Online businesses, 41
Online office suites, 87
Open data protocol (OData), 173

Open-source Android, 97
Open Virtual Format (OVF)
  Debian distributions, 287
  international standards, 287
  interoperability, 286
  LAMP stack, 287
  packaging format, 285
Operational expenses (OPEX), 76, 116
Outsourcing services
  definition, 139
  incentives
    capacity computation, 146
    cost, 140
    cost reduction, 146
    flexibility, 140, 147
    focus, 141
    skills, 141
  IT departments, 129–131
  risks
    access and identity management, 153
    certification, 151
    dependence, 142
    governance, 142
    liability, 145
    lock-in, 141
    security, 145
    service contract, 150
    service level agreement, 150
    technical risks, 149

P

Personal computing, 353
Plan-do-check-act (PDCA), 154, 158
Platform as a Service (PaaS), 53–54, 108
Private cloud, 111
Public cloud, 110
Public utility, 42, 63

Q

Quality assurance (QA) testing, 117
Quality of service (QoS), 337

R

Representational state transfer
    (REST), 175, 320
Resource-oriented architecture (ROA), 320

S

Scraping a screen, 170

Secure Sockets Layer (SSL), 103

Security assertion markup
     language (SAML), 153

Serial advanced technology attachment
     (SATA), 48

Service incident management, 185

Service knowledge management
     system (SKMS)
   architecture, 167
   AXELOS-accredited assessors, 167
   cloud and data collection, 179
   data collection and consolidation, 172
   data interpretation, 182
   data sources, 168
   IT service infrastructure and ITIL
     practice, 166
   presentation, 183

Service level agreement (SLA), 64, 122, 132

Service management
   goal of, 62
   importance, 60
   ITIL
     CCTA, 67
     common-cause
       variation, 67–68
     continual improvement, 70
     deming cycle, 69
     developers, 79
     special-cause variation, 67–68
     statistical quality control, 67
   service strategy
     financial management, 76
     methodology, 72
   value of service
     executive commitment, 66
     grassroots movement, 66
     ITIL training, 66
     participants, 66
     quality framework, 66
     service standards, 65
     utility, 63
     warranty, 63

Service orientation, 26

Service-oriented architecture (SOA)
   APIs, 320
   external interfaces, 205
   microservices, 320
   REST and SOAP, 320–321
   ROA, 320
   share services, 321

Service portfolio, 74

Service standards, 65

Service workflow and business process
     management
   alerts and events, 184
   change management, 185
   cloud implementation, 187
   "collect-and-display" applications, 188
   event correlation, 185–186
   management policies and rules, 186
   service incident management, 185
   SOAP architectures, 188
   unique management, 187

Six Sigma, 65

Smartphone, 85

SOAP, 188, 321

Software as a Service (SaaS), 53–54, 92, 109

Software-defined networks (SDNs), 337

Special-cause variation, 68

Storage area networks (SAN), 177

Streaming video services, 125

Sunk investments, 138

T

Tablet, 84

Technological Age, 9–10

TeleManagement Forum (TMF), 65

3G, 85

Total cost of ownership (TCO), 100

Total quality management (TQM), 65

Toyota production system (TPS), 71

Transmission control protocol/internet
     protocol (TCP/IP), 171

Transmission control protocol (TCP), 235

Transport layer security (TLS.), 103

U

UNIX operating systems, 52
Usage-based costing, 301
User datagram protocol (UDP), 235
Utility
    Carr's advice, 56
    cloud service models
        IaaS, 53
        PaaS, 53–54
        SaaS, 53–54
    commodity, 43
    definition, 42
    dry cleaning, 44
    electrical grid
        analogy, 47–48
        early adoption, 45
        pre-utility stage, 47
        productivity and electricity, 45
        utility computing, 47
    electrical utilities and
            computing, 55
    IT utilities
        computing consumers, 50
        computing providers, 49
        Internet. Consumers, 48
        network equipment and
            protocol, 48
        SATA interface, 48
        utility computing, 51
    notion of computing, 44
    technology, 44
    utility provider, 43
    virtualized computing, 54
Utility computing, 47, 51
Utility consumer, 43

V

Variable costs, 77
Virtualization, 353
    addressing
        MAC addresses, 277
        NAT, 278
        traditional integration, 277
    application/component, 270
    clouds, 254

clustering, 252
cumulative cost, 270
efficiency, 251
failover and
        performance, 282
flexibility, 253
gap analysis, 271
guest OS, 249
horizontal scaling, 281
innovation, 270
installation, 252
integration
    environment, 273
    physical server, 272
    service granularity, 274
    stateless services, 273
maintenance, 252
multi-user system, 251
OVF
    Debian distributions, 287
    international standards, 287
    interoperability, 286
    LAMP stack, 287
    packaging format, 285
paravirtualization, 249–250
physical resources, 251
requirements, 250
security
    administration and
        enforcement, 265
    hypervisor vulnerability, 265
    mobility, 266
    networking, 267
    privilege zones, 264
    proliferation, 266
snapshots, 254
third-party products, 271
vertical scaling, 280
virtual desktops, 254
virtual platform
    containers, 263
    hypervisors (see Virtual machine
        monitors (VMMs))
    LDoms, 262
    X86 rings, 255
Virtualized computing, 54
Virtual machine (VM), 52

Virtual machine monitors (VMMs)
   binary translation, 259
   general-purpose memory, 256
   paravirtualization, 260
   trap-and-emulate, 257
Virtual private networks (VPNs), 336
Von Neumann's EDVAC, 11

W, X, Y, Z

Waterfall development, 155–157
Web apps, 90
Workflow policies, 185
World Wide Web
             Consortium (W3C), 98

Get the eBook for only $5!

Why limit yourself?

Now you can take the weightless companion with you wherever you go and access your content on your PC, phone, tablet, or reader.

Since you've purchased this print book, we're happy to offer you the eBook in all 3 formats for just $5.

Convenient and fully searchable, the PDF version enables you to easily find and copy code—or perform examples by quickly toggling between instructions and applications. The MOBI format is ideal for your Kindle, while the ePUB can be utilized on a variety of mobile devices.

To learn more, go to www.apress.com/companion or contact support@apress.com.